LANGUAGE
IN THE
JUDICIAL PROCESS

LAW, SOCIETY, AND POLICY

Series Editors: Joel Feinberg, Travis Hirschi,
Bruce Sales, and David Wexler
University of Arizona

A Continuation Order Plan is available for this series. A continuation order will bring delivery of
each new volume immediately upon publication. Volumes are billed only upon actual shipment.
For further information please contact the publisher.

LANGUAGE
IN THE
JUDICIAL PROCESS

Edited by
Judith N. Levi
Northwestern University
Evanston, Illinois

and

Anne Graffam Walker
Forensic Linguistics Associates
Falls Church, Virginia

PLENUM PRESS • NEW YORK AND LONDON

Library of Congress Cataloging-in-Publication Data

Language in the judicial process / edited by Judith N. Levi and Anne
Graffam Walker.
        p.   cm. -- (Law, society, and policy ; v. 5)
    Includes bibliographical references and index.
    ISBN 0-306-43551-9
    1. Law--Language.   I. Levi, Judith N.   II. Walker, Anne Graffam.
III. Series.
K213.L36   1990
340'.014--dc20   90-45119
                                                            CIP

ISBN 0-306-43551-9

© 1990 Plenum Press, New York
A Division of Plenum Publishing Corporation
233 Spring Street, New York, N.Y. 10013

Printed in the United States of America

CONTRIBUTORS

SUSAN BERK-SELIGSON, Department of Hispanic Languages and Literatures, University of Pittsburgh, Pittsburgh, Pennsylvania 15260

JOHN M. CONLEY, School of Law, University of North Carolina, Chapel Hill, North Carolina 27599

PAUL DREW, Department of Sociology, University of York, Heslington, York Y01 5DD, England

BETHANY K. DUMAS, Department of English, University of Tennessee, Knoxville, Tennessee 37996-0430

WILLIAM L. F. FELSTINER, American Bar Foundation, 750 North Lake Shore Drive, Chicago, Illinois 60611

GEORGIA M. GREEN, Department of Linguistics, University of Illinois, Urbana, Illinois 61801

MICHAEL G. JOHNSON, Department of Psychology, University of Tennessee, Knoxville, Tennessee 37996-0900

JUDITH N. LEVI, Department of Linguistics, Northwestern University, Evanston, Illinois 60208

DOUGLAS W. MAYNARD, Department of Sociology, University of Wisconsin, Madison, Wisconsin 53706

WILLIAM M. O'BARR, Departments of Cultural Anthropology and Sociology, Duke University, Durham, North Carolina 27706

ELLEN F. PRINCE, Department of Linguistics, University of Pennsylvania, Philadelphia, Pennsylvania 19104

AUSTIN SARAT, Department of Political Science, Amherst College, Amherst, Massachusetts 01002

ANNE GRAFFAM WALKER, Forensic Linguistics Associates, 6404 Cavalier Corridor, Falls Church, Virginia 22044

FOREWORD

Legal realism is a powerful jurisprudential tradition which urges attention to social conditions and predicts their influence in the legal process. The relatively recent "social science in the law" phenomenon, in which social research is increasingly relied on to decide court cases is a direct result of realistic jurisprudence, which accords much significance in law to empirical reports about social behavior. The empirical research used by courts has not, however, commonly dealt with *language* as an influential variable. This volume of essays, coedited by Judith N. Levi and Anne Graffam Walker, will likely change that situation.

Language in the Judicial Process is a superb collection of original work which fits well into the realist tradition, and by focusing on language as a key variable, it establishes a new and provocative perspective on the legal process. The perspective it offers, and the data it presents, make this volume a valuable source of information both for judges and lawyers, who may be chiefly concerned with practice, and for legal scholars and social scientists who do basic research about law.

In this Foreword,[1] I will discuss the various important roles the research presented is likely to play in the legal process and will explore more fully its relationship to legal realism and to the Anglo-American common law system, which also values systematic reports of human experience. In doing so, my hope is to provide practitioners and scholars alike with a framework for understanding how the data of these essays will likely be employed by the courts.

---

[1] The assistance of John Monahan in preparing this Foreword is acknowledged, with appreciation. The editorial suggestions of Judith N. Levi and Anne Graffam Walker were also very helpful. Parts of this Foreword were first presented at the Conference on Language in the Judicial Process held at Georgetown University in July 1985.

The work presented in this book is a new phase of a now considerable movement to bring the methods and insights of social science to bear on the legal process. The origins of this effort are to be found in radical changes in legal thought that took place in the latter part of the nineteenth and early part of the twentieth centuries. American law until that period had been dominated by the belief that a particular, correct legal solution could be reached in every case by the application of logic to a set of self-evident principles. History suggests that judges constantly sought to ascertain and to follow these immutable principles, and the decision of a particular case was seen as incidental to the proper statement of applicable doctrine. This classical jurisprudence has been often described as "formal" because the process of deciding cases was understood as purely rational and deductive with the results apparently inevitable. An example of this view is provided by *Green v. Hudson River Rwy. Co.*, 28 Barb. 8 (N.Y. App. Div., 1858), *aff'd*, 41 N.Y. 294 (1866), in which a New York court refused to permit a husband whose wife was killed in a railroad accident to receive damages for the loss of her benefit and assistance to him. The court, citing precedents dating back to 1600, wrote, "I should have been happy in this case to have arrived at a different conclusion, but the law will not bend to accommodate our private views, or gratify our personal desires. I have no alternative but to administer the law as I find it—no dispensation from its injunctions to stand by its ancient landmarks." 28 Barb. 22 (N.Y. App. Div. 1858).

The classical view, however, was not completely dominant. Gradually, dissatisfaction became widespread, and the established view underwent changes. In general, these changes in legal philosophy reflected a loss of confidence in natural law theories and an increasing tendency to view law as a means of choosing social policy. The classical belief that the application of logic could determine a correct solution for every case gave way to the view that the answer to legal questions varies according to the social context. Hence the discovery and review of information about how society functions became more important, and the rational analysis of doctrine came to play a lesser role.

Three giants of American law, U.S. Supreme Court Justices Oliver Wendell Holmes and Louis Brandeis and Harvard Law School Dean Roscoe Pound, were instrumental in diminishing the classical view. Holmes and Pound provided compelling arguments that the true nature of law was sharply different from the classical concept because law was deeply involved with society (Holmes, 1881; Pound, 1912). As an attorney, Brandeis demonstrated the practical utility of abandoning the classical view by incorporating social research in his brief for the state in *Muller v. Oregon*, 208 U.S. 412 (1907). Eventually the national consensus about the nature of law and the work of lawyers changed. The typically formal and mechanical method of classical jurisprudence was replaced with the notion that law should, in large part, be concerned with making public policy. This revolt against formalism was called the Realist Movement and was led by faculty members at Yale Law School and Columbia University School of Law. They insisted that a new school of jurisprudence was forming, and during the 1930s they undertook to define—and defend—a "realistic" view. Karl Llewellyn, who was the most prominent member of this group, strongly endorsed the view that law was dynamic, constantly responding to changing social conditions (Llewellyn, 1931). Naturally, this view mandated the acquisition of reliable information about current social conditions as well as predictions about future trends. Eventually, realist jurisprudence, at least in modified form, became a core assumption, a preferred starting point in thinking about American law. Today, legal realism is pervasive. Indeed, remarkable support for this proposition is reported by Austin Sarat and William L. F. Felstiner in Chapter 5 of this volume, "Legal Realism in Lawyer–Client Communication." The attorneys Sarat and Felstiner studied communicated a very pure version of legal realism to their clients.

Two characteristics of the research reported in this volume make the work clearly a part of the legal realism tradition. First, the research is about a social variable, language, a pervasive and dynamic element of the legal process. According to the realist tradition, this is surely an appropriate subject for legal research because such investigations focus on human behavior related to the legal process. The particular selection of language as the focus of analysis is, however, comparatively new. Yet the case for linguistic analysis is decisively made by Judith N. Levi in Chapter 1, "The Study of Language in the Judicial Process." She persuasively argues that the multiple dimensions of language use in the legal process must be studied if we are to adequately understand how law functions. Indeed, Levi's case is so well made that the central importance of language in the legal process seems indisputable. It is surely remarkable that social scientists and legal scholars have, until recently, largely ignored the systematic study of language and law.

Second, the research reported here either concludes or at least strongly implies that the dynamic social factor of language has powerful influences in the legal process. This general conclusion is also consistent with typical realist predictions which hold that the outcome of legal proceedings is often— perhaps always—determined by social conditions. I was pleased to have a small part in some of the early studies in this field initiated by William M. O'Barr and conducted at Duke University. In this path-breaking work, O'Barr and his collaborators clearly demonstrated that language is a variable with noteworthy effects in the legal process. Their comparison of "power" versus "powerless" modes of speech showed that this linguistic distinction can have profound influence on the reactions of subjects to testimony, even when the apparent substance of the testimony is held constant. For example, a witness employing the powerless style is often judged to be less intelligent, convincing, and truthworthy than a witness employing the powerful style (Conley, O'Barr, & Lind, 1978). The study reported in Chapter 4 by O'Barr and his longtime collaborator, John M. Conley, "Litigant Satisfaction versus Legal Adequacy in Small Claims Courts Narratives," gives evidence of their continued excellent work in this new field. In this study, O'Barr and Conley focus on litigant testimony in small claims courts and examine just how the linguistic informality of these courts affects the satisfaction of parties and, in sometimes surprising ways, the outcome of cases.

O'Barr and Conley are not alone in demonstrating the power of spoken language in courtroom settings. Paul Drew's study, "Strategies in the Contest between Lawyer and Witness in Cross-Examination," reported in Chapter 2, shows how patterns of asking questions may be employed to diminish the credibility of witnesses in court. Two other studies in this volume also show the power of spoken language in courts. Significantly, both studies focus on actors commonly viewed as "neutral." The careful study by Susan Berk-Seligson, "Bilingual Court Proceedings: The Role of the Court Interpreter," which is reported in Chapter 6, shows that in bilingual proceedings, the presence of an interpreter creates powerful effects not present in monolingual litigation: the neutrality of the interpreter, which is assumed by courts, is rejected by the study. A similar and persuasive demonstration is made by Anne Graffam Walker in Chapter 7, "Language at Work in the Law: The Customs, Conventions, and Appellate Consequences of Court Reporting." Walker's chapter will end blithe reference to a "verbatim transcript" by debunking the idea that court reporters are neutral actors in the courtroom. Indeed, the Walker study shows that the production of transcripts is subject to considerable differences in behavior on the part of individual reporters. Yet, this work of court reporters, virtually free from systematic scrutiny, can be influential in surprising and fascinating ways. Extending the inquiry to the informal context of plea bargaining, Douglas W. Maynard's study, "Narratives and Narrative Structures in Plea Bargaining," reported in Chapter 3, shows the power of structural language choices in determining the negotiated outcome of cases. The conclusions of each of these studies are wholly consistent with the legal realism tradition because they point out the overwhelming importance of social conditions.

The belief that social research is significant in law, exemplified in the essays in this book, is also exemplified is the use of social science research by courts to decide cases. Within the past decade, American courts have turned to social science materials to an extent that is truly unprecedented. In our own research, my colleague John Monahan and I located, without difficulty, hundreds of cases in which judges and jurors have used social science materials to render significant decisions. For example, we found cases which applied social science research to issues involving discrimination, obscenity, trademarks, parole, bail, search and seizure, illegal aliens, battering parents, rapists, rape victims, eyewitness testimony, insanity, the Vietnam Stress Syndrome, school integration, mental hospitals, child custody, evidence, and jury size, to mention only some prominent categories. In short, we were able to find enough appellate cases to produce a traditional law school casebook (Monahan & Walker, 1985) devoted exclusively to the field of social science in law.

As a result of analyzing this wealth of material, we were led to propose that aspects of social research should be treated, for heuristic purposes, like case precedents, which record and give value to human experience in the Anglo-American common law system. This proposal is consistent with the realist view that empirical reports about human behavior—including the studies of language behavior in this book—are significant to the legal process. Having advanced this proposal, we then developed a three-part typology for classifying and then managing in the legal process the flood of social science research being used in court. The three categories in our typology correspond to three different ways of using social science research in legal cases: (1) the "social facts" use: research employed to prove (or disprove) case-specific facts; (2) the "social authority" use: research employed to make law; and (3) the "social framework" use: research employed to provide the context for case-specific factfinding (Monahan & Walker, 1988).[2]

Given these three categories, it follows that procedures for managing research in court should be tailored to fit these different uses. For example, in both the social authority and the social framework uses, conventional issues of "admissibility" would be eliminated because, we argue, the research material can be directly obtained, evaluated, and used by the court. Functional analysis of these two categories suggests a strong analogy to the use of precedent in a common law system. Precedent, likewise, can be directly obtained, evaluated, and used by the court. In our view, only the social fact use should present questions of admitting evidence. Here, we urge particular attention to the "relevance" of the research (Walker & Monahan, 1988). According to Federal Rule of Evidence 401, relevant evidence must speak to a fact which is "of consequence" in the case and must make that fact "more probable or less probable." The test should be met, simply put, if the research provides insight about a legally significant factual question.

Based on these earlier analyses and my reading of the studies in this book, I can confidently predict that certain kinds of linguistic research will be used in court to prove or disprove a specific fact which is important to the outcome of a case—the first category in our three-part typology. This social fact use is widespread (Walker & Monahan, 1988). For example, in *Palmer v. Schultz*, 616 F. Supp. 1540 (D.D.C. 1985), *rev'd*, 815 F.2d 84 (D.C. Cir. 1987),

---

[2] This is a summary of our views, intended primarily as an introduction for social scientists. More detailed statements are referred to below in the text.

female foreign service officers brought suit against the Secretary of State alleging sex discrimination. The plaintiffs used social science research to support their claim that differences in assignment and promotion of males and females was not likely to have resulted by chance—research presented to prove a fact specific to the case on trial.

Likewise, it seems inevitable that linguistic research will be used to prove particular disputed facts on trial. Indeed, the case study included in the essay by Georgia M. Green in Chapter 8, "Linguistic Analysis of Conversation as Evidence Regarding the Interpretation of Speech Events," is a very good example of the social fact use. The *methods* of conversational analysis described by Green and similar methods related by Ellen F. Prince in Chapter 9, "On the Use of Social Conversation as Evidence in a Court of Law," will almost surely be employed to decide future case-specific facts, although the particular *results* of these studies (or other studies in this book) will not be social facts in future cases because social fact research is crafted for particular cases. The theories and methods of Green and Prince (or other contributors) will be able to be employed to produce social facts for future cases.

It is also safe to predict, using the second category of the Monahan and Walker paradigm and considering the essays in this volume, that linguistic research will play a role in the lawmaking process itself. This social authority use is quite different from the social fact use because the research is not offered to prove a disputed fact but rather to assist the court in fashioning a rule of law that may apply in many cases (Monahan & Walker, 1986). The modern origin of the social authority use can certainly be traced to the U.S. Supreme Court decision in *Brown v. Board of Education*, 347 U.S. 483 (1954), which prohibited racial segregation in public schools. In writing an opinion for the Court, Chief Justice Warren cited a number of social science studies in the famous footnote 11. In the test of his opinion, Chief Justice Warren referred to the material in footnote 11 as "modern authority," thus describing this social research in much the same way other jurists might refer to case precedents. This particular use of social science research in *Brown*, and the social authority use, in general, remain controversial. Yet a lawmaking role for social research is fully consistent with realist jurisprudence, and it is virtually certain that linguistic research will be used in this important way. The research reported by Bethany K. Dumas in Chapter 11, "An Analysis of the Adequacy of Federally Mandated Cigarette Warnings," is a strong candidate to play a social authority role. For example, her conclusions about the objective adequacy of warning language could be used to influence the construction of a statute involving a warning label. A court might conclude that Congress intended to require, at least, language which measured up to such an objective standard.

A third safe prediction is that linguistic research will be used to establish what Monahan and I call *social frameworks*—baseline information which can assist judge or jury in deciding particular factual issues (Walker & Monahan, 1987). This comparatively new use of social research falls conceptually between the social fact use and the social authority use: The research is general in nature but is employed to prove case-specific facts. In *Arizona v. Chapple*, 135 Ariz. 281, 660 P.2d 1208 (1983), for example, the Arizona Supreme Court held that an Arizona trial court should have permitted an expert on eyewitness identification to testify in a murder trial where the outcome turned almost entirely on the accuracy of identification. The expert, Elizabeth F. Loftus, was prepared to present to the jury general research results regarding aspects of eyewitness identification in order to assist the jury in deciding whether to accept as correct the particular identification offered in the case. Thus general information was offered to assist in determining case-specific facts.

Linguistic research will certainly be employed in a similar way. For example, research like that reported by Michael G. Johnson in Chapter 10, "Language and Cognition in Products Liability," will be used to provide context for a case-specific decision of whether a particular product warning was understood by a particular person; the parallel with the eyewitness research is striking. Similarly, the results of research in conversational analysis, such as that reported by Green and Prince, might be used to provide context, instead of (or in addition to) providing social fact, as discussed above. According to the Monahan and Walker paradigm, this kind of linguistic evidence would be directly obtained and evaluated by the trial judge and presented to the jury by instruction. No expert would be required to testify directly because published reports, such as this book, would provide a reliable source for appropriate research. The evaluation task of the judiciary is obviously central to this proposed procedure, and we have suggested a series of tests for judicial use which are drawn from both the legal and social scientific traditions (Monahan & Walker, 1986).

In summary, the realist character of the research reported in this volume places it in the mainstream of modern American jurisprudence and suggests three important uses of these or similar research results to decide legal cases. The connection with legal realism leads to detailed proposals for incorporating these kinds of results in court proceedings. These management proposals are built on recognition that linguistic research about law, the social-science-in-law phenomenon, and the common law all value systematic reports of human experience. For social scientists, the prospect for substantial use of law and language research by courts should inspire continued commitment to quality work because some research results will produce dramatic human consequences. For attorneys, the responsibility is to use these materials creatively to advance the legitimate claims of their clients and, ultimately, the quality of the legal process itself. I predict their joint efforts will richly benefit the public interest.

1. REFERENCES

Conley, J., O'Barr, W. M., & Lind, E. A. (1978). The power of language: Presentational style in the courtroom. *Duke Law Journal, 1978,* 1375–1399.

Holmes, O. W. (1881). *The common law.* Boston: Little, Brown & Co.

Llewellyn, K. (1931). Some realism about realism—responding to Dean Pound. *Harvard Law Review, 44,* 1222–1256.

Monahan, J., & Walker, L. (1st ed. 1985; 2nd ed. in press). *Social science in law: Cases and materials.* New York: Foundation Press.

Monahan, J., & Walker, L. (1986). Social authority: Obtaining, evaluating, and establishing social science in law. *University of Pennsylvania Law Review, 134,* 477–517.

Monahan, J., & Walker, L. (1988). Social science research in law: A new paradigm. *American Psychologist, 43,* 465–472.

Pound, R. (1912). The scope and purpose of sociological jurisprudence. *Harvard Law Review, 25,* 489–516.

Walker, L., & Monahan, J. (1987). Social frameworks: A new use of social science in law. *Virginia Law Review, 73,* 559–598.

Walker, L., & Monahan, J. (1988). Social facts: Scientific methodology as legal precedent. *California Law Review, 76,* 877–896.

2. CASES CITED

Arizona v. Chapple, 135 Ariz. 281, 660 P.2d 1208 (1983).

Brown v. Board of Education, 347 U.S. 483 (1954).

Green v. Hudson River Rwy. Co., 28 Barb. 8 (N.Y. App. Div., 1858), *aff'd,* 41 N.Y. 294 (1866).

Muller v. Oregon, 208 U.S. 412 (1907).

Palmer v. Schultz, 616 F. Supp. 1540 (D.D.C. 1985), *rev'd,* 815 F.2d 84 (D.C. Cir. 1987).

LAURENS WALKER

T. Munford Boyd Professor of Law
School of Law
University of Virginia
Charlottesville, Virginia

PREFACE

1. ORIGINS OF THIS BOOK

This volume has its origins in the Conference on Language in the Judicial Process held at Georgetown University in July 1985 as part of the Linguistic Society of America Summer Institute. Funded in large part by the Law and Social Sciences Program of the National Science Foundation and organized by Anne Graffam Walker and Judith N. Levi, it was the first conference in the United States to bring together scholars from diverse disciplines whose common interest was the empirical investigation of phenomena in the new field of language and law.

The scholars who assembled at the conference to present their research came from eight distinct academic domains: anthropology, English, law, political science, psychology, sociolinguistics, sociology, and theoretical linguistics. Of the original 16 invited presentations, 9 have been revised, expanded, and edited for inclusion in this volume, together with two contributions on research not previously reported. They are gathered here in the belief that taken both singly and as a group, they provide special insights into the inseparability of linguistic and legal processes and can thus serve as models of and signposts for future research efforts.

The conference from which these papers come had several objectives, foremost among them being to share research findings with scholars of common interest. It was the first and remains so far the only such opportunity to do so because there was not then and still is not now any journal, newsletter, or national organization which could provide a centralized, systematic means for sharing scholarship on language and law. But allied with that primary purpose were other goals:

1. To demonstrate the productivity of law as a field for linguistic research
2. To illustrate the productivity of language as a focus for legal research
3. To represent the breadth of theoretical perspectives and methodologies that can be applied to such research
4. To stimulate critical thinking in the directions of both old and new research
5. To strengthen and expand the network of scholars active in this field
6. To call attention in general to this new discipline.

The conference was successful in the meeting of its goals, and this book is intended to reflect and extend that success, particularly in the direction of visibility because no matter how enthusiastic the participants, a one-time conference reaches only a limited audience. Although it is true that over the last decade, occasional courses in "language and law" have appeared in college curricula (and their numbers are growing) and occasional articles have found their way into academic journals, language and law as a coherent field remains relatively unrecognized in academia. In the legal community, moreover, it is still virtually unknown. The essential purpose of this collection, then, is to help remedy that situation by providing a text which can provide some of the visibility necessary to stimulate broader interest and research in this field.

2. ORGANIZATION OF THIS BOOK

We have divided this volume into four parts and an epilogue. Part I, by Judith N. Levi, provides a useful framework for what is to follow by giving the reader an historical perspective on and contemporary survey of the rapidly developing field of language and law. The three intermediate sections are devoted to empirical investigations and are divided roughly into groups representing a viewpoint which shifts gradually from the study of language as an integral part of the litigation process (e.g., its use in cross-examination and plea bargaining) to language as a potential subject of litigation (e.g., the wording of cigarette package warnings and spoken conversations as criminal evidence). The Epilogue, by Anne Graffam Walker, suggests directions for future research.

Chapter 1, "The Study of Language in the Judicial Process," serves as the reader's introduction to this new field. Judith N. Levi, who as unofficial chronicler and bibliographer for language and law brings to this volume an extensive knowledge of its literature, begins by discussing the intellectual value of research on language in the judicial process. She reviews some of the reasons behind its recent development as an area of study in the United States and analyzes the distribution of research efforts across three major categories: spoken language in legal settings, language as a subject of the law, and the written language of the law.

Part II, Analyzing Language in Legal Settings, comprises four chapters on spoken language in settings which range from criminal and small claims court proceedings (Chapters 2 and 4) to out-of-court negotiations and conversations (Chapters 3 and 5), thus nicely demonstrating gradational aspects of the important formality/informality dimension of language analysis. Within this dimension, each study attempts to discover how the structure of discourse varies according to the setting, situation, and participants.

The first two of the four chapters focus primarily on structural features of language as it is used in adversarial questioning between lawyer and witness (Drew) and in adversarial negotiations between legal professionals during plea bargaining (Maynard). In analyzing cross-examination, Paul Drew (Chapter 2, "Strategies in the Contest between Lawyer and Witness in Cross-Examination") identifies two structurally defined strategies—the use of contrasts and three-part descriptions—by which attorneys attempt to discredit the stories told by witnesses for the other side. Douglas W. Maynard (Chapter 3, "Narratives and Narrative Structure in Plea Bargaining") focuses not on witnesses on the stand but on attorneys behind the scene. His structural analysis of their plea bargaining narratives and his delineation of the functions which each component part of the narrative serves reveal interactional strategies whose skillful employment by attorneys is instrumental in a successful outcome.

Although William M. O'Barr and John M. Conley (Chapter 4, "Litigant Satisfaction versus Legal Adequacy in Small Claims Court Narratives") also analyze narratives in legal settings, their research perspective broadens to add the legal to the linguistic approach. Focusing on stories told by litigants in small claims courts, they use linguistics to examine the narratives for elements of internal structure (e.g., the use of passives in a litigant's account) and then compare those elements to standards for legally adequate narratives (e.g., demonstrating the responsibility of an agent for an act). They conclude that although litigants often feel more satisfied at being allowed to tell their stories in culturally familiar ways, the stories they tell do not always work to achieve "justice."

In the final chapter of this part, the emphasis shifts from the structure of language to the structuring of discourse. In a remarkable example of what can be done when social scientists are invited to observe the legal process "up close and personal," Austin Sarat and William L. F. Felstiner (Chapter 5, "Legal Realism in Lawyer–Client Communication") use language as a vehicle for discovering the legal philosophy of divorce lawyers in private conference with their clients. In identifying the philosophy as legal realism, the authors note that the evidence "suggests that one tier of the legal system, in this case, divorce lawyers, may work to unwind the bases of legitimation that other levels work to create."

In Part III, Transforming Language in Legal Proceedings, language is studied not just as an instrument in the legal process but as the *creative product* of two essential yet virtually invisible participants in the American legal system: the court interpreter (Berk-Seligson) and the court reporter (Walker). In both of these studies, the researchers are interested in the kind of changes that result when language is transformed from one manifestation or modality to another and in the implications these changes have for the judicial process. The studies are alike as well in their disclosure of the hidden power held by these language brokers whom legal professionals tend not to see. Susan Berk-Seligson (Chapter 6, "Bilingual Court Proceedings: The Role of the Court Interpreter") describes that power in terms of the control interpreters have over the flow of witness testimony and choices they make on whether and when to ask for clarification of attorneys' questions and witnesses' answers. Anne Graffam Walker (Chapter 7, "Language at Work in the Law: The Customs, Conventions, and Appellate Consequences of Court Reporting") identifies reporters' power as the choice of how to represent spoken legal proceedings in written form and demonstrates that the production of verbatim transcripts is a far more complex and ad hoc process than is generally recognized. Transcription, she argues, must be understood as an inherently *interpretive* process, one which will inevitably create discrepancies between the spoken testimony and the written record—discrepancies whose significance to the legal process is as yet little appreciated.

Although the studies in Part IV, Construing Language for Legal Purposes, are sharply divided between focus on the spoken and the written forms of language, they are united in their interest in how the meaning of a specific stretch of language, whether written or spoken, is interpreted by the law. In the first two contributions by Georgia M. Green and Ellen F. Prince, spoken language is the object of concern: Both investigators analyze surreptitiously tape-recorded social conversations which have been offered in criminal trials as evidence of speakers' intentions. In the final two chapters, by Michael G. Johnson and Bethany K. Dumas, written language which is printed on consumer products and intended to be read as a warning is investigated from the point of view of readers' interpretations.

Both Green and Prince write out of experience as consultants for the defense. Green begins her chapter (Chapter 8, "Linguistic Analysis of Conversation as Evidence Regarding the Interpretation of Speech Events") with an informative discussion of the principles of conversational analysis, follows with an illustration of a case for which she prepared an expert opinion, and concludes by addressing some of the legal and empirical issues that arise when expert linguistic testimony is offered as evidence in a trial. Prince (Chapter 9, "On the Use of Social Conversation as Evidence in a Court of

Law") uses her case analysis to demonstrate the legal consequences of combining unskilled transcription of recorded talk with uninformed interpretation of how social conversation works.

The final two chapters of this part take different approaches to a common subject: the interpretation of written warnings printed on consumer products. Michael G. Johnson (Chapter 10, "Language and Cognition in Products Liability"), working in the domain of psycholinguistics, suggests that the adequacy of consumer warnings can best be analyzed by reference both to the cognitive model of language comprehension which he proposes and to the legal concept of the fictional "reasonable man." In his conclusion, he offers some methodological suggestions concerning ways in which language experts and attorneys might work together to produce effective expert testimony in products liability cases. Bethany K. Dumas (Chapter 11, "An Analysis of the Adequacy of Federally Mandated Cigarette Warnings") first discusses warnings in terms of legal adequacy and then looks at them from the viewpoint of speech act theory. After presenting a detailed report of her empirical studies on consumer reactions to the health notices on cigarette packages, Dumas concludes by offering suggestions for strengthening existing warnings.

Despite the diversity of background and approach represented by these 10 studies, a common thread unites them: the demonstration of the value of applying empirical analysis to language as it actually occurs in the real world. Drew's discovery of structural regularities in what to a layman seems to be free-wheeling cross-examination and Maynard's discovery of the patterning of narrative elements during plea bargaining have added to our knowledge of language while deepening our understanding of the legal process. Careful analysis by O'Barr and Conley of the apparently unstructured stories which litigants present in small claims court led them to the linguistic discovery of patterned similarities and to the legally relevant realization that what the litigants achieve in psychological satisfaction, they often pay for in lack of legal adequacy.

By applying basic linguistic knowledge of how conversation works to the analysis of surreptitiously tape-recorded discourse, Green and Prince were able to demonstrate the absurdity of taking as gospel truth statements made during a social conversation; similarly, knowledge of how conversations are managed was an important component in Berk-Seligson's investigation of linguistic control exerted by interpreters over a legal process. An awareness of the importance of attitudes toward language made some of Walker's findings possible, and lawyers' attitudes toward the law were discoverable by Sarat and Felstiner through their investigation of naturally occurring law talk. Finally, Dumas' and Johnson's investigations of the question of what constitutes a legally adequate warning on consumer products both added to linguistic and psycholinguistic theory and helped to clarify the dimensions of a legal problem that will no doubt be with us for a long time.

The conference which gave rise to this collection of diverse yet cohesive studies was an interdisciplinary one; its audience should be as broad. Written in styles that are as free of jargon as possible, these studies are accessible to anyone interested in language and the judicial process: researchers, students, and professors in the social sciences, communication, and law; practicing lawyers and judges who want to gain new perspectives on their own professional universe; and lay readers who simply want to broaden their knowledge. We, the coeditors of this book, are pleased to invite the attention of them all to this new field.

ACKNOWLEDGMENTS

We are pleased to see this long journey to publication come to an end and to thank those who helped us along the way. The idea behind the conference which led to the book belonged to Deborah Tannen, then director of the LSA/TESOL 1985 Summer Institute. Georgetown University, through the offices of then Summer School Dean Gerald Sullivan, supplied the site and logistical support, and Grant No. SES–8420633 from the National Science Foundation provided much of the funding that made the conference possible. Felice Levine, Director of the NSF Law and Social Sciences Program, offered continuing encouragement as we moved toward publication as did our series editor, Bruce Sales. We are grateful for the help each one gave.

As coeditors, each of us would like to thank the other for the creative collaboration which made it possible to bring this book into reality. Editing is hard work; coediting is harder. It demands cooperation, mutual respect, tenacity, a great deal of time, and a continual willingness to learn. But the effort has brought its own rewards; drawing from our complementary backgrounds, we have learned a great deal from each other both about language and about law.

We have learned the most, however, from our contributors, and for them we reserve our deepest gratitude: There would be no book without them. Their scholarship has been an inspiration, their responsiveness to editorial suggestion has been rewarding, and their patience through this long process, a blessing. We consider our collaboration with them to have been productive; our hope now is that it will be judged a success.

CONTENTS

Part I

INTRODUCTION

Chapter 1

THE STUDY OF LANGUAGE
IN THE JUDICIAL PROCESS

JUDITH N. LEVI

1. INTRODUCTION

One of the distinguishing features of contemporary research on language in
the judicial process is the striking diversity of scholarly disciplines which have
begun to make significant contributions to this domain of inquiry. In this
volume alone, we find analyses by researchers trained in anthropology,
English literature, law, linguistics, political science, psychology, sociology—
and various combinations thereof. To be sure, the research reports have a
fundamental theme in common: a shared focus on some aspect of *language*
that has particular significance in the world of *law*. Nevertheless, we may
observe among the researchers intriguing differences which lend an unusual
richness and stimulating breadth to the field.

One important dimension of difference is the different values which
these researchers may place on the many variables in the "language and law"
equation. Thus *language* is the primary focus of one group of researchers, who
use the complex world of the law as a special context in which to explore
patterns of linguistic organization and use. For others, the primary interest is
in understanding *law and the judicial process*—in which case the analysis of
language is more an instrument for understanding the legal system than an

JUDITH N. LEVI • Department of Linguistics, Northwestern University, Evanston, Illinois
60208.

object of inquiry itself. For still others, the primary emphasis is on society or culture or human psychology, as each of these may be revealed through the study of human language in the context of our legal system.

One useful way to begin this chapter, then, is by reviewing the reasons why—despite significant differences in focus, training, methodologies, and ultimate objectives—the attention of social science scholars and legal professionals has converged to such a striking degree in the last two decades on the study of language and law.

1.1.   Value of This Research

The research reported on in this volume reflects the fundamental assumption that the study of the *language* of the judicial process is essential to achieving a better understanding of that process. Oddly enough, the validity of this assumption was hardly recognized until quite recently, despite the fact that language is *the* vehicle by means of which law is transmitted, interpreted, and executed in all cultures. The vehicle was apparently so ubiquitous and so natural a part of our daily lives that it was simply taken for granted, and therefore largely ignored, in earlier studies of judicial systems. In any case, the realization of its role as a highly significant variable in the workings of our courts has been slow in coming, with significant studies appearing only within the last 15 years or so.

Nevertheless, it does not take very extensive reflection to recognize the fact that the outcome of virtually *all* dimensions of the judicial process in its day-to-day applications is at least in part a function of what is said, by whom, to whom, and how. This is true regardless of whether we consider a potential arrest situation, a client consulting a lawyer, the conversations of plea bargaining, the multidimensional speech situation of a trial, or the entire appellate process. Yet the systematic and empirical study of this crucial dimension of the judicial process—the language dimension—was essentially unknown as recently as two decades ago. Even today the existence of this interdisciplinary field of scholarship remains unrecognized by many whose interests, both practical and theoretical, may be crucially at stake. Because interest in this subject has been so long delayed and because so little time has elapsed since the initial explorations of the 1970s, in many—perhaps most—areas of the law we *do not know* what is going on linguistically; we do not understand how the language used and the uses of language are affecting the outcomes of legal processes. We can only be sure that they are.

Legal processes are directly affected by language both in areas in which the law has explicit rules for governing language behavior and in other areas where the rules are either implicit or not to be found at all. For example, the legal system has rules governing language behavior in such diverse areas as the communication of a suspect's *Miranda* rights, the kinds of spoken evidence which are admissible in a trial, the right of individuals not fluent in English to a court interpreter, and even who may speak during a trial—and when—and who must keep silent. These laws, or rules, have presumably been instituted in order to further judicial objectives, but we do not have enough reliable empirical evidence to determine whether these objectives are in fact being served.[1] We do not know to what extent, if any, the intended effects are being realized, nor for that matter do we know whether the rules are producing some unintended effects as well, and if so, whether they are desirable, harmless, or detrimental.

In a number of other areas of the law in which language use affects the outcome of both formal and informal proceedings, rules are woefully inadequate—or entirely lacking—for facilitating the administration of justice in these areas. For example, we are only now starting to learn through empirical studies (such as Charrow & Charrow, 1979; Elwork, Alfini, & Sales, 1982) just how much jurors fail to understand the instructions given them by the judge before their deliberations. We also know very little about how dialectal differences among native speakers of English who are all participants in the same trial affect the trial outcome: what subtle, or not-so-subtle, effects does the accent, or vocabulary, or speaking style of a witness or defendant have upon the jurors or judge? (See O'Barr, 1982; Scherer, 1979; and Swett, 1969, for some pertinent discussion.) In the area of written language, we do not yet know (but only fear) to what extent the execrable language of government notices and forms adversely and *unequally* affects the ability of their intended audience to respond to them and thereby gain the benefits to which they are entitled. (See Benson, 1985; Felker, 1980; Walmsley, Scott, & Lehrer, 1981; and Wright, 1981.) In these areas and many more, a greater understanding of the language that permeates the judicial process will help us achieve a greater understanding of that process itself.

In an excellent overview of research on language and law (O'Barr, 1981), legal anthropologist William M. O'Barr articulates clearly one of the major paths by which research on the language of the judicial process can help us understand that process better. He explains that social science research is needed first of all to identify the many unexamined and possibly unwarranted assumptions about language that underlie the principles and practices of our legal system. Second, social science research is needed to subject these assumptions to rigorous empirical testing. And third, social scientists must lead the way to develop greater collaboration with legal scholars and practitioners to discover how relevant findings can be applied not only to further our intellectual understanding of the legal system—but also, where we can, to remedy its defects (O'Barr, 1981:402–404).

The task of using language to further our understanding of the legal

---

[1] See, for example, Brière, 1978; R. Johnson, 1984; and Vernon and Coley, 1978, on the communication of Miranda rights for nonnative speakers of English; Wallace, 1986, on admissibility of linguistic testimony about discourse; Pousada, 1979, on the right to a court interpreter; and Atkinson and Drew, 1979, and Walker, 1982, on rules constraining speech in trials.

system is not an easy one. But equally challenging is the task of using the legal system to increase our understanding of human language and language behavior. In considering law and language research in the latter perspective, we may begin by recognizing our legal system to be a highly elaborated network of interrelationships between language use, on the one hand, and social, economic, political, and even moral forces on the other. As a result, the legal domain offers linguists a special and indeed unique context which is especially appropriate for carrying out the kinds of pragmatic, functional, and contextually oriented research that constitute one of the major currents in linguistic research today. Moreover, the legal domain offers not just linguists but also sociologists, psychologists, political scientists, and other social scientists a unique *cultural* setting in which to explore such topics as language variables in social psychology, communicative competence, dispute resolution, storytelling in legal discourse, the semantics and pragmatics of persuasive language, gender differences in language and language behavior, and other subjects that are central to current social science research.

Much of this research develops ideas that are first suggested by the world of law itself and by the unusual features of this domain of discourse (e.g., the distinctive constraints on turn-taking and other aspects of speech behavior in a trial setting). But the world of law can also serve as a testing ground for hypotheses about natural language that are first developed, and tested, in nonlegal settings. In this case, the special qualities of the legal context can be used to great advantage to test our sometimes grandiose claims about the nature of language in general, by making us measure whether these claims do in fact encompass language in legal settings; even though these settings are linguistically and socially unusual, it is still natural language which is used there and which thus must be accounted for by our linguistic theories. Sometimes such testing will turn up distinctive features of language use that *are* a function of the specialized context, while at other times the phenomena analyzed may give us clues to universals of linguistic behavior which can help us improve our characterization of language patterns that are to be found in *all* social contexts.

One of the earliest examples of this kind of exploration is the work begun in the 1970s by the Duke University Law and Language Project, which set out to test (among other things) the claims proposed by a number of linguists (see, for example, Lakoff, 1975; Thorne & Henley, 1975) concerning the alleged differences between what we might call prototypical women's speech and prototypical men's speech (Lind & O'Barr, 1979; O'Barr, 1982). By testing these claims in a novel sociolinguistic context, namely, that of North Carolina courtrooms, the Duke team was led to develop a more satisfying categorical distinction that *was* of significance in analyzing the ways in which simulated jurors judged the speech of witnesses. Instead of characterizing the two styles of speech as a direct function of gender, the researchers proposed that a revised distinction be drawn in terms of *presentational styles*, with the contrast being that between a "power mode of speech" and a "powerless mode of speech." (The Duke research findings will be discussed in more detail in a later section of this chapter.) Thus certain general claims about language in our society were tested and refined, while at the same time further insight into the effects of language on the judicial process was attained. In similar ways, we can expect our understanding of both language and the judicial process to be further enriched in the years ahead as more scholars come to recognize the value of the legal domain for hypothesis testing in a variety of language-related domains.

Still another reason that the world of law represents a potentially fruitful context for linguistic analysis is the fact that it provides a strikingly wide range of discourse types and styles for the interested language scientist. Research published to date already encompasses considerable diversity, from the public discourse of the courtroom to the private discourse of lawyer–client consultations; from prepared talks such as jury summations to more spontaneous speech such as that of plea bargaining; from highly interactive sequences such as courtroom questioning to monologues like jury instructions read to a captive audience.[2]

In addition, because the house of law has many rooms, there are many levels of proceedings to attract the attention of social scientists: criminal courts, traffic courts, family courts, and small-claims courts; plea-bargaining conferences and out-of-court lawyer–lawyer conferences; lawyer–client interactions in legal aid settings and those in private offices; and even law school discourse, where the skills of maneuvering in the special language of this special world are first laboriously acquired (Philips, 1982). For social scientists interested in language and law, each of these settings and each of these levels offers a unique set of social, legal, and linguistic variables relevant to contemporary issues in social science research.

1.2. Historical Background

In the light of these reasons for social scientists to study language in the judicial process, one might well wonder why it is that social scientists have lingered so long outside this promising domain of study. One reason is simply the fact that even the much broader field of law and social science is itself quite young, hardly more than a few decades old. Another is the fact

---

[2] Representative research on these topics includes Atkinson and Drew, 1979, and O'Barr, 1982, on courtroom discourse; Bogoch and Danet, 1984, and Sarat and Felstiner, this volume, on lawyer–client interaction; Walter, 1988, on jury summations; Maynard, 1984, on plea bargaining discourse; Danet *et al.*, 1976, and Dunstan, 1980, on courtroom questioning; and Charrow and Charrow, 1979, and Elwork, Sales, and Alfini, 1982, on comprehensibility of jury instructions.

that for much of the past 30 years, linguists—who would be expected to have the most intense interest in language phenomena, wherever these are to be observed—were largely preoccupied with the analysis of language as a formal, self-contained system to be studied independently of so-called "performance factors," that is, independently of the real-life contexts in which human beings use language to communicate with each other. This approach was not one which would have much to contribute to the subject of this volume.

But instead of seeking more explanations for the *non*history of language and law studies in the United States before the 1970s, let us take a more positive direction at this point by considering some of the intellectual currents in linguistics and other social sciences which, independently and somewhat unexpectedly, began to flow together in the early 1970s to make possible the recent emergence of this now rapidly growing field.

In linguistics, one crucial change was that the focus of scholarly inquiry expanded considerably, moving beyond the traditional core subjects of phonology, morphology, and syntax, into the much less charted and more complex area of semantics, and thence still further out into the territory that we now call pragmatics. (For present purposes, we may define pragmatics as the study of contextual factors on which we all must draw extensively in order to construct our total understanding of an utterance, well beyond the meaning of the individual words themselves. These factors include such variables as time and place of the discourse, knowledge shared by speaker and hearer, prior discourse, the speaker's beliefs, and the hearer's assumptions about those beliefs.) One salutary result of this gradual enlargement of (and concomitant debate about) the boundaries of linguistics was a growing recognition that the study of language viewed solely as a collection of abstract, idealized objects suitable only for the most rigorous of formal analyses was *not* the only appropriate scholarly activity for a linguist to undertake. Rather, more and more linguists came to appreciate the importance of a research program which investigates the role of language as an instrument that human beings use in real-life situations to communicate with one another about topics of mutual concern. This restoration of a human-centered, naturalistic perspective on the functions as well as the structure of language is one of the major forces that has helped lead linguists to the domain of language and law.

A second significant trend in linguistics leading up to the last decade has been the continuing growth in the areas of psycholinguistics and sociolinguistics. Since both these subfields of linguistics are naturally concerned with many of the psychological and social variables that play such an important part in understanding the full dynamics of language used in legal contexts, it is not surprising that a great deal of the empirical research carried out to date by linguists in language and law has come from these two areas. Psycholinguistic work includes research on the influence of language on eyewitness testimony (e.g., Loftus, 1979), comprehension of jury instructions (e.g., the works cited earlier of Charrow & Charrow, 1979, and Elwork, Sales, & Alfini, 1982), readability of public documents (e.g., Chapter 1 in Felker, 1980), and issues pertaining to the adequacy of warning labels on consumer products (Dumas, this volume; Johnson, this volume). Sociolinguistic research includes studies of the social psychology of courtroom testimony (e.g., Lind & O'Barr, 1979), the problems faced by language minorities in dealing with the judicial process (e.g., Berk-Seligson, 1988, and this volume; Gumperz, 1982; Pousada, 1979), linguistic issues relevant to the sociology of the legal profession (e.g., Philips, 1982, 1984, 1985); and the manifold problems inherent in transforming the oral language of the courtroom into the written version of a transcript (Walker, 1985, 1987, and this volume). We shall return to a few of these topics very shortly.

A third relevant factor in the recent history of the linguistics profession is the development of several major conceptual categories and theories which have proven especially well suited to the investigation of legal discourse. Three of the most significant are:

1. *Speech act theory*, whose legal relevance is especially salient to linguistic behavior in areas like contracts (Schane, 1989; Tiersma, 1986), statutes (Kurzon, 1986), and verbal offenses, including defamation (Tiersma, 1987), threats to the life of the president (Danet, Hoffman, & Kermish, 1980), and solicitation to commit murder (Shuy, 1981)

2. *Conversational analysis*, already applied both to courtroom questioning sequences (Atkinson & Drew, 1979; Pomerantz & Atkinson, 1984; Drew, this volume) and to surreptitiously recorded conversations entered as evidence in criminal trials (Green, this volume; Prince, this volume; Shuy, 1981; Wallace, 1986)

3. The concept of *communicative competence*, drawing from the seminal work of anthropologist Dell Hymes (Hymes, 1972), a concept which has enormous potential value (insightfully discussed in B. Johnson, 1976) in helping us understand the subtle and complex sociocultural constraints on language use that make participation in courtroom discourse—and other kinds of legal language—such a difficult and frustrating experience for citizens without legal training (O'Barr & Conley, this volume; Walker, 1982, 1986).

These dynamic changes in the activities of research scholars in linguistics and related fields were, of course, fundamentally motivated and reinforced by the working assumption of these fields that it is *spoken language* rather than written language which is the primary object of study for contemporary language science, an assumption which, we may note, sets the social sciences apart from most legal scholarship and from most research in departments of English or other languages. This emphasis on naturally occurring speech as the target of investigation assumes additional significance when we consider that it is spoken language rather than written language which is the primary vehicle for communication in legal systems the world over; even in our own society and legal system, which are paper-ridden (and now also computer-driven) in many aspects, spoken language retains a preeminent role in official court proceedings, to say nothing of the multifaceted bargainings and negotiations that go on orally before, during, after, and in place of actual trial proceedings. As a result of these factors, it was only natural that linguists and other social scientists should have been increasingly drawn to the study of what legal scholar Walter Probert (1972a,b) has usefully dubbed "law talk," and it is in this new area of exploration that we can expect the diverse social sciences to make their most important contribution to expanding our understanding of the many roles that language plays in judicial processes.

While these changes were taking place in the field of linguistics, other intellectual shifts were occurring in a number of the other social sciences. To begin with, many anthropologists and sociologists have shared the interest of linguists in theories of communicative competence and in discourse analysis of various kinds, recognizing them as powerful intellectual tools for understanding a variety of cultural and social phenomena. And given the fact that anthropology, sociology, psychology, and political science had already developed research communities devoted to the study of legal systems in general (unlike linguistics, which is a newcomer to the field of law and social science), it is not surprising that these new intellectual directions should be increasingly represented in research efforts on language and law throughout the social sciences.

Another significant change that must be acknowledged here is the remarkable impact on language research that has resulted from the development and increased accessibility of sophisticated recording techniques, both audio and video. These technological developments have tremendously enhanced the ability of language scientists to perform quite complex multidimensional microanalyses of linguistic behavior (in legal settings as well as elsewhere) and to have their primary data remain accessible to colleagues for potential replication and verification of their findings.

In the area of epistemology, two additional theoretical developments that have influenced the work of social scientists to varying degrees are post-Wittgensteinian ordinary language philosophy (Pitkin, 1972), which has encouraged language scholars to "look for the meanings of verbal acts in the circumstances of their everyday use" (Dunstan, 1980:61), and the elaboration within the social sciences of alternatives to epistemological "positivism" which suggests that we can learn about the world by *discovering* an order which is inherent in the world itself. The new epistemological alternative claims that in learning about the world, individuals *construct* an order which they then attribute to the phenomena under observation but which may or may not be inherent in it. In this view, the process of observation and description is understood to be a process which is necessarily one of creative interpretation of the observed phenomena (which interpretation may then vary from observer to observer and from culture to culture), rather than one of quasi-objective "seeing" an order intrinsic to the object(s) observed. One result of this shift in epistemological perspective has been the development in sociology of ethnomethodological studies (Garfinkel, 1967, 1974), whose commitment to careful analysis of naturally occurring social interactions has proven to be especially suitable for the study of spoken language in legal settings (see, for example, Atkinson & Drew, 1979; Dunstan, 1980; Maynard, 1984; and the chapters by Drew and Maynard in this volume). Moreover, the ethnomethodologists' concern for regarding "even the most apparently mundane or ordinary events as puzzling enough to be worthy of serious analytic attention" in order not "to overlook, or take for granted, the very practices that they are aiming to identify and describe" (Pomerantz & Atkinson, 1984:287) is an especially powerful tool for counteracting the traditional tendency in legal scholarship to ignore the language dimension of the judicial process.[3]

One other factor that has led social scientists to study language in legal settings is the desire to investigate the validity of public and intraprofessional critiques of "the sociology of the professions," a subject which includes the language of legal professionals, which has been alleged to be elitist, exclusionary, mystifying, and/or oppressive. For those who wish to examine these claims from an empirical foundation rather than a purely ideological one, it is of course essential that one first observe and describe the object of potential criticism; and since that object is, in this case, language used in legal settings, one more motivation is added for researchers to take up the systematic analysis of that language.

Thus a variety of changing attitudes and possibilities—intellectual, technological, methodological, and social—have combined in the last two decades to produce the steadily intensifying interest in language and law, one result of which is the publication of this volume.

1.3.   Range of Current Research Topics

In the light of the above historical review, it seems appropriate to consider at this point just how the domain of social science research on language and law has taken shape over the last two decades; that is, what would a "surveyor's map" of the territory reveal in terms of such elements as broad outline, overall dimensions, internal and external boundaries, significant landmarks, and areas remaining *terra incognita*? To answer this question fairly concisely,

---

[3] For a concise summary of this development in sociology and its significance to the study of language in the courtroom, see Pomerantz and Atkinson, 1984.

we may consider the ways in which actual and potential research subjects might be arranged along a continuum of demonstrated scholarly interest, and thereby construct a set of three simple lists corresponding to those subjects which have been most studied (thus far), those least studied, and those falling in between.[4]

The research areas within language and law in which the most work has been published are the following:

1. Conversational analysis of language in legal settings, including studies of plea bargaining, courtroom discourse, and conversations entered as evidence in criminal trials
2. Linguistic factors affecting reliability of eyewitness testimony
3. Plain English studies (especially concerning the written language of legal documents and the oral language of jury instructions)
4. Presentational style and language attitudes in courtroom testimony.

In the category of subjects in which at least a promising start has been made, despite the distance left to travel, we find a larger number of topics, including the following:

1. Communicative competence in legal settings
2. Due process for language minorities
3. The language of lawyer–client interactions
4. The myth of the "verbatim" transcript and implications for the judicial process
5. Semantic and pragmatic issues in courtroom discourse
6. Storytelling as a model of courtroom discourse
7. Syntactic and discourse analysis of written legal language.

Finally, in the category of subjects which are excellent possibilities for fruitful research in this area but about which I can find very few (if any) published studies are the following:

1. Advertising language and FTC regulation
2. Free speech, symbolic speech, and the First Amendment
3. Judicial notions of linguistic authority (i.e., how do judges decide linguistic questions?)
4. Presuppositions and leading questions: the language of admissible evidence

---

[4] I should mention here that, in regard to these various lists and categories, I am speaking only of what is available in the social science literature because that is the domain of discourse for this chapter. I am certain that there are voluminous writings on some of these topics in the literature of other professions; for example, on advertising language in advertising journals, or on free speech and the First Amendment in legal journals. Nevertheless, these sets of publication have not been my concern and have thus not been covered in this review.

5. Problems of cross-cultural and cross-dialectal communication in legal settings
6. Speech act theory applied to verbal offenses.

These three lists reveal not only considerable variation in the quantity of published research among the different topics but also the striking qualitative diversity among the subjects constituting the broader research field. With this background in mind, the reader's attention is directed to Table 1, which offers additional detail concerning the content and organization of contemporary social science research in this area. As the arrangement of Table 1 suggests, research on language and law appears to fall within these three major categories: (1) the study of spoken language in legal settings; (2) the study of language as a subject of the law; and (3) the written language of the law. Although these three categories in principle might each encompass a comparably broad range of research questions, it happens that the largest part of contemporary research falls into the first category, namely, the study of spoken language in legal settings. As a result, it is from this category that three specific research topics will be featured in some detail in the three following sections.[5] The subjects which fall in the second and third categories—language as a subject of the law and the written language of the law—will be discussed thereafter, but more briefly, in a separate section.

2. LANGUAGE AND EYEWITNESS TESTIMONY

In the research area focusing on the reliability of eyewitness testimony, an area which includes both linguistic and nonlinguistic studies, one of the foremost researchers is Elizabeth F. Loftus, of the Department of Psychology at the University of Washington. Integrating the very extensive psychological literature on memory, which dates back over the last hundred years, with her own recent experimental studies, Loftus and her colleagues have identified a wide range of psychological and psycholinguistic factors that can alter the memory of an eyewitness between the time an event is observed and the time that testimony about that event is produced. The significance of this research is particularly telling in light of the fact that juries tend to give tremendous weight to an eyewitness account, weight that is in many cases far out of proportion to any chance of the testimony being actually reliable (Loftus, 1979:8–19).

Loftus's work on eyewitness testimony (see especially Loftus, 1979) recognizes that the phenomenon of memory must be analyzed as a three-stage process. Stage I is the acquisition and initial storage of information concerning an event; Stage II is the retention of this information over a period of time; and

[5] The content of Sections II and III is drawn from Levi, 1986; that of Section IV, from Levi, 1982b.

TABLE 1. Law and Language: Outline for Research

I. Spoken Language in Legal Settings
   A. Courtroom language: general
   B. Effects of language on eyewitness testimony
      1. Issues in memory acquisition, retention, retrieval
      2. Forms of questioning and their effects on memory
   C. Effects of language variation in the courtroom
      1. Language variation and witness credibility
      2. Language variation and attorney effectiveness
   D. Comprehensibility of jury instructions
   E. Semantic and pragmatic issues in legal discourse
      1. Courtroom discourse
      2. Discourse in other legal settings
   F. Communicative competence in legal settings
   G. Storytelling as a model of courtroom testimony
   H. The "verbatim" transcript: linguistic and legal issues
   I. The language of plea bargaining
   J. The language of lawyer–client interactions
II. Language as a Subject of the Law
   A. Rights of language minorities
      1. In general
      2. In public education
      3. In legal proceedings
      4. As citizens (especially in regard to government services)
   B. Verbal offenses
      1. Taped conversations as evidence in trials
      2. Defining individual verbal offenses (e.g., perjury, threats to the life of the President, defamation, libel and slander, solicitation to murder)
      3. Other
   C. Language issues in consumer protection
      1. Informed consent (e.g., consent forms, retainer agreements, package inserts for pharmaceuticals)
      2. Products liability (e.g., warning labels)
      3. Advertising language and the law (e.g., trademarks and copyright infringement, regulation of advertising language by the Federal Trade Commission)
      4. Effect of (in)comprehensibility on legal adequacy of mandated notices
   D. Free speech, symbolic speech, and the First Amendment
   E. Legal and judicial notions of linguistic authority
III. Law and Its Written Language
   A. Comprehensibility of written legal language
      1. What is and what is not "Plain English"
      2. Language in contracts
      3. Language in public documents and official notices
         a. Issues of adequate legal notice
         b. Issues of equal access to public services
      4. Language of laws and statutes
   B. Linguistic analyses (e.g., prosodic, semiotic, syntactic) of written legal language
   C. Problems in legal drafting and interpretation/construction
   D. Other issues (see also topics in I-H and II-C)

Stage III is the retrieval of information for verbal reporting. At each of these three stages, the mental processes of an individual can produce memories that differ in smaller or larger ways from the event that was the original stimulus.

During the first stage of direct observation and initial storage, the factors that influence an eyewitness' memory of an event are virtually all nonlinguistic; however, language can play a significant role in affecting the memory of eyewitnesses during both Stage II (memory storage) and Stage III (memory retrieval).

In one of the most intriguing and frequently cited experiments (Loftus & Palmer, 1974), Loftus and a colleague showed subjects a film of an automobile accident and then asked them questions about pertinent details, varying the wording to see its effect on both content and accuracy of subjects' recall. The first linguistically important discovery was that subjects who were asked, "About how fast were the cars going when they smashed into each other?" tended to report a significantly higher speed than subjects who were asked, "About how fast were the cars going when they hit each other?" It is reasonable to infer that the estimates of higher velocity were a function of the fact that the verb "smashed" carries a presupposition of a much more violent impact than that suggested by the verb "hit."

The second linguistically significant discovery was that this difference in lexical presupposition between the two verbs influenced other areas of the subjects' memory in addition to the obvious one of vehicular speed. For example, when the same subjects were questioned 1 week later, without any additional viewing of the film, and were asked (as one of a series of questions), "Did you see any broken glass?", subjects who had earlier heard the word *smashed* answered "yes" more than twice as frequently as those who had heard the same question with the word *hit* instead (Loftus, 1979:78)—even though in fact the film had shown no broken glass at all. This second discovery demonstrates that questions asked (or accounts read, or conversations heard) *while a memory is stored* (i.e., in Stage II) can change the form of the memory so that information recalled at a later date (i.e., in Stage III) will emerge in a form significantly different from that originally entered into memory.

During Stage II, the content of our stored memories can be changed not only by information derived from *external* sources but also by linguistically coded information created by our own thoughts. A number of psycholinguistic experiments reported by Loftus (1979:80–86) suggest that our stored memories can be altered by:

1. Labeling a particular object or situation with one word or phrase rather than another (Bornstein, 1974, 1976; Carmichael, Hogan, & Walter, 1932), causing us to recall the labeled category more clearly

2. Guessing with less than full confidence about part of a memory and later merging the content of that guess into what was until then a hazy or incomplete memory (Hastie, Landsman, & Loftus, 1978)

3. The "freezing effect" of repeating an earlier recollection until what was recalled only tentatively and incompletely at first becomes so familiar that one is convinced that the oft-repeated recollection is fully identical to what was actually seen originally (Kay, 1955).

In all these cases, it is the linguistic expressions that we choose in our own minds during Stage II that manifest a transforming power on the information first entered there.

During the third and final phase assigned to memory by psychological investigators, linguistic form and content continue to exert a powerful influence. Loftus reports (1979:90–94) on a series of experiments by others (Cady, 1924; Marquis, Marshall, & Oskamp, 1972; Snee & Lush, 1941) that show that the linguistic style of a witness' testimony—that is, free narrative versus answers to more or less directive questions—influences both the accuracy and the completeness of a witness' recollections. Specifically, the narrative form of response tends to produce the most accurate but not the most complete reporting, whereas a series of well-chosen questions has the opposite effect: coverage tends to be more complete, but responses are less accurate. This psycholinguistic research implies that the most accurate reporting by a witness will be achieved by asking the witness to deliver a narrative-style report first and then to fill in the gaps by means of a series of more specific questions. Any other procedure is likely to contribute to error in witness recall.

When we look at the specific wording of questions asked a witness during Stage III, we see once again that the presuppositions carried by individual words as small as *the* and *a* can significantly alter the content of a stored memory. In yet another automobile–accident–film experiment (Loftus & Zanni, 1975), Loftus and a colleague tested 100 subjects after viewing a film, using paired questions such as these: "Did you see a broken headlight?" versus "Did you see the broken headlight?" Loftus reports (1979:96):

> Witnesses who received the questions using "the" were much more likely to report having seen something that had not really appeared in the film. In the first experiment 15 percent in the "the" group said "yes" when asked about a nonexistent item, while only 7 percent in the "a" group made that error. In the second study the difference is even more striking: 20 percent versus 6 percent. On the other hand, witnesses who received the question with "a" were much more likely to respond "I don't know" both when the object had been present and when it had not.

The work by Loftus and others on the psychology of eyewitness memory has important potential application to legal practitioners and to psycholinguists alike. On the one hand, it shows some of the intriguing ways that language form and language content interact with other (nonlinguistic) mental processes as well as with nonlinguistic factors in a speaker's external environment. On the other hand, it suggests that lawyers and litigants need to understand more about the syntax, semantics, and pragmatics of courtroom questioning not only in order to win their own cases but in order to consider possible changes in the system of justice that might compensate in appropriate ways for the distorting effects of both linguistic and extralinguistic factors on the accuracy of courtroom testimony.[6]

3. LANGUAGE VARIATION IN THE COURTROOM

The second major research effort to be reported on in some detail in this review is the work of the Duke University Law and Language Project, mentioned briefly earlier in this chapter, which got underway with National Science Foundation support in 1974. The interdisciplinary team assembled at Duke some 15 years ago included three lawyers, two social psychologists, two anthropologists, and one linguist. The central hypothesis of the Duke research team was based in part on a substantial body of empirical research in social psychology and sociolinguistics carried out earlier and independently in nonlegal settings. These studies all suggested that our judgments of whether a person is telling the truth (of obvious significance in a courtroom setting) are heavily influenced by *linguistic* variables to which we react in that person's speech.

The Duke research group began by observing and tape recording over 150 hours of criminal trial proceedings in a North Carolina Superior Court. Both the observers' detailed notes and the audiorecordings were then analyzed, first to identify the significant dimensions of language variation among the lawyers and witnesses in these trials, and then to correlate the linguistic variables with different social variables observable in the courtroom. The hypotheses suggested by these observational analyses were then tested empirically in a series of simulated jury experiments, using both undergraduate and law-school students as subjects.

Stretches of actual courtroom dialogue between lawyers and witnesses were rerecorded by actors in several different versions, each of which illustrated one of the significant linguistic variables identified by the research team; different groups of subjects were then asked questions based on the particular version of the reenacted testimony that they had heard. Subjects were asked to rate witnesses for such personal qualities as competence, trustworthiness, and attractiveness; they were also asked to rate lawyers for such professional qualities as intelligence, fairness, skillfulness, and being in control. These social judgments were then analyzed to see how they cor-

[6] See Chapter 10 of Loftus, 1979, for some specific recommendations in this regard.

related with the three major dimensions of linguistic variation set up deliberately by the experimenters. These dimensions, all subsumable under the
broad heading of *speaking style*, are (1) power versus powerless speech, (2)
narrative versus fragmented testimony, and (3) perseverance versus acquiescence in simultaneous speech.

The first dimension, that of "power" versus "powerless" speech, corre-
sponds in general to the different speaking styles that linguists have observed
to be at least stereotypically associated with American (white) men and
American (white) women, respectively (Kramerae, 1981; Lakoff, 1975; Thorne
& Henley, 1975). Each of these styles is characterized by a distinctive set of
phonological, syntactic, semantic, and lexical features. The features associated with women's speech comprise a more tentative, deferential, polite,
exaggerated, indirect, and/or "emotional" style of speaking than the style
customarily linked to men's speech, which is considered to be more direct,
assertive, straightforward, and "rational"; as a result, the latter style is the one
we would expect to be taken more seriously and to be more persuasive—in a
court of law as well as in other settings—than the former.

The Duke research team included the set of features originally proposed
as characterizing women's speech among the variables to be examined in their
study of courtroom speech. However, when they found that use of the two
styles correlated much more directly with the status and social position than
with the speaker's sex (Erickson, Lind, Johnson, & O'Barr, 1978), they continued to investigate the effects of the two styles but changed the corresponding
terms to the "power" and "powerless" modes of speech.

The major research question at issue then became one of determining
how the use of these two styles of speech by witnesses would correlate with
simulated jurors' social evaluation of the witnesses because those social
evaluations in turn would affect the jurors' judgments of the witnesses'
credibility. Using the research methodology outlined above, and varying both
the sex and the speech style of the witness delivering testimony, the experimenters discovered that

> there are striking differences in the social evaluations produced by the power and
> powerless testimony. For both the male and female witnesses, the power speech
> testimony produced perceptions that the witness was more competent, attractive,
> trustworthy, dynamic, and convincing than did the powerless testimony. . . .
> These findings confirm that variation in the manner chosen by a witness for verbal
> expression may have strong effects on how those hearing the testimony evaluate the
> witness. (Lind & O'Barr, 1979:72)

In a second set of experiments, the Duke researchers sought to examine
how the difference between narrative and fragmented testimony would affect
juror evaluation of witnesses (Lind & O'Barr, 1979; see also O'Barr, 1982). The
hypothesis that the linguistic variable of long versus short answers in these
two styles of testimony would correlate highly with such social psychological
variables as control and respect was in general confirmed: Jurors tended to

respond more favorably to witnesses delivering narrative testimony than to witnesses forced into a more fragmented mode of speech. Presumably, this is in part because the jurors infer that the attorney would cede partial control of the linguistic interaction only to witnesses who command a certain amount of respect in the attorney's eyes. The implication once again is that the higher social evaluations accorded to these witnesses will correlate strongly with judgments of their credibility made by the jurors.

The third dimension examined in the Duke studies is called *perseverance and acquiescence in simultaneous speech*, in other words, who wins the linguistic tug-of-war when an attorney and a witness end up speaking at the same time. (In this set of experiments, the attorneys were all male.) The experimental results showed first, that *any* occurrence of simultaneous speech caused the subjects to view the attorney as having less control than in the case where there was no simultaneous speech at all. Second, subjects tended to rate the attorney as less intelligent and less fair to the witness when he persisted in simultaneous speech than when he permitted the witness to continue. On the other hand, significant differences were observed between male and female subjects when asked to evaluate the skill and competence of attorneys and witnesses, in exchanges involving the attorneys showing the most and least perseverance. One of these differences is that when the attorney persevered the most, male subjects tended to rank the attorney as more skillful and the witness as more competent, whereas female subjects ranked the attorney as less skillful and the witness as less competent and less likable (Lind & O'Barr, 1979; see also O'Barr, 1982).

To summarize the findings of the Duke University studies, it appears that for all three linguistic variables examined, judgments of witness credibility were made as a function of social psychological judgments about the witness, which in turn were significantly affected by the linguistic style in which the witness' testimony was delivered.

These findings are of relevance not only to scholarship in linguistics and social psychology but also to the study and practice of law. Current rules of evidence for courtroom testimony focus primarily, if not exclusively, on the content ("Is it relevant?") and the sources ("Are they reliable?") of the evidence provided by witnesses and do not take into account at all variation in "presentational style." It is not at all clear that the rules of evidence could, or should, take such a variable into consideration. Nevertheless, if the credibility of witnesses is as directly affected by linguistic variables as these studies suggest, then an appropriate next step for social scientists involved in this kind of research to take would be to consult with jurists and legal scholars on whether *any* component of legal practice and procedures—whether rules of evidence, instructions to jurors, or simply judicial conduct in "routine management of the trial" (O'Barr, 1982:117)—can realistically and productively be changed in such a way that psychologically biasing but legally irrelevant factors might be identified, and thus taken into account, in courtroom proceedings.

4. COMPREHENSIBILITY OF JURY INSTRUCTIONS

Within the broader area of the spoken language of the law, the third and last major research focus to be considered here is that of juror comprehension of judges' instructions. This subject has been studied most extensively by two different research teams. The first is that of Robert Charrow, a lawyer, and Veda Charrow, a psycholinguist, whose lengthy psycholinguistic study of the comprehensibility of jury instructions appeared in a *Columbia Law Review* article of 1979. The second team is that of psychologist Amiram Elwork, lawyer–psychologist Bruce D. Sales, and lawyer James J. Alfini, whose major research findings appeared in a series of articles between 1977 and 1982 (see, for example, Elwork, Sales, & Alfini, 1977; Elwork, Alfini, & Sales, 1982). These three researchers subsequently adapted their findings into a book (Elwork, Sales, & Alfini, 1982) explicitly intended to serve as a manual for legal practitioners on the art and science of rewriting jury instructions. For the sake of relative brevity, discussion in this chapter will concentrate primarily on the work of the former team.

The difficulty faced at the outset by these researchers is described by Charrow and Charrow as follows (Charrow & Charrow, 1979:1307):

> [T]here are major issues that have not been addressed. For one thing, although it is assumed that all "legalese" is incomprehensible, there is no real data, aside from anecdotes, to support this assumption or to elucidate the exact nature of the problem. There is no empirical evidence of the extent to which legal language is not understood, nor is there any data regarding those segments of the populations . . . that may *not* have problems comprehending legalese.
>
> As for the rewriting of legalese into "plain English," there are no criteria for determining what constitutes "plain English," and no empirically determined rules for rewriting. . . . Moreover, while the questions of what is "plain English" and what is "clear and understandable" will undoubtedly stimulate a flurry of litigation, the courts, at this time, appear to be ill-prepared to grapple with such questions. They lack the linguistic expertise and the necessary empirical tools to make sound determinations concerning clarity or comprehensibility.

In an attempt to make an empirical contribution to this legal and linguistic dilemma, the authors designed a set of psycholinguistic experiments in order to

1. Measure the actual difficulty of jury instructions for a typical jury audience
2. Discover whether individual linguistic features of the instructions could be isolated that were most responsible for the comprehension problems
3. Test to what extent rewritten instructions that reduced or eliminated the troublesome linguistic features *without* impairing legal adequacy would significantly increase juror comprehension (Charrow & Charrow, 1979:1309).

In Charrow and Charrow's experiments, legal material was drawn from the standard civil jury instructions prepared for use in California courts; experimental subjects were drawn from citizens called for jury duty in a Maryland county; and the basic testing methodology was an oral rephrasing task. Results from the first experiment suggested that certain vocabulary items and grammatical constructions were causing a disproportionate share of the comprehension problems. These results were then used to rewrite the instructions and run them through a second experiment, in which the same methodology was used on a different but comparable set of subjects.

One of the major discoveries of the Charrow and Charrow study was that legal jargon was not by any means the only barrier to comprehension on this task; rather, a number of grammatical constructions and discourse features contributed significantly to misunderstandings of the text. Some of the *grammatical constructions* identified as impeding comprehension were: nominalizations, vague and uncommon prepositional phrases, double or triple sets of negative words and phrases within a single clause, passive constructions (especially in subordinate clauses), and "word lists" or strings of closely related words connected by *and* or *or*. Some of the *discourse features* that seemed to adversely affect the subjects' ability to paraphrase instructions were poor organization within a paragraph (or its oral equivalent), apparently needless redundancy which may confuse the hearer rather than reinforce the message, and the stipulation of several related ideas without explicitly numbering them so as to indicate their relationship.

By isolating problematical linguistic features and by conducting statistical analyses of their results, Charrow and Charrow were able to measure the effects of particular grammatical and vocabulary changes as well as change in overall performance. The results varied in somewhat surprising ways, but the general effect of the rewriting was clearly positive, with average improvement in comprehension falling in the range of 35% to 40%. More specific results, obtained by analyzing the nine major categories of potentially difficult *grammatical* constructions, showed that the range of improvement varied widely; thus the increase in subjects' mean scores for accuracy varied in magnitude from 11% (for revised "word lists") to 45% (for revised nominalizations) to 81% (for revised passives in subordinate clauses) (1979:1372).

Although these results are certainly encouraging on the face of it, a more complete and thus more accurate picture emerges when we consider some of the other statistics provided by the researchers on the level of *actual* comprehension underlying the percentage increases. For example, although the rewritten instructions increased understanding of nominalization constructions by 45%, the actual rate of comprehension went from a depressingly low 31% to a not overwhelming 45%, indicating that even after the instructions had been improved, over half of the subjects' paraphrases of nominalizations were judged to be incorrect. In fact, for all nine of the grammatical constructions analyzed, the mean score correct before rewriting ranged from a low of 21% to a relative high of 43%, whereas rewriting the instructions produced a range of scores between 25% and 51%. Thus, although it is true that scores for each of the constructions went up as a result of the rewriting, for any given rewritten construction, anywhere from half to three-quarters of the subjects still failed to produce a paraphrase that could be scored as accurate.

Although it might be tempting to conclude from these discouraging achievement scores that rewriting jury instructions may not be worth the effort, it is more reasonable to interpret the findings as demonstrating that a single rewriting of the sort that Charrow and Charrow performed in these experiments will not necessarily suffice to raise performance levels to a more satisfactory level. Indeed, the authors themselves recognize the limitations of their experimental procedures, explicitly cautioning the reader in this way:

> [T]he rewritten instructions should not be viewed as model instructions, or as necessarily the best possible rewrites, but as instructions that have been systematically altered for experimental purposes. (1979:1329)

This should not be surprising to anyone who has ever attempted to rewrite complex instructions for a nontechnical audience; that task frequently requires not just tinkering with individual sentences but rather a thorough overhauling on a much more global level (followed by an appropriate series of field tests) in order to attain the level of comprehensibility desired.

One significant question in this context is just what a "desirable" level of comprehensibility would be in the setting of a jury trial—and how such a level might be decided. This question is patently not one for psycholinguistics alone but rather is an issue of public policy that must be addressed by the legal profession *in the light* of relevant empirical research.

Although Charrow and Charrow (1979) do not address this thorny question, the second team of researchers in this area—Elwork, Alfini, and Sales—have done just that. They report that they "decided to assume two possible standards of sufficient comprehensibility and judge our results against them" (Elwork, Alfini, & Sales, 1982:438). The first standard proposed and tested was:

> (1) that any given point of law "should" be understood by *at least two-thirds* of a 12-member jury (or eight out of 12 jurors) and (2) that this level of comprehension should be achieved in *at least eight out of 10 juries.* (1982:438)

The second standard was a still more demanding one (especially in view of the low initial scores attained by the subjects on the original version), incorporating these two more stringent criteria:

> (1) any given point of law "should" be understood by at least three-fourths of a 12-member jury (or nine out of 12 jurors), and (2) that this level of comprehension should be achieved in *at least nine out of 10 juries.* (1982:438)

One significant outcome of their research is the finding that both of the plausible levels of "sufficient comprehensibility" *could* indeed be attained by appropriate efforts at rewriting, although it was also clear that certain sections (typically, the ones that were the least understood at the outset) would need considerably more rewriting than others. The empirical results of this research team thus provide a valuable complement to the findings reported by Charrow and Charrow in suggesting appropriate directions to take—and methods to adopt—in attempting to improve this disturbing weakness in the functioning of jury trials.

Taken together, these studies on jury instructions are extremely useful in demonstrating not only that linguistic analysis of difficult legal language can be used to produce demonstrable improvement in juror comprehension—without sacrificing legal adequacy—but also that the need to achieve such improvement is compellingly strong, in view of the serious lack of understanding indicated by the subjects' initial performance in the experiments of both research teams.

As Charrow and Charrow point out (1979:1359):

> The ability of jurors to comprehend the charge adequately has obvious implications concerning the soundness of the jury system: if many jurors do not properly understand the laws that they are required to use in reaching their verdicts, it is possible that many verdicts are reached either without regard to the law or by using improper law.

Moreover, the problems created by juror misunderstandings of legal instructions affect not only the trial level but also higher levels of the judicial system because "the vitality of the appellate process depends, to a large extent, on the assumption that the jury instructions have been understood and properly applied" (Charrow & Charrow, 1979:1359).

Despite the serious implications of the empirical results just reported, the situation is actually a relatively hopeful one in view of the fact that jury instructions in many jurisdictions are periodically revised by standing committees for regular use by judges (Elwork *et al.*, 1982:7–12; Nieland, 1979) and the fact that detailed guidance for rewriting jury instructions, based on empirical research, is now available (Elwork *et al.*, 1982). Because of the growing social science literature on improving the comprehensibility of these instructions, increasing numbers of such committees are turning to this literature for assistance in rewriting their own "pattern instructions" (as they are known). In this area of the judicial process, then, an active interchange has already begun which serves to apply the results of empirical research on language and law to improve the administration of justice in this country.

The three areas just discussed—eyewitness testimony, effects of presentational style in the courtroom, and comprehensibility of jury instructions—provide three different perspectives on the ways in which spoken language may affect the proceedings in a formal trial situation. Two additional perspectives on this subject are provided by the chapters in this volume written by Berk-Seligson and by Drew, while the research possibilities inherent in the study of spoken language *outside* the formal courtroom are exemplified in the chapters by Maynard on plea bargaining, by O'Barr and Conley on the more informal small claims court, and by Sarat and Felstiner on conversations in the divorce lawyer's office. With the topic of spoken language in legal settings thus covered in considerable detail, we may now move on to consider, albeit in a more abbreviated manner, some of the dimensions of inquiry that fall within the other two broad categories of social science research, namely, (1) language as a subject of the law, and (2) the written language of the law.

5. OTHER AREAS OF CONTEMPORARY RESEARCH

The focus of this section is the research agenda suggested by the set of topics shown in Parts II and III of Table 1. In regard to the subject shown as the "rights of language minorities" (IIA in Table 1), we may note that this area concerns the relationship of a number of different groups to the legal process; these groups include speakers of other languages who have limited or no fluency in English, speakers of nonstandard dialects of English (e.g., Black English Vernacular, Caribbean or other varieties of English from outside the United States), and the deaf and hearing-impaired. All of these groups face obstacles to enjoying equal protection under the law, to attaining fuller access to government services and benefits to which they are legally entitled, and to ensuring a useful public education for their children. A relatively extensive body of research has been produced, especially in the last decade, concerning bilingual education programs and possibilities. However, much less social science research has been carried out, to my knowledge, on the obstacles faced by language minorities when they become involved in legal proceedings; this topic is, however, addressed informatively in Berk-Seligson, 1988, and in this volume; *Criminal Justice Newsletter* 16:13 (1985); Gumperz, 1982; and Pousada, 1979. (See also the relevant sections of Levi, 1982a, and Levi, 1985, for more bibliographic detail.)

The subject of "verbal offenses" (IIB in Table 1) is one of the least explored areas in all of Table 1, despite the considerable research appeal inherent in this category for linguists and others interested in speech act theory and its relevance to the real world; although the legal literature is certain to cover this topic extensively, systematic work by linguists on this subject has barely begun.[7]

A similar situation holds true for the subject listed as "advertising lan-

---

[7] See, however, Hancher, 1976, for an excellent starting place; as well as Kevelson, 1982, and Tiersma 1984, 1986, 1987—the latter being a series of analyses by one of several linguists who have become lawyers. The interested reader may also wish to consult Kurzon, 1986, a series of applications of speech act theory to written legal discourse, and Schane, 1989.

guage and the law" (IIC in Table 1). Just as the broader area of "language and the professions" is now attracting increasing research interest in the social sciences, especially in regard to the legal and medical professions, so is the subject of advertising language in general, although even here I know of only one major book by a linguist (Geis, 1982) and a small number of scattered articles and unpublished manuscripts (including Fillmore, 1975; Garfinkel, 1978; Langendoen, 1971). However, only some of these address to any degree the legal issues related to advertising language, such as the linguistic bases for regulations and decisions made by the FTC. The two chapters in this volume by Dumas and Johnson on warning labels on consumer products open up one additional, and somewhat related, area of inquiry, namely, the area of federally regulated "warning" language on consumer products. Like the issue of advertising language, this area is a potentially fruitful one for empirical investigation by social scientists from a variety of fields, including linguistics, psychology, sociology, and human factors engineering. The overall picture, however, indicates that the subjects grouped here under "language as a subject of the law" have thus far failed to attract much interest on the part of social scientists, despite the intriguing possibilities they suggest; the subjects identified in the second part of Table 1 thus constitute more of an outline for a future research program than a summing up of scholarly achievement to date.

The last major division of both actual and potential research represents the subject of *the written language of the law* (Part III of Table 1). This area is the one that most laypeople seem to associate with the term "language of the law," perhaps because written "legalese" (in such documents as insurance contracts, leases, bank statements, and tax forms) is the form of legal language which one encounters—and struggles with—most frequently in everyday life. And it is the *quality* of the written language in those documents which elicits intense reactions from many citizens, who feel that the language in those cases serves not as a means of, but rather as an obstacle to, effective communication. However, in contrast to the intense focus of the public at large on this form of legal language, social science researchers as a group have not devoted much attention to the issues it suggests, with the result that research efforts in this area turn out to be limited.

The research that *has* been published concentrates primarily on analyzing legal documents and texts, either for the purpose of improving their comprehensibility or for more purely theoretical purposes (e.g., stylistic and semiotic analyses). Thus we find the largest share of publications corresponding to the topics shown as IIIA and IIIB in Table 1 (namely "comprehensibility of written legal language" and "linguistic analyses of written legal language"), with other areas of potential interest to the general subject of written legal language, such as "problems in legal drafting and interpretation/construction" (listed as IIIC in Table 1) being more hypothetical than real as categories of contemporary research in the social sciences.

The subject of the language comprehension process is a central one within any of the disciplines which constitute cognitive science, including psychology, education, and linguistics. As a result, the literature on language comprehension in general is vast.[8] The question is what part, if any, of that body of literature constitutes empirical research that focuses primarily or exclusively on the written language of the legal domain. Fortunately for our purposes, it is now possible to identify a growing body of empirical work on legal language carried out by psychologists, psycholinguists, plain linguists, and others on the comprehensibility of different varieties of legal language.

An interesting subset of this work has come from the Document Design Center in Washington, DC, whose interdisciplinary research staff has produced a series of valuable analyses on the legal and bureaucratic issues relating to the concept of "plain English." The range of topics addressed by this group is suggested by the following partial listing of publications:

- *Understanding the Language of Documents Because Readability Formulas Don't* (Campbell & Holland, 1982)
- *Characteristics and Functions of Legal Language* (Charrow, Crandall, & Charrow, 1982)
- *Document Design: A Review of the Relevant Research* (Felker, 1980)
- *A Comparison of Prose and Algorithms for Presenting Complex Instructions* (Holland & Rose, 1981)
- *Readability* (Redish, 1979)
- *How to Write Regulations and Other Legal Documents in Clear English* (Redish, 1981)

As these titles suggest, the Document Design Center combines theoretical research on cognitive and perceptual issues in comprehension with applied work (e.g., consulting with businesses or government agencies on preparation or revision of specific forms and documents). The Center also serves an important role in disseminating its findings to legal practitioners, bureaucrats, businesspeople, and others in need of empirically supported and clearly expressed advice on improving the comprehensibility of language addressed to the public (including, though not limited to, legal language). The value of this work, if it is widely read and intelligently implemented, can hardly be overestimated.

In addition to studies focusing on the comprehensibility of written legal language, there appears to be a growing interest (or perhaps a recurring interest) in prosodic and other kinds of discourse analyses of legal texts, not necessarily for the purpose of changing legal writing but more overtly for the purpose of describing in more detail the nature of this particular linguistic domain. Some of this work is semiotic in approach, such as Goodrich's 1984

---

[8] For an introduction to the specific area of readability, a topic with considerable potential for applications to legal language, see Davison and Green, 1988.

survey article, "Law and Language: An Historical and Critical Introduction" (Goodrich, 1984). But the literature also includes syntactic, prosodic, rhetorical, strategical, and sociological analyses of written legal language, a significant sampling of which may be found in a special issue of *TEXT*, edited by Brenda Danet (Danet, 1984b); this issue is devoted entirely to studies of legal discourse and encompasses a variety of approaches and subjects on legal language in both written and oral form using data gathered in Britain, Israel, Sweden, the United States, and West Germany. Topics range from discourse analysis of British and American written texts (Kurzon, 1984; Vargas, 1984) to a sociolinguistic analysis of the syntax, semantics, and pragmatics of the speech of participants in an Israeli rape trial (Liebes-Plesner, 1984) and from an analysis of how communication patterns contribute to the construction of "legal reality" and "adjudicable" evidence in an inquisitorial hearing in West Germany (Caesar-Wolf, 1984) to a prosodic analysis of binominal expressions in legal Hebrew (comparable to such English doublets as *aid and abet* or *cease and desist*) as evidence of a psychologically motivated "poetization" of legal discourse (Danet, 1984a). Although some of these articles draw data from legal discourse and legal proceedings in other countries, for the most part the subjects addressed and the analyses provided do not appear to be fundamentally ethnocentric or language-specific in scope; rather, they appear to offer considerable potential for cross-cultural application to the study of patterns and processes observable when legal language assumes written form.

The written language of the law has drawn the attention—and often also the ire, disdain, and scorn—of both laypeople and legal professionals for centuries. In early American history, for example, Thomas Jefferson is on record as complaining (in 1774) about statutes

> which from verbosity, their endless tautologies, their involutions of case within case, and parenthesis within parenthesis, and their multiplied efforts at certainty, by *saids* and *aforesaids*, by *ors* and by *ands*, to make them more plain, are really rendered more perplexed and incomprehensible, not only to common readers, but to the lawyers themselves. (Jefferson [Lipscomb edition, 1905] 1:65, cited in Mellinkoff, 1963:253)

Although time alone has certainly not sufficed to ameliorate the problems of legal language addressed by Jefferson in his era, perhaps the variety of analytic styles exemplified in the research considered in the present section will contribute gradually to our understanding of the nature of written legal language and thereby, we may hope, to our ability to do something constructive about it.

6. CONCLUSION

This chapter has offered one representation of the broad range and appealing heterogeneity of contemporary work on language in legal contexts.

The chapters that follow in this volume further exemplify the rich array of research topics currently under investigation by social scientists.

Readers who wish to go beyond these topics may consult the two appendices to this chapter, which provide additional sources of information concerning contemporary research on language in the judicial process. In Appendix 1, the research topics identified in Table 1 are reorganized according to the subfield of linguistics to which they most closely belong; this arrangement will be of value to readers who wish to find out how specific subfields of linguistics, such as pragmatics or sociolinguistics, have been or might be applied to research on legal language. Appendix 2 presents a "beginner's reading list" for language in the judicial process, documenting a number of survey articles as well as a selection of book-length studies that have been published to date. In addition, bibliographical information for materials published by 1982 is available in Levi, 1982a, a lengthy topical bibliography organized by categories which closely parallel those of Table 1.

Although it is true that hundreds of articles and perhaps a score of books have already appeared on subjects relating to language and law, we must recognize that scholarly exploration of this field of inquiry has only just begun. We have not yet fully identified its internal and external boundaries; we have not yet penetrated to its depths, and although our mapping of the territory now includes a number of significant landmarks, we can expect that many more will be established as our work continues.

For example, we have noted that the lion's share of social science research in the United States has centered on spoken language in legal settings, and within that category, on spoken language in the courtroom. As scholarly exploration continues, we can expect that future research will broaden these studies into a fuller range of legally significant contexts beyond the formal arena of the courtroom and, in so doing, will inevitably deepen our understanding of the relationship of speech to judicial outcomes. Another important domain in which expanded research efforts by social scientists would be desirable is the area of laws pertaining to language use and language behavior; little explored thus far by social scientists, this category, in which language itself becomes a subject of the law, promises research opportunities which are both exciting in themselves and rich in their potential applicability to important issues of social policy. And last, there is much for us yet to learn about the written language of the law and such related issues as improving its comprehensibility, approaches to its interpretation, and analysis of its social impact.

As the contributions to this volume demonstrate, the first round of questions concerning the relationship of language to the judicial process has been posed and has received an initial set of answers. Our next task is to discover not only which answers need to be improved upon but which crucial questions have not yet even been asked. This intellectually intriguing and socially vital task will require that the research community in this inter-disciplinary field expand not only its numbers but also the breadth and depth of its inquiry. As members of the first sizable generation of scholars of law and language, we look forward to participating in, and being witness to, the discoveries to be made in the decades ahead.

APPENDIX 1: APPLICATIONS OF LINGUISTICS IN LEGAL DOMAINS

I.   Psycholinguistics
   A.   Psychology of memory: eyewitness testimony
   B.   Social psychology: language variation in courtroom
   C.   Psychology of language comprehension
      1.   Oral language (especially jury instructions)
      2.   Written language: forms, regulations, laws, contracts, notices, warning labels
II. Sociolinguistics
   A.   Language variation and social evaluation (see IB)
   B.   Language minorities and the law
      1.   Problems in legal processes
      2.   Problems in public education
      3.   Cross-dialectal problems for native speakers
   C.   Forensic dialectology (see VID)
   D.   Verbatim transcripts and issues of language modality (see IIID)
III. Pragmatics and Discourse Analysis
   A.   Speech act theory applied to legal discourse
      1.   Analysis of courtroom "questioning"
      2.   Verbal offenses
      3.   Regulation of advertising language
      4.   Analysis of contractual language
   B.   Conversational analysis
      1.   Taped conversations as evidence in trials
      2.   Plea bargaining
      3.   Discourse in other legal settings
   C.   Communicative competence in legal contexts
      1.   Parties in courtroom proceedings
      2.   Consumers as targets of advertising
      3.   Consumers in adhesion contracts
      4.   Evaluation of linguistic competence of nonnative speakers for various legal purposes
   D.   Speech versus writing: theoretical issues concerning the validity and quality of "verbatim" transcripts

IV. Semantics
   A. Lexical semantics issues in legal discourse and/or language in dispute (e.g., denotation, connotation, lexical presuppositions, ambiguity, vagueness, individual and dialectal variation)
   B. Sentential semantics issues (e.g., comprehension process of spoken and written language, devious language in contracts or advertising, legal construction issues)
V. Morphology and Syntax
   A. Courtroom questioning: forms and functions
   B. Comprehensibility of jury instructions
   C. Plain English and readability requirements
   D. Descriptions of legal morphology and syntax
VI. Phonetics and Phonology
   A. Forensic technology: voice identification and voice lie detection
   B. Speech differences (phonological) and social evaluation
   C. Phonetic/phonological similarities in determining brand name/ copyright infringement
   D. Forensic dialectology: voice identification by dialect

APPENDIX 2: MAJOR WORKS AND USEFUL BIBLIOGRAPHIES

Bibliographies

Kolin, P. C. & Marquardt, R. G. (1986). Research on legal writing: A bibliography. *Law Library Journal, 78* 492–517.
Levi, J. N. (1982). *Linguistics, Language, and Law: A Topical Bibliography.* Bloomington, IN: Indiana University Linguistics Club. (Out of print)
Levi, J. N. (1985). Rights of linguistic minorities in the United States: An introductory bibliography. *Language Planning Newsletter, 11*(3), 2–5.

Overview Articles

Danet, B. (1980). Language in the legal process. In R. L. Abel (Ed.), *Contemporary Issues in Law and Social Science* (special issue of *Law and Society Review*). *Law and Society Review, 14*(3) 445–564.
Levi, J. N. (1985). Applications of linguistics to the language of legal interactions. In P. Bjarkman & V. Raskin (Eds.), *The Real-World Linguist: Applications of Linguistics in the 1980s* (pp. 230–265). Norwood, NJ: Ablex.
Levi, J. N. (1989). The invisible network: Contemporary research in the USA on language and the legal process. In P. Pupier and J. Woehrling (Eds.), *Language and Law [Langue et Droit]: Proceedings of the First Conference of the*

International Institute of Comparative Linguistic Law (pp. 519–550). Montreal: Wilson & Lafleur.

O'Barr, W. M. (1981). The language of the law. In C. Ferguson & S. B. Heath (Eds.), *Language in the USA* (pp. 386–406). Cambridge: Cambridge University Press.

Books

Atkinson, J. M., & Drew, P. (1979). *Order in Court: The Organization of Verbal Behavior in Judicial Settings.* London: Macmillan.

Berk-Seligson, S. (1990). *The Bilingual Courtroom: Court Interpreters in the Judicial Process.* Chicago: University of Chicago Press.

Brigham, J. (1978). *Constitutional Language.* Westport, CT: Greenwood.

Bryant, M. (1962). *English in the Law Courts.* New York: Frederick Ungar.

Conley, J. M., & O'Barr, W. M. (1990). *Rules versus Relationships: The Ethnography of Legal Discourse.* Chicago: University of Chicago Press.

Danet, B. (Ed.). (1984). Special Issue: Studies of Legal Discourse. *TEXT: An Interdisciplinary Journal for the Study of Discourse,* 4(1/3).

Elwork, A., Sales, B. D., & Alfini, J. J. (1982). *Making Jury Instructions Understandable.* Charlottesville, VA: Michie.

Kurzon, D. (1986). *It is Hereby Performed. . .: Explorations in Legal Speech Acts.* Amsterdam/Philadelphia: John Benjamins.

Loftus, E. F. (1979). *Eyewitness Testimony.* Cambridge, MA: Harvard University Press.

Maynard, D. W. (1984). *Inside Plea Bargaining: The Language of Negotiation.* New York: Plenum Press.

Mellinkoff, D. (1963). *The Language of the Law.* Boston/Toronto: Little, Brown.

Mellinkoff, D. (1982). *Legal Writing: Sense and Nonsense.* New York: Charles Scribner's.

O'Barr, W. M. (1982). *Linguistic Evidence: Language, Power, and Strategy in the Courtroom* (in Studies on Law and Social Control Series). New York: Academic Press.

Pitkin, H. F. (1972). *Wittgenstein and Justice.* Berkeley and Los Angeles: University of California Press.

Tosi, O. (1979). *Voice Identification: Theory and Legal Applications.* Baltimore: University Park Press.

7. REFERENCES

Atkinson, J. M., & Drew, P. (1979). *Order in court: The organization of verbal behavior in judicial settings.* London: Macmillan.

Benson, R. W. (1985). The end of legalese: The game is over. *New York University Review of Law and Social Change,* 13(3), 519–573.

Berk-Seligson, S. (1988). The need for quality interpreting services in the courtroom. *The Courtroom Manager, 3*(2), 10–14 [Williamsburg, VA: National Association for Court Management].

Bogoch, B., & Danet, B. (1984). Challenge and control in lawyer-client interaction: A case study in an Israeli legal aid office. *TEXT, 4*(1–3), 249–275.

Bornstein, M. H. (1974). Perceptual generalization: A note on the peak shift. *Psychological Bulletin, 81,* 802–808.

Bornstein, M. H. (1976). Name codes and color memory. *American Journal of Psychology, 89,* 269–279.

Brière, E. (1978). Limited English speakers and the Miranda rights. *TESOL Quarterly, 12*(3), 235–245.

Cady, H. M. (1924). On the psychology of testimony. *American Journal of Psychology, 35,* 110–112.

Campbell, L., & Holland, V. M. (1982). Understanding the language of documents because readability formulas don't. In R. J. Di Pietro (Ed.), *Linguistics and the professions* (pp. 157–172). Norwood, NJ: Ablex.

Carmichael, L. C., Hogan, H. P., & Walter, A. A. (1932). Experimental study of the effect of language on the reproduction of visually perceived form. *Journal of Experimental Psychology, 15,* 73–86.

Caesar-Wolf, B. (1984). The construction of "adjudicable" evidence in a West German civil hearing. *TEXT, 4,* 193–224.

Charrow, R. P., & Charrow, V. R. (1979). Making legal language understandable: A psycholinguistic study of jury instructions. *Columbia Law Review, 79*(7), 1306–1374.

Charrow, V. R., Crandall, J. A., & Charrow, R. P. (1982). Characteristics and functions of legal language. In R. Kittredge & J. Lehrberger (Eds.), *Sublanguage: Studies of language in restricted semantic domains* (pp. 175–190). Berlin: Walter de Gruyter.

Criminal Justice Newsletter. July 1, 1985. Problems cited in greater use of court interpreters. Vol. 16, No. 13.

Danet, B. (1984a). The magic flute: A prosodic analysis of binomial expressions in legal Hebrew. *TEXT, 4,* 143–172.

Danet, B. (Ed.). (1984b). Special issue: Studies of legal discourse. *TEXT: An Interdisciplinary Journal for the Study of Discourse, 4*(1/3).

Danet, B., Hoffman, K. B., & Kermish, N. C. (1980). Threats to the life of the president: An analysis of linguistic issues. *Media Law and Practice, 1*(2), 180–190.

Danet, B., Hoffman, K. B., Kermish, N. C., Rafn, H. J., & Stayman, D. G. (1976). An ethnography of questioning in the courtroom. In R. W. Shuy & A. Shnukal (Eds.), *Language use and the uses of language* [N-WAVE V] (pp. 222–234). Washington, DC: Georgetown University Press.

Davison, A., & Green, G. M. (Eds.). (1988). *Linguistic complexity and text comprehension: Readability issues reconsidered.* Hillsdale, NJ: Erlbaum.

Dunstan, R. (1980). Contexts of coercion: Analyzing properties of courtroom "questions." *British Journal of Law and Society, 7,* 61–77.

Elwork, A., Alfini, J. J., & Sales, B. D. (1982). Toward understandable jury instructions. *Judicature 65*(8/9), 432–443.

Elwork, A., Sales, B. D., & Alfini, J. J. (1977). Juridic decisions: In ignorance of the law or in light of it? *Law and Human Behavior, 1,* 163–190.

Elwork, A., Sales, B. D., & Alfini, J. J. (1982). *Making jury instructions understandable.* Charlottesville, VA: Michie/Bobbs-Merrill.

Erickson, B., Lind, E. A., Johnson, B. C., & O'Barr, W. M. (1978). Speech style and impression formation in a court setting: The effects of "powerful" and "powerless" speech. *Journal of Experimental and Social Psychology, 14,* 226–279.

Felker, D. (1980). *Document design: A review of the relevant research.* Washington, DC: Document Design Center.

Fillmore, C. J. (1975). Prepared testimony—OTC [over-the-counter] drug advertising rule. Testimony delivered to the Federal Trade Commission. Unpublished manuscript version, 58 pp.

Garfinkel, A. D. (1978). *A sociolinguistic analysis of the language of advertising.* Unpublished doctoral dissertation, Georgetown University.

Garfinkel, H. (1967). *Studies in ethnomethodology.* Englewood Cliffs, NJ: Prentice-Hall.

Garfinkel, H. (1974). The origin of the term 'ethnomethodology.' In R. Turner (Ed.), *Ethnomethodology.* Harmondsworth, Middlesex: Penguin.

Geis, M. L. (1982). *The language of television advertising.* New York: Academic Press.

Goodrich, P. (1984). Law and language: An historical and critical introduction. *Journal of Law and Society, 11,* 173–206.

Gumperz, J. J. (1982). Fact and inference in courtroom testimony. In J. J. Gumperz (Ed.), *Language and social identity* (pp. 163–195). Cambridge: Cambridge University Press.

Hancher, M. (1976). Speech acts and the law. In R. W. Shuy & Shnukal, A. (Eds.), *Language use and the uses of language* [N-WAVE V] (pp. 245–256). Washington, DC: Georgetown University Press.

Hastie, R., Landsman, R., & Loftus, E. G. (1978). Eyewitness testimony: The dangers of guessing. *Jurimetrics Journal, 19,* 1–8.

Holland, M., & Rose, A. (1981). *A comparison of prose and algorithms for presenting complex instructions.* (Document Design Project Technical Report No. 17). Washington, DC: American Institutes for Research.

Hymes, D. (1972). Models of the interaction of language and social life. In J. J. Gumperz & D. Hymes (Eds.), *Directions in sociolinguistics: The ethnography of communication* (pp. 35–71). New York: Holt.

Jefferson, T. (1905). *The writings of Thomas Jefferson* (20 volumes). A. A. Lipscomb (Ed.). Washington, DC: Thomas Jefferson Memorial Association.

Johnson, B. (1976). Communicative competence in American trial courtrooms. *Centrum, 4*(2), 139–149.

Johnson, R. E. (1984). *Courtroom interaction and the application of linguistic arguments: An essay.* Unpublished manuscript. Washington, DC: Gallaudet College.

Kay, H. (1955). Learning and retaining verbal material. *British Journal of Psychology, 46,* 81–100.

Kevelson, R. (1982). Language and legal speech acts: Decisions. In R. J. Di Pietro (Ed.), *Linguistics in the professions* (pp. 121–132). Norwood, NJ: Ablex.

Kramarae, C. (1981). *Women and men speaking.* Rowley, MA: Newbury.

Kurzon, D. (1984). Themes, hyperthemes and the discourse structure of British legal texts. *TEXT, 4,* 31–56.

Kurzon, D. (1986). *It is hereby performed. . .: Explorations in legal speech acts.* Amsterdam/Philadelphia: John Benjamins.

Lakoff, R. (1975). *Language and woman's place.* New York: Harper & Row.

Langendoen, D. T. (1971). Linguistic practices of the Federal Trade Commission. *The Linguistic Reporter, 13*(2), 1–6.

Levi, J. N. (1982a). *Linguistics, language and the law: A topical bibliography.* Bloomington, IN: Indiana University Linguistics Club.

Levi, J. N. (1982b). *Language and law in the U.S.A.* Unpublished manuscript.

Levi, J. N. (1985). Rights of linguistic minorities in the United States: An introductory bibliography. *Language Planning Newsletter, 11*(3), 2–5.

Levi, J. N. (1986). Applications of linguistics to the language of legal interactions. In P. C. Bjarkman & V. Raskin, (Eds.), *The real-world linguist: Applications of linguistics in the 1980s* (pp. 230–265). Norwood, NJ: Ablex.

Liebes-Plesner, T. (1984). Rhetoric in the service of justice: The sociolinguistic construction of stereotypes in an Israeli rape trial. *TEXT, 4,* 173–192.

Lind, E. A., & O'Barr, W. M. (1979). The social significance of speech in the courtroom. In H. Giles & R. N. St. Clair (Eds.), *Language and social psychology* (pp. 66–87). Baltimore, MD: University Park Press. (Also published 1979. Oxford: Basil Blackwell.)

Loftus, E. F. (1979). *Eyewitness testimony*. Cambridge, MA: Harvard University Press.

Loftus, E. F., & Palmer, J. C. (1974). Reconstruction of automobile destruction: An example of the interaction between language and memory. *Journal of Verbal Learning and Verbal Behavior, 13*, 585–589.

Loftus, E. F., & Zanni, G. (1975). Eyewitness testimony: The influence of the wording of a question. *Bulletin of the Psychonomic Society, 5*, 86–88.

Marquis, K. H., Marshall, J., & Oskamp, S. (1972). Testimony validity as a function of question form, atmosphere and item difficulty. *Journal of Applied Social Psychology, 2*, 167–186.

Maynard, D. (1984). *Inside plea bargaining*. New York: Plenum Press.

Mellinkoff, D. (1963). *The language of the law*. Boston/Toronto: Little, Brown.

Nieland, R. G. (1979). *Pattern jury instructions: A critical look at a modern movement to improve the jury system*. Chicago: American Judicature Society.

O'Barr, W. M. (1981). The language of the law. In C. A. Ferguson & S. B. Heath (Eds.), *Language in the U.S.A.* (pp. 386–406). Cambridge: Cambridge University Press.

O'Barr, W. M. (1982). *Linguistic evidence: Language, power, and strategy in the courtroom*. New York: Academic Press.

Philips, S. U. (1982). The language socialization of lawyers: Acquiring the cant. In G. Spindler (Ed.), *Doing the ethnography of schooling* (pp. 176–209). New York: Holt, Rinehart & Winston.

Philips, S. U. (1984). The social organization of questions and answers in courtroom discourse: A study of changes of plea in an Arizona court. *TEXT, 4(1–3)*, 225–248.

Philips, S. U. (1985). Written and spoken law in the American courtroom: The taking of guilty pleas. To appear in S. U. Philips, *Ideological Diversity in Courtroom Discourse: Due Process Judicial Discretion in the Guilty Plea*. Norwood, NJ: Ablex.

Pitkin, H. F. (1972). *Wittgenstein and justice*. Berkeley: University of California Press.

Pomerantz, A., & Atkinson, J. M. (1984). Ethnomethodology, conversation analysis, and the study of courtroom interaction. In D. J. Müller, D. E. Blackman, & A. J. Chapman (Eds.), *Psychology and law* (pp. 283–297). Chichester, England: John Wiley.

Pousada, A. (1979). Interpreting for language minorities in the courts. In J. E. Alatis & R. Tucker (Eds.), *Language in public life (Georgetown University Round Table on Languages and Linguistics, 1979)* (pp. 186–208). Washington, DC: Georgetown University Press.

Probert, W. (1972a). *Law, language and communication*. Springfield, IL: Charles C Thomas.

Probert, W. (1972b). Words consciousness: Law and the control of language. *Case Western Reserve Law Review, 23*, 374–390.

Redish, J. C. (1979). *Readability*. Washington, DC: American Institutes for Research.

Redish, J. C. (1981). How to write regulations (and other legal documents) in clear English. In R. A. Givens (Ed.), *Drafting documents in plain language—1981*. New York: Practicing Law Institute.

Schane, S. A. (1989). A speech act analysis of consideration in contract law. In P. Pupier & J. Woehrling (Eds.), *Language and law* (pp. 581–590). Montreal: Wilson & Lafleur.

Scherer, K. (1979). Voice and speech correlates of perceived social influence in simulated juries. In H. Giles & R. St. Clair (Eds.), *Language and social psychology* (pp. 88–120). Oxford: Basil Blackwell. Also: (1978) Baltimore, MD: University Park Press.

Shuy, R. W. (1981). Topic as the unit of analysis in a criminal law case. In D. Tannen (Ed.), *Analyzing discourse: Text and talk* (pp. 113–126) [GURT 1981]. Washington, DC: Georgetown University Press.

Snee, T. J., & Lush, D. E. (1941). Interaction of the narrative and interrogatory methods of obtaining testimony. *The Journal of Psychology, 11*, 229–336.

Swett, D. H. (1969). Cultural bias in the American legal system. *Law and Society Review, 4(1)*, 79–110.

Thorne, B., & Henley, N. (Eds.). (1975). *Language and sex: Difference or dominance*. Rowley, MA: Newbury.

Tiersma, P. M. (1984). *The language of offer and acceptance*. Unpublished manuscript, Boalt School of Law, The University of California at Berkeley. [Uses speech act theory.]

Tiersma, P. M. (1986). The language of offer and acceptance: Speech acts and the question of intent. *California Law Review, 74*(1), 189–232.

Tiersma, P. M. (1987). The language of defamation. *Texas Law Review, 66*(2), 303–350.

Vargas, D. M. (1984). Two types of legal discourse: Transitivity in American appellate opinions and casebooks. *TEXT 4*, 9–30.

Vernon, M., & Coley, J. (1978). Violation of constitutional rights: The language-impaired person and the Miranda warnings. *Journal of Rehabilitation of the Deaf, 11*(4), 1–8.

Walker, A. G. (1982). Discourse rights of witnesses: Their circumscription in trial. *Sociolinguistic working papers* (No. 95). Austin, TX: Southwest Educational Development Laboratory.

Walker, A. G. (1985). *From oral to written: The "verbatim" transcription of legal proceedings*. Doctoral dissertation, Department of Linguistics, Georgetown University.

Walker, A. G. (1986). Linguistic manipulation, power, and the legal setting. In L. Kedar (Ed.), *Power through discourse* (pp. 57–80). Norwood, NJ: Ablex.

Walker, A. G. (1987). The verbatim record: The myth and the reality. In S. Fisher & A. Todd (Eds.), *Discourse and institutional authority: Medicine, education, and law* (pp. 205–222). Norwood, NJ: Ablex.

Wallace, W. D. (1986). The admissibility of expert testimony on the discourse analysis of recorded conversations. *University of Florida Law Review, 38*(1), 69–115.

Walmsley, S. A., Scott, K. M., & Lehrer, R. (1981). Effects of document simplification on the reading comprehension of the elderly. *Journal of Reading Behavior, 13*(3), 237–248.

Walter, B. (1988). *The jury summation as speech genre*. Amsterdam/Philadelphia: John Benjamins.

Wright, P. (1981). Is legal jargon a restrictive practice? In S. M. A. Lloyd-Bostock (Ed.), *Psychology in legal contexts* (pp. 121–145). London: Macmillan.

Part II

ANALYZING LANGUAGE
IN LEGAL SETTINGS

Chapter 2

STRATEGIES IN THE CONTEST BETWEEN LAWYER AND WITNESS IN CROSS-EXAMINATION

PAUL DREW

1. INTRODUCTION

There has been a burgeoning of research interest over the past decade in the use of language in courts, as well as in other institutional settings, as Levi documents in her contribution to this volume. Part of the stimulus for this has been the relatively recent movement among linguists toward studying naturally occurring language. While Chomsky's insistence on the primacy of investigating the formal syntactic and other properties of underlying linguistic competencies had such an ascendancy in the discipline, the *use* of language (performance) was relegated to a position of much less importance. The study of the structure of well-formed sentences, usually fabricated and detached from any sequences of discourse or from any other context, was preferred by many linguists over the empirical analysis of actual speech. A number of influences have, however, been responsible for a radical shift toward collecting (usually tape recording) and analyzing examples of what people actually say in communicating with one another. And because what people say and how they say it is generally affected by the context in which they are interacting,

PAUL DREW • Department of Sociology, University of York, Heslington, York YO1 5DD, England.

this movement to study naturally occurring speech has also fostered the development of research strategies, in such areas as sociolinguistics, discourse analysis, communication studies, and sociology, which better enable us to explore just how speech is influenced by the setting in which it takes place and how speakers use language to pursue certain organizational tasks or goals in particular settings. Nowhere are these influences, and the strategic uses of language, more clearly evident than in the courtroom.

In this chapter, I shall focus on aspects of the language used by witnesses and lawyers during cross-examination in American criminal trials.[1] I shall be particularly concerned to show that certain patterns of questioning are associated with attempts by counsel to undermine a (hostile) witness' evidence. Witnesses are, of course, generally cautious in the way they answer questions (as discussed in the next section), alive to the probability that counsel will try in various ways to upset their evidence. Despite that caution, counsel will indeed seek to elicit evidence in a way that is helpful to their side's case. My aim here is to show that in recordings of naturally occurring trials we can discern patterns of questioning that amount to techniques through which counsel attempt to rebut witnesses' stories, or in various ways reveal inconsistencies between parts of their testimony, or between their testimony and what may actually have occurred. These patterns/techniques of questioning are outlined and discussed in Sections 3 and 4.

2. CORRECTION IN COURTROOM CROSS-EXAMINATION

One of the reasons linguists, including Chomsky, have traditionally been skeptical of the value of investigating naturally occurring speech, instead favoring single well-formed but fabricated sentences as the primary unit of analysis, is that what people actually say often does not conform with the rules of proper syntax. What comes out of their mouths is a syntactic mess. And for traditional linguists the mess, the false starts, the unfinished clause or sentence, the hesitancies, the repetition of words are all, by the standards of linguistic competence, imperfections. They are the corrupt details of language use. Indeed when one looks at an accurately transcribed version of recorded conversation, for instance, it is frequently difficult to decipher. One of the "corrupt details" that most commonly disrupts the syntax and hence

[1] I am, as ever, very grateful to Brenda Danet of the Hebrew University of Jerusalem, and Mack O'Barr, of Duke University, North Carolina, for so generously making available to me recordings they made of criminal trials in courts in Boston and North Carolina, respectively. I am much in their debt because without access to their data my research on courtroom language would not be possible. The extracts cited from O'Barr's (i.e., 5, 18, and 19) data are modified versions of transcripts made by his research team. All other transcripts from trials (except extracts from published sources) I or those working with me have done.

creates the discontinuities that may make a transcript so puzzling, is self-repair. Quite recurrently, speakers may stop midturn or even midword in order to alter or correct something which they have just said. Some of the kinds of repairs which speakers quite frequently make in conversation, thereby disrupting the process of their own turn-at-talk, are illustrated in the following excerpts from transcripts of recorded conversations, using the transcription conventions of conversation analysis[2] (arrows in the left margin indicate the line(s) in the transcript where the feature under discussion appears).

(1) (NB:2:1:1)
B: Well <u>Brad</u> had tuh play <u>golf</u> uh <u>Thursdee</u>. So 'e ⌐-didn't take
A: └Oh:::::.
→ B: Sa-uh f-Fridee o:ff,

---

[2] These transcription conventions have been developed by Gail Jefferson and are summarized in Atkinson and Heritage (1984:18–xvi). Their use has been kept to a minimum in the extracts cited in this chapter, to make the data easier to follow. All the conversational extracts cited here were transcribed by Jefferson, except extract 2 that I transcribed.

Simplified key to transcription symbols used in text
a. Underlining, as in "Well <u>Brad</u>. . .", indicates emphasis.
b. Colons, as in "You ga::ve the defendant", mark the stretching of the preceding sound, in approximate proportion to the number of colons.
c. Commas, as in "Fridee o:ff,", indicate upward intonation of the last sound in the word.
d. Question marks, as in "a number of ph<u>o</u>ne calls?", indicate upward intonation over the whole word.
e. A period, as in "play <u>golf</u> uh Thursdee.", indicates downward intonation over the preceding word.
f. A square bracket thus ⌐B: So'e didn't take
                        └A: Oh:::::.

marks the precise position in a current speaker's talk where a next speaker starts up in overlap.
g. Equals signs, as in "we picked 'er: u:p=it w<u>a</u>sn't jus'...", indicates a run through with no discernible pause or 'beat' between parts of a speaker's turn, or between one speaker's turn and a next.
h. Numbers in parentheses thus   C: From the defendant?
                                      (0.2)
                                 W: Yeis
are lengths of pauses; a discernible but not measurable pause is indicated by (.).
i. A period in front of h, thus .hhhh, marks an audible inbreath, the length of inbreath being represented by the number of *h*'s.
j. Parentheses, as in "..to the door is that (what you're saying)", indicates some doubt about what's transcribed within the parentheses. Hence what is shown within the parentheses is the transcriber's 'best hearing'. If nothing appears within the parentheses, something is audibly being said, but the transcriber cannot make out what that might be.
k. Degree signs, thus °Mhm°, indicate talk that is especially softer or quieter than surrounding talk.

(2) (Northridge, ND:035)

D: Ahh stoopid .hhh Then she wants tih run away from ho:me 'n then we bri:ng 'er
→   ovuh our- I mean yuh know we picked 'er: u:p -=it wasn't jus' that y'know how
       her parents treat'er all the time. .mhhhhhm En so uh:m ( ) .hhh So then
→   hu-=th' nex' day: I min the sa::me day: (.) No we lef 'er at er granmothers house
       -she ran away tih her granmothers hou:se (.) yih know. . . .

(3) (JS:3)

→ E: hhh Well I don't- I'm not a great fan of this type of a:rt.
       There are certain ones that thet I like,

(4) (NB:VII:6–7)

→ Edna: Oh: god.I u:I k- I give uh- you know we gotta ch- we've gotta cra:ck in ar:
         beautiful new basin I to:ld ⌈-juh,
Margy: ⌊-Oh:::=

Margy: =I kno:: ⌈-w,
Edna: ⌊-(Bill) j'st gotta come'n putta new one the guy:'s gotta come en

       check it'n see::'v iv it's authennic thet it cra::cked'n all this bit yihknow,=

In some such instances, speakers correct an error they have just made; for
example, in extract 1 B's self-repair in "Sa-uh f-Fridee.." reveals her to have
been going to make a mistake about which day her husband worked and in 2
the speaker again gets a day wrong ("th' nex' day: I min the sa::me day:"). But
elsewhere it is not so much that an error is corrected, as that speakers begin to
say or describe something one way but interrupt themselves to change to an
alternative way of saying/describing it. For instance in 3 Edna has been asked
by her son what she thinks of a picture he has bought; it looks as though she
began to say, "Well I dont (like)" that type of art but changed it instead to the
more circumspect, less directly disapproving, "I'm not a great fan." In 2, D
changes "we bri:ng 'er ovuh.." to "we picked 'er: up" : and in 4 Edna was
probably about to say "we gotta ch(ip)", but alters this to "we've gotta cra:ck
in ar: beautiful new basin..", which is not only a more dramatic version of a
mishap (a crack in a handbasin being, presumably, more consequential than a
chip in it) but also better fitted to her story about their making an insurance
claim for a replacement. In these cases what is repaired is not so much wrong,
as less felicitous—for the purposes the speakers have—than the alternative
which they select to take its place. Thus speakers weigh and decide between
alternatives that although not being mutually exclusive (as in 1 where if it's
Friday, it could not have been Saturday), do not equally serve the speaker's
interactional purposes.

In ordinary conversation self-repairs such as those illustrated are very
frequent indeed. Speakers monitor their own talk and alter it, in its course,
with an eye not only to correcting errors but also to best serving the communicative effects they would like to produce (on self-repair in conversation, see
Schegloff, Jefferson, & Sacks, 1977 and Levelt, 1983). We might expect this

kind of conversational behavior to be evident in similar ways in courtroom discourse. However, my analysis of courtroom proceedings suggests that such self-repairs are comparatively infrequent, especially in witnesses' testimony. Even when witnesses are hesitant and having difficulty, perhaps because they are being put under pressure in cross-examination (examples of which will be shown later), they rather rarely perform the kind of self-repair evidenced in 1–4, in which a term first selected is then replaced by an alternative "better" term.

This is not, of course, because witnesses are being less careful about how they express themselves in court than they are in conversation. Indeed the reverse seems most likely; that is, they are being careful to avoid having subsequently to amend the versions they first proposed. If witnesses in court were to engage in the kind of self-repairs speakers do in 2 and 4, for instance, they could easily be challenged about the accuracy of their evidence (e.g., as to whether it was a chip or a crack), about their ability to recall (e.g., whether it was the same day or the day after)—thus raising questions about the verisimilitude, credibility, or consistency of their evidence and hence about their competence as witnesses. Even if an initial version were to be left uncompleted before being replaced with a "cleaned-up" version, that alteration might reveal enough of what the witness had been going to say, of what was partially verbalized, for that to be heard as the real version, and as some sort of Freudian "leakage" of the truth.[3] This may be observed in the following

---

[3] In this type of repair, a word partially verbalized and then, after only a very slight degree of error has been articulated, is replaced by a corrected version. In identifying this phenomenon, Jefferson notes that only just enough of the error has been spoken to make that first version potentially recognizable, but not enough to make it the talk's official business. So that if, for instance, that word (the error) is objectionable in some way, it is corrected in time for it not to be an officially complainable matter. However, Jefferson cites the following extract from a traffic court:

> *Defendant:* En I didn't read that ((description of violation police officer wrote on the
> → ticket)). When thuh ku-officer came up ⌈I s-
> *Judge:* ⌊'had traffic signal approximately thirty
> feet past of the cross-walk, when signal changed tuh red'.

About this Jefferson comments:

> While an occurrence like "thuh ku-officer . . ." may not be subject to official complaint, it appears that the judge is making his unhappiness with it manifest in an alternative way i.e., by interrupting the defendant mid-word in her correction. Whether or not "ku-" is an artifact of the 'cop/officer' alternation, or an anticipation error involving the subsequently appearing "came," the judge may hear it as a gross but still unofficial instance of the former and hear it as an insult. He may deal with both its grossness and its unofficial status by e.g., producing a rudeness, perhaps specifically a reciprocal rudeness to be heard as unofficially admonishing the defendant for her insult. (Jefferson, 1974:193–194)

Thus a partially verbalized error, although not officially part of the talk, may be recognizable for what it was going to be and may be oriented to in unofficial ways as that very object.

extract from a drug trial, in which the witness is a codefendant with her daughter on a charge of possessing heroin. During her cross-examination she mentions that her daughter has been in trouble with the police prior to this charge, at which point this sequence occurs.

(5) (O'B:WD:6)
Counsel: What kind of trouble
Witness: She was just found with some works in her pocket (   )
Counsel: Works eh now wher- where did you pick up the sla::ng expression works
Witness: I've heard it u:sed quite frequently=
Counsel: =What's meant by the term works
Witness: It means uh a nee:dle
      (1.6)
Counsel: A syringe?
Witness: Yes sir
Counsel: An cooker.
→ *Witness:* Ye- I don' know about the cooker
Counsel: Pardon
Witness: I don't know about the cooker

Having answered that "works" means a needle, the witness is prompted to agree that it includes also a syringe and is then asked whether in addition it means a "cooker." She provides what is plainly audible on the tape recording as something that is going to be an affirmative answer but cuts that off before completion, "Ye-"; she substitutes instead the answer that she does not know. By *not* confirming that she knows that the meaning of "works" includes "cooker," it appears that she is attempting—through a device to be discussed later in this chapter—to minimize her familiarity with an argot term used by drug addicts. However in the self repair "Ye- I don' know about the cooker," the witness may have been incautious enough to let slip enough of her first version for that to be revealed as possibly the "real" answer (i.e., that she does know that it also means "cooker"); thus in her subsequent version she might be considered to be dissembling or evasive.

This instance nicely illustrates the hazards of compromising one's testimony by amending or correcting an initial version. The infrequent occurrence in my data of this kind of revealing self-correction in witnesses' answers, relative to their enormous frequency in conversation, attests to witnesses being careful to produce just one version and to avoid having to amend or correct that version. Witnesses thereby appear to be cautious in avoiding the inadvertent leakages that can result from such self-corrections; in this way they may orient to the standards of veracity, consistency, and reliability that is required of legal testimony if it is to be credible. Thus we can already begin to see a basis in the details of language use, and especially in the details of its evident "messiness"—such as occurs in the work of self-repair—for showing

how very carefully witnesses attend to the context in which they are speaking
and orient to the necessary task of being cautious in the testimony they give.

The kind of repair illustrated in extract 5 and in the conversational extracts
1–4 is one in which a faulty item, an error or whatever, is corrected in the same
speaker turn as that in which the repairable fault first occurs. As mentioned
before, this kind of repair is rarely done by witnesses during cross-examination. In contrast, however, is another kind of repair that does occur very
frequently in cross-examination. In this a witness corrects a version of events
that has just been proposed by the cross-examining counsel in the formulation of the preceding question. These "next-turn other-corrections" (i.e.,
corrections of the other party's speech) bring us close to the heart of the
disputatious nature of cross-examination and the struggle in which prosecution and defense are engaged about how properly to depict the events at issue
in a trial. And in these other-corrections, witnesses continue to display a
marked cautiousness concerning testimony. Here are just some examples
from a portion of the transcript of a rape trial, in which the witness being
cross-examined is the alleged rape victim.

> (6) (BC:BD:Ou:1:2)
> *Counsel:* An' you went to a̱: uh (0.9) ah you went to a ba̱:r? in Boston (0.6) is that
> correct?
> (1.0)
→ *Witness:* It's a clu̱:b.

> (7) (BC:BD:ou:1:2)
> *Counsel:* It's where uh (.) uh (0.3) gi̱:rls and fella̱:s meet isn't it?
> (0.9)
→ *Witness:* People go̱: there.

> (8) (BC:BD:Ou:1:3)
> *Counsel:*An during that eve̱:ning: (0.6) uh: didn't mistuh ((name)) come over tuh sit
> with you̱
> (0.8)
→ *Witness:* Sat at our table.

> (9) (BC:BD:Ou:6:1)
> *Counsel:* Some distance back into theuh (.) into the wood wasn't it
> (0.5)
→ *Witness:* It was up the path I don't know how far

In each of the extracts, counsel proposes in his question some particular
version of an aspect of a scene: in 6 he describes the place where the witness
met the defendant, some months before the alleged rape, as a "bar"; and later
in 7 as somewhere where "girls and fellows meet." In 8 he describes the
defendant as having sat with her/her friends, and in 9 he states that on the
occasion of the rape the defendant had driven his car, in which the witness
was riding, off the road and some distance into a wood. In each case, the
witness avoids fully confirming counsel's version by embedding in her an-

swers a revised or repaired one.[4] So for example she revises "bar" to "club"; "girls and fellows meeting" to "people going"; "sit with you" to "sat at our table"; and "some distance into the wood" is changed to "up the path"—in each case trying to counter some fairly obvious inferences that might be made if counsel's version went unchallenged.[5]

The witness' answers display a marked cautiousness insofar as she takes a stand, through her other-repairs, on matters that might not otherwise, or in other forms of discourse, seem to make much of a difference. For instance, in a conversational setting, it may be doubted that in describing someone joining one at one's table for a drink, there is sufficient difference between that person's "sitting with one" and "sitting at one's table" for it to be worth troubling to insist on the latter description.[6] In such cases there is nothing intrinsically mutually exclusive about the two versions, the counsel's and the witness'. Thus bars may be situated in a club; "sitting with" someone can involve "sitting at" that person's table; and in the circumstances where driving up a path leads into a wood, either may serve as a description of where one was. However, in choosing not to let the counsel's versions pass unamended but to repair them by substituting alternatives of her own, the witness can be heard to attempt to correct some impression or implication that might be conveyed by the counsel's portrayal of the facts. She does this without directly negating his versions; that is, in these instances she does not use overtly negative components such as "No he did not sit with me, he sat at our table." The absence of such overt correction markers reflects her strategy of offering qualified, guarded versions, which oppose counsel's entirely through implicit or embedded properties of her alternative descriptions. Through this kind of repair in cross-examination, witnesses are being cautious not only about how events, actions, places, and the like material to the case are precisely to be described but also about the manner in which they correct the versions suggested by counsel. At this stage their corrections have more the appearance of putting the record straight than being directly disputatious.

3. STRATEGIES FOR REBUTTING WITNESSES' EVIDENCE: CONTRAST DEVICES

As might be expected, however, such attempts as these by witnesses rarely settle the matter because their embedded corrections of counsel's prior

---

[4] For a technical account of embedded corrections in conversations, see Jefferson (1987).

[5] Just prior to extract 6, counsel has noted, and had the witness confirm, that she was 18 years old at the time, which under Massachusetts law is too young to be served liquor in a public bar. In addition the connotations of "bar" are decidedly more "seedy" than those of "club," the latter implying membership.

[6] For a more general and theoretically situated argument on this point, see Levinson (1979, especially p. 374).

assertions are usually met by counsel's pursuing the matter so as to resist a witness' version. That is, counsel generally withholds supporting or concurring with a witness' alternative revised descriptions but instead pursues the matter at issue in questions that are designed ostensibly to clarify the matter, while doing so in such a way as to imply that the witness' evidence is open to doubt or is possibly incorrect or inconsistent.

This pursuit by counsel, exhibiting a nonacceptance of a witness' answers, can be illustrated in this further extract from the cross-examination of the alleged rape victim. The questions here concern an occasion on which the witness happened to meet the defendant in a bar/club, some months before the alleged rape. Counsel's purpose in this line of questioning is evidently to suggest that from this prior meeting, at least, the witness had grounds for knowing what the defendant's interest in her was (i.e., sexual); so that when on the evening of the alleged rape she agreed to go with him to eat somewhere, she should have known what to expect. Just before this extract begins, counsel has suggested that on this earlier occasion the defendant asked her to go out with him, to which the witness replied that she didn't remember whether or not he had asked her out.

```
(10) (Da:Ou:2:1)
  1    Counsel: W'l didn:'e a:sk you if uh: (.) on that night that uh::(.) he wanted
  2             you to be his gi:rl
  3             (0.5)
  4    Counsel: Didn'e ask you that?
  5             (2.5)
  6    Witness: I don't remember what he said to me tha'night
  7             (1.2)
  8    Counsel: Well yuh had some uh (p) (.) fairly lengthy conversations with thu
  9             defendant uh: did'n you?
 10             (0.7)
 11    Counsel: On that evening of February fourteenth?
 12             (1.0)
 13    Witness: We:ll we were all talkin
 14             (0.8)
 15    Counsel: Well you kne:w. at that ti:me. that the defendant was. in:terested (.)
 16             in you (.) did'n you?
 17             (1.3)
 18    Witness: He: asked me how a'bin: (un)
 19             (1.1)
 20    Witness: °J-° just stuff like that
→ 21    Counsel: Just asked yuh how (0.5) yud bi:n (0.3) but he kissed yuh good-
→ 22             nigh:t. (0.5) izzat righ:t.=
 23    Witness: =yeah=he asked me if he could?
 24             (1.4)
 25    Counsel: He asked if he could?
```

26   (0.4)
27   *Witness:* Uh hmm=
28   *Counsel:* =Kiss ya goodnigh:t
29   (1.0)
30   *Counsel:* An you said: (.) oh k̲ay? (0.6) izzat right?
31   *Witness:* Uh hmm
32   (2.0)
33   *Counsel:* ('n) is it your testimony̲ he only kissed yu o̲nce?
34   (0.4)
35   *Witness:* Uh hmm
36   (6.5)
37   *Counsel:* Now (.) subsequent to this: . . .

When the witness manages (in line 6) to avoid confirming that the defendant had on that occasion asked her to be his girl, counsel reformulates the matter by finding a different line of approach, proposing instead (in lines 8/9) that she had had some "fairly lengthy conversations with the defendant" that evening. The witness attempts to obstruct this line of questioning by the means discussed in the previous section, that is, by producing versions of her own that qualify and hence correct those of counsel. Thus she qualifies/repairs "fairly lengthy conversations with the defendant" to become instead "we were all talkin' "; and when counsel then suggests that she knew that the defendant was 'interested' in her, she offers instead only that "H̲e: asked me how I'(d) bi̲n: en (1.1) °j-° just stuff like that." Each of her answers is a repair of the counsel's description: In the first (line 13), she is attempting to correct the impression that she and the defendant had talked confidentially together for some while; and in her second answer (lines 18–20), her entirely embedded repair proposes that the defendant showed no more interest in her than that of a casual acquaintance, quite in contrast to counsel's suggestion that the defendant displayed more intimate interest. (For a more detailed analytic account of how her answers work in these ways, see Drew, 1985, and forthcoming.)

So far, then, the witness withholds confirming counsel's versions by producing alternative versions that convey quite different impressions about— and hence repair—the suggested intimacy between her and the defendant. Up to line 16 the defense counsel has persisted in his line of questioning by successively reformulating his depictions of that intimacy. However, when she again corrects his version (in her answer in lines 18–20), he pursues the matter by employing a device that attempts to rebut or undermine the version that the witness has been conveying in her repairs. In lines 21–22 counsel constructs a *contrast* between two things to which the witness has attested, specifically between the manner in which she claims he greeted her, "Just asked yuh how̲ (0.5) yud bi̲:n," and the manner of their farewell, "but he kissed yuh goodnigh̲:t" (which, 12 lines before this extract, she has confirmed he did).

The opportunity to bring together facts from prior testimony, to juxtapose them to make a point, is available only to the questioner in courtroom examinations, which gives the questioner an important means of control (for a discussion of which see Drew, forthcoming). In selecting the two facts cited to put together, counsel juxtaposes the claimed nonintimacy of the greeting (asking how one has been being a greeting between acquaintances) with the intimacy of the farewell (kissing goodnight). In view of the witness' characterization that their conversation was no more intimate than his greeting would suggest (explicit when she says in line 20 °j°-just stuff like that"), the contrast that counsel constructs now casts doubt on her characterization. It does so through the inconsistency between the two contrasting facts, an inconsistency that implicitly poses a puzzle that something more must have happened between the greeting and the farewell that could account for the intimacy of the latter, after they had seemingly begun on a nonintimate footing. It is, of course, exactly that damaging implication that the witness attempts to nullify, when in line 23 she adds to her confirmation an account as to how the defendant came to kiss her goodnight: "He asked me if he could." In the way she thus portrays the formality of the request, she attempts to lessen the otherwise apparent inconsistency between the greeting and parting (although in the way counsel subsequently treats that account, in lines 25–33, he manages to turn her account against her, by emphasizing the voluntariness with which she agreed to kiss the defendant).

The important point that I have sought to identify in this sequence of questions and answers is counsel's management of the question in lines 21–22; this is designed so as to produce a contrast that, in its damaging implications for some aspect of the witness' story, seeks to rebut or cast doubt on her version—in this instance, specifically as a means of pursuing his own version against her successive corrections of that version. Similar contrast structures have been found to be employed as rhetorical devices in argumentation in other settings besides courts, including political speeches (Atkinson, 1984, especially pp. 73–81; Heritage & Greatbatch, 1986), and disputes among scientists (Mulkay, 1984). Their recurrent use and forcefulness is particularly striking, however, in courtroom cross-examination. The following extract, also taken from the same rape trial, is a further instance of the use of a contrast device.[7]

(11) (Ou:45/2B:1)
Counsel: Now (.) subsequent to this: uh (0.6) uh you say you received uh (0.8) a number of phone ca:lls?
(0.7)

---

[7]Space prevents fuller illustration of the recurrence of this device's employment by counsel. Development of this issue and a fuller analytic account of how such contrast devices are built up and what they achieve interactionally in court cross-examination is to be found in Drew (forthcoming).

Witness: Yei:s
   (0.4)
Counsel: From the defendant?
   (0.2)
Witness: Yeis
   (0.8)
→ *Counsel:* And isn't is a fa:ct (t)uh (.) miss ——— that you have an un<u>li</u>sted telephone
   number?
   (0.3)
Witness: Yeis
   (1.2)
→ *Counsel:* An' you <u>ga::ve</u> the defendant your telephone number didn' you?
Witness: No: I didn't
   (0.3)
Counsel: You didn't give it to $\overline{\text{him}}$
Witness: No:.
   (10.2)
Counsel: Dur:ing the:seuh, ...

Such instances as 10 and 11 have a number of properties in common—properties that are associated with the interactional work that contrast devices employed by counsel may achieve. These properties may be summarized as follows. First, the contrast generates a puzzle out of apparently incongruent facts. For instance, in 11, it is first agreed that the defendant telephoned her on a number of occasions; counsel then manages the juxtaposition of her having an unlisted telephone number, with her claim not to have given him her number—the puzzle thus generated being, how else could he have obtained her number?

A second property is that the line of questioning is then terminated in such a fashion as to leave the puzzle unresolved: That is, counsel does not follow the matter up by asking a question that would allow the witness the opportunity to resolve the puzzle satisfactorily. It can readily be seen that in each case the puzzle conveys a damaging implication for the witness' testimony. For example, in 11 it might be inferred that she *must* have given the defendant her telephone number. And although there might be quite innocent explanations that would resolve the puzzle and that might be contrary to the damaging implications (e.g., that one of her friends had given him her telephone number), counsel terminates that line of questioning immediately after the contrast without inquiring further. Thus it may be noted that the last line in extracts 10 and 11 represents the opening of a new topic of the cross-examination. Counsel thereby manages to deny the witness the opportunity to provide such exculpatory explanations or to try to account for the apparent incongruity from her point of view. (It will be noticed that in 10 the witness creates that opportunity for herself, by adding an account to her answer, "Yeah," in line 23, as discussed.)

A third property of such contrasts is that the inferences that they generate and that are damaging to the witness' testimony are entirely *implicit*. The "incompleteness" exhibited in the contrast appears to be created in order to invite the audience, especially the jurors, to draw for themselves the damaging inferences that arise from the unadorned juxtaposition of the discrepant facts. This interpretation of the pragmatic strategy that may be behind this particular structural configuration of the discourse is supported by the fact that counsel leaves long pauses after the juxtaposition/contrast, before moving to questions about a next topic. These pauses last for 6.5 seconds in 10 and 10.2 seconds in 11; the pauses following other such contrast sequences in my data generally cluster in the 6–11 second range.

These are noticeably longer pauses than occur elsewhere in cross-examination. Their occurrence in this sequential environment, following contrasts, seems not only to mark the termination of one line of questioning but also to be designed to give the jury sufficient time to note and reflect on the implications which may be drawn from the contrast, to the discredit of the versions of events that the witness would have them believe.[8]

Through this sort of selective juxtaposition of apparently contradictory portions of testimony, counsel can exploit the asymmetrical nature of courtroom dialogue (i.e., the fact that counsel may return freely to prior testimony but witnesses may not) in order to implicitly suggest to the jury some damaging inferences concerning the veracity of the witness' answers and thus concerning his or her motives and actions. It is for this reason that the management of contrast devices, as exemplified in the extracts plays a special and central role primarily in hostile, disputatious questioning.

4. STRATEGIES FOR REBUTTING WITNESSES' EVIDENCE: THREE-PART DESCRIPTIONS

I want to turn now to another technique that counsel may employ in attempting to contest a witness' version of events by portraying these events

---

[8] Du Cann, in one of the leading British guides of advocacy, makes this related point. "During the rapid flow of question and answer in cross-examination the jury do not have much time to crystalize their impressions of the witness. The pause at the end of cross-examination may be the first opportunity for them to do so. The last question should therefore be one which will focus their attention on everything to the disadvantage of the cross-examined. . ." (Du Cann 1964:117). Du Cann is here quite explicitly noting the effect that a pause may be employed to achieve, although he focuses on its use at the end of cross-examination. The cases discussed here suggest a similar use of pauses at the end of a *phase* of cross-examination of a particular line, before moving to a next point.

rather differently. This technique is the use of a *three-part list* to describe some action, scene, or other element of testimony. To begin, let us return to the questioning in extract 5 in which counsel attempts to ascertain the extent of the witness' knowledge of the meaning of the word "works."

(5) (O'B:WD:6)
Counsel: What kind of trouble
Witness: She was just found with some works in her pocket (   )
Counsel: Works eh now wher- where did you pick up the sla::ng expression works
Witness: I've heard it u:sed quite frequently=
Counsel: =What's meant by the term works
1→ *Witness:* It means uh a ne̲e̲:dle
        (1.6)
2→ *Counsel:* A syringe?
Witness: Yes sir
3→ *Counsel:* An cooker.
Witness: Ye- I don' know about the cooker
Counsel: Pardon
Witness: I don't know about the cooker

It is possible here that the witness has perhaps inadvertently used a word which in the argot of regular drug users refers to the equipment used to prepare for injecting the drug.[9] In questioning her about its meaning, counsel's purpose is plainly to suggest that if she is familiar with the word's meaning, then her use of the argot is *prima facie* grounds for suspecting that she uses drugs, contrary to her story. As he questions her about her use of the word, she right away cites a secondhand source for it, "I've heard it used quite frequently," in an attempt to "disclaim" firsthand knowledge of such terminology. When questioned further, she volunteers that "works" means a needle and agrees that it also includes a syringe; but when he persists by asking if she knows it means a cooker, she appears to begin to confirm that she does with "Ye-", but cuts off in time to correct her answer to "I don' know about the cooker." In withholding confirmation that she knows "works" also means a cooker, the witness can be heard to circumscribe her knowledge to just the two prior items and hence to counter the implication that she is *fully* familiar with the argot of drug addicts.

It may not be happenstance that the counsel pressed her to agree to a third item, while she agreed to just two items but resisted the third. Research in conversation analysis, particularly by Jefferson (forthcoming), suggests that lists occurring in natural conversation are very frequently done in three parts. More important, three-partedness is a "basic structural principle" (Jefferson, 1990:89) to which speakers orient as a *normative* device, which is to

---

[9] For a detailed componential analysis of terms in the subcultural argot of drug users, based on his ethnographic study, see Agar (1973).

say that lists with less than three items may be treated as incomplete.[10] Two instances Jefferson cites from conversations are the following (in which square brackets identify each element of the triplet):

(12) (SPC)
Desk: And, ih- in general what we try to do is help people figure out [what the trouble is,] [what kind of help they need] [and get it for them.]
(13) (SBL)
Maybelle: I think if you [exercise it] [an' work at it]'[n studied it] you do become clairvoyant.

These cases offer particularly plain illustrations of Jefferson's finding that descriptions in conversation are commonly constructed in three parts. However, the rhetorical and symbolic significance of a tripartite structure for a wide range of types of discourse has been noted by other writers. Bettelheim, in his analysis of the psychological origins and impact of children's fairy stories, makes several references to the fact that the key symbolism of such tales is very frequently conveyed through their three-part character (Bettelheim, 1977). Atkinson (1984) and Heritage and Greatbatch (1986) have shown that politicians use three-part lists (among other devices) to elicit applause from their audience at critical junctures in their speeches. Jokes frequently employ the device of featuring three characters (e.g., the Englishman, Scotsman, and Irishman), in which a pattern of what the first two characters say or do is then confounded by the third character (Sacks, 1978). My own observations of advertising messages is that a product's merits are commonly depicted by three-part characterizations. At a different (perhaps higher?) level of discourse, the nature of the deity in the world's religions is frequently characterized as a trinity, as in Christianity's Holy Trinity of the Father, Son, and Holy Ghost; or Hinduism's Brahma, Vishnu, and Shiva, representing the creating, sustaining, and destroying functions of God. This striking pervasiveness of three-parted patterns across kinds of discourse, and across cultures, is perhaps responsible for the research beginning to take place in the cognitive and linguistic sciences to look into the technical bases for three-part categorizations as ways of conceptually organizing experience[11] (the title of Lakoff's book, *Women, Fire, and Dangerous Things* giving a clue to

---

[10] Jefferson notes that "three-partedness appears to have a 'programmatic relevance' for the construction of lists," evidence for which are two phenomena. First, if a speaker has only two items to include in a list, the third slot may be filled with a "generalized list completor," as in "And they had like a concession stand like at a fair where you can buy coke and popcorn *and that type of thing.*" An instance of this occurs in line 13 of extract 21. Second, speakers who have trouble coming up with a third item for a list are sometimes found to search for one until they discover one. In both these ways, Jefferson argues (forthcoming, pp. 66–68), speakers appear to orient to a "requirement" that a list, to be properly completed, needs a third part.
[11] Along with Jefferson, it was Sacks who first reported, at a technical interactional level, the three-partedness of lists in conversation and of stories told in conversation—including those stories that are jokes (see Sacks, 1978).

that; Lakoff, 1987). An indication of the relevance this has for the courtroom setting is suggested by the oath witnesses take to tell the truth, the whole truth, and nothing but the truth.[12]

An important point that emerges in part from Jefferson's finding that speakers may treat a list as incomplete until it has three parts is that listing three items is a way of expressing a generalization about a property that items in the list have in common (Lakoff, 1987:5). For reasons that I will not discuss in detail here, three is the minimum number of items necessary in order not merely to suggest but to establish or confirm a common property belonging (at least conceptually, if not physically) to categories that the list collects. To list two items is a way to be specific, to mean just these two; but to ascribe some generality to what is being described requires that the description be built in three parts. Thus we begin to get a sense of what is at issue in extract 5: In proposing a third item, "An' cooker," the counsel is looking to have the defendant display the fact that she knows generally (i.e., fully) what "works" means and hence is fully familiar with the argot of drug users. In contrast, by holding out at just two items, she is concerned to show that she does *not* know what "works" means in general (because what she says she has heard it used to refer to is just a needle and syringe).

The defendant's resistance to admitting knowledge of the third item here is closely paralleled by that of the witness in the following extract from a famous libel case heard at the Old Bailey in London in 1902 (the witness, Sievier, is the plaintiff in the case).

(14) (from Du Cann, 1964:131)
Hastings: Did you marry your first wife in 1882?
Sievier: Unfortunately for me, I did.
Hastings: Unfortunately for her, too. Did she divorce you in 1886, four years later?
Sievier: She did.
1→ *Hastings:* For desertion?
Sievier: Yes.
2→ *Hastings:* And adultery?
Sievier: Yes.
3→ *Hastings:* And cruelty?
Sievier: I know nothing about cruelty.
Hastings: I have her petition here . . .

Du Cann, in citing this extract as an example of the advocate's art, comments that "there is no particular style in its generally accepted sense about these questions, but putting them as three separate matters, piling them one upon the other, gains for this passage its particular effect" (Du Cann,

[12] Disraeli referred disparagingly to the legal mind as consisting "in illustrating the obvious, explaining the self-evident, and expatiating on the self-evident."

1964:131). But most importantly, it is evident from extracts 5 and 14 that in each case the witness orients to the 'generalizing' force of the three parts and apparently attempts to forestall that by denying the third item.

As further illustration of the relevance for language in legal settings and for legal rhetoric of this "generalizing" property of three-part lists, the following are extracts from the closing speech of the prosecution attorney in a murder trial. In 15, not only are three places cited where this crime is the most serious (Florida, United States, and the Bible), but the last of those is repeated three times.

(15) (MC:Peeley:CA:2)

Counsel: Mister R——— had the auda<u>city</u> (0.3) tuh stand up here and tell you about the most serious crime, (0.3) [in Flo<u>ri</u>da,] hh [in the United States,] (.) [and in the <u>bi</u>ble,] (0.9) the bible. (0.4) the bible which sez (0.7) <u>THOU</u> (0.2) <u>SHALT</u> (0.2) <u>not</u> (0.3) k(h)<u>ill</u>

In 16 the same attorney lists three things that the defense promised to show and that he contends they did not,[13] each item finishing with the refrain "didn't show you that"; he then contrasts what the defense failed to show with questioning either anything about the defense case might be reasonable; and again, "anything reasonable" is delivered in three parts.

(16) (MC:Peeley:CA:1) ((Prosecution's closing arguments))

Counsel: The defense, (.) said he was gonna show you things in opening statement, [=he was gonna show you, (.) that the defendant was a f:riend of the victim, didn't show tha:t,] (0.4) [that the victim was homosexual he had cocaine he had heroin he had drugs.=he never showed yuh thAt,] (0.3) [that W——— was a homosexual, (.) hh never showed yuh tha:t,] (0.5) [Is there a reasonable story? (0.3) on the other side?] [has mister R——— (0.7) raised anything reasonable?] (0.3) [anything reasonable (0.5) tuh keep the scales of justice from being tilted tih guilty?]

The appeal in extract 17 is constructed in a similar fashion; posing the rhetorical question whether any mercy was shown to the murder victim, the attorney lists "mercy," "feeling," and "remorse," each prefixed with the refrain "slightest bit." This lack of mercy is then contrasted with a description of the defendant's demeanor in court, and the refrain "You've seen him" is used to list three activities, "yawn," "laugh," and "smile."[14]

---

[13] The lawyer begins the second part of the list with "that the victim was homosexual. . ." and then completes that part with "he had cocaine he had heroin he had drugs"; the third item in the list is then "that W was a homosexual." It looks as though the first mention of "homosexual" was misplaced, and hence is being *replaced* by "he had cocaine he had heroin he had drugs," itself a three-part list; "homosexual" is then reintroduced as the third item, to complete the three-part list.

[14] A comparable instance in which a contrast is drawn between two sets of facts, each set consisting of three parts—but in which this is managed interactionally through questions and answers, rather than rhetorically in a speech as in 17—is to be found in Du Cann (1964). He cites

(17) (MC:Peeley:SR:4)

Counsel: Wuz any mercy shown to that old man= [the slightest bit uv mercy] [the slightest bit:t: of feeling] (.) [the slightest bit of remorse over what he had done,] (0.7) Never-you've never seen it. [You've seen him YAw:n] [you've seen him lau:gh] h [you've seen.him smile during this proceeding]= Have you ever seen himn weep. Never.

In each of extracts 15, 16, and 17, three-part lists are used as rhetorical devices to show fully, and hence to emphasize, how generally applicable is the quality being described (seriousness of the crime; defense's failure; the defendant's callousness). Now this generalizing property can also be employed to convey a sense of nonspecificity, or approximateness. Where for example the data in 5 show a witness trying to avoid the implication of *generality* carried by a set of three items, the data in 18 and 19 illustrate the use to which this property of generalizing may be put in estimating, rather than being specific or exact. This is quite explicit in the next extract, in which a police officer gives an estimate of how far away it was from a house that he discovered a drugs cache.

(18) (NC:O'B:WD:2:90)

Counsel: An' about how far: from the side uv the house (itself) (.)

Witness: From the side uv the house I'd say appro:ximately maybe fi:ve feet (0.4)

→   [fi:ve] [six] [seven] feet

Having used explicit terms of estimation, "appro:ximately maybe," the police officer then includes his estimate of the distance in a list of three, "fi:ve six

---

the opening of the cross-examination by the prosecution counsel Muir of the infamous poisoner Dr. Crippen; Crippen is accused of murdering his wife, which he denies, claiming to have last seen her alive late one night, after which (i.e., early next morning) she had disappeared. Muir opened the cross-examination by asking the following questions, the first three of which establish one point (that when last alone with his wife, she was alive), the next three establishing the contrasting point (i.e., that no one has seen her alive since).

(from Du Cann, 1980:106–107)

1→ *Muir:* On the early morning of the 1st February you were left alone in your house with your wife?

      Crippen: Yes.

2→ *Muir:* She was alive?

      Crippen: Yes.

3→ *Muir:* And well?

      Crippen: Yes.

1→ *Muir:* Do you know any person who has seen her alive since?

      Crippen: I do not.

2→ *Muir:* Do you know of any person in the world who has had a letter from her since?

      Crippen: I do not.

3→ *Muir:* Do you know of any person who can prove any fact showing that she ever left your house alive?

      Crippen: Absolutely not.

seven feet." And in extract 19 this "approximating/estimating" corollary of the generality conveyed in three-part lists is put to strategic interactional use by the prosecuting attorney in a speeding case.

(19) (O'B:MacA:3)
Counsel: All right what speed did your speedometer register
    (2.1)
Witness: It was thirdy five
→ *Counsel:* Exactly thirty five
Witness: That's right
→ *Counsel:* Not thirty six or thirty four.

When the defendant claims that he was doing 35 mph (in a 35-mph zone), counsel questions whether it was exactly 35 mph; and when that is confirmed, he attempts to undermine the defendant's precision by citing speeds 1 mph either side of 35 mph, thereby constructing a list of three speeds (34, 35, and 36) in order to suggest that 35 mph is more likely an estimate of an approximate speed.

I want to emphasize an important issue that I am beginning to develop here. In such extracts as 15, 16, and 17, the generalizing property of three-part descriptions is being used monologically for rhetorical purposes, in the manner in which, for example, a politician might use the same device in a speech. In extracts 5 and 14 counsel is doing much the same, although the rhetorical format—and hence effect—takes three questions and answers to achieve. So the *interactive* employment of the device, in addition to its monlogic use, is starting to emerge. This incipient interactive element comes to the fore in extract 19, in which the prosecuting attorney now actively works to reconstruct a singular into a three-part description. This interactive dimension is, specifically, that one can begin to see a struggle develop about whether a description will be limited, by citing one item (as in 19) or two items (as in 5 and 14), or will be generalized, or treated as an approximation by citing three items (as in 19). For example, in 19, a struggle is emerging between counsel and witness over just what the witness' testimony can be taken to amount to or what can be "pinned on" the witness' words. Thus the struggle over the "content" of the testimony is in part conducted through its form; that is, between a "generalizing"/"approximating" three-part description on the one hand, and a 'delimiting' less-than-three-part description on the other.

The centrality of this device in some struggles between counsel and witness over what the witness is saying is particularly well illustrated in some exchanges between prosecution and defendant in a murder trial. The defendant is accused of being an accessory to murder. The defendant's boyfriend had shot dead a male friend of theirs, after an incident in which the victim had knifed her boyfriend a few hours earlier in the day. She had accompanied her boyfriend to have his wound stitched at a hospital; the couple returned to their apartment where he collected a shotgun, after which they drove together to the victim's apartment. In an earlier part of the cross-examination focusing on how long they were together at the hospital, this exchange takes place.

```
(20) (Cheek:35-3A)
      1    Counsel: Yesterdeh (0.6) when you testifie::d that (0.3) you been in thu'
      2            hospital (about) a half hour (.) a:nd (you were mistaken) (0.3) is that
      3            correct,
      4            (3.2)
      5    Counsel: Remember testifying tuh that,
      6    Witness: I remember yesterday's u:hm (.) it could've bin fiftee:n twenny it
      7            could've been a half hour I-y- a liddle more a liddle less
      8            (0.6)
   →  9    Counsel: So. instead'uv'a half hour now between fifteen minutes and a half
   → 10            hour (0.3) that's (what you led to believe us)
     11            (0.4)
     12    Defense Counsel: 'Jection
     13            (1.8)
     14    Judge: No it may stand
     15    Counsel: (     )
     16    Witness: (Yes)
   → 17    Counsel: Fifteen minutes to a half ho:ur (0.3) is that what it is now
     18    Witness: O:kay: (hh) (.) well uh::
     19    Counsel: You don' (know)
     20    Witness: Yes. (.) u-uh mean NO
     21    Counsel: No=
     22    Witness: =i'was abou(t)-
     23            (2.0)
     24    Counsel: Wul how ⌈long
     25    Witness:          ⌊Twenty minutes I'm not sure. (bu-) -I don'know how
     26            long it takes fer anyone t'get stitched up . . . . .
```

In his first question in this extract, counsel seeks to exploit a possible inconsistency between the length of time the witness has just testified they were at the hospital and her earlier testimony (not included here) that they were at the hospital for about a half hour. He directly proposes (line 2) that she was mistaken in that earlier testimony. The defendant, on the other hand, in attempting to deflect the possible mistake/inconsistency, resists that imputation by including 'half an hour' in a three-part list designed to convey the very approximate nature of her estimate, in "it could've bin [fiftee:n] [twenny] it could've been a [half hour]" (lines 6–7), and adding the overt claim to approximateness, "a liddle more a liddle less." Here she is resisting counsel's attempt to pin her to a specific figure and she continues to do so when he persists (in lines 9–10) in trying to commit her to a difference between her earlier version, "So. instead' uv'a half hour" and the one she is now giving, "now between fifteen minutes and a half hour." Thus in this extract the struggle is between counsel's attempt to construe the timing she gave as more precise than the witness is willing to allow she had intended. She maintains the approximate nature of her estimate by representing it in the form of a three-part list of lengths of times, indicating the kind of time involved.

Later in the same cross-examination, another struggle occurs over the matter of how the witness knocked on the door to the victim's apartment. The prosecution alleges that she acted as an accessory to the murder in that, going ahead of her boyfriend, she persuaded the victim to open his door by knocking on it, thereby gaining admittance for her armed boyfriend. The witness, on the other hand, contends that she slipped out of their car unnoticed and went ahead in order to warn the victim that her boyfriend was coming with a gun, in an effort to enable the victim to escape. Fairly crucial to the difference between the two sides is the manner in which she knocked on the victim's door. Were she simply to have knocked in the regular fashion, that might be construed as having been intended to avoid arousing the victim's suspicions and hence to get him to open the door as he might to an ordinary caller. Her version, by contrast, is that she was banging on the door, and doing so continuously, while calling to him that it was her—"banging" being, of course, designed to display extreme urgency and hence to warn the victim that something was amiss. The contest in the following extract is then between the attempts by the counsel to portray her as having knocked on the victim's door in the usual way (i.e., without special urgency) and attempts by the defendant to depict herself as having constantly banged on the door in an effort to forewarn the victim of the danger.

(21) (Cheek:35A-2)

```
 1     Counsel: Then what happened
 2            (1.8)
 3     Witness: U::huh
 4            (4.0)
 5     Witness: I hear:d thuh (2.2) thuh lock the qu- nthuh=
 6     Counsel: = Right a:fter yih banged the second time? you knocked tw:ice? is
 7            that (fair tuh say)
 8            (2.8)
 9     Counsel: Y'knocked. in two groups, (.) is that fair tuh say
10            (3.9)
→ 11  Witness: I said I knocked ((Knocking sound, presumably by W))
12            (0.9)
→ 13  Witness: Banged whatever
14            (1.8)
15     Witness: uh Told'im it w'z me en all that, (0.3) then wai- ah waited a second
16            (.) (pt)u:hm (.) no-one came to th' door-(up) you know no ⌈one
                                                                         ⌊
17     Counsel:                                                          ⌊You
```

```
18    Counsel: waited a second, (  ⌐        )
                                   |
19    Witness:                     |I do- I don't (.) know. i's bin a long time I
20        don't 'f't'wz minutes or seconds.
21        (0.3)
22    Counsel: Why din'juh say so.
23        (1.2)
24    Counsel: 'Pro:ximat'ly- how much time in between (now) to the best of your
25        recollection,
26        (2.9)
27    Witness: ih'wuz-
28        (0.9)

      .
      .
      .    ((some lines omitted))
      .
      .

29    Counsel: Then what happ'n.
30        (1.2)
31    Witness: I heard thuh: (h) (.) foot- thuh click'v (.) of thuh lock
32    Counsel: Right after that second set of knocks.
33        (5.9)
34    Witness: Ah don' I don'know its bin so long bu(t)-u:hm
35        (1.8)
36    Witness: I don'know: how many secunds it wuz I don' remember I don't
37        even know how many it just seemed like it wuz a long time comin' tuh
38        th'door
39        (1.8)
→ 40    Counsel: You kno::cked (.) y'said something 'n you ⌐kno:cked agen
                                                          |
→ 41    Witness:                                          |°(Mhm)°
→ 42    Witness: An it jus::st (.) seemed like (th't) no-one came tih the door right at
43        that moment.
44    Counsel: At that moment af(t)erra second set of knocks no-one came tih the
45        door.
46    Witness: No-one came tih the door quick enough.
47    Counsel: (bh) No-one came to the door is that (what you're saying)
48    Witness: Oh kay ye- y'uo- mmhm
49    Counsel: Is it?
50    Witness: Yes,
51        (1.1)
52    Counsel: En then approximately how much time lapsed (0.5) before they
53        came to thuh door.
54    Witness: (Unp all in all I guess) about i'w'z a minute end a half I ⌐don-
                                                                          |
55    Counsel:                                                           |How
```

```
56        much time appro:xim't'ly after yer second set of knocks if you can
57        recall.
58   Witness: Oh (hh) uh:r
59        (2.1)
60   Witness: hhI can't recall. I-I can't reca ll  ⌐(    )
61   Counsel:                                      ⌊A minute
62        (4.1)
63   Witness: I(y)-I really can't recall I don't (.) have no ⌐:
→ 64   Counsel:                                            ⌊Remember  knocking
65        some more after the second set of knocks,
66        (5.0)
67   Witness: I don't know I was just c:onstantly ba:ngin' an' banging'=
68   Counsel: =(Didj'yu ) after the second set of knocks=
69   Witness: =I didn't say that I said:(n)'in the beginning I kept bangin' I don't
70        know how much-
71        (4.1)
72   Witness: How much uv tha:t uh:::m (1.0) when they answered thuh thuh door
73        I mean i k- I don't know?
```

The means by which the attorney implies that the defendant had knocked in such a manner as *not* to arouse the victim's suspicions is to propose (lines 6–7) that she knocked twice, thereby downgrading both the manner in which she struck the door and the frequency with which she did so. He thereby delimits her knocking to specifically "two groups" of knocks (line 9). The defendant responds with a three-part list, "I knocked (0.9) Banged whatever" (lines 11–13: on "whatever" as a generalized list completor and the use of such completors as the third part in lists, see Jefferson, forthcoming; 66–67). This three-part list now incorporates her preferred description, "banged," in a format designed to correct and challenge counsel's specificity, by conveying the generality—that is, persistence or continuousness—of her knocking/banging.

The cross-examination then turns to the issue of how long she was outside waiting for the victim to open his door. In the course of his questioning about that, counsel again depicts her as having knocked just twice when he asks (line 32), "Right after that second set of knocks." After a very long hesitation (line 33) (close to the length of pauses that occur after contrasts, as noted in the previous section), she offers the kind of reply that avoids confirming his version.[15] Counsel then pursues that in a question that manages to retain his version of her having knocked twice but in a format that elicits her implicit agreement. That is, he embeds the two sets of knocks into a descrip-

---

[15] For a discussion of such methods of avoiding confirming as the use of "don't know/don't remember," see Drew (forthcoming).

tion that lists three activities, "[You kno::cked] (.) [y'said something] 'n [you knocked agen]" (line 40). He manages in this way to use the format—and moreover the format she used earlier in lines 11–13—to depict the generality of her activity, while systematically holding on to his version of her having knocked in two groups. At just the point when it is clear that his description will be a three-part list, that is, when he has added "'n you," she overlaps quietly with an agreement token, "°Mhm°" (line 41) and then implicitly *endorses* the counsel's description by answering with a *continuation* of it, "An it jus::st (.) seemed like (Th't) no-one came tih the do̲o̲r" (lines 42–43).

This is the only point in the cross-examination concerned with this vital issue that the defendant seems to endorse or go along with her adversary's version of her having knocked twice. For example, when later (in lines 64–65) he reverts to talking about two set of knocks, she replies that she was "just c:onstantly ba:ngin' an' ba:ngin'." When he persists (line 68) by means of the phrase "after the second set of knocks," she has no hesitation in reproving him, "I didn't say that," and correcting him, "I said: (n)'m the beginning I kept bangin' I don't know how much-" (lines 69–70). So that when he is specific in delimiting her activity to just two sets of knocks, she withholds confirming and resists that version—except at just that point where counsel constructs the question in the form, at least, that might convey the generality of her knocking. She is thus brought to—perhaps "tricked" into—concurring with his version at this point in the cross-examination by his having packaged that version in line 40 in the format of a three-part characterization of her knocking that thus has the appearance of being sufficiently like her "generalizing" (i.e., continually knocking) for her to endorse. Her concession is only temporary because as soon as he leaves the 'cover' of the three-part construction of his version, she again resists his version of her having knocked twice.

Extracts 5, 19, 20, and 21 have thus illustrated the generalizing and approximating functions that three-part lists may serve in descriptions, in contrast to the specifying and delimiting functions of shorter lists. These extracts have also demonstrated how these alternatives may by employed strategically in the interactional contest between counsel and witness in cross-examination, as each party struggles to establish its version of how the events, action, and motivations that are at issue are to be properly described.

5. CONCLUSION

The extracts that have been considered throughout this chapter illustrate the considerable care that witnesses take to construct their answers so as best to exhibit and support the version of events they are trying to portray and to avoid endorsing those aspects of cross-examining counsel's versions that differ from or are detrimental to their own versions of 'the facts.' Witnesses are thus cautious in selecting those descriptions that may best serve their line or story. Some ways in which this caution is both manifested and managed have been considered in this chapter. For example, it is notable that witnesses rarely do the kinds of self-corrections that are common in ordinary conversation, the effect being that they thereby avoid both partially verbalized "errors" that might "give the game away" (see extract 5), and word/phrase substitutions that might be exploited by counsel as a basis for imputing uncertainty or unreliability to their accounts. The extracts considered have shown ways in which witnesses are ready to repair versions proposed by counsel in their questions, by producing amended or modified versions (often in embedded form) in their answers. In thus avoiding self-repair and engaging in other-repair, witnesses work to make descriptions count toward their preferred version of events about which they are being cross-examined.

On the other hand, it is, of course, the task of counsel in cross-examination to find ways of maneuvering around the cautiousness of witnesses in order to weaken or undermine their testimony. Although witnesses' purpose in being cautious is to convey their certainty and reliability and the consistency of their evidence, counsel seek in questioning to find ways to demonstrate the uncertainty, unreliability, or inconsistency—and possibly therefore the untruthfulness—of that same evidence. Therefore the management of "producing," of creating the impression of, unreliability and inconsistency is one central purpose of questioning in cross-examination. That is, inconsistency is not always a "natural" product of a witness' testimony but is often created by the way opposing counsel manages to construe how the witness has formulated that testimony. One of my aims in this chapter has been to analyze those methods through which questioning is designed to attempt to undermine testimony and/or to suggest points of inconsistency in evidence.

In particular, it seems that contrasts and three-part lists are two such methodic devices used in cross-examination. They are methodic insofar as they have specifiable properties and have interactional consequences to which participants can be seen to orient in their talk. Although they are devices that occur in language in a range of settings, from ordinary conversation to scientific texts and political communication, in the context of courtroom cross-examination, the 'persuasive' functions of contrasts and three-part lists are employed by counsel as resources in attempting to undermine and discredit witnesses' testimony. They are, however, different kinds of devices in this respect: the construction of contrasts is available only to the questioner (i.e., lawyer) because only the questioner has control over selecting which matters to raise, or to juxtapose. The generalizing and approximating properties of three-part lists, on the other hand, are available as resources to both lawyer and witness. As well as being used rhetorically by counsel in attempting to cast doubt on some point of evidence, or on the entire case of the other side, we have seen that three-part descriptions may be employed by witnesses in attempting to rebut versions being proposed by counsel. Thus they are an important resource in the construction of competing descriptions and hence in the struggle between the two sides in criminal court cases. It is to be hoped that further empirical analysis of naturally occurring interactions in courts will reveal other such underlying and scientifically observable regularities in the interactions between lawyers and witnesses and hence lead to the identification of other devices of practical reasoning and language use, devices that may play a strategic role in cross-examination.

6. REFERENCES

Agar, M. (1973). *Ripping and running.* New York: Academic Press.
Atkinson, J. M. (1984). *Our master's voices.* London: Methuen.
Atkinson, J. M., & Heritage, J. (1984). *Structures of social actions: Studies in conversation analysis.* Cambridge: Cambridge University Press.
Bettelheim, B. (1977). *The uses of enchantment: The meaning and importance of fairy tales.* New York: Random House.
Drew, P. (1985). Analyzing the use of language in courtroom interaction. In T. van Dijk (Ed.), *Handbook of discourse analysis Vol. 3 (Discourse and dialogue)* (pp. 133–147). London: Academic Press.
Drew, P. (forthcoming). Disputes in cross-examination. In P. Drew & J. Heritage (Eds.), *Talk at work.* Cambridge: Cambridge University Press.
Du Cann, R. (1964). *The art of the advocate.* Harmondsworth: Penguin.
Heritage, J., & Greatbatch, D. (1986). Generating applause: A study of rhetoric and response at party political conferences. *American Journal of Sociology, 92(1),* 110–157.
Jefferson, G. (1974). Error correction as an interactional resource. *Language in Society, 2,* 181–199.
Jefferson, G. (1987). On exposed and embedded correction in conversation. In G. Button and J. Lee (Eds.), *Talk and social organization* (pp. 86–100). Clevedon: Multilingual Matters.
Jefferson, G. (forthcoming). List construction as a task and resource. In G. Psathas (Ed.), *Interactional competence* (pp. 63–92). Norwood, NJ: Ablex.
Lakoff, G. (1987). *Women, fire, and dangerous things.* Chicago: University of Chicago Press.
Levelt, W. J. M. (1983). Monitoring and self-repair in speech. *Cognition, 14,* 41–104.
Levinson, S. (1979). Activity types and language. *Linguistics, 17,* 365–399.
Mulkay, M. (1984). Agreement and disagreement in conversations and letters. *Text, 5,* 201–227.
Page, L. (1943). *First steps in advocacy.* London: Faber and Faber.
Sacks, H. (1978). Some technical considerations of a dirty joke. In J. Schenkein (Ed.), *Studies in the organization of conversational interaction* (pp. 249–270). New York: Academic Press.
Schegloff, E., Jefferson, G., & Sacks, H. (1977). The preference for self-correction in the organization of repair in conversation. *Language, 53,* 361–382.

Chapter 3

NARRATIVES AND NARRATIVE STRUCTURE IN PLEA BARGAINING

DOUGLAS W. MAYNARD

1. INTRODUCTION

Recent interest in oral language and law (Atkinson & Drew, 1979; Danet, 1980; Levi, 1985; O'Barr, 1982; Pomerantz & Atkinson, 1984), repeating a characteristic of earlier research on criminal justice (cf. Newman, 1966:xiv, Rosett & Cressey, 1976), gives disproportionate attention to trials and formal proceedings rather than informal processes such as plea bargaining, even though it is in the give-and-take of the more casual setting that practitioners settle the bulk of cases coming before the courts. To be specific, the "explosion" of ethnographic research on plea bargaining during the last 15 years (Maynard, 1984:1) makes it abundantly clear that attorneys often present "facts" by telling stories about "what happened." However, although investigators have explored various dimensions of storytelling in the courtroom (Bennett & Feldman, 1981; O'Barr & Conley, 1985), narratives in the negotiational arena are unstudied and unexplicated.

A purpose of this chapter is to describe the structure of narratives and

DOUGLAS W. MAYNARD • Department of Sociology, University of Wisconsin, Madison, Wisconsin 53706.

analyze how this structure works in negotiations. Another purpose is theoretical. Probing the structure of narratives is also an exploration of the "interaction order" (Goffman, 1983) through which participants bring off plea bargaining as a situated activity. The interaction order can be contrasted with organizational, legal, and other possible orders. It has an integrity of its own that is not susceptible to influence from these other domains, although the interaction order can be, and is, systematically sensitive to organizational, legal, and other aspects of the social environment (Sacks, Schegloff, & Jefferson, 1974). The claim is not that narrative structure is itself a casual "variable" that explains bargaining *outcomes*. Rather, through narratives and narrative structure, as elements of a robust and impermeable interaction order, participants bring to life such factors as the law, organizational "roles," and even the identity of a defendant, as part of mundane negotiational discourse. It is through narrative that actors make decisions and effect "outcomes."

The data used for this analysis are audiotapes and transcripts of pretrial and settlement conferences recorded in a California municipal court. In all, nearly 10 hours of recordings in 52 cases were obtained, including 15 theft, 11 drunk driving, 8 battery, 3 drinking in public, 2 loitering offenses, and one case each of hit-and-run driving, resisting public officers, assault with a deadly weapon, removing vehicle parts, vandalism, and burglary. (In several cases, there was more than one charge; only the first charge for each case is listed here.) Some recordings involved a prosecutor and defense attorney; these took place in an unused jury room. Other negotiations included the judge and were recorded in chambers. Two judges, six public defenders, three private attorneys, and six district attorneys participated in the research. The corpus of cases was not systematic in the sense of being a probability sample. Rather, discussions in approximately one-eighth of all the cases handled during a 3-month period were recorded, as the logistics of recording various plea discussions within the courtroom would allow.

Generalizability of the analysis here derives from a presumption that patterns of talk and interaction reflect a common system of speaking and acting skills that participants acquire as users of natural language. Following procedures in conversation analysis (Sacks *et al.*, 1974:699), we can "extract" from plea bargaining talk those orderly discourse procedures phenomena that are independent of the particular court, particular kinds of cases, and particular negotiators. Moreover, narrative structures in plea bargaining can be regarded as specialized forms of storytelling procedures in ordinary conversation (Heritage, 1984:24). Such procedures may be modified in other settings, or with respect to felony bargaining, but that remains a matter for future investigation. Due to space limitations, I discuss only a small portion of the 52-case corpus. However the propositions about narrative structure apply to, and derive from, detailed, rigorous scrutiny and analysis of all cases and the narratives within them.

2. NARRATIVE STRUCTURE

Sociolinguists have provided a functional definition of narrative:[1] it matches the temporal sequence of experience and, by providing a main point, it serves personal interests of those in the social context where the narrative originates (Labov & Waletzky, 1967:13). However, as Robinson (1981:64–69) argues, it is difficult to assign an intrinsic point to a story. At the very least, the analyst has to take into account what a listener may make of a story, including, sometimes, nothing at all, and, at other times, many different things. Furthermore, tellers may produce stories precisely to discover, with recipients,[2] what evaluation should be made of it (Polanyi, 1979:214; Robinson, 1981:69–70).[3] And finally, the "same" story may have different meanings according to the group in which it is told (Sacks, 1975).

Other scholars have criticized the definitional approach because there is no universal agreement on what the functions of narrative are (Mishler, 1986:108, 155). Rather than providing a strict functional definition of stories and narratives, my strategy is to use a loose characterization to the effect that stories are ways of "packaging" or presenting the facts of one's own or another's experience (cf. Sacks, 1978:259). In Smith's (1980:232) terms, stories "minimally" and "generally" are "verbal acts consisting of someone telling someone else that something happened." Following conversation analysts, I will attend to structural matters.[4] Stories, in conversation, are distinguishable

[1] Prior research in both ordinary settings (e.g., (Labov & Waletzky, 1967; Sacks, 1978) and legal arenas (O'Barr & Conley, 1985) deals with the "personal narrative," wherein the teller of a story recounts his or her own past experience. Stories in plea bargaining involve other parties with whom the tellers are usually unacquainted and events with which the tellers have no direct experience. Thus these stories are parasitic on the tellings and writings of primary observers (offenders, witnesses, victims) and secondary interpreters (e.g., police). In contrast to "personal narratives," the phenomena for this study might be called "third person narratives."
[2] The terms "tellers," "recipients," "speakers," and "listeners" are used in this chapter to denote what Sacks (April 19, 1971:4) calls "conversational identities." Such identities are intrinsic to activities in talk (such as storytelling) and, according to West and Zimmerman (1985:116), contrast with "master statuses" (sex, race, age) that transcend particular occasions of discourse and with situated identities (student, salesperson, bus driver) that belong to particular settings.
[3] See also the definition of stories being about "remarkable" events (van Dijk, 1975), and Robinson's (1981:2–3) critical comment that "commonplace" events are, in appropriate circumstances, as tellable as the less common ones. And consider Sacks's (1984:418) proposal that even when one has a remarkable experience, its reporting is done in such a way as to be usual with respect to how others have had the same experience. In a sense, persons are only "entitled" to experiences as are conventionally available (Sacks, 1984:427).
[4] The structural approach here is also discussed by Agar (1980), who contrasts it with the hermeneutic or interpretive analysis of narrative and with his own concern with a narrator's cognitive schemata and what that reveals about them as persons. For an extension of the latter approach that uses concepts from the field of artificial intelligence, see Agar and Hobbs (1982). For an excellent review of a wide literature on narratives and narrative structure, see Mishler (1986:Chapter 4 and Appendix).

because they take up more than one utterance of talk; usual turn taking is suspended while the story is told (Ryave, 1978:131; Sacks, 1970:Lecture 2; 1975). Furthermore, a story is articulated with ongoing talk. At its beginning, it must be introduced into conversation, and, at its ending, it must be exited in such a way as to reengage or fit with other topical talk (Jefferson, 1978). Within the story itself, teller and recipient may trade turns, comments, glances, and other cues that make the storytelling a collaborative production (Jefferson, 1978; Ryave, 1978; Sacks, 1978). Attention to such matters in plea bargaining shows the following structure:

- A. Story entry devices by which participants warrant the telling of a story, such as
  Naming of the case
  Synopsis
  Transition to story
- B. The story itself, including
  A background segment
  An action report
  Reaction report
- C. Following the story, a defense segment, which consists of
  Denial
  Excuse

Both the reaction report and defense segment are devices by which a speaker offers to exit from the narrative and reengage turn-by-turn talk. The schematic here is very rough. As will be shown, not all negotiations contain these components nor necessarily in the order shown.

2.1. Story Entry Devices

Telling stories in any conversational arena is an activity that must be entered properly. In plea bargaining, participants go through an organized series of actions to arrive at the telling of a story. Regularly, one practitioner's naming of the case starts the plea bargaining session and may directly elicit a story:

(1) 1.011[5]
J1: Next we got John Gage
PD2: Well John Gage is a case that uh he's down at the dump and uh he's in the office where they got the money and the two guys apparently leave or turn their backs

---

[5] Numbers at the start of each excerpt refer to specific points in transcriptions of plea bargaining sessions. Tape recordings were transcribed according to the conversation analytic system devised by Gail Jefferson (e.g., 1978). Those conventions are designed to preserve and reproduce as much detail as possible from the actual conversations. In this chapter, excerpts are simplified

or something. When they come back money is missing. They don't know how much because they don't bother to ever keep track, they have no idea how much is in there ever. I assume that somebody regularly steals from those guys. They accuse my client, an' he says search me, which they do, right down to his toes, they search the horse he rode in on an' everything around him

Naming may also obtain a synopsis through which a speaker identifies the case, assesses or evaluates its worth, or exhibits the state of negotiations in such a way as to display a position on the matters to be told. The synopsis in the next example occurs at lines 2–4 and is followed by a story prefix (Jefferson, 1978:224; see the phrase between asterisks below):

(2) 31a.001
1   J1:   So two [charges] on Daniel Torres
2   PD2: Okay now Daniel Torres is a case where the d.a. 'n I had talked we still
3   haven't—we're not at loggerheads, we really haven't made up our minds
4   yet. *The facts basically are that* Torres and another young Mexican male
5   are in a place to buy beer . . .

The prefix operates with the synopsis to make a story's telling relevant and to project a subsequent utterance as the beginning of the story proper. Another device for properly introducing a story is the "prestory" sequence, in which a speaker requests to tell, and projects, a forthcoming story. Thus, in the next example, after naming the case (lines 1–2) and producing a synopsis (lines 3–6), PD1 requests to tell the story (asterisked utterance, line 8). Then, DA3 produces a go-ahead signal (line 9) that indicates his alignment as a recipient of the storytelling (Jefferson, 1978:219; Sacks, 1975:339–340).

(3) 1A.023
1   PD1: Um the only other one I have is Maria Zamora-Avila.
2   DA3: Sure Zamora hyphen Avila we've got a probation report on this
3   PD1: They're recommending straight probation but she's not gonna plead '
4   cause we have a good good defense.
5   DA3: Oh yeah?
6   PD1: Yeah It should be dismissed. [Referring to the contents of a file that DA3 is
7   reading:] Those are letters that other people've written about her charac-
8   ter. *Lemme briefly tell ya 'bout the case
9   DA3: Mm hmm
10   PD1: She goes inta Davidson's . . .

---

versions of the original transcription form. Following Labov and Fanshel (1977:40–41), excerpts contain some well-recognized dialect pronunciations, such as "ya" for you, etc. Also, personnel are labeled with abbreviations and numbers: J1 means Judge 1, PD2 = public defender 2, DA2 = district attorney 2, PA1 = private attorney 1, etc. All names of defendants, witnesses, attorneys, and others are pseuonyms.

Another type of prefacing sequence is where teller is invited to produce a story. This occurs in line 4 below, following the naming (line 1) and a synopsis (lines 2–3):

(4) 40a.005
1   J1:   Alberto Camina
2   PD2: Oh well this is a case where you heard the motion to suppress, made a bad
3   call in my opinion
4   J1:   What was it about
5   PD2: Okay. This is the guy who's in the car, stopped without taillights . . .

Thus instead of placing stories just anywhere in plea bargaining discourse, participants introduce them systematically. Moreover, one party does not unilaterally decide when a story is to be inserted in conversation; rather teller and recipient collaboratively provide for its production. Finally, synopses play a particularly significant role in the overall negotiations. Most often, as in examples 2, 3, and 4, they precede the story. In a few cases, if not in initial position, then they follow the story. In example 1, after telling what happened at the "dump" that led to his client being charged with theft, the PD remarked, "they don't have any case at all judge." Notice how the story there is built for this kind of "upshot" (Heritage & Watson, 1979). The use of synopses indicates that from the outset stories are not neutral renderings of "what happened" but aim toward or intend the kind of bargaining stance that teller ultimately takes. In example 2, PD2's characterization that he and the DA are "not at loggerheads, we haven't made up our minds yet" shows a willingness to deal. Indeed, after telling the story, he suggests that the defendant would plead guilty if the sentence would be a fine rather than time in jail. The PD in 3, as in 1, uses a synopsis to signal that he wants the case dismissed. The synopsis in 4 displays PD2's attitude toward a negative decision on an earlier motion to suppress the defendant's testimony and also anticipates a story-subsequent request for dismissal.

2.2. Stories

2.2.1. Background Segments

Initial utterances of a story regularly contain descriptions and formulations that "orient" recipients to the action report or core part of the story (Labov & Waletzky, 1967). That is, they provide a sense of who the main characters are and where activities occurred, in such a way as to allow appreciation of unfolding events in the body of the story (Sacks, 1970:Spring, lecture 7; cf. Goodwin, 1984). In technical terms, descriptions and formulations precede the action report in a "background" segment.

In a petty theft case, for instance, the PD produces the action-report part of his story (lines 7–9 below) after he describes the defendant as an employee of Sears and of a specific department within the store where a series of thefts had occurred. These person descriptions and locational formulations then provide the reference for deictic terms such as "they" (line 6) and "she" (lines 7–9), and for other indexicals such as "the room" (line 7), and "in" (line 9).

(5) 3.003

1   *J1:* Lemme come back ta Kathy Nelson
2   *PD3:* Um this is a very unusual petty theft your honor, uh Nelson's employed in
3   Sears and there's been some theft of employee purses and—
4   *J1:* She herself is an employee
5   *PD3:* She's employed and uh there's been some theft of employee purses,
6   employee money um from a little room that they have in the department
7   that she works in. And uh she goes back inta the room ta make some
8   phone calls and she sees a strange purse and she's lookin' in it an' the store
9   detective comes in and uh she gets busted . . .

In addition to placing persons at the scene where an offense occurred, background segments may also account for persons being at this scene. Thus, describing the defendant as an employee of Sears helps constitute a "course of action" (Sacks, 1972; Schutz, 1973; Zimmerman, 1974) that supplies a reason for her being at the location of the thefts (cf. Maynard, 1984:148–149). Similarly, although the store detective is not identified in the background segment, formulating Sears and the defendant's department as the locale of previous thievery also gives a particular sense to the detective's coming into the "room" (lines 8–9). Rather than being a random or fortuitous event, his presence is analyzable as part of a monitoring process, a reasonable course of action that is warranted not only by his membership in the category "store detective" but by the history of thefts in the defendant's department. Background segments place and account for parties in the alleged criminal action besides the defendant:

(6) 12.016
PD3: Um his girlfriend was in the car up ta 'bout five or ten minutes before uh the detention

Here, PD3 mentions the defendant's girlfriend, a "relational" category (Sacks, 1972) that explains her presence in the car. Generally, when a background segment contains descriptions of participants in a scene, they are not incidental members, but rather become principal characters in the forthcoming action reports, reaction reports, and/or defense segments (cf. Sacks, 1978:257). Thus, when PD3 continues the story in example 6 (see example 12), he reports the girlfriend as having spent time with the defendant before he was charged with drunk driving. Moreover, in the subsequent defense segment of the narrative, PD3 supports a denial of the accusation by quoting her version of the defendant's behavior. Finally, background segments may introduce objects that play a central role in the action report. In 5, PD3 refers to "some theft of employee purses," which suggests a history of stealing in the defendant's department and poses the "strange purse" (line 8) as a candidate, subsequent part of that history.

Background segments not only place and account for persons and objects in a scene, they also provide characterological information, answering the question, "What kind of person is this?" Thus, describing the defendant in example 5 as employed at Sears is important not only in explaining her presence in the situation but also in portraying her as a course-of-action "type." That the defendant is "employed" and working in the Sears store make her appear different from one who might be unemployed and wandering through the store. And the kind of person a defendant is proposed to be will become intimately related to the bargaining position that a negotiator displays. This is particularly clear in the Zamora–Avila case (see example 3 preceding):

(7) 1.014

1	PD1:	Situation is this. She's a sixty five year old lady, Mexic—speaks uh
2		Castillian Spanish, she's from Spain. Uh she goes into Davidson's. Oh
3		incidentally, by way of background, for twenty years she's worked in the
4		Catholic church at San Ramon as the housekeeper for the nuns an' the
5		fathers an' all this stuff, and uh very religious, well known. I've inter-
6		viewed half of San Ramon concerning her background. Wonderful lady,
7		no problems, sixty five years old.

In this case, analyzed in detail in Maynard (1984:126–134), the person descriptions (lines 1–7) work in conjunction with other negotiational devices to establish what PD1 considers to be the innocence of the defendant. And they do so in part by characterologically assessing the woman, in the public defender's terms, as "such a sweet little old lady, there's no jury in the world's gonna convict her." Eventually, as mentioned earlier, he proposes that the case be dismissed.

Thus, negotiators use background segments to depict a scene and persons and objects within it where action and counteraction take place. They describe and assess persons and objects with the effect of providing a particular understanding of what is related within the storytelling. Background segments are also constitutive parts of an overall bargaining position.

2.2.2. Action Reports

The action report is constituted by the temporally and sequentially ordered telling of those activities in which at least the defendant and perhaps others are involved until someone, usually an officer, reacts to what the defendant has done. Furthermore, the action report is often demarcated from the background segment by a change from a remote past to present events. In example 5, PD3 states that "there's been some thefts" (lines 3 and 5) and then tells what happened by saying, "she goes back into the room to make some phone calls and she sees a strange purse. . . ." In example 7, PD1 suggests that the defendant "worked" for 20 years as a housekeeper and then begins recounting more recent events with "She goes into Davidson's." But this verb shift is not the only demarcator, nor is it invariably present. More basic is a move from portraying biographical and other relatively durable matters to presenting situated information. Thus devices such as detailing a "history" of thefts (example 5), or listing actors including the defendant (example 5) and others (a companion, example 6) as involved in a course of action provide a temporal dimension to stories that is wider than and yet encompasses the focal moment of activity that resulted in arrest. Furthermore, portraying actors as "types," using categories such as employment status or age or nationality and making overall assessments or evaluations of an actor ("wonderful lady"), all propose transsituational elements to a scene, whereas the action report portrays just that which occurred at a specific time and place and gives the scene its particularity. A way that tellers mark a transition from the background section to the action report, then, is to introduce temporal formulations that indicate the boundedness of the focal activity (cf. Agar & Hobbs, 1982:13–14). The continuation of example 7 shows PD1 interjecting, between the background segment and the action report, "But on this particular occasion" (line 1 below). In example 11 following, PD3 inserts the phrase "On October first of this year" between the background and action components.

Action reports are therefore conversational objects with noticeable, participant-analyzable beginnings. They may also contain items that provide for their possible completion. In the Zamora–Avila case, the action report commences with "she goes into Davidson's" and ends with the defendant leaving the store.

(8) 1.023
```
1    PD1:  But on this particular occasion, she goes into Davidson's, goes into a
2          fitting room, takes two hundred dollars worth o' clothes, pins them up
3          underneath her dress, and leaves.
4          (1.2 seconds silence)
5    PD1:  And they pick her up outside, she's with a companion, they pick her up
6          outside and they uh cite her for petty theft, later discover how much was
7          involved and hit her with four eighty seven point one. [grand theft]
```

"Goes into" (line 1) and "leaves" (line 3) are contrasting terms that bracket the action report, and because "goes into" begins the report, it provides for "leaves" (line 3) as a possible completion.

Such completions are a kind of story-exit device; that is, they can invite a return to more general topical talk. The device here is met with silence (line 4). PD1 next produces a reaction report (lines 5–7), in which the PD tells of the defendant being apprehended and charged.[6] Thus, the story contains at least two candidate completions, which show how action and reaction reports can be distinguishable components of narrative structure. In example 5, however, it is only by way of the reaction report that story exit is noticeable. The defendant is depicted as in the midst of an activity ("looking in" the purse) that is not itself a recognizable completion point when "the store detective comes in and she gets busted."

2.2.3. Reaction Reports

Reaction reports in plea bargaining portray unresolved, incomplete conflict between a defendant and accuser, who may be an actual party ("the detective") or, more abstractly, the "police," the "prosecution," or even "they." This way of proposing completion of a story may be unique to the plea bargaining context as compared with conversational storytelling. Labov and Waletzky (1967) suggest that "normal form" narratives in everyday environments contain some "complicating action" and then a "resolution" of the complication that constitutes the ending of the narrative. Because of their brevity, the following examples are selected from Labov and Waletzky's 14-set corpus of elicited storytellings to illustrate the pattern:

(9) Labov and Waletzky, 1967:16, example 5
Questioner: Were you ever in a situation where you were in serious danger of being killed?
Subject: Yes.
Questioner: What happened?
Subject: I don't really like to talk about it.
Questioner: Well, tell me as much about it as you can?
Subject: Well, this person had a little too much to drink, and he attacked me, and the friend came in, and she stopped it.

(10) Labov and Waletzky, 1967:18, example 10
Questioner: Did you ever see anybody get beat up real bad?
Subject: I know a boy name Harry. Another boy threw a bottle at him right in the head, and he had to get seven stitches.

Each of these stories[7] portrays conflict that, in structural terms, constitutes the "complicating action" and then reaches some "resolution" or completion in

---

[6] An interesting transition occurs between the action and reaction report. That is, the action report triggers the reaction report by characterizing the defendant's activity in such a way as to provide the grounds for official intervention. Where the police were or how they got there is not indicated (cf. Sacks, Fall 1965:Lecture 7, p. 3).

[7] These are elicited rather than spontaneously told stories, but the question that invites them may constrain only the substance of the story rather than its structure. On substantive and structural differences between stories in interviews (elicited) and those in conversation (spontaneous), see Wolfson (1982:61–71).

both cases (Labov & Waletzky, 1967).[8] Notice that example 9 has a kind of reaction report ("she stopped it"), but it still indicates at least a temporary end to the situation. In contrast, plea bargaining reaction reports necessarily imply further steps to reach resolution.

Reaction reports are mostly found in utterances that explicitly formulate police or prosecutor response to the defendant's activity, as in example 8, lines 5–7. However, tellers can depict reactions by different, more implicit means. That is, they may give no overt reaction report and instead provide enough information for a recipient to infer it. Thus, in the next example, the attorney does not produce an explicit reaction report. Instead, the action report (lines 4–8), that contains the plaintiffs' version of events, gives enough information so that a recipient of the story can realize the authorities' likely reaction:

(11) 21.007

1	PA3:	The undisputed facts are that my client is an accountant, he conducts a
2		business in his home out in Woodenville. One night on October first of this
3		year, two people were parking about a hundred yards from his house. He
4		went out of his house 'n went down and exchanged some words with those
5		people, and the dispute is over what those were. The uh people in the car
6		say that he came and beat on the window and told 'em ta get the fuck outta
7		there and that he was a member of the county foot patrol. What my client—
8	DA:	That he was an Officer from the county foot patrol.
9	PA3:	What my client will say is that he went down there and told them that he
10		wanted them to leave, that he was going to call the Woodenville foot patrol
11		or the county sheriff's if he didn't. And the uh, well the gist of the whole
12		thing, it's just who's telling the truth, the two victims or my client and our
13		other witness.

This mode of indirect reporting employs what Sacks (1964–1965, lecture 1) has called a "proper sequence." Listeners to a story know that once one event has occurred, or a series of events has occurred, then something else correctly follows; that is, they know how things should occur in a particular context. In particular, PA3 quotes those descriptive terms from the plaintiff's version of events that display the legally sanctionable nature of the defendant's behavior (see lines 6–7). (The defendant was charged, under Section 146 of the California penal code, with falsely representing himself as a police officer and under Section 415 with "using offensive words inherently likely to produce violent reaction.") Given this display and recipients' orientation to a proper sequence, it is not necessary for a speaker to produce an overt reaction report. Instead, the teller relies on recipients' sense of the grounds upon which police are

[8] Evidence that spontaneously told stories often embody "complicating action" and "resolution" stages can be found in other places. In an article by Jefferson (1978:237–245), see example (25), in which Roger tells a story regarding "voodoo," a car that drag-raced "every car" in the valley, "polished them off one after another," and then "turns aroun'n goes home." See also Sacks's (1978:258) analysis of a dirty joke, which contains a puzzle whose resolution is interpreted from the punchline.

called to some scene (Sacks, 1964–1965, lecture 1:6) by using characterizations of behavior that evoke report, arrest, and charge as normal and natural consequences of the behavior.

Such characterizations do not work alone to implicitly convey the legal reaction to a defendant's activity; they work in conjunction with narrative structure. In the prior example (11), PA3 suspended the action report and euphemistically described the dispute (lines 4–5: the defendant "exchanged some words with those people, and the dispute is over what those were"). It is partly due to the action being suspended that a reaction report is cued and expected. In the next example, the implicit reaction report is evoked by the manner in which the teller fashions the background segment:

(12) 12.016

1	PD3:	Um his girlfriend was in the car up ta 'bout five or ten minutes before uh
2		the detention. He'd had something to drink seven, seven thirty at night,
3		he had three beers, and uh he had a little whiskey in the day, went to sleep,
4		woke up to take her to work, drops her off at work, he's got his kid with 'im
5		an' he's driving home? And um, he says I was not doing anything wrong,
6		said I didn't feel the alcohol, I wasn't under the influence . . .

In this excerpt, the action report (lines 4–5) reaches a possible completion ("he's driving home?", line 5) and is not followed by a reaction report. What follows the story is the defense portion of the narrative. And unlike the prior example, the action report is not itself clearly formulated so as to project arrest as an inevitable consequence of the events within it. Yet recipients can infer the police reaction as having occurred just when the defendant is driving home. This is possible because PD3 mentioned the "detention" in the background segment and placed the defendant's girlfriend in the car before that detention. Therefore, when PD3 reports the defendant "dropping her off at work," one of the next expected events is the detention, which recipient "builds in" or inferentially supplies as part of the story that teller "drops" or leaves out (Sacks, Fall 1965:Lecture 7).

Stories in my plea bargaining data invariably end with a depiction of conflict between various accusers and the accused, whether this depiction derives from an explicit or implicit reaction report. This conflict is comparable to what Labov and Waletzky (1967) refer to as the "complication" of a personal narrative in ordinary conversation. The "resolution" that is the normal end to such narratives does not occur in plea bargaining stories precisely because resolution must be the *outcome* of negotiations, rather than part of the stories told within the process. As Robinson (1981:75) argues, to encompass the resolution phase of some narratives, we have to expand "our concepts of form to include the entire narrative interaction." Or as Goodwin (1982:799) states it, stories can be "embedded in social processes extending beyond the immediate social encounter." In plea bargaining, if negotiators succeed in determining a disposition for the case, then the story has reached its resolution. If they decide to go to trial, then resolution is put off for one more narrative round, and the negotiations have become another segment in the unfolding story.

2.3. Defense Segments

Defense segments in plea bargaining appear as two basic types: denials and excuses. Denials, on the one hand, propose that an alleged wrongdoing on the part of the defendant did not occur. Consider the continuation of example 12:

(13) 12.016

1	PD3:	An um, he says I was not doing anything wrong, said I didn't feel the
2		alcohol, I wasn't under the influence, and she says, well I was in the car
3		with him, I would've taken the car myself if I thought he couldn't drive. If
4		I thought his driving was impaired or he was doin' somethin' wrong, I
5		would've driven. I didn't need him.

Here, statements of both the defendant and his girlfriend counter the allegation of drunk driving.

Excuses, on the other hand, admit that some wrongdoing has occurred and propose an explanation that mitigates the defendant's culpability or responsibility for the act (cf. Scott & Lyman, 1968:47; Emerson, 1969:153–155). Thus, in the Zamora–Avila case, after recounting the defendant's arrest, the public defender produces a long explanation for her behavior:

(14) 1.036

1	PD1:	She had no explanation except to say that she was sorry, her companion
2		with whom she lives is here in court today, says that night, SHE, the
3		companion was crying saying— look what've you done why are you
4		doing this an' all the lady could say is what've I done? y'know what've I
5		done? It wasn't til the next day that she realized when she found the ticket
6		in her purse that the police had given her what she had done. And then in
7		subsequent investigation, uh it was discovered that she had taken two
8		different drugs, one for her arthritic condition, she'd taken more than
9		what she should've, and another drug, combined them which was im-
10		proper, and was obviously under the influence of drugs
11	J1:	What're the drugs, ya got any idea
12	PD1:	Darvoset
13	J1:	Yeah
14	PD1:	and seconal. Now I've checked with the county pathologist and he's
15		researched the thing out. He says that if those drugs are mixed, it will
16		cause a state of confusion, delirium, and put the person in a situation
17		where they just in a dream world, don't know what in the world they're
18		doing. I've also talked with a pharmacist at Middleton Medical who says
19		the exact same thing

Although this is not the whole of the defense attorney's argument,[9] the segment shows that he does not question the wrongfulness of the act. Indeed, he depicts her companion and the defendant as shocked and puzzled by what she had "done" and by "the ticket" (lines 3–7). Not denying the delict, PD1 provides an excuse for it.

Ultimately, both denials and excuses may be a claim of innocence for the defendant, but within the narrative they operate in very different ways.[10] Defenses by denial, on the one hand, retrospectively reconstruct the nature of behavior first depicted in an action report. In example 11, the defense component offers an alternative version of what the defendant said to the plaintiffs who were in a car parked outside his house. In 13, the denial suggests the inculpability of the defendant's conduct as he was "driving home" from taking his girlfriend to work. Excuses, on the other hand, leave an action report relatively intact and provide a causal reason for what happened that focuses on a defendant's subjective state. Denials and excuses, we shall see, are also different in their sequential consequences. Recipients of a narrative treat them in contrastive ways.

3. THE USE OF NARRATIVE COMPONENTS

Narrative structure in plea bargaining comprises a set of devices by which attorneys introduce a story, present it, and then exit from the telling. That is, at least in these data, a narrative can consist of (1) story-entry devices, such as invitations, requests, synopses, and prefixes, through which participants relevantly tell the story; (2) the story itself, which may contain a background segment, action report, and reaction report; and (3) a defense segment that marks the end of the narrative.

That a narrative "can" consist of these components and subcomponents means that it does not necessarily contain them all nor in that specific order. Stated positively, narratives in plea bargaining display variation in the use and ordering of these basic devices. In general, the variability in the use of components and subcomponents reflects their employment for specific purposes, situations, and audiences (Robinson, 1981:74). Having completed our analysis of basic narrative structure, we can now consider the significance of this variability, by examining (1) patterns whereby narratives and narrative

---

[9] For a more complete analysis and transcript of this case, see Maynard (1984).

[10] In a study of trial discourse, Atkinson and Drew (1979:139) also discuss two basic types of "defenses" that witnesses produce to avoid or reduce the blame implicit in a counselor's allegations. Witnesses use justifications in an attempt to forestall blame, and they employ accounts to reject the premise that they could have performed the action they are faulted for not taking. In the discourse, there are separate and ordered "slots" where the two kinds of defenses appear. By virtue of the organization of blaming sequences, speakers may use both kinds.

components are distributed in negotiations, and (2) how narratives and components work to set boundaries for negotiation.

3.1. On the Distribution of Stories and Other Narrative Components

In the 52-case corpus of plea negotiations, only 12, or less than one-fourth, contain stories in which attorneys orally present the facts of what happened to one another. Furthermore, the data include 24 offenses that a defense attorney and prosecutor discussed on their own and 34 in which the judge participated.[11] Comparing the two sets of cases shows that attorneys tell stories when the judge is present but not very often to each other. In only 1 of the 24 lawyer-only negotiations is there a narrative; the other 11 narratives all occur in negotiations with the judge present. This asymmetry does not mean that lawyers are uninterested in the facts. Instead, it reflects familiarity with or immediate access to police and other sources of information, such as the stories of defendants, victims, witnesses, and others (Meehan, 1986; Smith, 1974). In fact, the one situation in which a defense attorney does tell a story to the prosecutor with no judge present occurs because the DA is newly assigned to the case.

That is not the end of the matter, for negotiations without full-blown narratives may nonetheless contain narrative components. Thus, bargaining in 9 cases contains a defense segment and in 8 cases a background component. All 17 of these cases are ones with which the attorneys and judge demonstrate familiarity, and the defense or backgrounding components are introduced in the context of making or rejecting offers for disposition. The following examples illustrate the two usages.

3.1.1. Using a Defense Component

In a case where the defendant is charged with "resisting public officers" and possessing marijuana, negotiations open with the DA offering to dismiss the second charge in exchange for the defendant's pleading guilty to the first and spending two weekends in jail. The PD rejects the offer on the basis of the defendant's denials of specific alleged acts:

(15) 7.012 (Simplified)
PD2: Well I can just about tell ya what he's gonna say, and that's no. And uh he'd get two weekends if he lost this trial, he might get more. Now he didn't throw any beer cans at any police officer. Uh he was at a place where there was quite a disturbance, lots of people. Uh if they got the right guy and if he threw beer cans

[11] The total is 58 rather than 52 because 6 cases were discussed and taped in two locales—once between a defense attorney and prosecutor only and once among the attorneys and the judge.

I suppose that the weekends are uh reasonable . . . but he says he didn't do it
and uh that wouldn't settle the case

Subsequently, PD2 suggests that his client would plead guilty for a fine, and
that counteroffer eventually succeeds.

3.1.2. Using a Background Segment

In a case of drunk driving (no. 9 in the corpus), the DA proposes to reduce
the charge to reckless driving but with a regular drunk driving penalty. The
PD's response is to say the defendant, Walter Larson, is "concerned" with
what even this conviction "might do to his security clearance one day, he's
going for his master's or his doctorate." On this basis, the PD rejected the DA's
proposal. The DA held to his position, based partly on a review of the police
report, which stated that the defendant's driving was extremely erratic. Subsequent to this, the PD asked for a lesser penalty because the standard one
was so "punishing" and "undignified" for his defendant. The DA also refused
that appeal, and the defendant eventually pleaded guilty and received the
standard punishment. In a theft case (no. 10), the defendant, David Johnson,
had taken a decal that permitted him to park at his college. During negotiations, the PD did not dispute the defendant's having taken the decal but noted
that he was a student at the college with no prior record and asked that he be
given a suspended sentence rather than time in jail. The DA and judge
granted his request.

As these examples show, defense segments that deny or excuse a person's
behavior and/or background components that identify the defendant in particular ways may be disjoined from the rest of a narrative to justify a given
bargaining position. This demonstrates how negotiations are parasitic on the
tellings and writings of primary observers (offenders, witnesses, victims) and
secondary interpreters (e.g., police). The dependence of a negotiator's narrative on other parties' prior stories is sometimes marked or signaled during the
opening of talk on a particular case:

(16) 13.017
PD4: If you wanna read it over I can explain ta you what he says happened which is uh
actually very plausible

Thus the successive tellings a given occurrence goes through before some
version is delivered in the plea bargaining context would be an interesting
topic for study were it possible to gather the necessary data. Of particular
importance in understanding the complete narration of an event is the police
report as a socially constructed "documentary reality" (Smith, 1974) and one
that aims for particular readings in contexts other than that in which it was
written (Meehan, 1986). Most significant, dependence of a negotiator's dis-

course on textual tellings shows that stories, although not necessarily delivered orally, are nonetheless an embedded feature of all plea negotiations.

3.1.3. Who Uses Narrative Components

The distribution of narratives and narrative components reveals that, predominately, defense attorneys tell stories or introduce other aspects of narrative structure, such as background or defense segments, into the discourse. For example, in all but one of the 12 negotiations in this corpus that contain stories, defense attorneys were the narrators. District attorneys thus tend to be recipients, responding to specific components of the telling. This is consistent with the "relative passivity" of prosecutors (Feeley, 1979:177; Mather, 1979:70, 94), who seem to assume that standard penalties are appropriate for most cases and leave it to defense attorneys to convince them otherwise in particular cases or, in other words, to make an argument that a given case is not an instance of a "normal" crime (Sudnow, 1965).[12] Significantly, the one narrative told by a district attorney ends not with a defense segment but rather with the reaction report. The generalization from this is not that prosecutors are precluded from telling stories nor that defense attorneys are required to do so, as if these behaviors were part of their role obligations. Rather, by looking at the deployment of narratives and narrative structure, it is possible to describe the means by which interactants make visible those categorical identities in and through actual talk. In part, one enacts the identity of defense attorney by using narratives and narrative components, including defense segments, in asking for some disposition. Another brings off the identity of district attorney largely by responding in specific ways to a narrative or its components or by telling narratives without defense segments.

3.2. Setting the Boundaries of Negotiation

Speakers' use of narratives and narrative components and recipients' specific ways of dealing with these components result in four patterns of negotiational discourse: routine processing, assessing character, disputing facts, and arguing subjectivity.

3.2.1. Routine Processing

In some plea negotiations, a prosecuting or defense attorney may open by soliciting, or requesting to make, an offer. The lawyer thereby proposes that the case is "routine" enough to permit immediate focus on charging and

---

[12] See the discussion of these matters in Maynard (1984:151, fn. 7).

sentencing issues (Maynard, 1984:107). Such a focus becomes possible, Mather (1979:57–58) indicates, when prosecution and defense "converge" in their assessments of the case by "reading" police reports and other documents in the same way. However, this is only part of what makes "routine processing" possible. In the following example, a defendant was charged with engaging in a "speed contest," a misdemeanor. The attorneys eventually agree to reduce the charge to an infraction ("forty five in a twenty five," line 6).

(17) 33.004
1   PD2: Okay. Ya wanna make an offer in that case
2   DA3: I have so little use for these uh, dumb uh [9 seconds of silence while DA3
3   reads file] I can't intelligently make an offer in that case 'cause I have no
4   idea whether it's a bankrupt uh, you know sometimes they hear the
5   scratch uh y'know, little squealer
6   PD2: Forty five in a twenty five, I mean you know what are we doin' here
7   DA3: I'll be happy uh— would you give me forty five in a twenty five on that?
8   PD2: Twenty five dollar fine
9   DA3: How 'bout a fifty dollar fine
10 PD2: How 'bout a twenty five dollar (heh) fine (heh) real misdemeanors go for
11   fifty dollars
12 DA3: How 'bout thirty five
13 PD2: Eh yeah, I think that's not a bad deal

In line 1, PD2 solicits an offer from DA3, who, while reading the file, formulates the case as "dumb" (line 2) and as possibly "bankrupt" (line 4). These characterizations suggest that he considered the case, in Mather's (1979) words, as light (in terms of seriousness) and weak (in terms of evidence). Similarly, after DA3 counters PD2's proposal of a $25 fine (line 8) by suggesting $50 (line 9), PD2 holds to his original proposal and downgrades the case with an ironic statement, "real misdemeanors go for fifty dollars" (lines 10–11). In a sense, it asks for or confirms an understanding of the case as light and weak, as if this would be the synopsis that PD2 would use if he himself were to tell the story from the file. In ultimately agreeing to a compromise, the DA aligns himself with this characterization. Notice also that the judge may produce such synopses in the context of routine processing, as in this example:

(18) 47.001
1   J1: Next is Jerry Romney, which is a 23109b (speed contest)
2   PD2: Ya we haven't discussed that yet but if you'll take a speeding and thirty
3   five dollars
4   (silence)
5   J1: Oh I'm sure the people'll do that, right?
6   (silence)
7   J1: Looks like it's just breaking traction
8   DA3: Sure, sure.
9   PD2: Okay, we'll do that

Twice the DA responds with silence when asked to accept a proposal (lines 2–3, and 5), and after the second time, the judge produces a synopsis which downgrades the offense (line 7). In the data, this represents a characteristic form of participation for the judge, and suggests again that a way of "doing" a particular identity is to insert narrative components at sequential junctures in the negotiations. By producing a suggested upshot of a case's narrative rendering after one party makes a proposal, the judge may urge the recipient to reply in a specific way. Here, the DA does indeed assent to the judge's proposed synopsis and accepts the PD's offer. Cases of routine processing may involve a convergence or "concerting of expectations" (Schelling, 1963:93), but, as these examples also show, such convergence depends on negotiators' reading of others' previously told and written stories, which is embedded in discursive negotiations over charge and sentence.

3.2.2. Assessing Character

Another pattern involves the use of narrative background segments that assess the defendant's character. As with cases of routine processing, a defense attorney does not dispute the action of the defendant or the appropriateness of a legal reaction. Rather, an appeal for leniency is based sheerly on the good character and difficult circumstances of the defendant. The question for the DA is whether character and circumstances need to be taken into account, and if so, to what extent. Sometimes he decides negatively, as in the Walter Larson drunk-driving case mentioned. The DA's concern with the "weaving" of the defendant's car prior to arrest seemed to override the importance of the PD's backgrounding information. Sometimes, however, the DA reacts positively, as in the David Johnson decal theft and in the following shoplifting case:

(19) 39.101
PD2: She is advanced middle aged eastern lady. This is the lady who sends her son back east to go to med school, the son is killed, her husband leaves her, uh she lives in an apartment with no furniture, uh she attempts suicide. She knew what she was doing when she took it. I just don't think that uh considering her age 'n her mental state that uh she's a fit candidate for—that she will fit in well with the jail population, and if she could do some uh service work
DA3: Sure

Notice that the defense attorney admits the woman's culpability in a way that depends upon common knowledge (understanding what "it" was that she took requires such knowledge) and indicates the participants' familiarity with "what happened." He simultaneously uses descriptions of the defendant to argue against jail time and for the alternative penalty, which the DA grants. In each of these cases, the PD presents person descriptions and character assessments that the DA does not dispute. The descriptions and assessments justify bargaining proposals (cf. Maynard, 1984:137), and prosecutors deal with the backgrounding information by granting or denying these proposals.

3.2.3. Disputing Facts

A third pattern includes those cases in which an attorney uses a defense component that is a denial. In these, the defense segment reconstitutes the "facts" of the case (whether presented in an attorney's story or in the police reports) and the properness of a legal reaction as matters for dispute within the bargaining episode. Consider example 15 again, where PD2 introduced a denial when rejecting the DA's suggestion that his client plead guilty to "resisting public officers" and be sentenced to two weekends in jail. That is, PD2 argued that his client did not resist officers by throwing beer cans. That defense rendered questionable the police report and resulted in a discussion of the facts of the case. The district attorney then noted (but this is not reproduced here) that the defendant allegedly threw beer "bottles" and not "cans" (as the PD had characterized the objects). And when PD2 countered DA1's offer with a proposal for a lesser charge and fine, this occurred:

(20) 7.077
DA1: I can't see it, not when the officer has to sit through and go through bottles bein' thrown at him, and he says he saw your man do it

Not surprisingly, the outcome of the negotiations is at least partially tied to which version of the event participants regard as the "real" one. In this case, DA1 favored the police account and did not relent on reducing the charge, although he did offer a penalty of a fine rather than time in jail (and the defendant pleaded guilty).

The way in which denying defenses render action reports equivocal is also apparent when attorneys, rather than relying on the police report, produce a story during negotiations. Returning to example 11, the case in which the defendant was charged with representing himself as an officer and with using offensive words, we can note that PA3 uses a story prefix (line 1) that marks subsequent utterances as containing "undisputed facts." He then produces a background segment (lines 1–2), and an action report (lines 3–7) with an implicit reaction report. Within this action report, PA3 refers to an exchange of "some words" between the defendant and the plaintiffs and characterizes those words as the subject of "the dispute" (line 5). Next, PA3 reports what "the people in the car say" (lines 6–7) and, in the defense component (lines 9–11), "what my client will say." All of this renders "what happened" as very uncertain. Thus the PA formulates the gist or synopsis of the story as "who's telling the truth, the two victims or my client and our other witness."

How do attorneys determine who is telling the truth? The DA's strategy, this case, was to introduce further background information:

(21) 21.035
DA3: It would appear that the defendant has called the foot patrol a number of times
on prior occasions complaining about people parked there, he seems to have, I
dunno, from the face of things, I would say an inordinate concern for the
possibility the people park in front of his house may be burglars . . .

Thus, even as the use of a denying defense component calls into question
"what happened," determining the facts of the case may entail reconsidera-
tion of "who" the defendant is in an attempt to ascertain a possible motive that
would fit with one version of the event as opposed to another. Here, noting the
defendant's history of complaints may be the DA's way of picturing a type of
person who would impersonate a police officer. The PD, on the other hand,
continued to point out inconsistencies in the victim's account of the event and
suggested the possibility that they "misunderstood" his client. That is, rather
than arguing over the character of the defendant, he—as it turns out, successfully—attempted to discredit the opposing version of what happened. In
the end, the district attorney dismissed the case. In summary, then, introducing a denying defense means that attorneys do not take a story of what
happened at face value; instead they may seek to reconcile alternative versions
and do so through suggesting different scenarios and backgrounds for the
focal event.

3.2.4. Arguing Subjectivity

A last pattern in the use of narrative components derives from excusing
defenses, which largely leave a depiction of "what happened" intact and seek
to provide an exculpatory reason for the defendant's behavior. Consider yet
another case of shoplifting. The private attorney (PA2) here represents two
defendants:

(22) 20.013
1   *PA2:* . . . an it was one o' these things where they went to a grocery store, did
2   not have a cart, they're pickin' up items, and uh a few of 'em happened to
3   fall in the pockets, they get up ta pay for it they're payin' for it, they buy
4   twenty dollars worth of uh groceries and uh uhm just—they claim they
5   didn't— they neglected to think about the other small items that they had,
6   which it was a bottle of Visine which was in their pants pocket.
7   (1 second silence)
8   *PA2:* So uh they were picked up for simple petty theft.
9   *DA3:* Well to be absolutely precise uh the co-defendant with mister Winter told
10   the store employees that uh he in effect intended to steal it.

PA2's narrative contains an action report (lines 1–4) and an implicit reaction
report that can be filled in at the point where the defendants are "payin' for
it . . .," and it turns out that they "neglected to think about the other small

items" (lines 4–5). Lines 5–6, which identify what the small items were, also constitute the defense segment; they represent an excuse for the defendants' behavior. This segment (lines 4–6), furthermore, is a possible completion for the narrative: It is point where the recipient could demonstrate an understanding of the narrative's import (Jefferson, 1978). Next is a silence (line 7), however, which indicates a lack of turn transition. PA2 then formulates an explicit reaction report (line 8), a "secondary ending" (Jefferson, 1978:231) through which PA2 more strongly proposes closing the narrative and returning to a system of turn taking that is partially suspended during the narrative proper. When DA3 takes his turn, he rejects the excuse (lines 9–10) by arguing that the intent of at least one of the defendants was different from PA2's characterization. Later, he also refuses each of a series of lesser charges and penalties suggested by PD1 as alternatives to a guilty plea and the standard shoplifting penalty (see the discussion in Maynard, 1984:95–96). That is, both defendants pleaded guilty and received 24 hours in the county jail.

The vulnerability of excuses derives from their dependence on assertions about a party's subjectivity (cf. Coulter, 1979). Instead of directly occasioning talk regarding "what happened," as occurs with denying defenses, an attorney's employment of excuses involves inferences regarding the defendant's intentional or psychological state. When a claim is simply made that a defendant did not form the intent to commit the wrongful act, as in the prior example, that seems to be a relatively weak defense, which may be why the PA in this case achieved no compromise. Clear evidence for the weakness of such subjectivity statements exists in the case of employee theft at Sears (example 5). Upon hearing PD2's narrative defense component wherein it is acknowledged that the defendant was going through the purses but had "no intention of stealing anything," the judge produces a negative assessment:

(23) 3.049
    J1: Why was she even foolin' with the purses
    PD3: Well she says she didn't recognize the purses, she was wondering what they
         were doin' in there an' she was looking through the purses when the guy
         came in
→   J1: Boy that's a bad excuse
    PD3: Um that's the only excuse that she's got

Stronger excuses, it seems, are those that propose external or internal processes as interfering with a defendant's subjectivity and capacity for forming intent. Thus, in the Zamora–Avila shoplifting case (examples 7, 8, 14), the PD proposed that the ingestion of drugs incapacitated the defendant. Still, the case fits a pattern wherein the use of an excusing defense occasions a dispute over the defendant's psychological state. When the district attorney in this case responds to PD1's telling, he questions neither the backgrounding information nor the action and reaction reports; instead, he attacks the excuse:

(24) 1.121

DA1: . . . I just can't believe that the drug is—if the drug affects you that badly you're gonna do something bizarre, in other words you're gonna walk out swingin' around your arm or carryin' out bananas in your ear or something crazy. Here she was extremely sophisticated, go into the dressing room, pin it up underneath her coat, uh her dress like that. Uh I just can't buy it

Stated differently, the DA does not directly dispute "who" the woman is or "what" she did but rather argues against the defense attorney's depictions of her subjective state and capacity to form intent. Of course, this can indirectly call into question the character of the defendant and can invite a different, retrospective interpretation of the "facts" as told during the story proper. Nevertheless, the PD, telling his story several times as the case was continued over a period of weeks, stuck to his portrayal and interpretation of events and eventually won a dismissal.

3.3. Summary

Narratives in plea bargaining are structured aspects of the discourse through which attorneys present or rely on versions of "what happened" in a way that is sensitive to the social situation, including who their audience is and what the knowledge states of its members are. Thus some negotiations contain no narratives, and others include only narrative components or sub-components. When coparticipants are familiar with a case or when they regard it as routine, they may proceed directly to deciding charge and sentence or may use background or defense segments to justify a bargaining position. And when narratives or their components appear in plea bargaining, it is usually defense attorneys who tell them. Prosecutors and judges may also produce components, but in particular ways. This suggests that narratives and their components may be devices for "doing" the identities by which principal actors in the discourse are known.

Narratives and narrative structure permit plea negotiations to proceed in a systematic fashion, in four basic ways. In routine processing, participants depend on stories that have been textually constructed in police and other documents and, in deciding charge and sentence, may claim particular understandings of cases on the basis of synoptic upshots. In cases of character assessment, where participants similarly rely on police reports, an attorney may introduce background information regarding the defendant into the negotiations as a way of justifying a bargaining position. Rather than disputing the assessment, the other negotiator simply accepts or rejects the dispositional proposal it supports. When attorneys deploy a narrative component that denies an offense, it sets up a negotiational dispute over "what happened." That may mean discussing alternative versions of the facts and also reconsidering who the defendant is in terms of identity and character. Finally, where a defense attorney uses an excusing defense as part of the narrative, that regularly results in arguments over what the subjective state of the defendant was during commission of the offense. Such arguments may indirectly recast the character of the defendant and the nature of the act. In all, then, their use of narratives and narrative structure partially establishes what participants will and will not discuss when utilizing "bargaining sequences" to decide matters of charge and sentencing (Maynard, 1984:Chapters 4, 5, and 8).

4. THEORETICAL IMPLICATIONS

Narratives have a structure that is organized independently of outside or exogenous social and legal factors. This structure is part of the interaction order that bargaining participants simultaneously produce and confront in the ways that they talk and behave with one another. In this view, neither "what happened" nor "who" the defendant is, nor the criminal justice process and the law as institutions are constraining or influencing the interaction order. Rather, through narrative and other interactional structures, participants constitute the reality of facts, character, rules, and law as features of situated activity. An initial step in explicating this assertion can be made with an analogy between plea bargaining and science. Both enterprises are devoted to making propositions about events in the world and to drawing conclusions from those propositions. Both are seemingly constrained in a variety of ways. They are to be responsible to the actual sequence of events. They determine this actuality in relation to a body of law, on the one hand, or scientific procedure, on the other. Laws also help specify appropriate remedies, whereas scientific procedures dictate how to report results and conduct further investigations. In the realm of science, Landau (1984) argues that narrative has an unsuspected influence on perceptions of the world, on determining significant events, and even on methods of investigation. Across their various paleoanthropological accounts of human evolution, for instance, scientists have followed several narrative principles. They organize events into intelligible stories with beginnings, middles, and ends. Furthermore, scientists define individual evolutionary episodes as "turning points," "crises," and "transitions." Finally, they select and arrange worldly matters into chronological and causal sequences that are narrative in origin. Thus, it is possible that "scientific explanations apparently based on natural laws are actually a function of narrative procedures" (Landau, 1984:267). The point of Landau's suggestive analysis is not to discredit science or to somehow rectify the narrative forms through which scientists perform their enterprise and report their results. Rather, it is to take narratives seriously with respect to understanding how they are used in the process of discovery and experimentation.

4.1. Plea Bargaining, Defendant Characteristics, and Other "Factors"

By the same token, a focus on narrative forms in plea bargaining should not imply that attorneys are "only" telling stories or that they are producing fictionalized accounts of legal offenses or that they are somehow distorting facts. As Schudson (1982:98) observes: "Their function is less to increase or decrease the truth value of messages they convey than to shape and narrow the range of what kinds of truths can be told." Understanding narratives in plea bargaining means appreciating how participants bring facts, biography, law, and other matters to bear on the decision-making process. They do so through narrative structure: by introducing stories into negotiations with synopses, prefaces, prefixes, and the like; by telling stories with background segments, action and reaction reports; and by producing defense segments in characteristic ways. The "normal form" of plea bargaining narratives suggests that attorneys orient to offenses as acts committed by persons with distinct characters who engage in conduct that elicits a more or less reasonable legal reaction. Defense attorneys can claim innocence for their client by denying that the behavior occurred or by excusing it with reference to the defendant's unintending subjective state. They use such defenses to ask for some lesser charge or sentence or for dismissal. Prosecutors and, to some extent, judges, also employ narratives and narrative components, but differently from defense attorneys. In all, stories are not a neutral rendering of what happened but rather aim for some synoptic upshot. Even if participants do not produce a full narrative, they rely on textual stories from police documents and can deploy narrative components, including synopses, background segments, and defenses as they bargain over charge and sentence. All of this suggests that attorneys may scan the material available to them as a "case" for its "storyable" characteristics (cf. Sacks, 1984:417), seeking just that which is presentable in narrative form and that which will be most effective in supporting their respective bargaining positions (cf. Spencer, 1984:223–224).

Therefore, traditional concerns with the influence of various legal, organizational, and other "factors" on plea bargaining outcomes must be supplanted (Maynard, 1984:Chapter 7). We need an understanding of how the organization of "talk-in-interaction" (Schegloff, 1987) makes an independent, integral contribution of its own to outcomes. Abstract factors, such as the character of the defendant, organizational roles, and the law do not influence decisions so much as the narrative structure of plea bargaining affects how participants bring those matters into play. We know, for instance, that descriptions of persons depend upon an infinite variety of potentially relevant categorical and evaluative background factors. In producing person descriptions in conversation, however, participants orient neither to a principal of "correctness' (Sharrock & Turner, 1980:20) nor of simple "adequacy" (Atkinson & Drew, 1979:137). Rather, they select factors and assemble them in context with one another and within discourse activities such as praising, blaming, insulting, justifying, and so on (Atkinson & Drew, 1979; Labov, 1972; Maynard, 1984:137–139). In plea bargaining, participants use descriptions of defendants in background segments of narratives to proffer a sense of persons so as inform what is to be made of what they have done. With the stories they accompany, they are ultimately employed to argue for and against various dispositions. "Who" a defendant is thus depends partly on how an attorney assembles a subset of the infinite variety of things that could be said about a defendant to support a particular bargaining stance. Or for another instance of how abstract factors are brought into play, we have seen that negotiators, rather than acting out roles, enact or provide for the visibility of their organizational identities in and through the details of their talk, that is, by producing characteristic narrative components at particular sequential junctures in the negotiations. Finally, although the role of law has barely been touched upon here, there are clear directions for further research. That is, if bargaining occurs in "the shadow of the law" (Mnookin & Kornhauser, 1979), studies of narrative may show just what kind of shadow the law casts, for it is in the process of producing narratives that participants interactively take that law into account (cf. Erlanger, Chambliss, & Melli, 1987:599). The law operates as a "context of accountability" (Rawls, 1987); it is only through a sensitivity to legal stipulations that participants can muster background components, defense, and other devices for making and responding to proposals for disposition. In short, future investigations concerned with the "law in action" can attend to how attorneys *use* laws in forming narratives and narrative components during negotiations.

In general, then, "who" a defendant is and what legal, organizational, and other factors enter a decision depend, in large measure, upon how they become relevant within the narratives that attorneys collaboratively build. To paraphrase Smith (1980:229), the major features of a case are not prior to or independent of narratives; they come to life through narrative practices by which a teller makes them manifest and a listener makes inferences and responds accordingly. Thus more attention needs to be paid to the conversational and interactional order in legal settings; rather than seeing cases, laws, organizations, or roles determining how participants talk and act, we need to conceptualize cases, the setting, and their features as a function of the interaction order.[13]

---

[13] And it should be clear that narratives are only one aspect of that order. In plea bargaining, narratives work in conjunction with bargaining sequences and other negotiational devices to bring about concrete decisions and outcomes. See, for example, the analysis in Emerson (1983:445) regarding how attorneys "invoke the treatment accorded prior cases as a lever for negotiating the outcome of the current one." Such a device can make a "larger organizationally determined whole" (Emerson, 1983:425) specifically relevant for a case at hand by operating in conjunction with the case narrative an attorney builds.

4.2. The Reflexivity of Stories and Plea Bargaining

Unlike stories in everyday conversation, those in plea bargaining portray conflict that is not yet resolved. Plea bargaining narratives thereby exhibit a reflexive relationship between actors and the stories they tell. That is, narratives are a resource in and for plea bargaining, which is itself a feature of those selfsame narratives. Even while attorneys present what has happened (an action report), how it was responded to (a reaction report), and what a defense might be, they themselves have become part of the drama, part of the process by which some resolution is to be reached.

Prior literature depicts the main participants in plea bargaining as engaging in exchange and reciprocity on the basis of how they mutually decide facts and character (e.g., Alschuler, 1975; Feeley, 1979). Plea bargaining, in this view, is a way of rendering substantive justice, although investigators acknowledge that work load and bureaucratic demands diminish defense attorneys' sense of duty to their clients so that "accommodation and compromise" rather than "adversary combat" characterize negotiations (Rosett & Cressey, 1976:127–128). In emphasizing cognitive appraisals of cases to the neglect of everyday routines and experiences in which participants become embedded (Maynard, 1984:170), this may be an overrationalistic approach to understanding negotiations. If participants are part of the narratives they present, the implications are different. They are motivated to present stories as effectively as possible as an interactional matter. That is, from within an experience, participants are often oriented to producing it as a course of action that will turn out to be a "good story" (cf. Sacks, 1984:417). Insofar as good stories are those that involve winning rather than losing,[14] attorneys will be interested in more than mutually deciding facts and character or engaging in exchange or meeting their bureaucratic mandate. As part of a still unfolding narrative, lawyers are provided with a structural incentive to be alert to legal, extralegal, personal, and other innumerable elements of a case that can be built into the story in such a way as to justify and induce the granting of a favorable disposition.

As Goffman (1983:8) argues, the work of organizations gets done face-to-face and is therefore susceptible to interactional effects. Persuasion is one such effect; as negotiational devices, narratives can be "performed" in such a way as to be more or less compelling or convincing (Bauman, 1977:26; Labov, 1982:230). Consider again the Zamora–Avila case, in which a woman was charged with the theft of clothes. Although the prosecutor adamantly disagreed with the PD's defense regarding the influence of drugs on his client, he ultimately granted the PD's proposal to dismiss the case. His decision derived

---

[14] See the discussions in Buckle and Buckle (1977:150–152) and Mather (1979:96–97) regarding how lawyers are evaluated in terms of whether they "win" or "lose" negotiations.

from an assessment, based on the PD's narrative, about what would happen at trial. It was as if the story the PD told was a rehearsal for a similar courtroom presentation, and, in the DA's view, it was one that would be convincing to a jury (Maynard, 1984:114; 133–134). Thus, whatever the merits of the case and the legal grounds for dismissing it, the PD's narrative casting had to be done in such a way as to provide compelling support for his proposal. Case characteristics and legal matters, then, are not irrelevant, but neither are they self-invoking or self-evident features of the negotiational process. Rather, to paraphrase Heritage (1984:290), they are "talked into being" by way of narrative and narrative structure. As an aspect of the interaction order, this structure shapes the content of the case and clearly *effects* the course of negotiations. The exact ways in which it also *affects* outcomes cannot be ascertained until more is known regarding narrative and other structured aspects of negotiational interaction.[15] In short, it seems that a lawyer requires both legal and conversational competence, and we need more understanding of the latter kind of skill to fully appreciate how bargaining results come about.

5. CONCLUSION

Comparative research on bargaining narratives would be beneficial and would involve studying narratives in different plea bargaining settings, such as those wherein felony offenses are discussed. Also relevant are negotiations in other legal arenas, including civil cases such as divorce (e.g., Erlanger *et al.*, 1987; Mnookin & Kornhauser, 1979). Comparisons should also be made between narratives in legal contexts and those in ordinary conversation. Plea bargaining narratives may be less "idle" than everyday stories, to the extent that they more regularly continue to unfold in the process of being told. We also need more understanding of textual narratives on which negotiators depend (cf. Spencer, 1984) and which are largely absent in the everyday context. Contrasts such as O'Barr and Conley (1985) have drawn regarding the legal adequacy of narratives in everyday conversation and those that seem effective in small claims court are informative. And most intriguing would be a comparison between how events are told in plea bargaining and how they are presented at trial. We know that trial narratives are elicited and pieced together through question-and-answer sequences (Atkinson & Drew, 1979; see especially pp. 61–62, 76–77), whereas plea bargaining stories are told more spontaneously and uninterruptedly. Trial discourse therefore structures narrative events differently from plea bargaining discourse, in terms of length, amount of detail, ordering of segments, and so on (cf. Wolfson, 1982:61–71).

---

[15] See Schegloff's (1987:228) remarks on how modes of conversational organization constitute a context for bodies of knowledge and other interactional products.

And, parties at some remove from the original event tell plea bargaining stories, whereas trials involve direct participants. The question for future research might be, how consequential are these differences for the depiction of reality and the rendering of justice in each arena?

ACKNOWLEDGMENT.   An earlier version of this paper appeared in *Law and Society Review*, Volume 22, No. 3 (September, 1988). I would like to thank Steve Clayman, Robert Kidder, Judith Levi, and Anne Walker for helpful comments.

6. REFERENCES

Agar, M. (1980). Stories, background knowledge, and themes: Problems in the analysis of life history narrative. *American Ethnologist, 7*, 223–239.

Agar, M., & Hobbs, J. R. (1982). Interpreting discourse: Coherence and the analysis of ethnographic interviews. *Discourse Processes, 5*, 1–32.

Alschuler, A. (1975). The defense attorney's role in plea bargaining. *The Yale Law Journal, 84*, 1179–1314.

Atkinson, J. M., & Drew, P. (1979). *Order in court*. London: Macmillan Press, Ltd.

Bauman, R. (1977). Verbal art as performance. In R. Bauman (Ed.), *Verbal art as performance* (pp. 3–58). Rowley, MA: Newbury House.

Bennett, W. L., & Feldman, M. S. (1981). *Reconstructing reality in the courtroom*. New Brunswick, NJ: Rutgers University Press.

Buckle, S. R. T., & Buckle, L. G. (1977). *Bargaining for justice: Case disposition and reform in the criminal courts*. New York: Praeger.

Coulter, J. (1979). *The social construction of mind: Studies in ethnomethodology and linguistic philosophy*. Totowa, NJ: Rowman and Littlefield.

Danet, B. (1980). Language in the legal process. *Law and Society Review, 14*, 445–564.

Emerson, R. (1969). *Judging delinquents: Context and process in juvenile court*. Chicago: Aldine.

Emerson, R. (1983). Holistic effects in social control decision-making. *Law and Society Review, 17*, 425–455.

Erlanger, H. S., Chambliss, E., & Melli, M. S. (1987). Participation and flexibility in informal processes: Cautions from the divorce context. *Law and Society Review, 21*, 585–604.

Feeley, M. (1979). *The process is the punishment*. New York: Russell Sage Foundation.

Goffman, E. (1983). The interaction order. *American Sociological Review, 48*, 1–17.

Goodwin, C. (1984). Notes on story structure and the organization of participation. In J. M. Atkinson & J. Heritage (Eds.), *Structures of social action* (pp 225–246). Cambridge: Cambridge University Press.

Goodwin, M. H. (1982). 'Instigating:' Storytelling as social process. *American Ethnologist, 9*, 799–819.

Heritage, J. (1984). *Garfinkel and ethnomethodology*. Cambridge, England: Polity Press.

Heritage, J. C., & Watson, J. R. (1979). Formulations as conversational objects. In G. Psathas (Ed.), *Everyday language: Studies in ethnomethodology* (pp. 123–162). New York: Irvington.

Jefferson, G. (1978). Sequential aspects of storytelling in conversation. In J. Schenkein (Ed.), *Studies in the organization of conversational interaction* (pp. 219–248). New York: Academic Press.

Labov, W. (1972). *Language in the inner city*. Philadelphia: University of Pennsylvania Press.

Labov, W. (1982). Speech actions and reactions in personal narrative. In D. Tannen (Ed.), *Analyzing discourse: Text and talk* (pp. 219–247). Washington, DC: Georgetown University Press.

Labov, W., & Fanshel, D. (1977). *Therapeutic discourse*. New York: Academic Press.

Labov, W., & Waletzky, J. (1967). Narrative analysis. In J. Helm (Ed.), *Proceedings of the American Ethnological Society: Essays on the verbal and visual arts* (pp. 12–44). Seattle: University of Washington Press.

Landau, M. (1984, July). Human evolution as narrative. *American Scientist, 72,* 262.

Levi, J. N. (1985). *Language and the law in the U.S.A.: A guided tour.* Paper read at National Science Foundation conference, Language in the Judicial Process. Washington, DC: Georgetown University.

Mather, L. M. (1979). *Plea bargaining or trial? The process of criminal case disposition.* Lexington, MA: Lexington Books.

Maynard, D. W. (1984). *Inside plea bargaining: The language of negotiation.* New York: Plenum Press.

Meehan, A. J. (1986). Record-keeping practices in the policing of juveniles. *Urban Life, 15,* 70–102.

Mishler, E. (1986). *Research interviewing: Context and narrative.* Cambridge: Harvard University Press.

Mnookin, R. H., & Kornhauser, L. (1979). Bargaining in the shadow of the law. *Yale Law Journal, 88,* 950–997.

Newman, D. J. (1966). *Conviction: The determination of guilt or innocence without trial.* Boston: Little, Brown, and Co.

O'Barr, W. M. (1982). *Linguistic evidence: Language, power, and strategy in the courtroom.* New York: Academic Press.

O'Barr, W. M., & Conley, J. (1985). Litigant satisfaction versus legal adequacy in small claims court narratives. *Law and Society Review, 19,* 661–701.

Polanyi, L. (1979). So what's the point? *Semiotica, 25,* 207–241.

Pomerantz, A. (1984). Agreeing and disagreeing with assessments: Some features of preferred/dispreferred turn shapes. In J. M. Atkinson & J. Heritage (Eds.), *Structures of social action* (pp. 57–101). Cambridge, England: Cambridge University Press.

Pomerantz, A., & Atkinson, J. M. (1984). Ethnomethodology, conversation analysis, and the study of courtroom interaction. In D. J. Muller, D. E. Blackam, & A. J. Chapman (Eds.), *Psychology and Law* (pp. 283–297). New York: John Wiley.

Rawls, A. (1987). The interaction order sui generis: Goffman's contribution to social theory. *Sociological Theory, 5,* 136–149.

Robinson, J. A. (1981). Personal narratives reconsidered. *Journal of American Folklore, 94,* 58–85.

Rosett, A., & D. R. Cressey (1976). *Justice by consent: Plea bargains in the american courthouse.* Philadelphia: J. B. Lippincott.

Ryave, A. L. (1978). On the achievement of a series of stories. In J. Schenkein (Ed.), *Studies in the organization of conversational interaction* (pp. 113–132). New York: Academic Press.

Sacks, H. (1964–1972). Unpublished lecture notes. Irvine: University of California.

Sacks, H. (1972). Notes on police assessment of moral character. In D. Sudnow (Ed.), *Studies in social interaction* (pp. 280–293). New York: The Free Press.

Sacks, H. (1975). An analysis of the course of a joke's telling in conversation. In R. Baumann & J. Sherzer (Eds.), *Explorations in the ethnography of speaking* (pp. 337–353). Cambridge: Cambridge University Press.

Sacks, H. (1978). Some technical considerations of a dirty joke. In J. Schenkein (Ed.), *Studies in the organization of conversational interaction* (pp. 249–269). New York: Academic Press.

Sacks, H. (1984). On doing 'being ordinary'. In J. M. Atkinson & J. Heritage (Eds.), *Structures of social action* (pp. 413–429). Cambridge, England: Cambridge University Press.

Sacks, H., Schegloff, E. A., & Jefferson, G. (1974). A simplest systematics for the organization of turn-taking for conversation. *Language, 4,* 696–735.

Schegloff, E. A. (1987). Between macro and micro: Contexts and other connections. In J. Alexander, B. Giesen, R. Munch, & N. J. Smelser (Eds.) *The micro-macro link* (pp. 207–234). Berkeley: University of California Press.

Schelling, T. C. (1963). *The strategy of conflict.* Cambridge: Harvard University Press.

Schegloff, E. A., & H. Sacks (1974). Opening up closings. In R. Turner (Ed.), *Ethnomethodology* (pp. 233–264). London: Penguin.

Sharrock, W. W., & Turner, R. (1980). Observation, esoteric knowledge, and automobiles. *Human Studies, 3*, 19–31.

Schudson, M. (1982). The politics of narrative form: The emergence of news conventions in print and television. *Daedelus, 111*, 97–112.

Schutz, A. (1973). *Collected papers I: The problem of social reality*. The Hague: Martinus Nijhoff.

Scott, M. B., & Lyman, S. M. (1968). Accounts. *American Sociological Review, 33*, 46–62.

Smith, B. H. (1980). Narrative versions, narrative theories. *Critical Inquiry, 7*, 213–236.

Smith, D. (1974). The social construction of documentary reality. *Sociological Inquiry, 4*, 257–268.

Spencer, J. W. (1984). Conducting presentencing investigations: From discourse to textual summaries. *Urban Life, 13*, 207–227.

Sudnow, D. (1965). Normal crimes: Sociological features of the penal code in a public defender's office. *Social Problems, 12*, 255–283.

van Dijk, T. A. (1975). Action, action description, and narrative. *New Literary History, 6*, 273–294.

West, C., & Zimmerman, D. H. (1985). Gender, language, and discourse. In T. A. van Dijk (Ed.), *Handbook of discourse analysis, volume 4: Discourse analysis in society* (pp. 103–124). London: Academic Press.

Wolfson, N. (1982). *CHP: The conversational historical present in American English narrative*. Dordrecht, The Netherlands: Foris Publications.

Zimmerman, D. H. (1974). Fact as a practical accomplishment. In R. Turner (Ed.), *Ethnomethodology* (pp. 128–143). London: Penguin.

Chapter 4

LITIGANT SATISFACTION VERSUS LEGAL ADEQUACY IN SMALL CLAIMS COURT NARRATIVES

WILLIAM M. O'BARR and JOHN M. CONLEY

1. INTRODUCTION

For more than half a century, the label "small claims" has been applied to a wide range of judicial procedures intended to achieve the simple and economical resolution of disputes involving limited amounts of money (Ruhnka & Weller, 1978:1–5). Despite their differences, small claims courts share a number of common elements, such as simplified procedures, reduced costs, limited rights to appeal, and the opportunity for litigants to appear without lawyers (Steele, 1981:330). Most research on small claims courts focuses on the parties involved or on the characteristics and outcomes of the cases brought. This chapter has a different focus. We are concerned with how the informality of small claims court procedures affects the ways in which litigants tell their stories. This focus yields significant insights into the way that disputants conceive of their problems and devise strategies to resolve them while at the

Reprinted from *Law & Society Review*, Volume 19, Number 4, Copyright © 1985 The Law and Society Association. Reprinted by permission.

WILLIAM M. O'BARR • Departments of Cultural Anthropology and Sociology, Duke University, Durham, North Carolina 27706.   JOHN M. CONLEY • School of Law, University of North Carolina, Chapel Hill, North Carolina 27599.

same time raising questions about the efficiency and fairness of the small claims court as an adjudicative forum.

Analysis of the form as well as the content of small claims narratives reveals the powerful effect of the evidentiary constraints found in ordinary litigation. Small claims litigants indulge in a variety of everyday storytelling practices that would be forbidden in most formal courts. It appears that the opportunity to tell a story in everyday terms to an authoritative decision maker enhances litigant satisfaction with small claims courts, but this ability and the resulting satisfaction may have a hidden cost. Our study of the structure of small claims narratives indicates that many accounts of disputed events that are entirely adequate by the standards of ordinary conversation prove to be legally inadequate because of judicial assumptions about how a story must be told and how blame must be assessed. In particular, unassisted lay witnesses seldom impart to their narratives the deductive, hypothesis-testing structure with which judges[1] are most familiar and often fail to assess responsibility for events in question in the way that the law requires. Although the legal inadequacy of narratives may influence the disposition of cases, and although legal inadequacy often results from correctable problems of form or substance, these issues appear not to be recognized in most instances by either litigants or magistrates.

2. THEORETICAL BACKGROUND

Three sets of theoretical concerns led us to conclude that the way that litigants in small claims courts present accounts of their problems would be worth researching. First, our prior research on the use of language in more formal courts (Conley, O'Barr, & Lind, 1978; O'Barr, 1982) focused on participants' language strategies as a means of understanding the actual workings of the courtroom. Research on styles of testifying had made us keenly aware of the many problems witnesses face when their everyday conventions for giving accounts are frustrated by evidentiary restrictions. Recognition of these problems led us to wonder whether litigants might talk differently about their problems in a legal environment where such constraints were missing. This interest led directly to small claims courts that, like more formal courts, resolve disputes according to rules of law, but that, unlike more formal courts, do so with greatly relaxed rules of evidence and procedure.

Second, the small claims and alternative dispute resolution literature, while containing little explicit analysis of speech, is replete with references to

---

[1] The term "judge" is used for convenience. It is meant to include various types of legal decision makers, some of whom, like arbitrators, may not formally be judges.

the significance of language in the resolution of disputes. For example, Mather and Yngvesson (1980–1981:777) note that disputes undergo *rephrasing* (that is, "some kind of formulation into a public discourse") early in the disputing process. Subsequently, the disputants endeavor to frame the dispute in recognized, coherent paradigms of argument (Mather & Yngvesson, 1980–1981:780–781). Mather and Yngvesson contend that an important feature in all social conflict is a struggle over these paradigms. Moreover, they emphasize that where there is a written legal code and an official language of disputing, the ability to manipulate that language becomes an important determinant of the relative power of the parties.

Other researchers, approaching the significance of language from a somewhat different perspective, have noted the influence of speaking opportunities on disputants' attitudes toward the process. Yngvesson and Hennessey (1974–1975:260) observed that the opportunity for self-expression seemed to contribute to disputants' willingness to compromise; Abel (1982: 284) made the related point that small claims courts "allow grievants to let off steam, performing an expressive rather than an instrumental function" and thereby help to neutralize social conflict. These statements are consistent with the observation of Arno (1985) that, for some disputants, the opportunity for structured verbal interaction with a person in a position of authority is the most important aspect of the disputing process. They are also consistent with anecdotal evidence reported by both lawyers (e.g., Kulat, 1984; Weinstein, 1977:521) and social scientists (e.g., McFadgen, 1972:46–48) to the effect that disputants are frustrated by legal rules that limit their speaking opportunities and prefer forums that put fewer limits on the form and duration of narratives.

Third, we see our work as adding to previous research in the relatively new field of language and law. The relation of language and law has attracted the attention of researchers in such diverse disciplines as anthropology, sociology, linguistics, psychology, speech communication, and law, and most of their work has been empirical in orientation. The general question of interest to most researchers is how a focus on language can illuminate legal processes. Topics that have been researched include such diverse, but related, issues as the comprehensibility of jury instructions (Charrow & Charrow, 1979; Sales, Elwork, & Alfini, 1977), the influence of question form on testimony (Danet, 1980; Loftus, 1979), and the effects of variations in speech style on the evaluation of testimony (Conley et al., 1978; O'Barr, 1982). Within this research orientation, some attention has also been devoted to the nature of the testimony given in legal proceedings. For example, Atkinson and Drew (1979), using the microanalytic approach of conversation analysis, have examined how speech in court differs from everyday conversation, with particular attention to the attribution of blame and responsibility in courtroom examinations. Other microanalytic studies have further demonstrated how the conversation analysis approach can shed light on the nature of accounts given in legal contexts (see, for example, Drew, 1985; Pomerantz, 1978; Pomerantz & Atkinson, 1984).

Using a broader orientation to the trial process, Bennett and Feldman (1981) have attempted to understand legal decision making by considering how jurors make sense of evidence presented by various witnesses in response to attorneys' questions. They argue that jurors reconstruct the evidence as "stories" and make decisions about the truthfulness of these stories on the basis of their structural characteristics. In her review of their work, Philips (1983) points to some significant deficiencies in it. The concept "story" is never clearly defined, and the similarities of legal reasoning to everyday judgmental processes are exaggerated while critical differences between courtroom proceedings and ordinary decision making are underemphasized or ignored. Nevertheless, Bennett and Feldman's effort to study the trial as a whole is important, for it reminds researchers in the field of law and language not to lose sight of the trial as an entity in their attempt to understand its constituent parts.

Within the field of law and language, as this brief review suggests, attention has been given to microlevel interactive encounters at one extreme and to macrolevel cognitive schemata at the other. Little research, however, has focused on processes that fall between these extremes. We have chosen individual litigant narratives[2] as the unit of analysis in an initial attempt to understand and explain such middle-level linguistic phenomena.

To summarize, the significance of language in the disputing process has been widely recognized: It is a strategic weapon in the framing and presentation of disputes, and the way in which it is controlled by the forum may affect the attitudes of the participants toward the dispute resolution process. Moreover, the detailed study of language in legal and quasi-legal contexts has been shown to be a source of invaluable information about the functioning, fairness, and effectiveness of the institutions being studied. We hope to add to this body of knowledge by investigating language in a context where its significance has often been presumed or recognized but seldom documented or studied.

[2] The terms "account," "narrative," and "story" have been used somewhat interchangeably to refer to the telling of the particulars of an act, occurrence, or course of events by a witness in court. In our use of these terms, we seek to draw an analytic distinction between two aspects of a telling. A witness' "story" or "account" refers to the totality of the telling by any particular witness, even though the telling may not occur as a relatively uninterrupted or unbroken segment within a trial. "Narrative," by contrast, refers to a telling that occurs in a relatively uninterrupted manner, with the witness having an opportunity to determine both the form and the substance of the telling. An interesting finding is that most litigants come to court with a narrative that they want to tell and usually find a way to present it. In this article, we are concerned with both aspects of the way litigants talk about troubles in small claims courts. Differences in terminology reflect which aspect or aspects we are considering at any particular time.

3. RESTRICTIONS ON NARRATIVES IN FORMAL COURTS

Motivated by the research just reviewed and by our own prior experience studying formal courts, we decided to examine in detail the use that small claims litigants make of the opportunity to present their positions in a relatively unconstrained fashion. More specifically, our intention was to analyze the structure of the narratives told by small claims litigants. We were interested in what patterns could be observed in such narratives, especially what they might reveal about the litigants' goals and strategies and about the fairness and effectiveness of the small claims court as an institution.

When we began the present research, we already had access to over 100 hours of tapes and transcripts of criminal proceedings in the North Carolina Superior Court. The tapes had been collected in the mid-1970s in the course of a study on the strategic use of language in formal courts (Conley *et al.*, 1978; O'Barr, 1982). We began this study by reviewing our existing data, paying particular attention to the structure of witnesses' narratives in these more formal courts. We recognized, of course, that the law of evidence places substantial restrictions on the length and scope of witness narratives and that any narratives we found in our sample would necessarily differ from everyday storytelling conventions. We suspected, however, that by examining instances in which evidentiary restraints were placed on witness narratives, we would be able to make useful inferences about how witnesses would structure their narratives in the absence of such restraints. We therefore focused on narratives that engendered evidentiary objections, following Llewellen and Hoebel's (1941) dictum that situations in which a system breaks down often yield the most interesting information about the nature of the system.

Our analysis of our earlier data repeatedly confirmed the intuition that lay witnesses come to formal courts with a repertoire of narrative customs and strategies that are often frustrated, directly or indirectly, by the operation of the law of evidence. Consider, for example, the following constraints that are imposed on witnesses in most American formal courts:

1. A witness may not ordinarily repeat what other persons have said about the events being reported.
2. A witness may not speculate about how the situations or events being reported may have appeared to other people or from other perspectives.
3. A witness may not ordinarily comment on his or her reactions to, or feelings and beliefs about, events being reported.
4. In responding to a question, a witness is ordinarily restricted in digressing from the subject of the question to introduce information about he or she believes critical as a preface or qualification.

5. A witness may not normally incorporate into his or her account any suppositions about the state of mind of the persons involved in the events being reported.
6. Value judgments and opinions by lay witnesses are generally disfavored.
7. Emphasis through repetition of information is restricted.
8. Substantive information may not be conveyed through gestures alone.
9. A witness is generally forbidden to make observations about the questions asked or to comment on the process of testifying itself.

These restrictions and prohibitions are supported by the statutory or common law of evidence or by unwritten custom widely followed in formal courts. Yet reflection on how we ordinarily speak suggests that each forbidden practice is common, if not essential, in everyday narration.

It appears that frustration and dissatisfaction are inevitable results of such constraints. One federal trial judge has commented at some length on the fact that litigants frequently feel dissatisfied because the trial process does not afford them a fair chance to tell their stories (Weinstein, 1977). He reports that greater satisfaction for litigants in small claims procedures seems to be related to the absence of formal rules of evidence. On the basis of his experience, Weinstein believes that

> allowing litigants to introduce evidence relatively freely and to rely on hearsay, provided the opponent can call the declarant and otherwise attack him with a minimum of barriers, tends to tranquilize them. This truism is demonstrated repeatedly in magistrates' courts where a complaining witness pours out his heart to an attentive judge and then, having had his day in court, withdraws the complaint. (1977:521)

Carlen (1976) reports that the experience of litigants and witnesses in Britain has been similar. The rules governing courtroom procedure, Carlen notes, place defendants in positions where they must plead their cases or give supporting testimony in a manner that is "quite divorced from the conventions of everyday life outside the courtroom" (1976:24) and where the logic of the legal process is opposed to "commonsense interpretations" (1976:85).

These observations are confirmed by conversations we have had with courtroom witnesses. Witnesses—both parties to the dispute and others—complained about their inability to convey their versions of the facts at issue. Many even went so far as to assert afterwards that they would never have taken their cases to court or agreed to testify if they had realized ahead of time how little opportunity they would have to tell their stories.

The source of this frustration is obvious from segments of superior court testimony we collected in which a witness' narrative efforts engender objections. In each instance, the agendas of the witness and the court conflict.

Although the witness attempts to tell the story on his or her own terms, the court will hear the evidence only when it is structured in ways alien to the day-to-day lives of most of those who testify.

Texts 1–5 illustrate several difficulties that witnesses encounter. Texts 1 and 2 are drawn from a vehicular homicide case in which an allegedly drunk driver was charged with running a red light and colliding with an ambulance. As a result, a heart attack victim on her way to the hospital was thrown out into the street and killed. In Texts 1 and 2, the witness is an ambulance attendant who was riding in the back of the vehicle with the patient. In the testimony quoted, the prosecution is attempting to establish that the patient was alive before the collision and died as a result of it. This witness has already run into difficulty several times for attempting to report what others said.

The account given in Text 1 differs in important ways from the type of account that one would expect in ordinary discourse, where the speaker has greater control over the organization of his story and where reports of conversations are common.

Text 1[3]

W: Well, I went, uh, Mr. N told me to go outside.

L_2: Object.

W: Well, I . . .

J: Just describe the physical act of what was done. Not what was said, but what actually transpired.

W: Well, I wasn't really doing anything in relation to the patient. Mr. N was doing all that.

L_2: Did you go, did you go back, did you return, return to the emergency vehicle?

W: I returned to the emergency vehicle.

The objection sequence in Text 1 occurs precisely at the point where the witness attempts to do what he would ordinarily do. The problem (and hence the objection) occurs as a result of the witness' attempt to use everyday discourse rules in the courtroom. When he violates the rule that reporting a conversation (hearsay, from the perspective of the law) is not ordinarily allowed, an objection occurs. As in this instance, evidence conventions (read: *the rules of courtroom discourse*) are seldom explained in any detail to those who must conform to them. At most, witnesses receive some instruction from attorneys in the course of pretrial preparation.

[3] Texts 1–5 are excerpts from trials we studied in a North Carolina superior court under a grant from the Law and Social Science Program of the National Science Foundation (GS-42742). Texts 6–12 are excerpts from small claims trials in North Carolina and Colorado. Readers can determine which state each small claims trial is drawn from by the difference between the terminology used for the judges in the two states: *magistrate* in North Carolina and *referee* in Colorado. Names, dates, and locations have been changed to preserve the anonymity of the persons whose cases we discuss.

In Text 2, the same witness attempts to state the source of his knowledge and finds that, because he heard it from someone else, it is disallowed. He comes up against two proscriptive rules. The first limits nonexpert witnesses to their firsthand knowledge. The second, the hearsay rule, holds that firsthand knowledge to what another has said is not a permissible basis for testimony offered to prove the truth of what the other has said; in the example, the color of the victim's lips.[4]

Text 2
L_1: Were her lips blue at the time?
W: Uh, I don't remember. I think that, uh, the patient's family said they were blue.
L_2: Object to what the family said.
J: Sustained.

Text 3 presents a somewhat different hearsay problem. The text is taken from an armed robbery trial; the convenience store clerk who was held up is attempting to describe the car in which the robber fled. In her first answer, the witness acknowledges the hearsay source of the information, and the judge excludes it. The second answer, which omits any reference to the source, is allowed to stand. This text shows a good deal about the curious workings of the court. The witness has already stated that she knew the year of manufacture of the car because someone had told her. Yet the witness' testimony about the year of manufacture, which had been excluded when its hearsay basis was mentioned, is allowed to stand when presented in language that suggests firsthand knowledge.

Text 3
L_1: Now could you describe the year or approximate year?
W: Uh, seventy—, I was told seventy-three.
L_2: Object, your honor, to what she was told.
J: Sustained as to what she was told. Disabuse your minds of that, members of the jury. It is not competent.
L_1: Could you describe whether it looked like a new or an old car?
W: Well, it was seventy-three then. It was a seventy-three Pontiac.

Texts 1–3 are typical of instances of reported conversations that occur in formal courts and are treated as hearsay. These texts suggest that in some respects at least witnesses often attempt to tell their stories in courts as they

---

[4] These rules are thought to promote accurate fact finding because the law of evidence presumes that cross-examination of witnesses will resolve most questions about testimonial reliability by allowing the judge and jury to evaluate the witness' credibility and the plausibility of the witness' story. When a witness testifies only about personal observations, the witness may be cross-examined about everything that is reported. When a witness reports what someone else has said, however, the cross-examiner can only investigate whether the present witness is reporting the other person's statement accurately. The declarant's state of mind and the factual accuracy of the declarant's report cannot be probed.

might tell them in everyday situations, and they are often frustrated in the attempt. If witnesses did not tend to report conversations in their testimony, the rule of hearsay would not be needed; in any event, there would not be such frequent objections resulting from attempts to keep secondhand information out of testimonial accounts.

Evidentiary rules regarding the expression of opinions and conclusions in the course of testimony also cause frequent problems. Except in the case of expert witnesses, the law of evidence expresses a strong preference for concrete descriptive testimony. Lay opinions and conclusions are not necessarily impermissible, but they are frequently restricted. Judges have considerable discretion here.[5]

Text 4 illustrates the problem that many witnesses have in adapting to this preference for concrete testimony. The witness is a woman who has filed a criminal complaint against her father, alleging that when drunk he threatened her mother with a gun. In the quoted testimony, she is attempting to describe his behavior on a particular occasion. Rather than describing the behavior in concrete terms, however, she summarizes it in a conclusory fashion ("he gets uglier and uglier"). Moreover, she does not limit her account to events that she observed on the occasion in question but appears to generalize from observations she made on other occasions when he was drunk ("After he gets a certain amount of drink in him"). Although such generalization may be common in everyday conversation, it is unacceptable in court, because the law usually does not permit a witness to prove what happened on one occasion by reference to other, similar occasions. In this objection sequence, the basis for the objection is not explained to the witness. Nor does the witness show any understanding of the objection sequence; rather she ignores it and proceeds with her account.[6]

Text 4

W: . . . After he gets a certain amount of drink in him, he gets uglier and uglier and he does become very violent.

L_2: Objection, if your honor please.

J: Objection sustained.

W: Anyhow, I was afraid—about the gun. That's what petrified me.

---

[5] Lay opinions and conclusions are most often permitted when there is no simple way to describe a particular event: for example, a lay witness will usually be permitted to offer the opinion that another person appeared to be drunk without reciting all the observed physical characteristics that prompted that conclusion. Witnesses who qualify as experts are allowed to give opinions about matters within their fields of expertise. The circumstances under which opinions are admissible in the federal courts are described in Fed. R. Evid. 701-5.

[6] In this instance, the witness's "anyhow" suggests that she means something like "I didn't understand what you said, but I will continue with what I was attempting to say." This interpretation is supported by other instances of similar reactions by witnesses to objections in comments like "Can I answer?" and "I beg your pardon."

Text 5 contains a similar objection sequence, but this time the judge provides some explanation of his ruling on the objection. In this excerpt, which is taken from an appeal of a speeding ticket, the police officer who stopped the defendant is attempting to account for the events in question by referring to what often happens in similar situations. As in Text 4, the testimony is disallowed. Note that the judge's remarks are directed to the jury and not to the witness who has made the "mistake." As in most such instances, no instruction is given to the witness about the legal problem he has encountered in testifying. Consequently, witnesses do not understand such "errors," and our transcripts show witnesses making them repeatedly (cf. Atkinson & Drew, 1979:209–215).

Text 5

L_2: After you entered the fifty-five zone, what happened next?

W: Um, our cars have the electronic siren and I tapped it a few times hoping he would pull over because, uh, sometimes when people decide to run they wait till they get to open road and so I was trying to get him to stop . . .

L_2: Objection. Motion to strike.

J: Sustained as to what people sometimes do. Disabuse your minds of that, members of the jury. It is not competent. Motion to strike is allowed.

The law of evidence is in one sense epistemological: It reflects the law's views on what constitutes a fact and what sources of information are reliable. These views are in turn imposed on the form and content of the accounts that witnesses are allowed to give in court. Texts 1 through 5 provide evidence that witnesses come to court with their own epistemological assumptions and that these assumptions often conflict with the ones embodied in the law of evidence. Witnesses' reactions to objection sequences suggest that they have little understanding of the nature of this conflict and that the explanations offered by the courts do little to enlighten them about why the law deems their narratives unacceptable. These kinds of difficulties in telling stories in court may contribute to the frequently reported dissatisfaction of witnesses with the formal judicial process.

These observations about problems with testifying under the rules of evidence suggested several specific questions for our study of small claims narratives. First, we believed that small claims narratives would be a fertile source of information about those "folk" approaches to narration that are apparently frustrated by formal court procedures.[7] Are there, for example, consistencies in the way that lay litigants structure legal narratives? Can

[7] Although small claims courts do not impose formal rules of evidence and procedure, there are rules, or at least customs, that control many aspects of litigants' behavior. For example, witnesses may not talk indefinitely, nor may they interrupt each other. Such rules and customs vary from court to court, from magistrate to magistrate, and even from day to day. In the tapes we collected, however, these rules and customs were never observed to frustrate witnesses in their efforts to present uninterrupted narratives.

narratives tell us anything about how litigants conceptualize their problems or about how they define their objectives in coming to small claims court? Second, we suspected that the relaxation of many of the evidentiary constraints on narration might affect litigant satisfaction with the process and hoped that the detailed analysis of litigants' speech might shed light on this issue. Finally, we wondered whether the removal of formal constraints on witness narratives might create its own set of problems even as it ameliorated, at least on a superficial level, some of the dissatisfaction that was so evident in formal courts.

4. THE SMALL CLAIMS STUDY: METHODS

We began the research with an ethnographic study of two small claims courts. Pursuant to confidentiality agreements with the respective courts, we observed and taped 30 small claims cases in Durham, North Carolina, and 25 cases in Denver, Colorado.[8] Durham is a city of about 100,000 people, but the Durham court's jurisdiction also includes many rural areas of Durham County. We also observed but did not tape 3 days of trials in Orange County, North Carolina, a less urban county adjacent to Durham in which the main campus of the University of North Carolina is located. In Durham, small claims trials are held in a small office, and the parties in each case generally remain outside in a waiting room prior to the beginning of the trial. In Denver, trials are conducted in a larger courtroom that is usually crowded with the parties to several cases. At least one of the researchers was present during all taped proceedings, observing and making notes to facilitate the study of the tapes. During breaks in the trial calendar, we had many opportunities to ask questions of the magistrates and engage in informal discussions. In both jurisdictions, litigants were informed at the start of each trial that we were observers conducting an academic study, but we believe that we were largely ignored by most litigants, who were necessarily more concerned with their cases.

In North Carolina, small claims courts have jurisdiction over civil matters in which the amount in controversy is less than $1,000 (N.C. Gen. Stat. §§ 7A-210-232; Guth, 1983). The cases are heard by full-time appointed magis-

[8] We defined a "case" as an adversary proceeding in which at least one party appeared and which led to a judgment, either after trial or by default. In the courts we studied if the defendant fails to appear, the plaintiff is still required to testify in support of his or her case before a judgment is entered, but the defendant is automatically awarded a default judgment if the plaintiff fails to appear. We observed a few instances in which a single plaintiff, typically a landlord, obtained judgments simultaneously against several defendants who did not appear; we counted such an instance as a single case. In the Durham court, we also observed 22 "transactions," which we defined as other interactions between a "consumer" and the magistrate that did not fit the definition of a case. Such interactions were possible in Durham because people could walk directly into the magistrate's office/courtroom. In Denver, consumer inquiries were all handled by a clerk's office.

trates whose duties include both hearing small claims cases and handling such criminal matters as issuing search and arrest warrants and setting bond. These magistrates need not be lawyers, and most are not. We observed six different magistrates in Durham and Orange Counties, one of whom had a law degree, although he was not admitted to the North Carolina bar (see Guth, 1983; Haemmel, 1973). North Carolina magistrates are permitted but not required to follow the rules of evidence. A recent survey indicates that evidentiary constraints are rarely if ever imposed (Bashor, 1985). North Carolina small claims courts permit lawyers, but the parties were represented by counsel in only one of the 30 cases we observed.

Colorado small claims courts also have jurisdiction over civil cases involving less than $1,000. The judges, or referees, are appointed by the chief judge of the local county court and must be admitted to the bar. Lawyers are generally not allowed to appear; in most instances, if a party wants to be represented by a lawyer, the case is transferred to the county court. The rules of evidence and procedure are not observed (Colo. Rev. Stat. §§ 13-6-407-416).

Following the collection of audiotape recordings in the two jurisdictions, we prepared transcripts for each of the trials. Our method for analyzing the trials was inspired by the group workshop technique used by many conversation analysts. In our analytic sessions, we were joined by three or four other researchers trained in law, social science, or both.

A typical session focused on a trial segment selected in advance, usually a single litigant's narrative as we have defined it (see note 2). Participants listened several times to the tape (often as many as five or six playings) and were furnished with a transcript similar to those prepared by court reporters. Following the playings of the tape, each participant spent 20 minutes or so writing notes about those features of the narrative that were of particular interest to him or her. The remainder of each session, usually 60 to 90 minutes, was devoted to a round-table discussion of our respective observations.[9]

The issues discussed in this article were among the most frequently recurring themes in our analytic sessions. The only prior agreement among the participants was to focus general attention on the matter of how small claims narratives differ in form and substance from testimony given in more formal legal settings. Such issues as deductive versus inductive narrative structure and the manner in which litigants assess responsibility repeatedly attracted analytic attention; indeed, a striking aspect of the sessions was the participants' high degree of agreement about the narratives.

Approaching the data in this manner allowed us to focus on the issues that the data suggest are important to the trial participants themselves.

[9] We wish to thank the following persons for their participation in the Duke–UNC Law and Language Research Seminar during 1984–1985: Ron Butters, Chris Bashor, Roy Baroff, Mark Childress, Lynda Flanagan, Susan Hirsch, Tom Jarvis, and Sylvia Servas. The group analytic method was suggested by Max Atkinson based on data analytic techniques commonly used by conversation analysts.

Inferences about litigant satisfaction resulting from the opportunity to tell one's story, for example, are based primarily on litigants' linguistic behavior in responding to the opportunity and secondarily on their comments about the process of testifying. Our conclusions about the adequacy of some of the narratives from the perspective of legal decision makers are similarly based primarily on the reactions of magistrates during the trial and secondarily on their out-of-court discussions with us about particular cases.

Our method is fundamentally similar to conversation analysis in that recordings of naturally occurring (institutional) speech are the primary source of data. We also rely on the native-speaker competence of the researcher as a principal tool for the analysis of the data. Thus we share with conversation analysts the convictions that the best evidence for the study of the social consequences of speech lies in speech behavior itself and that this evidence is readily accessible to other members of the speech community.

Our method differs from most conversation analysis in that we deal with significantly larger units of data. Whereas conversation analysts frequently work on brief exchanges that commonly occur in everyday conversation, the narratives and accounts we analyze are often several minutes in duration. We work with such larger units of data for two reasons. First, the unit of the narrative is a natural one in small claims court: When witnesses are invited to tell their stories, they commonly respond with substantial narratives. Second, although we recognize that many important details of speech may be overlooked when such larger units are analyzed, it is also true that certain features are not discernible when approached with a narrow turn-by-turn focus. The major issues discussed in this chapter—the structure of narratives and the assessment of responsibility—can only be studied by examining complete accounts given by witnesses.

Our approach differs in one further significant way from much of the work done in the conversation analytic tradition. Our specific goal is to understand the social and legal implications of the data we analyze rather than to further understanding of conversation itself. Accordingly, we strive to ensure that our inferences are firmly grounded in the linguistic data available to us, but we consider the implications of these inferences for such issues as the fairness of small claims courts and their place in the larger social order rather than for a general theory about how conversation proceeds.

5. LEGAL NARRATIVES WITHOUT EVIDENTIARY CONSTRAINTS

The small claims courts we observed allowed litigants to tell their stories without evidentiary constraints.[10] Witnesses' accounts in these courts were

---

[10] Over the course of 55 cases, we observed an evidentiary restriction being imposed only once, when a magistrate excluded a document as hearsay on his own initiative.

indeed more like everyday speech than the accounts heard in the regular trial court. Accounts in small claims court include reported conversations and expressions of opinions as well as such other features as metapragmatic comments on the process of testifying and various organizational devices related to longer and more flexible narratives. Moreover, these accounts embody lay models of *legal adequacy*.

Our tapes are replete with evidence that small claims litigants realize that the opportunity to tell a judge a relatively uninterrupted story is a rare one. In an eviction action, for example, the defendant, a law school graduate who had fallen on hard times and was in arrears on his rent, recognized that he had no legal defense to the eviction. Nonetheless, he took several minutes to relate all his troubles to the magistrate, finally commenting that it had been worth the effort to come to court and that it had "at least [made him] feel better." In another case, the plaintiff sought to recover some personal property that his former wife had retained after their divorce. After a long trial marked by several emotional exchanges among husband, wife, and two sons, the magistrate ruled against him. His closing remarks indicated that he understood the ruling and felt that the trial itself had been a useful, if not therapeutic, exercise.

Other expressions of such sentiments could be cited. The most telling bit of evidence, however, may be simply the fact that *every* litigant we observed responded to the magistrate's invitation to speak by giving a narrative description of the situation. The invitation to speak was typically in the form of a question such as "Why are you here?" or "Why have you brought this matter to the court?"[11] Litigants, however, invariably responded not by answering the questions in a narrow sense but by commencing a chronological narrative of the dispute as they perceived it. The scope of these narratives often went far beyond the facts that the court was empowered to adjudicate.

All of this suggests that, from the litigant's perspective, the opportunity for unconstrained narrative is an important component of small claims court procedure. Litigants uniformly take advantage of the opportunity to talk, apparently viewing narration as an appropriate small claims strategy, and some even offer unsolicited favorable comments about this aspect of the procedure. These findings are consistent with Abel's (1982:284) view that small claims courts neutralize conflict by allowing grievants "to let off steam."

Text 6 illustrates a typical account given in a small claims court. The plaintiff (Norris), a black man in his 20s, is a highly paid, skilled industrial

---

[11] The opening questions used by the North Carolina magistrates included: "At this time, Miss H, if you want to state to the court the reason you're bringing this action against the defendant"; "Mr. E, do you have any statement at this time concerning this matter?"; "OK, Miss S, do you wish to stand on the complaint as read or do you want to elaborate on that as read?" The single referee whom we observed in Denver frequently asked a series of specific questions to open the hearing but always issued an open-ended invitation to speak, such as, "From you what is there that I can learn that will help me decide this case?"

worker. He alleged that a suit he bought from a store was damaged when he got it back from its first dry cleaning. He sued both the cleaner and the store, asking the court to decide whether the damage resulted from defective material or negligent cleaning and to award damages against the appropriate defendant. The magistrate severed the cases against the two defendants, first hearing evidence against the cleaner. The cleaner had sent the suit for analysis to the International Fabricare Institute, which reported in writing that the material was defective. The magistrate accepted this report as conclusive. The manager of the cleaning establishment then testified for the plaintiff in his case against the clothing store. The court accepted the argument of the store manager that the manufacturer was at fault and ordered the case continued while the store attempted to gain a refund from the manufacturer. Text 6 contains the plaintiff's initial presentation of his case against the cleaner.

Text 6

Magistrate: OK, Mr. Norris, if you want to state to the court the reason you are bringing this action against NDE Company.

Norris: Uh, the reason I am bringing this action against NDE Company, I, got a suit, bought a suit from Feldman's around the last of May, I wore the suit one time, and I sent it to the laundry to have it, have it cleaned, and I, they send the suit back to me, the suit, well I can show it to Your Honor.

Magistrate: OK, show it to Mr. Cashwell also.

Norris: The suit come back to me like this here [*pointing to spot on suit*], like it had maybe, I thought maybe, it wasn't enough heat on it.

Magistrate: Uh, huh.

Norris: Mr. Rogers at the laundry, he told me that it was a defect in the material that was in the suit. He—I, I, I brought the suit home and I wore it and I seen this here [*indicating spot*] that it was on there so I took the suit off and I told my wife, "Well, we goin' send it back to the laundry the next day." This is the laundry ticket [*indicating ticket*] where they redone the suit. See, they didn't put this tag here on there till the second time I got the suit, OK. This first time I got it—the suit—they just had it in the plastic. I thought it was OK until I seen it, so I sent it back to the laundry and I was talking to a Mr. Rogers and he said that, uh, that the suit was— it was a defect in the material—he say, "What about waiting two weeks?" So I spent time out of work going back and forth talking to Mr. Rogers, and he put this on, on [*pointing to paper attached to suit in the plastic bag*], on the suit about the second time I picked it up. He said, "Well,"—you can see that [*indicating paper*]— he said, "Well, it's probably a defect in the material." He said, "What I'll do, I'll send it off and I'll have it analyzed and when it come back," he said, "if we're in the fault," he said, "we'll send—we'll, uh, refund your money." So I was waiting at the time two weeks, I'm hoping that maybe they'd find the fault and pay me my money, but he said that—"I can't pay you no money." He's given me, when the suit come back, he gave me this information here [*holding up several pages*].

The narrator provides three types of evidence within his account. First, he produces *documents* that support his story. Second, he calls "*witnesses*" by performing their parts. Third, he introduces *physical evidence*, the suit itself. In an everyday account, some of these might not have been included. Their inclusion in the plaintiff's testimony hints at his conception of legal adequacy. These features of the narrative suggest that the plaintiff believes that written records are more powerful pieces of evidence than his recollections; that the words of others speak for themselves more forcefully than his own paraphrases or interpretations; and that physical evidence is especially useful because it can "speak" for itself. Analyzed in this manner, relatively unconstrained narratives offered as evidence to the court reveal lay models of the kinds of accounts that are appropriate and sufficient to prove a defendant's responsibility.

Other interesting features of this account include the perspective from which it is told, the performance of the story, and its structural features. The story is told from a frequently shifting perspective, sometimes from the vantage of the narrator's home and other times from the vantage of the cleaner's. Deictic markers[12] give clues to the perspective throughout the story. Abelson (1975) argues that a story told from a single vantage point[13] is easier to comprehend, but accounts given in small claims courts suggest that narrators do not follow this principle. In fact, the shifting of vantage points in an account is common in both small claims and more formal courts. In the latter, however, a shift away from the speaker's past vantage points is likely to occasion an objection that the witness is engaging in speculation or reporting hearsay.

One may well ask what significance the shifting of perspective has in a narrative, if, following Abelson, we assume that accounts containing multiple points of view are more difficult for listeners to comprehend. Having looked through a large number of accounts without discovering any discernible pattern regarding the vantage point from which stories are told, we have two hypotheses about what may be occurring.

First, multiple vantage points may reflect the natural tendency of the narrator to triangulate on the events being described. Narrators ordinarily tell stories from many perspectives. As listeners, we are taken from scene to scene, we hear the relevant parties "speak," and we may even get privileged information about the motives and thoughts of various parties to the action. Abelson's study of consistency in perspective was a laboratory study. There is

---

[12] Deictic markers are linguistic features that speakers use to anchor themselves in discourse with respect to place and time (e.g., Fillmore, 1971; Jarvella & Klein, 1982). Our earlier research in formal courts revealed that witnesses frequently orient themselves by using such contrasting deictic pairs as *here* and *there*, *this* and *that*, and *come* and *go*, often to the apparent confusion and consternation of the court. (Much of this confusion may stem from judges' concerns about producing a clear and unambiguous record in the transcript.)

[13] Although Abelson uses the term "point of view" to mean the vantage point from which the narrator tells the story, we use the term "vantage point" in order not to confuse this aspect of a narrative with what is commonly referred to as point of view in literary studies (e.g., omniscient first-person narrative, third-person interior monologue, etc.).

no reason to suggest that his findings about consistency of perspective and corresponding ease of comprehension are incorrect, but there is also no reason to assume that the artificial situation studied in the laboratory actually replicates the way people tell stories in natural settings.

Second, as Wolfson (1982) found in her study of the conversational historical present tense in English, it may well be that the shift of perspective is more important than the actual perspective that is assumed. Following Wolfson, we suggest that the shifting of perspective serves to highlight the story and hold the listener's attention. (The reader is invited to test Wolfson's theory by reformulating Text 6 so that it is told from a single perspective.)

Another interesting aspect of the account contained in Text 6 is the fact that the narrator performs the story by assuming the voices of the actors in it, rather than by merely relating it in some more distant or indirect manner. Students of folklore know from the writings of Hymes (1981) and others that the "breakthrough into performance" is considered in many cultures to be an important feature of persuasive narratives.[14] Although adequate and acceptable stories may be rendered without performance, it is generally true across cultures that those narrators who perform stories in telling them are perceived as giving better accounts. If this is true, then one of the consequences of the evidentiary constraints that proscribe performance by eliminating testimony relating to what other persons have said is to reduce the rhetorical force of the account. It may well be that those who are accustomed to performing stories and who are not allowed to do so give testimony that appears particularly uninteresting or even incredible.

Tannen (1981) suggests that major differences exist between stories told in oral and literate cultures. One such difference she reports is the tendency for accounts to be performed in oral cultures and to be related in literate cultures according to the rules of written discourse, which places a higher value on consistency of vantage point. Accordingly, we suspect that some persons within a pluralistic culture such as our own may tend toward the oral mode of narration, whereas others may be more familiar with the literate mode. Small claims courts, which have relaxed rules of evidence, allow and tolerate either mode, whereas more formal courts, based as they are on the literate tradition and its recordkeeping requirements, follow the biases of the literate tradition. Under these circumstances, it is easy to understand why many people feel constrained and inhibited by the formalities of courts of record and why they may prefer the informality of small claims courts.

Another feature of the account in Text 6 is its chronological organization. Although chronology might be expected as an organizational device for legal accounts, there are many situations in which accounts are not chronologically

---

[14] "Breakthrough into performance" refers to the situation in which a narrator shifts from third-person reporting to enactment of a story by speaking the parts of the characters rather than merely reporting what they said.

ordered. Perhaps the most common occurrence of nonchronological accounts is in cross-examination. Trial practice manuals advise lawyers to break chronology in order to unsettle witnesses. At the same time, they caution that presentation of facts out of chronological order may have the effect of confusing the jury or conveying the impression that the lawyer is disorganized (Bailey & Rothblatt, 1971:192, 200–201; Keeton, 1973:23; McElhaney, 1974:27). The naturalness of chronological ordering is suggested by the fact that trial practice manuals give advice on when not to follow it. By contrast, most direct examinations tend to be chronologically ordered because of the legal necessity to demonstrate that the witness has the requisite firsthand knowledge of the evidence to be introduced—what lawyers call "laying a proper foundation." Equally important, however, is the fact that chronology is related to our cultural understanding of causality (i.e., event A must precede event B if A is a cause of B).

In small claims courts, most narratives are organized chronologically. For most witnesses the difficult decision is where to begin and end the account. The form of the invitation to testify does not seem to provide much assistance with respect to where to begin. In Text 6, for example, the magistrate invites the witness to state his reason for bringing the action. In Text 7, which is drawn from a case arising out of a boundary dispute between landowners, a fuller invitation is issued, yet there is no appreciable difference between the accounts that these different types of invitations elicit. It is also the case that witnesses sometimes embark on long chronological narratives in response to highly specific factual questions.[15]

Text 7

Referee: Now likewise as a witness for the plaintiff, you've heard everything that has been said and you're closely related to all of this, and I believe you understand that, uh, your mother is, uh, alleging right to recover for the expenses that she's incurred over this long history and also she, it's her opinion that in the process she's been harassed and annoyed and all of that and she's seeking recovery for that as well. Now you're as familiar with this perhaps as anyone. From you, what is there that I can learn that will help me decide this case?

Tom: Uh, as you can see from the pictures of the trees that there were several trees on the Barretts' property that a particular tree grows underground and up onto other people's property. Uh, under the fence line and all the way up against the foundation of the house, these sumac trees have grown and spread out and, if I can point out something here [*pointing to photograph*], uh, this is the particular tree . . .

Referee: In such a way that the defendant can see it as well.

[15] One of us (WMO) also serves as a mediator in a community dispute settlement center. Similar difficulties are common in mediation sessions. Mediators comment that parties often start "in the middle" of their stories. On being invited to give their side of the case, disputants often ask for guidance with a question like "How far back do you want me to begin?" In this particular center, mediators are taught to respond to such inquiries with a noncommittal answer like "As far back as you think necessary," leaving the decision up to the narrator.

Tom: These have grown up from their property onto our side of the house, OK, and they were removed by me. These, this is where the hedge line was, but now it is grown up with the same sumac trees that came out of their back yard and off of their property, and these are the trees that my mom was talking about having to cut after the hedge was actually dead and gone. There have been, um, a couple of instances where I, days where I went out and cut down the trees that had grown under the fence and it started to grow all over our yard and against the foundation, and poisoned those trees. They grew up through a bush that we had there and, uh, so there are several instances where I've had to go out and cut those trees and dig out and poison them, uh, to get them to stop growing on our property and then they grew up in the hedge area and then the hedge was removed and taken out. Um, it was a very poor choice of shrubs—something that spreads all over the, you know, area. Uh, the, uh, trees have dropped, you know, there's one [*indicating picture*] like that already. There's another picture with the trees growing up on the property and that's after they've already been cut several times. Um, and the big trees—you can see there—keep dropping things and the bushes keep growing through the fence which is onto our property, onto my mom's property.

Notice also that after his narrative began, the witness received few clues about when to continue and when to quit. Atkinson (personal communication) has suggested that magistrates in British small claims courts give cues about continuing through response tokens such as "yes" and "I see." In the small claims courts that we studied, such tokens are infrequent, and witnesses are left more to their own devices with regard to how long to continue. In these circumstances witnesses tend to employ turn preservation techniques that allow them to continue speaking, usually until they decide that their stories are complete. Look, for example, at the use of the connective "and" in the narrative in Text 8, which is taken from a negligence case arising out of a collision between a car and a moped. Several times, the witness reaches a point where the listener might reasonably conclude that the story is over. The witness preserves his speaking turn with an "and," which is followed by another segment of the narrative. In addition, at several points in his narrative the witness employs rising intonation in an apparent request for acknowledgment and understanding. Because the magistrate gives no verbal response on any of these occasions, the witness is required to continue without the response he has requested. In formal court proceedings, the witness need not be concerned about where to begin and end, because the interrogating lawyer manages the allocation of speaking turns.

Text 8[16]

Magistrate: You tell your, please tell your story. She tells her story, then we decide. OK?

---

[16] Two additional transcribing conventions are used in this text. First, discernible pauses are indicated (in tenths of seconds) in parentheses throughout the text. Second, rising intonation is marked with an upward arrow at the end of the phrasal segment containing the intonational contour.

Fisher: All right. Uh, there's a, there's a four-way intersection here in Durham up close by the Oyster Bar, and we was making a left-hand turn. . .

Nancy: Mmhmm.

Fisher: and, um, was pulling into, as we turned in—it's a short, very short distance, fifty foot, seventy-five foot, something like that where there's a parking area ↑ (1.0) to be parked at. We, she turned on the left turn, uh, the right turn signal to make a right-hand turn into the parking lot ↑ (1.0), and we started, the front, the front end of the car was into the, um, little uprise to get onto the parking lot area ↑ (1.0), and when we did, first thing I know of, something hit me behind, the arm, pushed my arm up into the mirror, and then my arm come back into the car, (1.5) and then maybe I looked back to see what was going on and here's this lady on a moped all over us (2.0). And we had stopped right there in the road, and, um, she was on the ground, and Nancy went ahead and put the car into the parking lot to get us out of the middle of the road, and we got out to see what we could do to help the woman. And (1.0) about twenty minutes later, I guess, the Durham cop—police—finally come up, (1.0) and they, we went after they wrote out the summons for both of us to come to court and then—me and Nancy and Miss Devlin here to come to court— and we did. And we thought it was to get the money to fix the repairs for the car which what we found out was the only thing that done there was charged with a traffic violation. (1.5) And we was told—we asked the, uh, not the arresting officer, the man that was there,

Nancy: Carl.

Fisher: and he said we could, um, bring it to civil court or whatever ↑ (1.5), to get, to get, um, to get the payments for the damages. (2.0) And that's—we, come down here and we was told where to go to talk to the lady, and she told us what to do and she's apparently set up a date to come here. ↑ (1.5) And that's all we was told. We didn't [*inaudible*] anything else about the car . . .

Magistrate: Anything else? You want to add to that?

Nancy: No.

6. THE LEGAL ADEQUACY OF UNAIDED WITNESS NARRATIVES

The most significant of the problems faced by small claims litigants relates to the legal adequacy of their narratives. We use the term "legal adequacy" to refer to a narrative's form and content rather than to its impact on the outcome of a case. While it would be interesting to investigate whether particular narrative styles correlate with favorable case outcomes, we do not have sufficient data for that purpose. Legally inadequate narratives are for our purposes narratives that differ substantially in form and content from the accounts that judges are accustomed to dealing with by training and experience. There are three sources of information concerning the legal adequacy of individual narratives: the comments of the magistrates during extensive interviews before and after the cases observed, the training and experience of one of the authors (JMC) as a trial lawyer, and the reactions of the magistrates to certain types of narratives during the hearing of cases. The third category of data is the most significant, because it is drawn from actual courtroom discourse rather than from the after-the-fact reflections of participants or observers.

From a common sense perspective, the plaintiff in Text 6 appears to give an adequate account of why one of the two defendants should be held responsible for the damages to his suit. It is evident from an examination of the suit that it has been damaged. There are three possible responsible agents: the man himself, the cleaner, and the store and/or manufacturer. In describing his own behavior, the man excludes himself, at least by implication, because he says nothing that suggests he is to blame. When he concludes, he apparently believes that he has given the court an adequate basis for finding against either or both of the defendants.

Despite the commonsense appeal of his story, the man received no compensation for his damaged suit. The cleaner presented an exonerating report from a purported expert, and the magistrate accepted it without question. The cleaner's representative, a middle-aged white man, then testified for the plaintiff, stating that the material in the suit was defective. This testimony shifted the burden to the store, whose representative, a young well-dressed black man, quickly persuaded the magistrate that the fault must lie with the manufacturer, which had not been sued. The man was told to come back later, after the store had tried to work things out with the manufacturer.

It is difficult to see in what respect the man's case fell short. From a legal standpoint, he acted properly in joining the two defendants and asserting that one must be held responsible. Even if one accepts the cleaner's "expert" report at face value, as the magistrate did, the man would seem to have a valid warranty claim against the store, to which the ultimate responsibility of the manufacturer should be no defense. The shortcoming appears to be not in the legal theory adopted but in the structure of the narrative itself.

It may be significant that in his narrative, the man proceeded as if the facts would speak for themselves. In particular, he never dealt explicitly with the issues of blame, responsibility, and agency. The assessment of responsibility for the damage he has suffered is accomplished only to the extent that the listener can draw inferences from the facts recounted. In this respect, his approach might reasonably be characterized as inductive. He does not lay out a theory of the case for testing. Rather, he presents the facts he considers relevant and expects them to lead to a conclusion.

Compare the man's narrative with the case as a lawyer might have presented it in a formal trial or even in an argument to a small claims court magistrate. The lawyer would not have added any facts; on the contrary, some information, such as the reported conversation with the plaintiff's wife, might have been deleted. What the lawyer would have done is to begin the presentation with an opening statement that posited a hypothesis about who was responsible. The evidence would have been organized around that hypothesis, and the case would have concluded with an argument that emphasized the ways in which the evidence demonstrated the validity of the hypothesis. In contrast to the man's inductive approach, a lawyer would have organized the case as a deductive experiment in which the issue of responsibility was addressed directly.

In light of the result, it is interesting to note that both defendants dealt explicitly with the allocation of responsibility. The cleaner had his expert's report, whereas the store manager laid the blame on the absent manufacturer. The significant point may not be that the defendants were correct in their theories but simply that each defendant articulated a theory of responsibility in the deductive form familiar to lawyers and legal decision makers. A litigant who is unable to structure his or her case in this familiar form may be at a serious disadvantage.

The point is further illustrated by a text taken from a case brought by a middle-aged white woman against a garage owner, a white man in his early 30s. The woman claimed that she—or, rather, a "friend" of hers—had bought a rebuilt car engine from the defendant, that the engine had never worked properly, and that as a result she had spent hundreds of dollars on oil, her transmission had been damaged, and she had lost her job when she was unable to get to work. She testified later in the case that her life had ultimately deteriorated to the point where she had been evicted from her apartment for nonpayment of rent and was sleeping in the disabled car.

A lawyer would probably characterize this as a breach of contract or breach of warranty case in which the plaintiff sought two kinds of damages: direct (the money paid for the engine) and consequential (the money paid for oil and compensation for the loss of job and eviction). The magistrate accepted the defendant's argument that the language on the bill of sale limited his liability and ordered him to refund the price of the engine—something that he had apparently been willing to do all along.

Text 9

Magistrate: OK. At this time, Miss Harrell, if you want to state to the court the reason you're bringing this action against the defendant.

Harrell: Well, on January the third, a friend of mind paid, uh, him $312 for a motor for my car. It was installed the seventh of January, and for a week—first week after that it was leaking oil all—everywhere around the lifters and all around the motor on the other side and there was a big puddle of oil in my yard. Every time the car was stopped it was leaking oil. I went back on the following Friday and told him about it, he—one of his mechanics told me to try some gaskets. So I went down and got the gaskets, came back, he reimbursed me for the bill for that, and the gaskets were installed. Um, two hours later, I decided to drive it up the street to see how it was doing, and it started knocking and making all kinds of noises, and since then, well, I have been back and forth over there. One of his mechanics even checked it out, it was smoking and everything else. And since then I have put over two hundred thirty-some dollars worth of oil in the car. It has damaged my transmission, uh, I've had it checked by a number of mechanics that said the motor was bad and it—uh, it was—the vacuum lines were intact, they, um, everything was checked on that and it has caused the transmission to—quite a bit of damage to that, and, um, so it's, um it's been one thing after another. I called him, and, um, about the middle of March. I was calling him every day just about. Or two or three times a week anyway, and had to call him to remind him to find me a motor, and always—he, um, I offered to take my old motor back if they had, had been able to do anything with it, work on that, do anything with it, he didn't want to do that. This motor has, he said, has 62,000 miles on it, which is 162,000 and all the mechanics that I have contacted, you know, they've checked it out, the transmission, everything, said that the motor was bad and there was not enough vacuum coming from the motor to cause the transmission to change. I've had to put no transmission fluid in there, uh, it's, um, it's, um, it's just not, it's not changing, and it's, it's really played, uh, a havoc with my, um, livelihood.

Once again, this is an inductive narrative in which the litigant relates a series of facts from a highly personal point of view. Listening to her story, the audience hears in detail how the malfunctioning engine has intruded on and virtually destroyed her life.

Despite its compelling quality, the woman's narrative has one significant shortcoming. The facts that she relates include little information about the contractual relationship between her and the garage owner. In particular, she fails to say explicitly why the garage owner should bear responsibility for her troubles. With respect to the relationship, all we learn is that an unidentified friend paid for a motor for her car. She then describes a number of things that the garage owner did: He apparently talked to her on several occasions, he paid for new gaskets, he had his mechanic install them, he had the mechanic check the car on a subsequent occasion, and he failed to respond to further telephone calls. She does not explain, however, how the owner incurred an obligation *to her*, what the nature of the obligation was, in what respect he failed to live up to his obligation, and how his failure caused her troubles. (On the contrary, to the extent that she describes the owner's behavior, one might conclude that he behaved reasonably well.) The problem, put in somewhat different terms, is that she has failed to blame the owner in a legally significant way. In fact, it can be argued that if there is in the narrative an active agent that the woman explicitly blames for her troubles, it is the engine itself.

After the woman completed her narrative, the magistrate asked several questions and then turned to the garage owner for his account. The owner was an experienced businessman who ran the garage with his father. He did not respond to the woman's recounting of her troubles. Instead, he talked about his limited legal duty to the woman, as evidenced by the written form contract that he produced, and asserted that he had met that limited duty, making specific reference to actions that he had taken and offers that he had made. The magistrate accepted his characterization of the relationship without question or discussion.

A particularly striking feature of this case, and one that it shares with a number of others we studied, is that the parties talk past each other. Neither contradicts what the other says. Rather, each takes a different approach to recounting a problem whose essential facts do not seem to be in dispute. The woman's approach was personalized and inductive. She described her troubles in detail, but she failed to provide all the components of a legally sufficient account and to arrange her story in a way that would be familiar to a legal decision maker. The owner provided the missing elements of the case. His approach was deductive: He explained the relationship between the parties, gave his version of the legal obligations that the relationship imposed, and referred to selected facts that suggested that he had not violated his legal obligations. The structure that he imposed on the facts was accepted by the magistrate. From a legal standpoint, this may well have been the appropriate structure. In any event, because it was the only alternative offered to the magistrate, the defendant seems to have gained a substantial advantage by proposing it.

Like other litigants we observed, the plaintiffs in these cases tell about the problems that have brought them to court, but they often fail to place blame or responsibility explicitly on any other party in a legally acceptable way. They may talk about the action and the acted upon without identifying any responsible human agent. Examples of this include such statements as:

> The rent started falling behind.
> The tools got stolen.
> I got injured.

The legal system cannot deal easily or adequately with such situations, because the law's theory is that a plaintiff must show the defendant as an *agent*, an *action*, and themselves as *recipient of the action*, as well as a causal link between the action of the agent and the harm the plaintiff has suffered. In small claims courts, however, plaintiffs often avoid dealing with agency even though the issue is critical for the legal process (e.g., Text 8). This finding is understandable when we compare small claims narratives to how people talk about trouble in everyday conversations.

The analysis of everyday conversations shows that people concerned with blame and responsibility tend to talk about these issues and to assess responsibility in interactive sequences rather than to attribute blame directly or unambiguously. In her study of blaming, Pomerantz (1978)[17] shows how

---

[17] For further discussion of how talk about trouble occurs in nonlegal everyday contexts, see Jefferson (1980).

people talk about troubles in everyday conversational contexts. She found That when trouble-tellers fail to deal with the issue of agency, those they are conversing with seek further information that clarifies agency. For example, a speaker reporting that his car blew up is asked what he did to it. In another of Pomerantz's examples, a woman complaining that her face hurts is asked what another person did to her to cause her face to hurt. These instances show the recurrent pattern of an interactive search for agency—in order to assess responsibility or place blame—when problems are described without the specification of a responsible agent. Often missing in small claims courts is this interactive search for responsibility, which is typical of everyday trouble tellings. By contrast, in more formal courts where rules of evidence apply and attorneys structure the telling of troubles by litigants, it is part of the lawyers' role to state a theory of responsibility.[18]

7. THE ROLE OF THE MAGISTRATE IN SHAPING NARRATIVES

In Texts 6 through 9, witnesses present accounts of their problems without the intervention of the magistrate. In each instance, the magistrate issues an invitation to speak, and the witness responds with a lengthy and largely uninterrupted narrative. In other cases studied, the magistrate plays a far more active role in eliciting and directing testimony, with the resulting account of the events in question emerging as the product of a dialogue between magistrate and witness. As the texts that follow illustrate, the effect of the magistrate's participation is often to provide the legal structure and explicit assessment of blame that is lacking in many unquestioned lay accounts.

Texts 10 and 11 are drawn from a case brought by the owner of a brass bed against a moving company that allegedly damaged the bed. Both the plaintiff and the representative of the company are white men in their 30s. Factually, the case is strikingly similar to the one described in Text 6. The plaintiff claimed that the movers scratched the bed while moving it and then damaged the finish by treating the scratch with a chemical. This had all happened about 6 months before the trial; during the interim, the moving company had sent the bed to a furniture repair shop, and it had remained there while the parties tried repeatedly but unsuccessfully to settle their differences. The small claims referee heard the two witnesses, examined the bed, and awarded the

---

[18] Attribution of responsibility in an interactive context can also be seen in Texts 1–3. In Text 1, the witness is attempting to deflect responsibility by explaining his action as a response to a request by another person rather than as a result of his own volition. In Texts 2 and 3, the witnesses seek to place responsibility for potentially important information they knew on those who told it to them. In these instances, the interactive setting of the courtroom—clearly different from the everyday contexts Pomerantz describes—prevents the diffusion or deflection of responsibility and requires individuals to take responsibility for their actions and knowledge.

plaintiff compensation for the damage, although he denied a claim for the replacement cost of the bed.

In Texts 10 and 11, the plaintiff's case is presented in two very different ways. In the early part of the case (Text 10), the referee asks the plaintiff a series of highly specific questions. It is clear from this dialogue that the referee, himself a lawyer, has already constructed a legal theory of the case, which he is proceeding to test. He views it as a bailment, which involves entrusting one's property to another, such as a mover, mechanic, or parking garage, for a fee. If the property is not returned in its original condition, the recipient or bailee is liable for any loss in value or for the replacement cost of the property if it has been destroyed.

Text 10

Referee: When did this move take place?

Allen: It took place at the end of April, sir. April 1984.

Referee: 84? And it's obvious this must or was this, uh, commercial property from a, uh, retail store or otherwise? Or was it personal . . .

Allen: It was personal, uh, property from my, uh, former, prior, uh, the prior place of residence to my new place.

Referee: And, did the defendant, was the defendant hired to move you?

Allen: Yes sir.

Referee: And in that process, according to the complaint, and by reason of some of the preliminaries in this case are more or less admitted that the move was accomplished and yes there was some damage and when did you turn the headboard back to the defendant for examination or repairs?

Allen: Approximately a week after, uh, I moved.

Referee: All right, sir.

Allen: Right around that time.

Referee: Did they pick it up or did, uh, you deliver it to them?

Allen: Well, Harry, uh, attempted to repair it, it at home with the, uh, a kind of a chemical. I don't know exactly what the name is but the chemical, uh, removed the, uh, finish, the lacquer finish. Therefore, it was decided to take it out to, uh, a place where it could be refinished.

After the completion of this dialogue, the referee invited the mover's representative "to respond and to further develop your defense or your answer," and he replied with a lengthy narrative. The representative did not refute any of the facts alleged by the plaintiff. Instead, he began by talking about how he and his boss had acted in good faith by trying to help the plaintiff even though he had failed to complain within the time specified by the contract. He talked about his friendly relationship with the plaintiff and concluded by deflecting responsibility for the damage toward the furniture repair shop. Following this portion of the trial, the plaintiff responded as follows to the referee's request for "anything additional, by way of conclusion."

Text 11

Referee: Back to you Mr. Allen as the plaintiff. Anything additional by way of conclusion?

Allen: Your honor, only that, that, I, I find some discrepancy in the position of the firm. When I spoke to Mr. Jefferson three weeks ago, uh, and at that time, I, I asked the reason I, I called them was look, um, I, I've been dealing pretty well, uh, with Harry, you know, with his employee. I had no, no problem. I think the most unpleasant experience was with Colorado Antique Finishing. Uh, but we've been able to talk with each other. And, and I said, there are some, some salient facts which he should be aware of. Uh, that I had gotten delivery without the proper assembly, that the buffing marks were there, that folks admitted, uh, that it had taken many months and I wanted to know if, if, uh, I said, "Can we resolve it?" and he said, "Yeah," I think, "you know we'll try to resolve it." In fact he was suggesting that I get a hold of some other firm that might rebuff it and he says, "We can work something out." I attempted to do so and, and I, I called several firms in, uh, here in Denver and, and it's, it's a complicated, uh, process, I guess. They, they to rebuff it they would have to do the thing over again and I called him back and I gave him the, the prices on that. I also gave him the price of what a, the new headboard costs. He called me back to say that he felt that it was worth no more than $65 and that he would be willing to settle at that point, keep the, uh, headboard, and give $65, which I thought was an absurdity, especially if you, uh, price the, uh, this particular headboard. So I find some discrepancy in saying things are OK but willing to pay $65 and then, and then keep my headboard and probably sell it for a higher amount. I'm not saying that Harry, uh, you know, said that. I got that directly from Mr. Jefferson. I think many months have passed on this thing. I sure waited a long time for that, uh, silly headboard. I'm beginning to have some feelings about it myself and the reason I'm fighting so hard is that if I don't get something back there at home, my wife was gonna, you know, really take care of me. So, uh, that's, that's practically [*inaudible*] to her, and it's so [*inaudible*] but I think you know, your honor, that, uh, uh, I have been very patient in it, that, uh, we take care of our things. We have no children. We take care of our things and make sure that they're in good shape and uh, that's, that's the way we like to keep them, and, and that's why we called and that's why we're unhappy with the shape that's in and we feel that, uh, once they accepted responsibility for it, then they should see that responsibility through, and if they felt strongly that, uh, we had no case in the matter that they shouldn't have accepted responsibility and simply said, "Allen, you're going to have to live with your scratch." I guess that's my case, your honor.

Like most others we observed, this narrative is chronological and inductive in structure. It deals with the issue of responsibility, but in a very different way than the referee dealt with it in his earlier questions. The plaintiff does not present the theory of absolute responsibility (bailment) that the referee seemed to be pursuing; rather, at the end of the narrative, he apparently acquiesces in the defendant's view that the mover assumed responsibility for the damage only by making a gratuitous offer of help. He seems almost to agree with the proposition that the mover could have avoided all responsibility simply by ignoring his complaint. Note particularly his characterization of the mover's settlement offer as "an absurdity." The implication is that the mover's offer of help created a relationship and that each party then assumed a duty of socially reasonable behavior toward the other. As long as this duty was met, he felt that he had no grievance. When the mover breached the duty by making the "absurd" offer, the plaintiff, prodded by his wife, concluded that it was time to assert his complaint.[19] At this point the plaintiff sees in the defendant's cooperative actions an admission of responsibility.

The plaintiff thus gives an inductive account of his grievance, in the course of which he sets out a complex theory of responsibility. While the theory may be marginally adequate as a legal matter (compare the duty of reasonable care imposed on a rescuer), it bears little relation to the theory adopted by the referee. It therefore seems questionable whether the plaintiff would have fared any better than his counterpart in the case of the damaged suit (Text 6) if he had had to rely solely on his unaided narrative. Unlike the owner of the damaged suit, however, this plaintiff had the benefit of a referee who was willing and able to develop a theory of responsibility, frame the case in deductive terms, and then test the hypothesis developed against the evidence.

Text 12 presents another situation where the judge and the litigants pursue different agendas. As the text suggests, the case was brought against the parents of a teenage driver who had collided with and damaged the plaintiff's car. The magistrate, who has already heard from the plaintiff, is now attempting to impose a legal structure on the parent's position. In his questions, he breaks the problem down into three components: (1) the boy's legal liability for causing the collision; (2) the parents' legal liability for the actions of their minor child; and (3) the extent of the damages for which they might be liable. The referee's questions suggest that he assumes that point 1 will not be contested because the boy is not in court and the parents were not eyewitnesses to the accident and that point 2 is beyond dispute as an established rule of law. He apparently believes that the parents have come to court solely to contest the amount of the damages sought by the plaintiff.

Text 12

Referee: Have you any questions as to the liability of parents for minors under ordinary circumstances?

Mr. F: Uh, in some cases because, uh, what chance do we have when he doesn't mind us, you know?

---

[19] The wife's behind-the-scenes role in the case seems crucial. One might conclude from the plaintiff's narrative that but for the domestic discord his inaction was provoking, there would have been no case. Instances such as this support Abel's (1982) suggestion that small claims proceedings often distort social reality by forcing litigants to view multifaceted problems as simple disputes between the parties who are actually in court.

Referee: Well sir, that's, that's nothing that I can decide here today. There's a case has been filed. It appears that a case has been filed against two parents for the operation of a motor vehicle owned by the parents and in the possession of the minor, uh, son of the party. An accident arose and there was damage.

Mr. F: Well . . .

Referee: Now we're back to this again. Were either one of you there at this time?

Mr. F: No.

Referee: So you have no knowledge as to how it happened?

Mr. F: No.

Referee: Basically the question is this, and I understand your concerns that the driver should pay but that's, he's not a party to this and cannot be a party, uh, because of his age. He may have obligations to you. That's not before the court today. But are you concerned only with the dollar amount of what this is going to conclude to us?

Mrs. F: No. We're concerned with that also, but we don't feel that we're responsible. We feel that he should have to be responsible for it.

Referee: All right, well you're bypassing the question now. Are you saying that it, the accident was not the fault of your son?

Mrs. F: No, we're not saying that. We don't know whose fault it was.

Referee: All right. We don't know. Then maybe that answers the next question, which is how this all got started. Uh, do you deny that it was your son's fault?

Mr. F: Could be. His friend loaned him the car.

Referee: Well, at the accident when this thing happened, are you admitting, let's phrase it that way, are you admitting that it was your son's fault?

Mr. F: Yeah, I admit that.

. . . .[testimony from plaintiff]

Referee: Back to the defendants. Anything additional?

Mr. F: Well, you know, I can see paying for the rental car and everything else. That was $157.27. But this, uh, this Holt, you know. Uh, I think he just typed up something since it was a friend of Sally's and everything else. You know, this is a kind of large amount for, you know, a short time. Three thousand miles. That's a thousand miles, you know, a month, but it's, I really don't know. I'd just like to see Carl pay for and, you know, get it off my back. We don't have much control over it. We don't. . .

Referee: What restraints were there placed on Carl as to the use of the vehicle?

Mr. F: I didn't even know his friend loaned him the car, gave him the keys, you know, where he was going or nothing else. We don't let him drive our car.

Referee: Logical question from the opposition with attorneys present would be why. We won't get into that. That will conclude the testimony. . . .

It can be inferred from the parents' answers that they have come to court with a different view of the significance of the issues in the case. In particular, they are prepared to discuss the broader social issue of whether parents should be "responsible" (contrast the referee's use of "fault" and "liability") for the actions of a child "when he doesn't mind us." After a series of specific questions from the referee, the parents admit "fault" as the law defines it, but it is unclear whether even then they appreciate the divergence between their agenda and that of the court. Finally, after the plaintiff has testified, the parents address themselves briefly to the single issue of concern to the court, the dollar value of the damage. The father comments on the fairness of the rental fee that a friend of the plaintiff charged her but reverts quickly to the issue that is of greatest importance to him, the responsibility of the parents for the actions of uncontrollable children. The referee might have intervened to pursue the rental fee issue but does not do so; instead, after his provocative comment about what might have happened "with attorneys present," he concludes the testimony and goes on to render judgment for the plaintiff.

Texts 10, 11, and 12 are similar to other cases we observed in which the magistrate or referee intervened to take an active role in developing the testimony of one or both of the parties. Two important points emerge from these cases. First, the timing and content of the magistrates' remarks and questions indicate that they have found many of the witnesses' narratives to be legally inadequate in the sense of not containing the information necessary to support a legal judgment, or at least not containing that information in a form they find useful. In Text 12, the problem is primarily one of content: The defendants insist on discussing a problem that the magistrate believes is not for him to solve. In Texts 10 and 11, by contrast, the differences between the unaided narrative and the elicited account relate as much to the way in which information is presented as to the information itself.

Second, these cases highlight the critical role of the magistrate. They suggest that most of the problems encountered by lay litigants, whether substantive or stylistic, can be resolved by a magistrate who has the time, inclination, and ability to intervene. At this stage in our research, we are not in a position to comment on the frequency with which magistrates intervene or the circumstances under which they do so, except to say that intervention is sporadic and that some magistrates appear to intervene more than others. As Texts 10, 11, and 12 illustrate, magistrates intervene sometimes to restructure testimony for the apparent benefit of the witness and sometimes to resolve an issue that the witness seems determined to avoid. Important questions for further research include whether identifiable characteristics of witnesses or their behavior correlate with different kinds of magistrate intervention, and whether the likelihood and nature of intervention by particular magistrates correlate with features of their background or training.

We hesitate at this point to speculate about cause and effect in the outcomes of cases. Thus far, we have worked as ethnographers describing *how* a system works; questions about the frequency of certain features remain open for more detailed quantitative analysis. Nonetheless, we have been impressed by the range of cases in which a credible narrative that appears to contain the elements of a legal claim has failed to evoke a sympathetic response from the magistrate or referee. Our suspicion in some of these cases is that the fatal flaw in the narrative is the party's failure to develop a theory of responsibility and present it in the deductive, hypothesis-testing form that is most familiar to legal decision makers. In a formal court trial, the lawyer performs this function, and it is left to the judge or jury simply to test the hypothesis against the evidence. The role of the small claims court magistrate, like that of the judge or jury in formal court, is to apply the law to the facts. However, the small claims court magistrate must not only perform this evaluative function but must also develop the hypothesis to be evaluated, all in the course of a brief hearing, aided only by a one- or two-sentence complaint.[20] This may be asking too much, particularly when the magistrate lacks legal training or experience.

8. SOME ETHNOGRAPHIC CONCLUSIONS ABOUT ACCOUNTS IN SMALL CLAIMS COURTS

We have employed several texts drawn from cases we observed and taped to illustrate the range of our findings. Several points that these texts have in common are particularly significant. First, each speaker employs certain narrative devices that have been found by other researchers to recur in noninstitutional, everyday narrative contexts. Speakers thus appear to bring to the court the same narrative strategies that they use in ordinary social interaction. Second, many of the more common features of small claims narratives violate the rules of evidence in force in formal courts. As we suspected in reviewing the formal court transcripts, the law of evidence is in

---

[20] The statements of complaint filed in the Colorado cases we discuss in this article are typical. The following statements are taken verbatim and in full from the complaint forms filed by plaintiffs (italicized words are printed on the summons and complaint form provided by the clerk's office):

The Defendant owes me $35.00 + 286.00 *for the following reasons*: For Damage received to my automobile on Nov. 11, 1983 in McNichols Arena Parking lot. Plus the cost of Filing in Adams & Arapahoe counties 35.00 total.

The Defendant owes me $256.60 *for the following reasons*: I worked for the defendants as line cook for one week at (est 57 hours) rate of $4.50 per hour during est week of August 10, 1984. I have one witness that was told I would get $4.50 an hour and that I was a line cook. Plus 50% $128.25.

The Defendant owes me $400 *for the following reasons*: At the beginning of June, 1984 defendant took our Queen-size brass headboard for repair after damaging the finish. Headboard has not been refinished nor assembled properly as of this date. It is in the possession of University Movers or their agent in this matter. It has not been delivered to me in either proper repair or reassembly. I am seeking replacement headboard of identical type and manufacture.

The Defendant owes me $200.00 *for the following reasons*: Damages to my car '73' ply duster.

The Defendant owes me $500.00 *for the following reasons*: payment of phone bill.

frequent conflict with many of the conventions of everyday speech. Our data suggest that evidentiary constraints may preclude many of the narrative features that speakers in courtroom contexts view as most important. Third, our data indicate that this narrative freedom is a mixed blessing, as many cases seem to turn on legal inadequacies in litigant narratives of which the litigants seem totally unaware.

In particular, the data show that witnesses giving testimony in small claims courts often lack any understanding that the law imposes highly specific requirements on narratives. In presenting accounts in court, witnesses rely on the conventions of everyday narratives about trouble and their informal cultural assumptions about justice. From the law's perspective, such accounts often have disabling shortcomings. For example, it is common to find accounts that fail to include a full theory of the case that links an *agent* with an *action* that caused harm to the plaintiff. Because the court functions to test hypotheses about relations among agents, actions, and recipients of the action, it is unable to respond affirmatively when accounts are incomplete. Failure to generate a complete hypothesis for testing against the facts to be presented may result in losing the case.

Findings such as these complement research already done on small claims courts and suggest directions for further investigation. The detailed analysis of how disputes are presented in small claims court adds to our understanding of the origin and evolution of disputes (Miller & Sarat, 1980–1981) and the social, psychological, and linguistic processes through which grievances are transformed into active disputes (Coates & Penrod, 1980–1981; Felstiner, Abel, & Sarat, 1980–1981; Mather & Yngvesson, 1980–1981). These findings also have relevance for broader questions of legal and social policy. For example, Abel (1982) analyzed small claims courts and other alternative dispute-resolution procedures as mechanisms of social and political control. The findings of this study explicate some of the means through which such control is exercised. The approach used in this research may be similarly useful to those who have expressed concerns about the balance of power between small claims litigants (e.g., Nader, 1979), for the analysis of what is said in court provides an empirical perspective on this problem.

Perhaps the most significant policy question raised by this research relates to the social distribution of the ability to formulate legally adequate narratives. It may be the case that certain categories of litigants are less prone to present legally adequate narratives and accounts. If such differences exist and follow ethnic, racial, or gender lines, new and important questions would arise about the fairness of present small claims court procedures and about possible reforms such as assistance both before and during trials. The need to consider such issues is suggested by the findings reported in this chapter, but additional research is clearly needed to further our understanding of these matters.

The frequent complaint of witnesses who have testified in formal courts that they did not get an adequate opportunity to tell their story takes on a new light in the small claims context. Small claims courts, operating without the formalities of the rules of evidence, do indeed allow accounts to be given in a relatively unconstrained manner so that people generally feel that these courts allow them the storytelling opportunity denied in more formal courts. However, a new and potentially more serious problem emerges when plaintiffs fail to give accounts that deal adequately with issues of blame, responsibility, and agency and to present them in a deductive framework that the court can test against the evidence presented. This may be a mechanism by which informal procedures substitute expressive satisfaction for the enforcement of rights.

ACKNOWLEDGMENTS. The research reported here is a joint project. The authors alternate priority of authorship in their publications. The research was supported by grants from the National Institute for Dispute Resolution, the Research Council of Duke University, and the Law Center Foundation of the University of North Carolina. We acknowledge with appreciation the assistance of the officials of the small claims courts of Durham, North Carolina, and Denver, Colorado, and of the persons whose cases we studied. Earlier versions of some portions of this article were reported at the Law and Society Association meetings in San Diego in June 1985 and at a conference on Language and the Judicial Process funded by the National Science Foundation and held at Georgetown University in July 1985.

9. REFERENCES

Abel, R. L. (1982). *The Politics of Informal Justice*. New York: Academic Press.

Abelson, R. P. (1975). Does a story understander need a point of view? In R. Schank & B. L. Nash-Webber (Eds.), *Theoretical issues in natural language processing* (pp. 154–157). Cambridge, MA: M.I.T. Press.

Arno, A. (1985). Structural communication and control communication: An interactionist perspective on legal and customary procedures for conflict management. *American Anthropologist, 87,* 40–55.

Atkinson, J. M., & Drew, P. (1979). *Order in court*. Atlantic Highlands, NJ: Humanities Press.

Bailey, F. L., & Rothblatt, H. B. (1971). *Successful techniques for criminal trials*. Rochester, NY: The Lawyers Co-Operative Publishing Company.

Bashor, C. R. (1985). Small claims procedure in North Carolina. *Popular Government, 51,* 35–43.

Bennett, W. L., & Feldman, M. B. (1981). *Reconstructing reality in the courtroom*. New Brunswick, NJ: Rutgers University Press.

Carlen, P. (1976). *Magistrates' justice*. London: Martin Robertson.

Charrow, R. P., & Charrow, V. R. (1979). Making legal language understandable: A psycholinguistic study of jury instructions. *Columbia Law Review, 79,* 1306–1374.

Coates, D., & Penrod, S. (1980–1981). Social psychology and the emergence of disputes. *Law & Society Review, 15,* 655–680.

Conley, J. M., O'Barr, W. M., & Lind, E. A. (1978). The power of language: Presentational style in the courtroom. *Duke Law Journal, 6,* 1375–1399.

Danet, B. (1980). Language in the legal process. *Law & Society Review, 14,* 445–564.

Drew, P. (1985). *Disputes in courtroom cross-examination: "Contrasting versions" in a rape trial.* Paper presented at the Conference on Language and the Judicial Process, Georgetown University.

Felstiner, W. L. F., Abel, R. L., & Sarat, A. (1980–1981). The emergence and transformation of disputes: Naming, blaming, claiming. . . . *Law & Society Review, 15,* 631–654.

Fillmore, C. S. (1971). *Santa Clara Lectures on Deixis.* Bloomington: Indiana University Linguistics Club.

Guth, D. A. (1983). *Suing in North Carolina small claims court: A practical guide.* Charlottesville, VA: Michie.

Haemmel, W. G. (1973). The North Carolina small claims court: An empirical study. *Wake Forest Law Review, 9,* 503–519.

Hymes, D. (1981). *"In vain I tried to tell you": Essays in Native American ethnopoetics.* Philadelphia: University of Pennsylvania Press.

Jarvella, R. J., & Klein, W. (1982). *Speech, place, and action: Studies in deixis and related topics.* Chichester, England: Wiley.

Jefferson, G. (1980). *Final report to the (British) SSRC on the analysis of conversation in which "troubles" and "anxieties" are expressed.* Mimeographed.

Keeton, R. E. (1973). *Trial tactics and methods* (2nd ed.). Boston: Little, Brown.

Kulat, R. (1984). Hairy tales from Chicago's pro se court where you don't need a lawyer to help solve life's more vexing problems. *Student Lawyer, 13,* 14–15.

Llewellen, K. N., & Hoebel, E. A. (1941). *The Cheyenne way: Conflict and case law in primitive jurisprudence.* Norman: University of Oklahoma Press.

Loftus, E. (1979). *Eyewitness testimony.* Cambridge, MA: Harvard University Press.

Mather, L., & Yngvesson, B. (1980–1981). Language, audience, and the transformation of disputes. *Law & Society Review, 15,* 775–821.

McElhaney, J. W. (1974). *Effective trials, problems, and materials.* St. Paul, MN: West Publishing Co.

McFadgen, T. (1972). *Dispute resolution in the small claims context: Adjudication, arbitration, or conciliation?* LL.M. thesis, Harvard University.

Miller, R. E., & Sarat, A. (1980–1981). Grievances, claims, and disputes: Assessing the adversary culture. *Law & Society Review, 15,* 525–566.

Nader, L. (1979). Disputing without the force of law. *Yale Law Journal, 88,* 998–1021.

O'Barr, W. M. (1982). *Linguistic evidence.* New York: Academic Press.

Philips, S. U. (1983). Review of *Reconstructing Reality in the Courtroom,* by W. Lance Bennett and Martha S. Feldman. *Language in Society, 12,* 514–517.

Pomerantz, A. (1978). Attributions of responsibility: Blamings. *Sociology, 12,* 115–121.

Pomerantz, A., & Atkinson, J. M. (1984). Ethnomethodology, conversation analysis, and the study of courtroom interaction. In D. J. Muller, D. E. Blackman, & A. J. Chapman (Eds.), *Psychology and law: Topics from an international conference* (pp. 283–297). Chichester, England: Wiley.

Ruhnka, J. C. & Weller, S. (1978). *Small claims courts: A national examination.* Williamsburg, VA: National Center for State Courts.

Sales, B. D., Elwork, A., & Alfini, J. J. (1977). Improving jury instructions. In B. D. Sales (Ed.), *Perspectives in law and psychology, Vol. 1: The criminal justice system* (pp. 23–90). New York: Plenum Press.

Steele, E. H. (1981). The historical context of small claims court. *American Bar Foundation Research Journal, 1981,* 293–376.

Tannen, D. (Ed.). (1981). *Spoken and written language: Exploring orality and literacy.* Norwood, NJ: Ablex.

Weinstein, J. (1977). The Ohio and federal rules of evidence. *Capital University Law Review, 15,* 517–547.

Wolfson, N. (1982). *CHP: The conversational historical present in American English narrative*. Dordrecht, The Netherlands: Foris Publishers.
Yngvesson, B., & Hennessey, P. (1974–1975). Small claims, complex disputes: A review of the small claims literature. *Law & Society Review, 9*, 219–274.

10. STATUTES CITED

Colo. Rev. Stat. 13-6-407-416.
Fed. R. Evid. 701-5.
N.C. Gen. Stat. 7A-210-232.

Chapter 5

LEGAL REALISM IN LAWYER–CLIENT COMMUNICATION

AUSTIN SARAT and WILLIAM L. F. FELSTINER

1. INTRODUCTION

Legal materials have often been used to examine issues of general interest in the analysis of language and language use. Traditionally the study of law and language has concentrated on statutes, formal decisions, legal instruments, or documents used in legal procedures (see Rodell, 1939; Christie, 1964; Mellinkoff, 1963; Brigham, 1978). Particular attention has been given to questions of whether legal language is distinct from other language forms (Stone, 1981) and whether legal language can, and should, be simplified and thus made more accessible to non-lawyers (see Arnold, 1935:66).

Recently, students of law and language have gone beyond written law to scrutinize what Probert (1972) calls "law talk." This effort requires listening to the language of the law as it is spoken in courtrooms, courthouse halls, lawyers' offices, and in the interaction of legal officials and citizens in informal settings. As Martin Shapiro (1981:1201) argues:

> We have both deliberately and unconsciously treated law talk as the talk of judges to other judges and to lawyers contemplating future litigation. . . . But the two principal talks of lawyers are lawyer to client (counseling) and lawyer to lawyer (negotiating). We have assumed without empirical investigation that these two talks

AUSTIN SARAT • Department of Political Science, Amherst College, Amherst, Massachusetts 01002.   WILLIAM L. F. FELSTINER • American Bar Foundation, 750 North Lake Shore Drive, Chicago, Illinois 60611.

are so heavily determined by judge to judge and judge to lawyer talk that we may study the case law tail rather than the counseling and negotiating dog. What if we began our study of law with the proposition that law is not what judges say in the reports but what lawyers say—to one another and to clients—in their offices?. . . Such an approach would give us a more accurate description of law as it is.

Problems in securing access to these informal settings have limited the development of our understanding of the law talk that Shapiro considers crucial. (for exceptions see Maynard, 1984; Cain, 1979; Hosticka, 1979; Bogoch & Danet, 1984; Caesar-Wolf, 1984; Sarat & Felstiner, 1986). The law talk that it has been possible to observe has proved to be much less formal, technical, jargon-filled, complex, mysterious, coherent, or dramatic than the language of the written law or talk in the courtroom (see Bennett & Feldman, 1981).

Most analysis of law talk retains the focus on law as a vehicle for the study of language and on the nature, quality, and comprehensibility of the language used (see Atkinson & Drew, 1979; Danet & Bogoch, 1980; Sales *et al.*, 1977). The focus of this chapter is not on what one can learn about language by looking at law but on what one can learn about law by looking at talk about law. We examine lawyer–client conversations as a vehicle for discovering the pictures, or images, of law that are conveyed from legal professionals to lay people. Our data are drawn from a larger study of lawyer–client interaction in divorce cases (see Sarat & Felstiner, 1986) carried out over a period of 33 months in two sites, one in Massachusetts and one in California. This effort consisted in following one side of 40 cases, ideally from the first lawyer–client interview until the divorce was final. We followed these cases by observing and tape recording lawyer–client sessions, attending court and mediation hearings and trials, and interviewing both lawyers and clients about those events. One hundred fifteen lawyer–client conferences were tape recorded.[1]

---

[1] A major obstacle to, and accomplishment of, this research was securing access to the lawyer–client conferences. In order to devise a strategy to overcome that problem we interviewed a dozen lawyers concerning divorce practice generally and specifically on the question of access. Although their predictions and advice varied, they suggested that it would be important to mobilize relevant judges and try to convince lawyers that they were selected for some positive reason. In addition they suggested that the lawyer–client privilege was not likely to be a practical barrier for most lawyers.

The second step was to mobilize judicial support. In California the appropriate judge seemed to be the presiding judge of the local court; in Massachusetts there was only one relevant judge, the judge of the family court. Both judges said the research sounded interesting; they provided a list of appropriate lawyers and said we could say to lawyers that they thought the research was unobjectionable.

The process of securing lawyer participation began by compiling a list of all of the lawyers in each community who did a substantial amount of divorce work. In each instance, the list eventually contained about 40 names. The list was constructed by asking judges, mediators, and lawyers to name the principal divorce lawyers in the area. We stopped trying to add names to the list when additional inquiries were not providing new names. All of the lawyers on each list were asked to cooperate in the research. Most agreed, but only slightly more than one-quarter in each site actually produced one or more clients willing to participate in the research. Identification of

In this chapter we describe the content of one kind of law talk, namely talk about the law itself, talk in which lawyer and client speak about the nature of the legal process, the competence and motives of lawyers and legal officials, and the grounds on which legal decisions are made. The picture of the legal system that the lawyer conveys to the client is made up of remarks about many subjects; statements about the legal process as a whole, about ingredients of the process such as trials, about legal officials, about other lawyers generally, about the other lawyer in the case at hand, about law's implicit rules of relevance, and about the nature of legal education.

The law talk that we examine is spoken by lawyers to people involved in official legal proceedings. Yet it is a special kind of law talk in that it is, of necessity, self-reflective and self-referential; it is the law, or one part thereof, speaking of itself. It is, in our view, a particularly consequential genre of law talk because of its obvious influence on the way clients perceive and think about the legal system. For clients, lawyers provide an important source of information about the substance of law and legal rights and help them relate legal rules and procedures to individual problems. Although clients may have highly varied feelings about their lawyer's performance, one would expect most to be predisposed to accept their lawyer's descriptions and evaluations of the legal system as informed and accurate.

Law talk in the lawyer's office helps to constitute and/or decode a legal ideology, a set of meanings contained or embodied in the practices of law. What lawyers tell clients may reveal or construct such an ideology at two levels (Trubek, 1984). The first involves what lawyers themselves say about law and legal process. Descriptions, attributions, and explanations of legal events, processes, and practices may rationalize or attack the coherence of, and thereby legitimate or delegitimate, the legal order. At the second level, what the lawyer says about the nature of legal rights, the proper course of client conduct, the justifications of particular actions, and the range of legally appropriate expectations may express world views that are embedded in the legal order. It is in the lawyer's office that clients are instructed in the meaning of law and in the meaning of social relations contained in law and legal practices.

2. MODES OF DISCOURSE ABOUT LAW

In this chapter we examine conversations between lawyers and clients about the status of rules, the roles and motivations of legal officials, and the

---

clients was left to the lawyers except that they were to focus on cases that promised to involve several lawyer–client meetings. The samples of lawyers and clients are not representative of all divorce lawyers and clients. The research strategy approximates more closely that of an anthropologist studying a community than survey research.

fairness and utility of law. We attempt to categorize those conversations in terms of three modes of discourse that contain generalizations about law and the legal system; these three modes of discourse are commonly known as "formalism," "equity," and "realism." They focus on, and highlight, particular elements that some scholars argue can be used to characterize the entire legal process. Although these elements are on occasion used to organize ostensibly coherent and complete portraits of the legal process, we recognize that the legal process is always too situational, varied, contingent, political, flawed, and ambiguous to be accurately described by any of such discrete pictures. As we examine the talk between lawyer and client, we explore how they use and draw upon elements and points of emphasis from formalism, equity, and realism.

2.1. Formalism

The formalist model of legal discourse—what others have called the "classical style" (Mensch, 1982) or positivism (Simon, 1975)—begins by differentiating law and power. Law is presented as both different from, and able to control, the exercise of power in political or social life. Law is a rule system, and rules determine how law operates, procedures work, and decisions are made. Rule determinacy insures that the legal process will itself be orderly, regular, and predictable and that legal decisions will be made impartially, fairly, and in a nonarbitrary fashion. The formalist model portrays individual legal actors as highly constrained by a regimen of clearly articulated rules; it is a world where rules matter, but people do not (Noonan, 1976). Judicial discretion is, in this discourse, minimal and inconsequential. As Dicey (1939:198) argued, rule determinacy insures "the absolute supremacy or predominance of regular law as opposed to the influence of arbitrary power, and excludes the existence of arbitrariness, of prerogative, or even of wide discretionary authority." By embracing an interpretation of law based on rule determinacy, formalists seek to promote legal universality and equal treatment. Where rules are the same and facts are identical, comparable results should be produced regardless of the circumstances of particular litigants, the inclinations or interests of legal officials, or differences in the location or jurisdiction of the decision-making forum. What should matter most, according to formalist discourse, is what rules say and mean. Arguments about fairness, purpose, or utility are, for the formalist, as out of place as are arguments about the self-interest, convenience, or political views of legal actors (see Unger, 1976:204).

The place of lawyers in formalist discourse arises from "the strangeness of law" and the fact that "rules are not easily apprehensible" (Simon, 1975:41). The function of the lawyer is to decode the rules, to explain how they apply to the client's particular situation, and to present the facts and applicable rules with clarity sufficient to insure their recognition by the lawyer on the other side (in which case a settlement, without judicial intervention, should be reached) or in an official forum (in which case a favorable decision should be secured). The result in any dispute is, in the formalist view, "determined by the autonomous operation of the system of rules" (Simon, 1975:41; see also Nonet & Selznick, 1978). Finally, in formalist discourse, lawyers are neutral; their own values and views are not allowed to influence either how they advise their clients or how they present their cases. They act as partisan agents of the interests articulated by their clients, and they neither formulate nor transform those interests.

2.2. Equity

The movement from formalist discourse to the language of equity shifts rules from the center to the boundaries of the legal process. Rules constrain decision makers by embodying standards and norms that point in general directions but do not require or direct particular results. Discretion is at the heart of the discourse of equity and is both inevitable and desirable (see, for example, Davis, 1971:43). It is inevitable because no rule system can be sufficiently clear or comprehensive to provide predictable and certain outcomes and because language is always given meaning as it is used. Discretion is desirable because it allows flexibility and responsiveness to individual circumstances. The discourse of equity emphasizes the capacity and willingness of the legal process to accommodate particular persons with particular problems.

Where the formalist stresses the limited range of law, the language of equity portrays a system with much looser rules of relevance, a system in which legal decision makers look closely at the circumstances and concerns of the people with whom they deal (see Mather & Yngvesson, 1980–1981). Where formalism emphasizes the desirability of the impartial, technically competent judge, equity favors a conscientious, concerned, and above all, wise arbiter. The emphasis is less on the definition of legal rights and obligations than on finding out as much as possible about the problems and people brought to law in order to arrive at solutions that are substantively just. The language of equity portrays a legal process populated with legal officials dedicated to doing the "right" thing (Weber, 1954:Chapter X; see also Feeley, 1979:283–290; and Noonan, 1976:Chapter 1).

In the model of equity, the job of the lawyer is to inquire in the broadest possible way into the circumstances that give rise to particular problems. More important, lawyers, like judges, must attend to the task of identifying the right solution to those problems. They therefore should try to elicit and demonstrate what social norms define as right, and, although there may be competing definitions of right in particular cases, lawyers should expect of, and accord to, each other a reasoned and reasonable, open-minded and curious, careful and competent consideration of each case. Because legal rules are indeterminate, the legal process works on the basis of the commitments of its major participants to doing justice.

2.3. Realism[2]

The realist emphasis reverses the relationship of rules and people envisioned by formalists. Instead of determining legal procedures and choices, rules are used by legal officials as instruments through which their personal or political purposes can be achieved or as justifications invoked after the fact to rationalize results that also reflect the judge's idiosyncrasies, economic background, personal prejudices, or political commitments. For at least one version of realism,

> There will be a right if, and only if, the court finds for the plaintiff or declares the statute unconstitutional. What the court cites as the reason for the decision or the existence of a right is, in fact, only the result. (Mensch, 1982:27)

Because legal realists believe that rules are only one of many elements affecting decisions, they consider discretion to be ubiquitous. Nevertheless legal actors are limited, by factors external to law including history, circumstance, the need to maintain organizations, or to fulfill expectations of others with whom they have continuing relations. It is to these personal or organizational factors that judges and other legal actors are most attentive. Bureaucratic routine, local custom, or the strengths and weaknesses of strategically placed people govern the legal process. As a result, that process is described by realists as no more orderly and predictable than the social order itself.

Realist description of the way judicial decisions are made is quite judge-centered. Repudiating the view that court decisions are dictated by the autonomous operation of legal rules or are shaped through a process in which the overriding concern is fairness to people, realism insists that what courts do reveals "in large part an exercise of power on the part of the judge" (Simon, 1975:65). In so doing, realists break down the separation of law and power that is so much a part of formalism. Such a judge-centered view of law may, although it need not (see Singer, 1984), make law and legal decisions seem quite unpredictable and inconsistent with decisions in similar cases or on similar matters and as varying from one judge to the next.

In contrast to the theoreticians of formalism and equity, realists stress that the job of the lawyer is to tie rules closely to facts, to acquaint clients with the nature of the legal process, and to help them accommodate to its needs as

---

[2] The realism that we describe is a reconstruction and an amalgam that combines elements drawn from the original realists (for a description, see Kalman, 1986) and from contemporary heirs of the realists in the sociology of law and critical legal studies.

well as to its routines and requirements. The image of equity, of a legal process bending to serve the interest of justice in particular cases, is rejected as naive. Because the workings of the system depend on the idiosyncrasies of its key people, or its indigenous routines and conventions, what the lawyer offers is local knowledge, familiarity with people and conventions as well as strict attention to facts. Lawyers become a kind of broker between a local legal system in which they are a continuing participant and clients with whom they have at best episodic relations (see Blumberg, 1967). In Blumberg's view, the client is always a potential enemy capable of making demands and insisting on actions that might disrupt regular practices or upset judges and other lawyers whose good will is necessary to the effective practice of law. From this perspective, legal practice requires neither expert knowledge of rules nor a particularly strong sense of fair play and substantive justice; instead, it requires pragmatism, an ability to cultivate personal relationship with key people, skills in finding ways to appeal to known prejudices, making mutually advantageous deals with nominal opponents, and playing by "rules" known only to experienced insiders.

3. THE DISCOURSE ABOUT LAW IN THE DIVORCE LAWYER'S OFFICE

From these abstract descriptions of different points of emphasis in legal discourse we move to describe the law talk that we actually observed in divorce lawyers' offices. Although that talk generally begins with a brief explanation by the lawyer to the client of divorce procedures as they are presented in statutes, most lawyer–client talk about law comes in response to questions or remarks by the client. The lawyers we studied clearly do not think of themselves as legal educators, nor do they deliver set lectures on the nature of the legal process. Instead, lawyer descriptions and characterizations of law are prompted by client inquiries about why something did or did not happen or when clients want their lawyers' views about what might or will happen. Thus the species of talk we are considering is one of explanation or justification. This kind of talk occurs when lawyers introduce characterizations of law, the legal process, and the motivations of its central actors (see Scott & Lyman, 1968) while responding to a client's request to give an account of, or make a prediction about, some event.

The most prominent feature of talk about law we observed in the divorce lawyer's office is an emphasis on people rather than rules. This discourse acquaints the client with a process in which particular people exercise considerable discretionary power. As one Massachusetts lawyer put it in describing the way the local court operates, "there really are no rules here, just people: the judge, the lawyers, the litigants." Of these people, none is more important than the judge. Law talk in the lawyer's office is focused on judicial powers, personalities, predispositions, and idiosyncrasies. The message to the client is that it is the judge, not the law, that really counts.

Client: His [the judge's] decision is basically whether the two of us should be divorced or not. Is the settlement of the property also going to be a part of that?

Lawyer: Oh, yes. Absolutely. That's what he is there for. He doesn't just grant the divorce to somebody, he also makes all the decisions relative to property distribution, alimony, and support. A probate judge also has an immense amount of power and authority, an immense amount. Probably more than any other type of judge in the Commonwealth. Superior Court judges have a lot of authority but Probate Court judge even more because he's dealing with a marriage . . . people . . . he deals with people's lives in a very significant manner. And he has authority to reach and dispose of pretty much as he deems fit within certain limits but very undefined limits. Anything, any property at all . . . however acquired and in whosever name . . . so long as it is part of the marital estate. And marital estate does not mean it has to be in both names. If that house were just in your name and you owned it fully, he could still give it to her if he felt that that was what he should do, okay. Although he would have less of a battle on it . . . but nevertheless he could still do it.

This talk is a classic example of legal realism in which the legal process of divorce is portrayed as a highly discretionary procedure circumscribed loosely, if at all, by rules the efficacy of which are in doubt. The message from lawyers to clients is, however, not simply that the judge is central in importance but that not all judges are alike; it matters who the judge is. Lawyers often compare judges and suggest that another judge would have acted in a different way. Law talk turns discretion into difference.

In one Massachusetts case, a lawyer drew the following comparison between the judge in the probate court where he usually practiced and the judge handling this particular client's case.

Client: If I were a judge and people, if I order people twice to do certain things and they still refused with no good legal justification to refuse to produce those things, I would bring the hammer down . . . gavel down . . . and say that's it. I've heard enough of this nonsense . . .

Lawyer: Well, I think Judge X would have done that. I think probably most other judges would have done that. Remember, too, that this judge is brand new. Maybe he just hasn't had this happen to him before and doesn't know what to do about it. Of course I think he should consult with other judges at that point and find out what they would do. Okay. And maybe he has. . . . Frankly, as I told you before . . . I think Judge Y would have said . . . all right . . . or I'm going to have a hearing and I'm going to make a decision in this case. Period. And Judge X hasn't deemed it fit to do that yet. Maybe he will. Maybe he will. . . .

This comparison, and others like it, suggest that lawyers believe that judicial decisions are determined by neither a set of general rules nor a commitment to substantive justice. Instead, what counts is the experience or disposition of individual judges.

Although some judges are deemed by the lawyers in our sample to be better than others, and although better judges are said to be "smart" or "experienced" or "savvy" or "reasonable," the clear tendency of the talk about judges is to call into question their skill, dedication, and concern. Frequently they are described as lazy, uninterested in the people who appear before them, and intellectually unsophisticated. Among the words most frequently used to characterize judges is "arbitrary." Note, for instance, the validating response of one lawyer to his client's evaluation of the judge in his case.

Client: I say he's a little scatterbrained. He looks arbitrary to a layman. He looks arbitrary.

Lawyer: Well, you've heard not just me, you've heard other lawyers in this town say the same thing in the hallway.

This same lawyer discussing another judge in a different case suggests that even a judge whom he respects may be capable of making a decision that seems to ignore both the litigants' past behavior and the legal rules relevant to that behavior. In this conversation, in which the client is being prepared for a hearing, the lawyer goes to some lengths to encourage the client to adopt a particular manner in the courtroom.

Lawyer: But you sit there somewhat respectful. Do the same thing in this courtroom, okay? Hands in front of you are just fine, or on the table, just fine. I don't care, but don't cross your legs. Okay. I asked you not to do that. If you do it I'll probably nudge you in the shoulder and ask you to stop crossing your legs. Okay? No arms over the back of the chair. Okay?

Client: [Sits up very straight]

Lawyer: That's all right. You look nice and neat and scared that way, that's okay. But sit up with your arms and hands in front of you; I don't care where they go, but in front of you, and without the crossed legs. Okay? And then one other thing I ask of you. Don't go like this [lawyer puts face in his hands]. Okay? If you want go like this [folds arms in front], or like this [puts hands in lap], or anything, but don't go like this [puts face in hands]. Okay? No matter how tired you are tomorrow morning I want you to look pretty alert. It's best if you can just remember to keep your hands on the table or in your lap, and you'll be all set. Okay? Why? Why am I asking you to do this? Only because the judge will be looking at you Okay? And he's going to make a decision, a fairly important one, and I don't want that decision to be influenced just by the way you sit.

Client: Like, he don't care.

Lawyer: Well, he might, if he doesn't like you. Okay? And even if he doesn't like you but you look concerned and you're interested, he'll probably go your way anyway. Okay? Judges are people, and well, I'll tell you, we might as well play the odds rather than have some surprises develop just because the judge doesn't like the way you're sitting. Okay?

Client: Some would do that.

Lawyer: Yup, some do. I don't think this judge is like that. I have a lot more respect for him than that but if we play the game this way all the time, then there's no problem. We just, we know we're doing it right and when it's all done and over with then you can go out and get drunk and have a hell of a time and say "All right, it's all over!" But we treat it with some solemnity, some, certainly integrity, and a hell of a lot of respect. Okay, you show that to the judge and we should be in good shape. Okay?

In explaining why he is talking about such things as posture and dress, the lawyer suggests that he is guarding against the possibility that the judge's decision may be "influenced just by the way you sit." Although this may be at the extreme, law talk is peppered with references to extralegal factors that might influence judges. What is portrayed to clients is a discretionary process in which judges are influenced by a wide range of factors, many of which are neither contemplated nor acknowledged by the written law. Lawyers play upon client expectations that judicial decisions should be highly constrained by the law on the books and introduce the notion that there is a gap between law on the books and law in action (for a full statement of this idea see Pound, 1917).

Although judges can, according to these lawyers, be influenced by the details of client dress or behavior in the courtroom, much law talk explains that judges are incapable of grasping the nuances and subtleties of legal argument, are uninterested in the details of particular cases, and adopt positions that are hard to understand. As a California lawyer said in explaining a judge's ruling:

> Ever since I've been practicing law in Pacificola, I've had—I like him; I respect him; he's a hard worker; and I think he's very, very honest; I supported him in his campaigns, so on and so forth—but I have had difficulty understanding how . . . [he] thinks. It is—and I have an analogy that I thought of today. While my jury panel was on a break, I went in to watch him, and there was a district attorney that he was questioning. They were going to sentence some guy—it was a probation revocation—they were going to sentence him to county jail. The district attorney had earlier argued that he ought to be sent to the state prison. The judge turns to the district attorney and says, "Well, now, when I send him to county jail, I want to do this, this, this, this, this, but this is my problem; I don't know if I can do this, do this, do this." And the district attorney started to help him with his problem, then said "Wait a minute; I don't know what I'm doing. I don't want him to go to county jail; this guy belongs in state prison; I think he belongs in state prison; you just said you were going to think about sending him to county jail, and now you want me to tell you how to do it; I think you're wrong, and I'm not going to tell you how to do it wrong." Now those weren't his exact words, but then the judge had some more chin music and then continued it for another day, so that he could think it over. And he had an excuse. He said, "Well, I need some more evidence on this, and I need some. . . ." And I talked to the district attorney afterwards, and I said, "It was so clear to me what was going on. It was as though you, as one side, say, judge, the way I see this case it's matter of $5 + 5 + 5$ divided by $3 = 5$. Now, you have made a

tentative ruling where you say, 5 + 5 + 5 = 14. Now, you want me to tell you how you
come up with a right answer after you've made the first false conclusion. And I
can't do it." And that's what happened. He just . . .

This discussion suggests that the judge's ruling, like the county jail sentence,
rested on a "first false conclusion." What that conclusion is the lawyer never
does say. But in the course of constructing the narrative about the sentencing
hearing, the lawyer suggests that the mind of the judge is unfathomable, that
the judge was at best confused, that the district attorney, at least for a moment,
did not know his own interests and that, in the end, time was wasted pursuing
a course of action based upon a mistaken premise.

Judges, these divorce lawyers suggest, may not have the requisite qualifications or knowledge to make the decisions that law expects them to make.
Although this is widely recognized to be a problem in child custody cases
(Chambers, 1984), the lawyers indicate that it may also be relevant to the more
common task of dividing marital assets.

Lawyer: Here's the problem. . . . What they really ought to do in domestic law is every
judge who hears domestic law ought to have, literally, a CPA, or somebody
familiar with financial data, compare for him or her something before the case to
say somehow there is magic going on here. Like I had a guy last year who before
he separated he was running $67,000 a month through his accountant. Separation
time and he runs $3,000 through the accountant. My theory to the judge was,
judge I don't know how the hell he works his finances but he did it last month, tell
him to do it again. The judge says, "Look buddy, however you did the magic, do
the magic again." Very often a judge won't do that. A judge won't say, "Oh I see
what's happened, you had a small . . . as you say, on the outer limits of middle
class anyway and all of a sudden you have two households." They don't think
even logically to say where's the money going to come from. . . . It's really very
difficult to explain to the judge how it all goes because they are not very interested
in it. We don't have a family law court here. In other words, you may be second on
the calendar in two weeks and the first guy on the calendar is going away for
murder. And so when your case comes up it's, "Well what's the problem here." I
mean there's one judge over there that says no matter what papers you turn in, he
looks at you and says, "What's this case all about." What did I turn all those papers
in for if you are asking me?

In this discussion, judges not only lack particular expertise but are again
made to appear uninterested, inattentive, and unprepared. As another lawyer put it, they "don't want to make tough decisions." This aversion to
difficult problems is directly related to judicial decision-making patterns. As
this same lawyer explained to a client involved in a custody battle: If a court
sees "a good mother and a good father and it's easier for them just to say . . .
it's easier to say, well, leave it status quo."

This pattern may be as true for property decisions as for child custody
matters.

Client: Okay. On the property, I suggested to her—we were going to go purchase value, but it didn't work—so I suggested that we just take everything, except the cars and piano, and take 50% of their value.

Lawyer: Whatever arbitration system you choose is better than the judge. I'll tell you what the judges are doing recently. It's garage-sale time. You come to them with a list of items and they simply say, I'm holding a garage sale at your house on Saturday; you're in charge.

The image of the "garage sale" is hardly the picture that either formalist discourse or the language of equity would tolerate. Moreover, what lawyers suggest is that the inattentiveness, insensitivity, and incompetence of judges must be taken into account in deciding how to process cases. As this lawyer says, "whatever arbitration system you choose is better than the judge." For him, settlements allow for fuller, more careful consideration than is available in a contested trial before a judge.

Client: So I could go back to court if I went back to teaching?

Lawyer: Sure.

Client: And say I don't make that much money; I can't handle it.

Lawyer: Sure.

Client: And see what happens.

Lawyer: Right.

Client: If we went to court.

Lawyer: If you went to court. In other words, the rules are essentially different if you don't involve the court. My theory is, at trial you usually get a much more rigid decision. It's more workable never to have to go to trial. But there are certain things that won't work.

Client: And so you're saying, it's really in my best interest to stay away from trial.

Lawyer: It's in everybody's best interests. It's very costly. The judges are not tolerant of subtleties or innuendoes. All they want is they want you out the door, and the rulings are usually gross. They're gross rulings. They don't consider and factor in the subtleties of what the people are trying to do.

In other words, in this lawyer's view, the intolerance of judges and their desire to get things "out the door" means that it is in everyone's best interest to avoid going to trial.

What do lawyers say in their offices when they move from discussions of particular judges to evaluations of the efficiency, fairness, and social utility of law in general and the legal process of divorce in particular? There are virtually no positive characterizations in our data. Lawyers rarely either defend the legal system or make positive claims about the values to which it aspires and the results that can be achieved through it. In the context of divorce cases, at least, lawyers do not serve as apologists for or defenders of the legal order in which they participate. Instead, law talk suggests distance between lawyer and legal order with the former portrayed as struggling valiantly within a process that seems neither equitable nor just. As one California lawyer said after an extended discussion of the difficulty of obtaining an equitable division of the marital assets and of the unsatisfying choice of continuing to try to negotiate an agreement or going to court,

> Well, my hat's off to you, . . . I mean it's very frustrating, uh, you know, I mean, basically you come to somebody who's supposed to help you, and I am giving you the choice of being frustrated all summer, pay me a thousand, or you can have heartache in July and pay me five thousand. I mean, you know, the words coming out of my mouth are ludicrous, on their face, except, somehow it has to end.

This lawyer positions himself as unable to do his job because of circumstances beyond his control. The choice available for the client is frustration at the hands of his wife or "heartache" at the hands of a judge. There is, however, no escape allowed because "it has to end." The best that the legal process is able to offer is a choice between two different kinds of pain; there is no effort to describe the logic or underlying rationality of a process that would pose such a choice. It is simply labeled "ludicrous."

In the lawyer's office, cost is often alleged to be the major determinant of legal results. As one Massachusetts lawyer explained to a client in a contentious divorce in which the wife's wealthy family was paying her lawyer,

> *Lawyer:* I'm not just making this up. I'm telling you very frankly it appears as though he's [the wife's lawyer] doing a $10,000 case. That's just the way it is. Your . . . no matter who you go to you can't afford a $10,000 case. Can't do it. And that's part of the injustice of the American legal system but I'm not going to do as much work as he is at the moment. I can't . . . I'm just not equipped to do it. If you were to give me $10,000 I would drop everything, drop everything and work 40 hours a week, but I can't based on what you can afford.

Lawyers tell clients that, in the "American legal system" you get what you pay for, and suggest that they probably can't afford the "justice" that they seek.

Not only is the legal process described as costly and biased in favor of those who can pay, there are, in addition, repeated descriptions of its frustratingly slow pace. In a California case, a lawyer refers to "hopelessly crowded court calendars" and the "hopelessly slow judicial process"; the repeated use of "hopelessly" suggests resignation in the face of an insurmountable problem. In a Massachusetts case, the client's frustration at the pace of his case is reinforced by his lawyer:

> *Client:* Oh yeah. No, I intend, I intend to write a letter at the end of all this to Ayatollah Khomeini, and tell him whether he should be proud of his judicial system in Iran, or if he should feel very sorry, because depending on how he handles this the Western style, I would feel very, I would feel proud of Khomeini, or I would feel very bad about the way he deals with it. Because I've had a taste of the Western style judicial system, and I certainly hear by word of mouth the Khomeini style. At least his is very decisive.

Lawyer: Swift.

Client: Yes, even swift, you know. He listens to witnesses, and decides within a day, okay, how things are going to be. And sometimes even shorter.

Lawyer: Well, I want you to understand too, well, it's not typically swift in this country.

A costly and slow process might be justifiable if it were fair, reliably protected important individual rights, or responded to important human concerns. However, law talk makes problematic whether the legal process is even designed to meet those goals. As one lawyer and client discuss what they ought to ask for in trying to negotiate a settlement, the client says:

Client: Sure. I mean, that's as much as can be expected, I believe. Am I right in that?

Lawyer: I think so, too. I think that that effects a good settlement. Well, it effects an equal division. I don't know—is a legal settlement a fair settlement? It gets the legal aspects of the case over.

The lawyer's doubts seem clear. Is a good settlement the same as the equal division that the law requires? This uncertainty is resolved, rhetorically, by his reference to the resolution of "the legal aspects" of the case. His words suggest that a legal resolution cannot be counted on to advance the ends of fairness nor resolve other aspects of "the case."

Such other aspects of divorce cases and the law's attitude toward them become the focus of an extended discussion between a lawyer and a male client who wants to arrange shared custody of a young child who was, at the time, living with her mother in Florida.

Client: Most important of all to me is the present and the future of the development of the relationship between me and my daughter, the right of my daughter to have access to her father and the right of me to have access to my daughter. It's a right that both my daughter and I have to protect for the future . . . especially given the pathology that I am aware of in her family. . . . I want to retain joint custody although I am willing to negotiate the actual day to day responsibilities for my daughter.

Lawyer: You are ignoring the fact that she's a thousand miles away. That's fine and that is very workable if two people can work it out together and they both live in the same general location. She's a thousand miles away. . . . The child I'm certain is going to stay in Florida. You talk about all these things it's fine. . . . The child's going to be in Florida. You are not going to be able to do it unless you are with the child in Florida. Now you talk about all the things you want to develop in your relationship with the child. The court is not going to get into that. The court is going to award custody of the child to one person and visitation rights to the other person and that's it. They are not going to lay down any sort of guidelines concerning your relationship with your daughter, your wife's relationship with your daughter and the way your wife feels with you and vice versa concerning your daughter. It's going to be custody and it's going to be visitation rights. And that's that.

Client: Are you aware of how people . . . people mind of the children . . . what the people live? They don't have two homes or two sets of friends . . . they have more than two and they go out to each house and that is exactly what I am getting for my daughter to have access to the Jewish culture from my wife and my wife's family because she has that right being born to my wife and to have access to my culture Latin, Hispanic whatever label you want to have it. She'll have a set of friends there and a set of friends here. She is very young and for as long as she's young I'm willing to have the lesser amount of time but as she grows I would like to have the opportunity for me and for her to develop a relationship . . . for her to have the best of two worlds. Rather the best and the worst . . . or the worse or one of them. That's what happened to my wife. I'm a psychologist and very much aware with the body of research . . . studies of that type of development. . . . I am concerned and have the bases for it. So the fact is that something should be done.

Lawyer: I don't want to. . . . I realize how you're looking at it. But you've got to realize how I'm looking at it . . . how the law's going to treat it. The law is not going to go into that at all. It's going to be a custody order and a visitation order and perhaps a child support order.

What is most important for the client is not the custody or visitation order. That is simply the means available for insuring his continued involvement in the life of his child. The court, he is told, is "not going to get into that"; it is not going to attend to the nature of the relationship that he wishes to develop with his child. The client asserts that his concerns are based not only on his desires but on scientific evidence as to what is best for children. He believes that because he is concerned and because he has "the bases" for that concern, something should be done. The response is a repeated reminder that the court will neither be guided by those concerns nor even attend to them.

Even if the concerns of this client exceed the capacity of the law it is, nevertheless, clear that such law talk sends the message that the law's agenda is narrow and unresponsive. Such conversations incorporate an instruction about the distance between law and society not just because of the limited efficacy of legal rules but because of the law's limited concerns. Again the idea of a gap emerges. Only here the gap is not between what the law says and what judges do; it is, instead, between what judges do, or are willing to do, and what clients' want. Law, and legal officials have, according to the lawyers we observed, a truncated perspective. This truncated perspective has special importance because there is frequently a clash between the client's agenda and the lawyer's version of what the law will do, a clash in which the client's version is broader than the law's alleged competence. In reaction, lawyers readily acknowledge the special and limited nature of legal justice.

Client: Well, I mean, I'm a liberal. Right? A liberal dream is that you will find social justice, and so here was this statement that it was possible to fight injustice, and you were going to protect me from horrible things like judicial abuse. So that's uh, it was really nice. . . . But as you say, if you want justice in this society, you look somewhere other than the court. I believe that's what you were saying to Bob.

Lawyer: Yeah, that's what I said. Ultimate justice, that is.

Although lawyers may be able to fight "judicial abuse," this California lawyer juxtaposes legal and "ultimate" justice. The person seeking such a final accounting is clearly not going to be fully satisfied by a system that focuses much more narrowly. The law talk of the lawyer's office seeks to teach clients to come to terms with that reality by limiting their demands on law and by looking elsewhere for satisfaction or consolation. As one lawyer advised his client,

Lawyer: It's an ongoing battle. . . . My partner and I have a phrase. I don't know if I told you this before, but he found it in this Federal case down in Alabama, Georgia or somewhere where this Federal judge had this very difficult case, very difficult problem, and he didn't really have an answer, either. He had to come up with a decision so he gave his decision and then he said, he kind of excused himself on the decision by saying, life in all its fullness has the answer and he added, I think he added anyway, that none of us really live life to its fullest. In other words who knows if he's right. Who knows what the answer is?

Client: My favorite word is that justice is in the eye of the beholder. . . .

Lawyer: And that's true too. So, life in all its fullness. My partner and I say that to each other almost daily.

This law talk acknowledges simultaneously the indeterminacy of legal rules and the limited competence of judges (even judges may not have answers), directs the client to look elsewhere for answers to his problems and conveys doubts as to whether these answers can be found.

4. CONCLUSION

Law talk in the divorce lawyer's office is one of the ways through which the divorce process is experienced by clients, most of whom are not well informed about the legal process generally or the steps involved in getting a divorce (see Griffiths, 1986). Lawyers provide information and tell clients what the law requires and what may be expected from it. Although clients do have some direct experience of the legal process of divorce (they go to court, attend hearings, read orders and other documents), they are, because of their lack of information and experience, dependent on their lawyers for explanation and interpretation of events as they unfold. Law talk provides an interpretive frame for clients; it helps them understand the workings of the law and gives them an insider's view of legal processes in action.

At the beginning of this chapter we discussed three different visions of the legal process: formalism, equity, and realism. Our observation of law talk in the divorce lawyer's office suggests that the preponderant emphasis, the interpretive frame usually presented to the client, resembles most closely the realist style. Law talk is, in the first instance, replete with rule skepticism (Frank, 1949). Indeed, although a new generation of critical scholars is devoting itself to proving the proposition that legal rules are indeterminate and, in so doing, to demystifying the claims of legal formalism (see, for example, Singer, 1984), divorce lawyers seem routinely to be engaged in this same project as they counsel clients.

There is, of course, nothing surprising about the lawyer's rejection of formalist discourse. Divorce law is based on general guidelines rather than precise rules, and it invites a wide range of judicial discretion.[3] Yet the talk about law in the divorce lawyer's office is only slightly more compatible with the discourse of equity than it is with formalism. Although that talk acknowledges the centrality of people, especially the judge and the opposing lawyer, it does not encourage the view that legal officials give careful consideration to the litigants' needs, to tailoring results to particular cases, or that they are much interested in doing justice. Law talk places people at the center of the legal process of divorce and then proceeds to characterize them as uninterested in the litigants' priorities, lacking important qualifications, prone to arbitrary or inexplicable actions, making decisions on the basis of a variety of legally irrelevant factors, indulging their own personal prejudices, and/or caught up in "bureaucratic" routines that are either excessively technical and detailed or incomplete, rigid, and routinized.

Yet the lawyer must, at the same time that he creates doubts about the legal process, give the client some reason to rely on him. Thus the lawyer's emphasis on insider status. Nothing is guaranteed, but the best chance for success rests with those who are familiar with local practice and who have a working relationship with officials who wield local power. The interests of the professional, in this instance, depart from the interests of the legal system. These lawyers construct a picture of the legal process that fixes the client's dependency on them, while it jeopardizes their trust in any part of the system beyond them.

In a legal order whose legitimacy allegedly rests on the claims of formalism and, to a lesser extent, on the claims of equity, the law talk of the divorce lawyer's office might, if internalized by clients, be quite politically significant.[4] Such talk may be partially responsible for the oft-noted finding that people who use legal processes tend, no matter how favorable the results of

---

[3] We recognize that the fit between discourse and practice may be different from one legal area to another. The more codified legal doctrine in a legal field, the closer may be the correspondence to a formalist model. This hypothesis is simply another way of saying that the more rules, the less discretion, and the less discretion, the less lawyers are cynical about rules and judges. Testing this hypothesis requires study of lawyer–client conversation across legal fields.

[4] It is, of course, quite likely that clients do not believe the picture of legal process presented by lawyers and sooner or later conclude that it is developed for its instrumental value (see Sarat & Felstiner, 1986:127), and that they come to believe that lawyers, like therapists, adopt roles that are situationally useful (cf. Bosk, 1979:103–110 on the role of horror stories in the social control of surgeons).

their encounter, to have a less positive view of the law than those with no direct experience (see Sarat, 1977). By examining actual conversations between lawyer and client we can see that law talk in the divorce lawyer's office characterizes legal process in ways that contradict the expectations that people have about law. If the presentation of a formalist front is necessary to legitimate the legal order, then what we and others have captured in descriptions of the legal process as it is experienced at the street level (see, e.g., Merry, 1984) suggests that one tier of the legal system, in this case divorce lawyers, may work to unwind the bases of legitimation that other levels work to create.

ACKNOWLEDGMENTS.   The research on which this chapter is based was supported in part by the National Science Foundation Program in Law and Social Science under Grants No. SES–8110483 and 8510422. We appreciate the helpful comments of Anne Graffam Walker, Judith Levi, Susan Silbey, Laura Kalman, and Terence Halliday.

5. REFERENCES

Arnold, Thurman. (1935). *The symbols of government*. New Haven: Yale University Press.
Atkinson, J. Maxwell, & Drew, Paul. (1979). *Order in court*. London: Macmillan.
Bennett, W. Lance, & Feldman, Martha. (1981). *Reconstructing reality in the courtroom*. New Brunswick: Rutgers University Press.
Blumberg, Abraham. (1967). The practice of law as a confidence game. *Law & Society Review, 1*, 15.
Bogoch, Bryna, & Danet, Brenda. (1984). Challenge and control in lawyer/client interaction, A case study in an Israeli legal office. *TEXT, 4*(1/3), 249–275.
Bosk, Charles. (1979). *Forgive and remember: Managing medical failure*. Chicago: University of Chicago Press.
Brigham, John. (1978). *Constitutional language*. Westport: Greenwood Press.
Caesar-Wolf, Beatrice. (1984). *Professionalized lawyer/client interaction: An exemplary case study of a divorce consultation*, unpublished paper, on file with the authors.
Cain, Maureen. (1979). The general practice lawyer and the client, *International Journal of the Sociology of Law, 1*, 331.
Chambers, David. (1984). *Rethinking the substantive rules for child-custody disputes in divorce*, unpublished paper.
Christie, George. (1964). Vagueness and legal language. *Minnesota Law Review, 48*, 888.
Danet, Brenda, & Bogoch, Bryna. (1980). Fixed fight or free for all. *British Journal of Law and Society, 1*, 36.
Davis, Kenneth. (1971). *Discretionary justice*. Urbana: University of Illinois Press.
Dicey, A. V. (1939). *Introduction to the study of the law of the constitution* (9th ed.). London: Macmillan.
Edelman, Murray. (1977). *Political language*. New York: Academic Press.
Feeley, Malcolm. (1979). *The process is the punishment*. New York: Russell Sage Foundation.
Frank, Jerome. (1949). *Courts on trial*. Princeton: Princeton University Press.
Griffiths, John. (1986). What do Dutch lawyers actually do in divorce cases. *Law & Society Review, 20*, 135.
Hosticka, Carl. (1979). We don't care about what happened, we only care about what is going to happen. *Social Problems, 26*, 599.

Kalman, Laura. (1986). *Legal realism at Yale*. Chapel Hill: University of North Carolina Press.
Mather, Lynn, & Yngvesson, Barbara. (1980–1981). Language, audience and the transformation of disputes. *Law & Society Review, 15*, 775.
Maynard, Douglas. (1984). Inside plea bargaining. New York: Plenum Press.
Mellinkoff, David. (1963). *The language of the law*. Boston: Little, Brown.
Mensch, Ellen. (1982). The history of mainstream legal thought. In David Kairys (Ed.), *The politics of law* (pp. 18–39). New York: Pantheon.
Merry, Sally. (1985). Concepts of law and justice among working class Americans. *Legal Studies Forum, 9*, 59.
Nonet, Philippe, & Selznick, Philip. (1978). *Law and society in transition*. New York: Harper & Row.
Noonan, John. (1976). *Persons and masks of the law*. New York: Farrar, Straus & Giroux.
Pound, Roscoe. (1917). The limits of effective legal action. *International Journal of Ethics, 27*, 150.
Probert, Walter. (1972). *Law, language and communication*. Springfield, IL: Charles C Thomas.
Rodell, Fred. (1939). *Woe unto you, lawyers!* New York: Renol and Hitchcock.
Sales, Bruce. (1977). Improving comprehension for jury instructions. In Bruce Sales (Ed.), *Perspectives in law and psychology* (pp. 23–90). New York: Plenum Press.
Sarat, Austin. (1977). Studying American legal culture. *Law & Society Review, 11*, 427.
Sarat, Austin, & Felstiner, William. (1986). Law and strategy in the divorce lawyer's office. *Law & Society Review, 20*, 93.
Scott, Marvin, & Lyman, Stanford. (1968). Accounts. *American Sociological Review, 33*, 1.
Shapiro, Martin. (1981). On the regrettable decline of law French. *Yale Law Journal, 90*, 1198.
Simon, William. (1975). The ideology of advocacy. *Wisconsin Law Review, 1975*, 30.
Singer, Joseph. (1984). The player and the cards. *Yale Law Journal, 94*, 1.
Stone, Christopher. (1981). From a language perspective. *Yale Law Journal, 90*, 1149.
Trubek, David. (1984). Where the action is: Critical legal studies and empiricism. *Stanford Law Review, 36*, 575.
Unger, Roberto. (1976). *Law in modern society*. New York: Free Press.
Weber, Max. (1954). *On law in economy and society*. Max Rheinstein (Ed.). New York: Simon and Schuster.

Part III

TRANSFORMING LANGUAGE IN LEGAL PROCEEDINGS

Chapter 6

BILINGUAL COURT PROCEEDINGS
The Role of the Court Interpreter[1]

SUSAN BERK-SELIGSON

1. INTRODUCTION

Ethnographers interested in linguistic behavior have long looked at speaker role as a key variable in determining what a person will say in a given situation and how he or she will say it (Hymes, 1962, 1972). Participants in a particular linguistic setting have various sorts of expectations regarding the verbal behavior of other participants. This chapter intends to explore the verbal behavior of a relatively new participant in what is typically a highly ritualized linguistic setting: the courtroom. It intends to demonstrate that what is expected in terms of verbal behavior on the part of an official verbal participant in the courtroom is far from fulfilled. Specifically, the chapter analyzes

[1] This is a revised version of a paper presented at the Symposium on Law and Language, Georgetown University, July 26–28, 1985. The project has been supported by the National Science Foundation (grant SES 8114717 and SES 8341766). The investigator wishes to thank all those court personnel who so generously cooperated with the project, the judges, attorneys, clerks, bailiffs, and most especially, the interpreters, without whom the research could not have been carried out. In order to protect their anonymity, however, these persons will remain unnamed. Furthermore, in order to ensure the anonymity of all those persons involved in the court cases referred to in this chapter, all the names of persons, places, and courts have intentionally been changed or left unidentified.

SUSAN BERK-SELIGSON • Department of Hispanic Languages and Literatures, University of Pittsburgh, Pittsburgh, Pennsylvania 15260.

the behavior of the foreign language court interpreter and tries to show what it is that the social setting would require of her,[2] and why it is that these expectations in reality are not fulfilled.

It is the thesis of this chapter that the American legal system would like the court interpreter to be physically invisible and vocally silent, if that were at all possible. That is to say, ideally she should not exist as a distinct verbal participant in her own right during the course of a judicial proceeding. In effect, she is meant to speak solely in place of the other participants in the courtroom, those considered to legitimately hold the right to speak: the attorneys, witnesses, plaintiffs, defendants, and the judge. The interpreter must perform this function whenever English speech needs to be interpreted into a foreign language for the benefit of non-English-speaking witness or defendant, and whenever foreign language testimony must be interpreted into English for the benefit of the judge, attorneys, and jury. It will be shown in this chapter why the expectations of the judicial system cannot be met, and that in fact, the court interpreter plays a far more active verbal role than the system could ever imagine. Finally, it will be shown that the interpreter's verbal role is very much tied to the linguistic control of "legitimate" participants in judicial proceedings, a degree of control that often is tantamount to linguistic coercion.

2. LANGUAGE AND POWER IN THE COURTROOM

One of the most prevalent beliefs held by court personnel is that bilingually conducted judicial proceedings—that is, proceedings carried out with the assistance of a foreign language interpreter—are in no way different from normal, monolingually conducted proceedings. Apparently, as far as many judges, attorneys, court clerks and bailiffs are concerned, the presence of the court interpreter at a proceeding has no impact of its own on the progression of a judicial event. It is the thesis of this chapter that this prevalent judicial assumption is fallacious and that the presence of the foreign language court interpreter does indeed alter the normal flow of events in the courtroom. In particular, it will be shown that the court interpreter behaves as an intrusive element in the courtroom setting, despite the fact that court authorities would prefer that she be completely unobtrusive. It is ironic that, although much of this obtrusiveness is caused unwittingly by the interpreter's own behavior, to a large degree it is magnified unintentionally by judges and attorneys on the one hand, and by witnesses, plaintiffs, and defendants on the other.

The intrusiveness of the interpreter has serious implications for those

---

[2] Interpreters will be referred to with the feminine pronoun, "she," as it has been found by this investigator that the majority of court interpreters are women.

who wish to control the testimony of witnesses and defendants. Scholars involved in research on language in legal settings have shown that control over a testifying witness or defendant resides in attorneys (Atkinson & Drew, 1979; Danet & Kermish, 1978; Danet & Bogoch, 1980; Danet et al., 1980; Dunstan, 1980) and in judges (Philips, 1979). Because of the very nature of their job, interpreters unintentionally interfere with attorneys' and judges' examination routines, exerting their own sort of control over testimony. As will be shown, one important aspect of this control is the ability to make testifying witnesses speak before they are ready to, and to prevent them from speaking when they are about to speak. Because this kind of coercive power on the part of the interpreter is a new variable in the American courtroom, then it must be recognized as a significant new variable in courtroom discourse alongside of the power that has already been shown to reside in attorneys and judges.

Danet and her colleagues (Danet & Kermish, 1978; Danet et al., 1980) have found that attorney questions vary in the degree to which they control witnesses' answers. In their research they present a typology of coerciveness, in which different question forms can be seen to be differentially coercive in the type of answer that they tend to elicit. For example, declarative questions such as tag questions ("You did it, didn't you"), which are considered to fit into the category of "leading question," are found by Danet and her associates to be the most highly coercive (i.e., they strongly limit the witness' choice of acceptable answers and even suggest the answers), whereas open-ended wh-questions (questions phrased with words such as "who," "what," "where," "when," and "why") are low in their coercive power. One measure of question coerciveness used by Danet is length of answer: The more coercive the type of question, the shorter the answer. Highly coercive questions such as tags tend to produce "yes/no" type answers, which are generally short utterances (e.g., "Yes," "Yes, I was," "No, he didn't"). Answers to open-ended questions tend to be longer in that they produce either lengthier sentences, as measured by number of words per sentence or sentences strung together in a narrative discourse format.

The work of Dunstan (1980) and Atkinson and Drew (1979), which analyzes the language of attorney/witness interaction in British trial courts, finds that the power of attorneys over testifying witnesses cannot be limited to the factor of question form but must be seen to derive from larger contextual factors. Starting from an ethnomethodological viewpoint and using notions from the theory of conversational analysis developed by Sacks, Schegloff, and Jefferson (1974) and from the theory of conversational implicature developed by Grice (1975), Dunstan, Atkinson, and Drew see the coercive power of attorneys as being exercised through the structuring of question/answer sequences over a series of turns. Dunstan (1980), for example, shows how an attorney's repetition of a question during different points in his or her examination of a witness conveys an impression to others listening that he or she finds her or his answers less than truthful. Dunstan, Atkinson, and Drew find that in addition to repetitions, a number of other linguistic strategies that fit into the category of paralinguistics (e.g., pauses, interruptions, repetitions) and suprasegmentals (e.g., voice pitch, tempo) can also be seen as being subject to manipulation by attorneys as they exercise their power over the witnesses whom they are questioning.

One of the major variables in witness testimony that is controlled by attorneys is the length of answer permitted. Danet *et al.* (1980) have found length of answer to be related to question coerciveness, as has been noted. O'Barr and his colleagues Conley, Erickson, and Lind have observed that "long, narrative answers by witnesses are possible only when lawyers relinquish some control, allowing more leeway to witnesses in answering questions" (O'Barr, 1982:77). Trial practice manuals, recognizing this fact, recommend that "lawyers should allow their own witnesses some opportunity for narrative answers and should restrict opposition witnesses to brief answers as much as possible" (O'Barr, 1982:77).

An additional factor in attorney control over witness testimony is the role played by interruptions and simultaneous speech. The studies of O'Barr, Conley, and Lind (O'Barr, 1982) show that whenever overlapping speech occurs between an attorney and a witness, the attorney is perceived as having less control over the presentation of testimony, and the witness is perceived as being more powerful and more in control. In short, the perception of simulated juries is "that an attorney loses control whenever simultaneous speech occurs in the courtroom" (O'Barr, 1982:90). The impression that the lawyer has lost control in such situations does not necessarily mean that he or she has lost control of the situation in reality, because attorneys can and do use such speech events to their advantage. They often knowingly yield to witnesses in a moment of simultaneous speech or refuse to yield to them. Each tactic has its costs and benefits, however, as O'Barr and his colleagues have observed.

When judges take on the role of examiner, as is normally the case in arraignments, changes of plea, and sentencings, then it is they who hold the controlling power over the person who must answer under oath. In these cases it is the defendant who is being questioned. The work of Philips (1979) concludes that the syntactic form of the judge's questions (e.g., yes/no questions vs. *wh-* questions) greatly affects the nature of the answers that those questions will elicit. For example, yes/no questions tend to elicit short answers, whereas *wh-* questions generally produce lengthier answers, as is true for attorney questions as well. In change of plea proceedings, for instance, the differences in judges' questioning style will result in a difference between defendants' merely assenting to a factual basis for the crimes with which they are charged and the defendants' providing the facts themselves.

Whereas it may be expected that an examining attorney or judge would have the power to control a testifying witness' or defendant's answer, it is a less obvious fact that to some degree those testifying hold their own measure of linguistic power over their answers. Specifically, they have the ability to use "powerful" testimony style as opposed to "powerless" style (Conley *et al.*, 1978; Erickson *et al.*, 1978; Lind *et al.*, 1978; Lind & O'Barr, 1979; O'Barr & Atkins, 1980; O'Barr & Conley, 1976; O'Barr & Lind, 1981; O'Barr *et al.*, 1976). The notion of powerless speech style grew out of the observation of O'Barr and his colleagues that some witnesses testify in a speech style that earlier research by R. Lakoff (1975) had identified as a stereotypical "women's speech style." It is a style comprising the relatively frequent use of a set of linguistic features, including polite forms ("sir," "ma'am," "please"), hedges ("sort of," "a little"), hesitation forms (pause fillers, such as "uh," "um,"); and meaningless particles, such as "oh," "well," "you see"). O'Barr renamed this speech style as the "powerless" mode of testifying and called the contrasting style, in which these features are relatively uncommon, the "power" mode. The experimental studies of these researchers have found that powerless testimony style is by no means restricted to women, but rather, that it is characteristic of speakers of low socioeconomic backgrounds. Furthermore, these scholars have found that witnesses who testify in the powerless mode as opposed to a style lacking these features, the power mode, are evaluated less positively by mock jurors on a variety of social/psychological scales (e.g., convincingness, truthfulness, intelligence, and competence). Although the proclivity to answer questions in powerful versus powerless testimony style is greatly determined by the socioeconomic characteristics of the witness, to the extent that witnesses are capable of speaking in powerful style, to that extent do they hold power over their own testimony, and consequently, over the impression that they make on jurors. It should be pointed out, however, that witnesses are far less likely to be conscious of their speaking style than are attorneys. Attorneys make use of a deliberate, well-practiced form of control when they examine witnesses. Witnesses generally are novices at speaking on the stand. Thus the power that witnesses bring with them to the examination process resides in whether they are fortunate enough to come naturally equipped with the powerful speech style.

The preceding discussion has explored the various sources of linguistic power that attorneys, judges, and testifying witnesses, defendants, and plaintiffs bring with them to the courtroom. What this chapter will demonstrate is that the court interpreter in a number of ways weakens the control that these persons have over testimony as it emerges. Consequently, interpreters will be shown to exert an influence on the very progression of a judicial proceeding.

3. THE BILINGUAL COURTROOM

What is referred to here as the "bilingual courtroom" is the courtroom in which a court-appointed interpreter is assigned to a non-English-speaking

defendant or witness.[3] The use of foreign language interpreters is commonplace today in American cities and towns having sizable non-English-speaking populations, and interpreters are used in such areas in all judicial tiers:
federal, state, and municipal, alike. In the fiscal year 1982, 31,128 proceedings
were conducted with the aid of an interpreter in federal courts alone (Berreby,
1982:24). In fact, the impetus for the ever-growing use of foreign language
interpreters in all courts comes from the enactment of a law that applies to
federal courts only. In October 1978, with the enactment of Public Law 95-539,
the court interpreter became an official entity in U.S. district courts. The Court
Interpreters Act provides for the appointment of interpreters in all criminal
and civil cases initiated by the federal government in federal courts. However,
many states have taken their own measures to ensure equal justice for the
non-English-speaking in state-level courts. These measures range from
amendments to the state constitution (e.g., the case of California and New
Mexico), to statutes (e.g., Arizona, Colorado, Illinois, Massachusetts, Minnesota, New York, and Texas), and judicial regulations (e.g., the California
Evidence code).

   This chapter restricts itself to the analysis of the Spanish/English bilingual courtroom. The focus on Spanish interpreting arises from the fact that
Spanish is heard more frequently than any other foreign language in American courtrooms. In 1982, in a federal courthouse located in a northeastern
metropolis, 684 interpreted proceedings were conducted in Spanish, whereas
in the same courthouse the total number of interpreted proceedings for all
other foreign languages combined amounted to 233.[4] In other words, there
were three times as many Spanish interpreted proceedings as there were
interpreted proceedings for all the other languages combined. In 1984, for the
nation as a whole, Spanish constituted 91% of all court interpreting at the
federal court level (see Table 1). In the U.S. Southwest, the proportion of
Spanish court interpreting compared to the interpreting of other languages is
even higher because of the demographic importance of the Hispanic population in that region.

---

[3] Courts do allow for privately paid interpreters, a practice that also falls under the purview of a
bilingual courtroom. It is relatively unusual, however, for individuals to pay for interpreters
privately, however, because most defendants whose cases require the services of a foreign
language interpreter are indigent. During the course of the fieldwork for this project, only in one
instance was a privately paid interpreter used. The case involved international drug trafficking.
[4] The statistics for the courthouse in question come from the annual log kept by the chief of court
interpreting/translating services of this particular courthouse. Each entry in the log represents a
"docketable" appearance of an interpreter, that is, it reflects the appearance of an interpreter at
one single proceeding (e.g., an arraignment, a change of plea hearing, a sentencing, a morning
session of a trial). It is in this way that events are listed on the daily courthouse docket, or
schedule. The numbers in the log are listed in terms of docketable events because it is upon this
basis that payment is made to free-lance interpreters for their work. Permanent full-time
interpreters of the court, however, are paid on a fixed, annual salary basis.

TABLE 1. Fiscal Year 1984 Interpreter Statistics[a]

As reported by district courts		As reported by district courts		As reported by bankruptcy courts	
Language	Number of times used	Language	Number of times used	Language	Number of times used
Spanish	38,807	Tongan	13	Spanish	19
Italian	368	Ibo	12	Korean	3
Haitian Creole	344	Filipino	12	Japanese	1
Arabic	326	Laotian	12		
French	266	Hmong	12		
Chinese	200	Bengali	11		
Thai	192	Taiwanese	11		
Korean	187	Turkish	11		
Urdu	148	Hungarian	9		
Navaho	147	Swedish	9		
Yoruba	119	Yugoslavian	9		
Portuguese	102	Carolinian	5		
Cantonese	93	Papago	5		
Mandarin	92	Cambodian	4		
German	90	Macedonian	4		
Russian	71	Malai	4		
Punjabi	59	Sicilian	4		
Japanese	55	Albanian	3		
Farsi	50	Nepali	3		
Armenian	49	Romanian	3		
Chamorro	45	Tamil	3		
Vietnamese	34	Bangla	2		
Greek	30	Dutch	2		
Sign (for deaf)	29	Edo	2		
Czech	27	Lakota	2		
Hindi	25	Lebanese	2		
Serbo-Croatian	23	Ashish	1		
Polish	20	Bulgarian	1		
Hebrew	17	Tewa	1		
Tagalog	17	Yavapi	1		
Apache	16				

[a]This table is taken from the Hearing before the Subcommittee on the Constitution of the Committee on the Judiciary, United States Senate, Ninety-ninth Congress, Second Session, on S. 1853, A Bill to Amend the Court Interpreters Act of 1978, February 25, 1986, Serial No. J-99-88 (p. 261). It should be noted that the data in this table are derived from the records of court interpreting offices and reflect a failure to collapse language categories that in fact represent different varieties of the same language (such as the listing of Chinese in four different ways: Chinese, Cantonese, Mandarin, and Taiwanese). Nevertheless, even if these varieties were to be collapsed, the table would still demonstrate an overwhelming preponderance of Spanish interpreting in United States federal district courts.

The findings presented in this chapter are derived from ethnolinguistic observation carried out by this investigator in the fall of 1982 and spring of 1983. Spanish/English interpreted proceedings were observed and tape-recorded over a 7-month period, primarily in the U.S. Southwest but also in a northeastern metropolis, nearly all of them being criminal cases. A total of 114 hours of judicial proceedings involving the use of an interpreter were taped. These proceedings included initial appearances, arraignments, preliminary hearings, changes of plea, full trials, and sentencings—in short, the complete gamut of proceedings that a criminal defendant might undergo. Beyond observation and taping, the fieldwork involved interviewing interpreters, lawyers, and judges. Observation and taping were conducted in two federal courthouses, three state-level courthouses, two municipal courthouses, and two justice of the peace courts. During the months of fieldwork, 18 interpreters were observed, 12 of whom were women and 6 of whom were men. Of the 18, 6 were federally certified interpreters (i.e., they had passed the federal court interpreters examination), 6 were full-time court employees who worked strictly in the capacity of interpreter for their court, another 6 were court employees who worked primarily in some capacity other than interpreter (e.g., bailiff, clerk). A final 6 were free-lance interpreters who either worked through a private agency or who were self-employed and who could be called to a courthouse at a moment's notice.

4. HOW ATTENTION IS SHIFTED TO THE INTERPRETER BY COURT PROCEEDINGS AND BY OTHER PARTIES

4.1. Consciousness of the Presence of the Court Interpreter

When an interpreter is at work during a judicial proceeding, she is not simply "part of the furniture" of the courtroom. She does not simply melt into the woodwork, even though judges would prefer that she do so. Rather, attention is constantly drawn to her for a number of reasons. As the following sections will demonstrate, some of the reasons have to do with the actions of the judge and the attorneys, whereas others have to do with the behavior of the interpreter herself.

4.1.1. How Judges and Attorneys Draw Attention to the Interpreter

From the moment an interpreter begins functioning as an interpreter at a judicial proceeding, attention is directed toward her. Before she is permitted to begin her work in any given courtroom at any stage of a case pending before the court, the interpreter must be sworn in. Interpreters are required to swear an oath to the effect that they will interpret to the best of their ability, as accurately as possible, the proceeding at hand. This sworn statement must be made in each courtroom in which the interpreter is scheduled to interpret. It means being sworn in several times a day and raises the very possibility that her interpretation might not always be accurate. Thus the requirement of the court that the interpreter must take an oath in open court calls attention to the interpreter from the outset of a proceeding.

The issue of interpreter accuracy, which is raised by the swearing-in process, becomes salient when interpretations given by court interpreters are challenged in the course of the proceeding. The challenge is usually made by bilingual attorneys. When such cases arise, the interpreter is put on the stand as a witness and must testify as to the accuracy of her choice of words. If the routine, daily swearing-in process itself calls attention to the interpreter, then the challenging of an interpreter's interpretations throws an even brighter spotlight on her. It certainly acts to make other persons in the courtroom aware that the interpreter is not a computerlike translating machine, one that needs only to be plugged in at will. It calls attention to the fact that the interpreter is a person who has developed a set of skills to a greater or lesser degree, and, additionally, that she is a person whose integrity cannot automatically be taken for granted. She is held accountable for the accuracy of her interpreting.

Interpreters are asked to testify not only to the accuracy of their own interpretations but to that of other interpreters as well, when disputes arise. A common situation in which interpreters are made to give expert testimony is in cases in which the translation of documents and formulaic statements is called into question. One federal court interpreter (personal communication) has had to testify as to the accuracy of the Spanish translation of a "consent to search" form used by the Federal Drug Enforcement Administration. This form allows federal drug enforcement officials to search a person and his premises without a regular search warrant. The person who is to be searched must sign that he has been "requested" to consent to a search of his person and premises. One Spanish translation of this form used the word *requerir*, "require," rather than an equivalent of the verb "request," such as *pedir*. The result of this poor translation was an attempt on the part of the defense attorney to have the case against his client dismissed on the grounds that the client had not been given a valid "consent to search" form to sign.

In another case (Reese & Reese, 1984), the improper translation of the Miranda rights was at issue. In *People v. Díaz* (1983) 140 Cal. App. 3d 812, report Reese and Reese (1984), the court ruled that the defendant had not been effectively advised of his rights because of an inadequate translation of the fourth branch of the Miranda rights. In English, that right reads as follows: "If you cannot afford to hire a lawyer, one will be appointed to represent you before any questioning, if you wish one." The California Highway Patrol Miranda Card had the following translation printed on it: "Si no puede conseguir un abogado, se le puede nombrar uno antes de que le hagan preguntas." Two certified court interpreters testified that the translation was inaccurate because it did not imply that if a person could not *afford* a lawyer, one would be appointed to represent him. The court agreed with the interpreters, acknowledging that the Spanish word *conseguir*, "obtain," did not convey the idea intended by the Miranda rights, namely that indigent defendants have a right to be represented by an attorney *at no cost to them*, if they cannot pay for one. The court, relying on the expert testimony of the two interpreters, came to the following conclusion (Reese & Reese, 1984:5):

> If the phrase "sin pagar" (meaning "without pay" or "without paying") had been used in the advisement in question, appellant would certainly have been adequately advised that indigent status would entitle him to appointed counsel. In so stating, we recognize that frequently there is no single word in a foreign language which carries the identical meaning of a single word in the English language. In this regard, we examined four different Spanish translations (including the California Highway Patrol card used in this case) of the Miranda advisement at issue. We discovered that none of the translations were identical. However, unlike the California Highway Patrol's translation, those translations which used the word "conseguir" also contained additional qualifying phrases such as "sin pagar."

Apparently, at the heart of this questioning of the accuracy of the Miranda rights translation is the translator's rendition of the word "afford." Whereas dictionaries do list near equivalents, such as *costearse*, apparently the translator of the document in question had not been familiar with this lexical item or with some other satisfactory gloss. Critical to this case is the difference in meaning between the words "afford" and "obtain" (the English equivalent of the Spanish word used in the translation, *conseguir*): "afford" implies "capable of paying," whereas "obtain" carries no such implication. One rendition found to be satisfactory by the judge quoted above is to add to the verb *conseguir* the additional phrase *sin pagar*.

4.1.1a. The Voir Dire. Even when interpreters are not in the limelight of the witness stand but are merely sitting unobtrusively at the defense counsel table doing simultaneous interpreting, judges bring the interpreter to the attention of others in the courtroom.[5] Nowhere is this more explicitly done

---

[5] Court interpreters are expected to be competent in three distinct interpreting modes: simultaneous, consecutive, and summary. In the simultaneous mode the interpreter's voice overlaps with that of the person whose speech she is interpreting, but her rendition in the target language lags behind the source language utterance by relatively short intervals, such as a phrase or a clause. This mode is intended for use at the defense counsel table, for the benefit of the defendant, and is carried out in whispered tones. Consecutive interpreting, in contrast, is done aloud for the entire court to hear and is the mode recommended for use at the witness stand when a non-English-speaking or hearing-impaired witness testifies. The consecutive mode requires that there be no overlapping speech between speaker and interpreter: The interpreter must wait for the speaker to fall silent before she begins her interpretation. In reality, because consecutive interpreting relies on high recall of everything that has been said, whenever witnesses or defendants answer in long, narrative-style format, interpreters resort to interrupt-

than during jury selection. References to the presence of the court interpreter and questions regarding the attitudes of prospective jurors toward the use of an interpreter during bilingual trials are a regular feature of the *voir dire*, that is, the questioning of prospective jurors for purposes of selection to the jury panel. Judges generally begin questioning the pool of juror candidates in this regard by formally introducing the interpreter to them. This is usually done at the time when the attorneys are introduced by name to the prospective jurors. Just as the attorneys must be identified to jurors, so too, must the interpreter, whose presence at the defense table must somehow be accounted for. Otherwise the jury might conclude that she is an attorney herself, a member of the defense team. The following example comes from the *voir dire* of a federal narcotics trial:[6]

1.
Judge: All right. Now the defendant before you is Mr. Juan Carlos Ortega. Would you
   mind standing up? (pause) And also face these folks back here. All right, any of
   you know Mr. Ortega? All right, thank you. Uh, the, uh, defendant is represented
   by Mr. John Turner, T-U-R-N-E-R. Any of you know Mr. Turner? And now, sitting
   with, uh the defendant, Mr. Ortega, Mrs. Alicia Calderón, who's the interpreter, . . . Spanish interpreter. All right, now the government is represented by
   Mr. William M. Donelly, and he's an assistant United States Attorney here in the
   First district of El Paso. Sitting with him is a drug enforcement agent, Miss Kelly
   Porter. Uh, any of you know either of them?

The judge might then briefly explain the role of the interpreter and go on to ask if any of the prospective jurors have any objection to the use of an interpreter during the trial or would feel uncomfortable about her carrying out this task. The following example is typical of the *voir dire* questions that were asked at trials observed by this investigator:

---

ing them in order to be able to interpret accurately and not miss any linguistic substance. Note taking is generally practiced by interpreters during consecutive interpreting. The third interpret- ing mode, summary interpreting, departs from the other two verbatim-type methods in that it allows the interpreter to summarize long stretches of speech into their most salient points. This mode is generally allowed when lawyers and judges talk to each other rather than to a jury (e.g., during the presenting of motions).

[6] The tape recordings were transcribed by two groups of trained student transcribers. Monolingual English-speaking assistants transcribed the English portions of the tapes, and Spanish-
   dominant or relatively balanced bilingual Hispanic students transcribed only the Spanish
   portions (i.e., the Spanish testimony of witnesses and defendants and the interpretations into
   Spanish of the court interpreter). Each transcript was checked for accuracy by someone other
   than the person who had transcribed it, to ensure the highest possible quality of transcription.
      The transcriptions to some extent follow the format developed by conversational analyst
   pioneers, Sacks, Schegloff, and Jefferson (1974). Thus, all hesitation phenomena were transcribed, extra heavy word stress indicated by underlining, and simultaneous speech indicated
   by a latching symbol [[].

Judge: Now you'll notice the defendant is having this translated for him into Spanish. Would the fact that uh, he, he, uh speaks Spanish, and not English, would that affect your ability to be absolutely, to be absolutely fair? And to the uh, government?

In one federal trial that was observed, the judge did not include in the *voir dire* any questions regarding the use of an interpreter, yet a prospective juror raised the issue as one that was problematical for her. The following interchange took place between judge and prospective juror:

2.

Judge [addressing panel of jurors]: Very often in questioning a jury I miss the most important question, as to whether or not you can sit as a completely fair and impartial juror. It would be nice if we had a little crystal ball we could look into and know, uh what you are thinking right now. Maybe I wouldn't wanna know. [Laughter from jurors.] But, it might be helpful to us, uh, in determining whether you can sit as a completely fair and impartial juror. So whether I refer to it in any way whatsoever, let me ask you if you can think of any reason why you could not sit and be a completely fair and impartial juror. And maybe you might think, "Well, this might sound silly and I really don't want to, uh, state it," but if you think of anything, tell us about it. Thank you. Yes?

Prospective juror: Your honor, I work with deaf people as an interpreter, a volunteer interpreter, and I know the problems that are involved in, lacking verbal communication, and it really bothers me that they, the defendants do not speak English and have to,—no reflection on the interpreter—but it depends solely on the interpreter, for their understanding.

Judge: Of what is going on here?

Prospective juror: Yes, ma'am, and what is happening.

Judge: It used t'be in the, in the, just about five or six years ago we didn't even have an interpreter in the courtroom.

Prospective juror: I know [laughing].

Judge: It is, it is difficult, uh, of course, it's acceptable and it's legal the way it's done and, uh, I think we have one of the best interpreters, uh,

Prospective juror: Yes, ma'am.

Judge: You agree with that, too?

Prospective juror: I agree, but I also deal with deaf people and I know that many times they tell you they understand and they don't.

Judge: Well are you, uh [pause], are you uh telling me that you, you're not sure you can be fair and impartial or uh. . .

Prospective juror: I'm telling you I don't,—I think it would influence me greatly, yes, ma'am.

Judge: Uh, of course, what is going to be testified to has already occurred. All of what is going on here is just an interpretation of what the witnesses say. Uh, it doesn't affect the act itself or the alleged act itself or anything of that nature, which to me is a little different than, uh, if we were just starting with the, all the acts now. I'm not trying t'influence you, but I am not sure that that would affect you, uh, in deciding the case. Yes?

Defense attorney: Can I say something your honor?

Judge: Sure.

Defense attorney: They both speak English, but they're more comfortable with their entire language in Spanish, too, in the courtroom.

Judge: Does that affect you in any way?

Prospective juror: No, that satisfies me.

Judge: Thank you, and I really appreciate your speaking out.

What the *voir dire* sequence in 2 shows is that a jury candidate has called extra attention to the interpretation process, attention of an unflattering kind. She has implied that interpreting is not always as effective as persons are led to believe. Her comments raise the whole issue of whether interpreting should be carried out in the first place and cast doubt on the validity of the interpretation that is to follow.[7] Interestingly, because of the objection raised by the prospective juror, one piece of information regarding the co-defendants emerges: They understand and speak English but feel more comfortable hearing Spanish in addition to English. This type of situation, where the defendant is bilingual but asks to have an interpreter by his side throughout the trial, occurs frequently. Judges approve such requests sometimes in order to avoid the risk of a future appeal should the trial end in a conviction because failure to be provided with an interpreter is a frequently used ground for appeals (e.g., *State v. Vasquez*, 1942). The fact that the defendants in this particular case understand English well emerged publicly only because of the

---

[7] Although court interpreting may seem to be the only solution to the problem of enabling linguistic minorities to understand the language of the court, another solution that has been proposed is to conduct the entire judicial proceeding in the language of the defendant. In a case that was considered before the Supreme Court of Canada (*Mercure v. A. G. Saskatchewan*, 1988) lawyers for the appellant, André Mercure, argued that as a French speaker being tried in an English-speaking judicial jurisdiction of Canada, Mercure had the right to have the entire trial conducted in French. This would have entailed the presence of a French-speaking presiding judge and French-speaking attorneys. Mercure's lawyers used a number of arguments to demonstrate that the interpreting process is inherently imperfect insofar as it is bound to fall short when it comes to conveying nuances of meaning. The Canadian Supreme Court rejected these arguments, stating that Mercure had been given a fair trial in Saskatchewan, the trial having been conducted with the assistance of a court-appointed interpreter.

Whereas such a case is less likely to come up in the United States, given the nonofficial status of the Spanish language at the national level and in most state legislatures (New Mexico being one exception to the general rule), in reality all-Spanish judicial proceedings do in fact go on in the United States. These are usually conducted in low-level courts (e.g., justice of the peace courts, municipal courts), located in Spanish-speaking *barrios* (neighborhoods of high Hispanic concentration) or small towns where Hispanics make up the overwhelming majority of the population. This occurs when the judge, attorneys, defendants, and witnesses are all Spanish speakers, and the judge is willing to conduct the proceeding in this manner. Such proceedings do not make use of a court reporter but are tape-recorded instead, so that an English translation may later be made based upon the recording, the translation in turn becoming an official transcript for the court record.

hesitancy expressed by the prospective juror. The whole issue of whether the interpreter should be there at all was thus inadvertently raised by the jury candidate and became even more subject to question as a result of the attorney's efforts to allay the woman's qualms. In effect, the comments of the prospective juror inadvertently opened up a can of worms regarding the use of a court interpreter in that trial.

4.1.1b. Addressing the Interpreter Rather Than the Witness or Defendant. Judges and attorneys alike inadvertently draw attention to the interpreter by departing from one of the standard rules for addressing interpreter-assisted witnesses or defendants. That rule, as formulated by the Texas Judiciary Interpreters Association, for example, states (Texas Judiciary Interpreters Association, n.d.:2):

> The interpretation shall be conducted in the first and second person, as if the interpreter did not exist. The non-English speaking client should be informed of this, so as to avoid confusion. For instance, the question should be "What is your name?" NOT "Ask him what his name is." Likewise, the interpreter shall respond for the client "My name is. . ." NOT "He says his name is. . ."

Similarly, the guidelines proposed by the California Judicial Council (Standards of Judicial Administration, sec. 18.1, 1981) instruct interpreters in the following way: "All statements made in the first person should be interpreted in the first person. For example, a statement or question should not be introduced with the words, 'He says. . .' " Furthermore, in the instructions to counsel, the guidelines state that "All questions by counsel examining a non-English speaking witness should be directed to the witness and not the interpreter. For example, do not say, 'Ask him if. . . .' "

Many lawyers, particularly those who have never examined a witness through an interpreter, are clearly not aware of this basic approach to asking questions of a non-English-speaking witness. However, even attorneys and judges who have worked frequently with interpreters will sometimes lapse into addressing the interpreter rather than the witness or defendant. This usually comes about during moments of confusion and frustration, when the examiner has asked the same question more than once but is not getting an appropriate reply to his question. Typically, this occurs during arraignments and changes of plea, when the judge explains to the defendant the alternative pleas that are available to him and the consequences of choosing one versus another. The following sequence of questions and answers, taken from a change of plea proceeding, illustrates a typical situation in which the interpreter is suddenly addressed directly by the judge or attorney and is requested to ask the defendant a particular question. Here, rather than lapsing unconsciously into directly addressing the interpreter, the attorney deliberately asks permission of the judge to speak directly to the interpreter.

3.

Judge: All right, what is your plea to count two, "guilty" or "not guilty"?

Interpreter: Bien, ¿cómo se declara Ud. del cargo número dos, "culpable" o "no culpable"?

Defendant: ¿De la, que la traía? Sí.

Interpreter: Of having brought it? Yes.

Judge: Now, now what you're charged with in count two is having the cocaine, having possession of it with intent to distribute it, that is, to give it to somebody else, or to sell it or,. . .

Interpreter: De lo que la acusan en el cargo número dos, es de haber tenido en su poder la cocaína, de haber tenido posesión con intención de distribuirla, o sea dársela a alguna otra persona.

Defendant: De distribuirla, no.

Interpreter: Not to distribute it.

Judge: Mrs. García, tell me, were you going, what were you gonna do with that cocaine you had?

Interpreter: Bueno, señora García, dígame una cosa, ¿y qué iba Ud. a hacer con esa cocaína que traía?

Defendant: La iba a dar. En el aeropuerto.

Interpreter: I was going to give it at the airport.

Judge: All right now, so what do you plead, "guilty" or "not guilty" to that charge two?

Interpreter: Bien, ahora, entonces, ¿cómo se declara Ud., "culpable" o "no culpable" de ese cargo número dos?

Defendant: ¿De posesión?

Interpreter: Of the possession?

Judge: Yes, what are you, guilty or not guilty?

Defendant: Sí, porque lo traía.

Interpreter: ¿Culpable o no culpable, señora?

Defendant: ¿Cómo?

Interpreter: What?

Judge: Culpable [said in Spanish], excuse me, guilty or not guilty?

Interpreter: [slowly and distinctly] ¿Culpable o no culpable?

Defendant: Sí, porque yo lo traía.

Interpreter: Yes, because I had it.

Judge: See, you must either tell me you are guilty or not guilty. Do you plead guilty?

Interpreter: No, tiene Ud. que decirme o que es culpable, o que no es culpable.

Defendant: Sí, porque lo tenía.

Interpreter: Yes, because I had it.

Defense attorney: Judge, can I me—, merely tell her, she doesn't seem to explain it to her, she must say it out loud to the judge that she is guilty or not guilty?

Interpreter: ¿Podría yo decirle? [*addressing defendant*]. Parece, tiene Ud. que decirle al juez que es Ud. culpable o que no es culpable.

Defendant: Sí.

Interpreter: Yes.

→ *Defense attorney [addressing interpreter]:* So she's gotta say it, tell her to say it.
→ *Interpreter:* O sea que tiene Ud. que decirlo. ¡Dígalo! ¿Qué es?
Defense attorney: Say it!
Interpreter: ¡Dígalo!
Judge: Can you say the word "culpable"?[8]
Interpreter: ¿Puede Ud. decir la palabra "culpable"?
Defendant: Culpable, ¡ah, sí!
Interpreter: Guilty, oh yes!
Judge: Is that what you are? Are you guilty?
Interpreter: ¿Eso es lo que es, es Ud. realmente culpable?
Defendant: Sí, culpable.
Interpreter: Yes, guilty.
Judge: Now, you're making this plea of guilty voluntarily and of your own free will?
Interpreter: Ahora, se está Ud. declarando culpable voluntariamente de su propia
     voluntad?
Defendant: Sí.
Interpreter: Yes.

It should be stressed that the situation presented is characterized by increasing frustration and irritation on the part of the judge and a mounting tension in the defense attorney, who is trying to effectuate the change of plea as smoothly as possible. The failure on the part of the defendant to produce the word "guilty" eventually leads the judge to prompt the defendant, and to go so far as to use the Spanish equivalent of the word "guilty" ("Can you say the word *culpable?*"). This particular type of confusion, where a defendant or a witness answers yes/no to a wh- type of question (i.e., a type of question requiring more substantive information for an answer), is very common in proceedings involving the non-English-speaking. It is particularly problematical during the plea and change of plea, where the court insists upon the defendant's stating the words "guilty" or "not guilty."

As can be seen in the instance cited, when communications break down between the examiner and the defendant, the examiner will temporarily dispense with the norm of speaking directly to the defendant through the interpreter, and instead, will talk to the interpreter, instructing her to convey the question to the party undergoing examination ("So she's gotta say it, tell her to say it"). Thus the examiner will violate the basic rules for questioning a defendant or witness through an interpreter. This, in turn, forces the interpreter into the position of giving instructions to the witness or defendant, which fundamentally alters the nature of her prescribed role in court. Instead of merely rendering speech from the source language into the target lan-

---

[8] Note that the judge is uttering the Spanish word [kulpáble] at this point. The spelling in Spanish happens to be homographic with the English word "culpable."

guage, she becomes an active verbal participant in the interaction, one who, from an observer's vantage point, appears to be initiating dialogue with the person under oath.

In lower-level courts, particularly municipal courts, the active participation of the interpreter is even greater. There, attorneys, and judges as well, will concede to the interpreter a degree of authority that officially is restricted to attorneys. This transfer of attorneylike functions to the interpreter is a result of the absence of defense attorneys at various sorts of municipal proceedings. For instance, during the course of traffic arraignments, a proceeding that sometimes is combined with sentencings, judges rely heavily on interpreters to process the cases. In the case cited next, the judge asks the interpreter her opinion as to whether the defendant has understood the charges against her:

4.

> *Judge:* All right, uhm, I'm gonna find you guilty because I believe that,—when you crossed over,—the two cars had to,—stop or slow down,—and they had the right of way to go through without stopping,—that when you crossed over,—you violated their right of way to keep going without interruption.
>
> *Interpreter:* Entonces la voy a encontrar culpable porque creo que Ud. cuando cruzó la carretera había dos carros que tuvieron que detenerse o detener su velocidad y estos dos carros tenían el derecho de paso de, de, sin tener que detenerse. Cuando Ud. cruzó Ud. violó su derecho de paso de poder continuar sin tener que, sin tener interrupción de
>
> *Defendant:* Yo tenía buen rato en la "middle line" esperando. Yo tenía buen rato esperando en el "middle line" cuando el oficial
>
> *Interpreter:* I'd been, uh, I'd been waiting at the. uh middle lane for a while when the officer
>
> → *Judge [addressing interpreter]:* Do you feel that she understands the charge or not?
> → *Interpreter [addressing judge]:* Yes, your honor.
> *Defendant:* Yes, I understand.

In this case, the defendant is bilingual, although a dominant Spanish speaker. The violation of the norm that interpreters should speak only on behalf of another speaker seems to lead the defendant to break the rule that defendants and witnesses are supposed to follow, namely speak only when you have been addressed directly. Thus the defendant answers the judge, even though she has not been spoken to during the interchange. At a moment such as this, then, once one rule of procedure has been broken, other rules of verbal interaction fall by the wayside as well, and so the entire routine of question/answer sequences has been temporarily halted. There has been, in effect, a temporary reinterpretation of the arraignment format, and this is a direct consequence of the judge's abandoning the court's own norms regarding the role of the interpreter. According to those norms, the judge should not have asked the interpreter whether she believed that the defendant had understood the charges. Rather, he should have addressed his question to the defendant directly, using the interpreter as an interpreter, and not as an active third party to the interaction.

5. THE INTERPRETER'S OWN ATTENTION-DRAWING BEHAVIOR

Interpreters try their best to be as inconspicuous as possible during courtroom proceedings. They are fully aware that they are not supposed to make their presence felt and that everyone's attention ought to be riveted on the speakers for whom they are interpreting. Nevertheless, circumstances arise in which the interpreter feels she must intrude upon the proceeding, and this usually occurs when she recognizes a problem of interpreting.

It must be emphasized that professional court interpreters are expected to interpret verbatim what a speaker has said.[9] This means that if an attorney or judge has made any linguistic errors in the formulation of a question or statement, theoretically it is the interpreter's duty to interpret the erroneously worded English utterance into as close an equivalent as possible in the target language, in this case Spanish. Similarly, if a witness or defendant in his reply to a question answers improperly (e.g., tangentially, off-target), the interpreter's obligation is to interpret that response to the nearest English equivalent, even though the outcome potentially may sound evasive or even nonsensical to those in the courtroom. Clearly, accurately interpreting a witness' off-target reply will put the interpreter into a certain jeopardy: She runs the risk of looking incompetent herself. In other words, if an interpreter correctly interprets a poorly worded answer, it is very possible that the monolingual judge or attorney might assume that a faulty interpretation has been made. Furthermore, if the interpreter is highly professional, she will not succumb to the temptation of switching from the first-person pronoun to a third-person reference to the witness (i.e., she will refrain from prefacing her interpretation with the phrase, "He says that. . ."). Consequently, when a good interpreter is

---

[9] The notion that court interpreting must be verbatim, that is, precise and a hi-fidelity rendition of the source language utterance, is emphasized in court interpreter training workshops and seminars. At sessions of the California Court Interpreters Association conferences, for example, and at intensive court interpreting institutes such as the University of Arizona Summer Institute for Court Interpretation, which this investigator attended in June–July 1983, the need for hi-fidelity accuracy is stressed constantly. It is precisely the verbatim quality of court interpreting that distinguishes it from conference interpreting and escort interpreting. The former chief interpreter of the United Nations, Theodore Fagan, commented (University of Arizona Summer Institute for Court Interpretation, June, 1983) on the distinction between the type of interpreting done at the United Nations and that expected in court, namely that the former regularly involves the interpreter's embellishment and improvement upon source language statements, whereas the latter does not allow for any alterations on the source language utterance. Fagan ultimately came to serve as a consultant on the team that created the first Federal Court Interpreters certification examination.

interpreting for a noncomprehending witness or defendant, she must bear the burden of often sounding stupid, inept, and incompetent. Often this impression accompanies a reply of *No comprendo*, or, "I don't understand." Attorneys and judges at times are not certain if the interpreter is speaking for herself, or interpreting for the witness or defendant. Jurors, who have far less experience in observing interpreters at work, may even more easily jump to the conclusion that the English statement "I don't understand" is a statement originating with the interpreter rather than with the Spanish speaker.

5.1. Interpreter Attempts to Clarify Witnesses' or Defendants' Answers and Attorneys' Questions

When a witness or defendant clearly is confused and keeps responding to a question in a meaningless fashion, even highly professional interpreters may interject themselves into the court record. This is usually done by asking the judge for permission to speak in order to explain to the attorney and to the judge the source of the witness'/defendant's confusion. In effect, the interpreter tries to clarify the witness'/defendant's answer.

Probably the most common context in which Spanish speakers answer a question in a nonmeaningful manner is during the plea and change of plea. Very often, as in Example 3, a defendant will respond "Sí" to the judge's question, "How do you plead, 'guilty' or 'not guilty'?" Sometimes, as in 3, it is the lawyer or judge who tells the interpreter to clarify the confusion of the defendant or witness. At other times, however, the interpreter herself takes the initiative to talk to the person undergoing examination. According to accepted practice, this should be done only after the interpreter has obtained permission from the judge to do so. Most interpreters are aware of court protocol, however, and know that before they attempt conversation with a testifying witness or defendant, they must first be granted permission from the judge.

5.2. Clarifying the Attorney's Questions

Interpreters frequently address themselves to the examining attorney for clarification of a question that has just been asked. Often the interpreter's need for clarification is simply a matter of not having heard the question clearly, or else one of not having noted down a sufficient portion of the question to be able to render a complete interpretation of it.[10] The following examples reflect the attorney-directed request for clarification:

---

[10] Note taking is a crucial element in consecutive interpreting because interpreters know that they cannot rely entirely on memory alone for accurate interpreting in this mode. Note-taking skills, therefore, are a regular feature of court interpreter training programs.

5.

Prosecuting attorney: And did the pilot ask you to pay him any money in Caño Seco?
Interpreter: Y el piloto le pidió a Ud. que le pagara algo de dinero en Caño Seco, en Caño Seco?
Witness: Sí, todos le pagamos.
Interpreter: Yes, all of us paid him.
Prosecuting attorney: How much did you pay in?
Interpreter: ¿Cuánto le pagó cada uno de Uds.?
Witness: Ochocientos.
Interpreter: Eight-hundred each of us.
Prosecuting attorney: Did you protest this payment?
→ *Interpreter [addressing attorney]:* Did you "protest," sir, "protest"?
→ *Prosecuting attorney [addressing interpreter]:* Yes.
Interpreter: ¿Protestaron Uds. de este pago, seño—, señorita?
Witness: No.
Interpreter: No.

6.

Defense attorney: Did you tell the border patrol agents that Mr. Durán first approached you while you were staying at the hotel?
→ *Interpreter [addressing attorney]:* Well, you were "standing" or "staying," sir?
Defense attorney [addressing interpreter]: Staying.

7.

Prosecuting attorney: After you were arrested by the police, were you interviewed by anybody?
→ *Interpreter [addressing attorney]:* How's that, sir?
Prosecuting attorney [addressing interpreter]: "Interview."
Interpreter: Después de que Ud. fue arrestado por la policía le hizo a Ud. alguien una entrevista? ¿Le hizo una?
Interpreter [addressing attorney]: I don't think he understood the word "interview," sir.
Prosecuting attorney [addressing interpreter]: Okay. Ah, discussions.
Interpreter: Después de que lo arrestaron a Ud. ¿tuvo Ud. alguna plática con alguna persona, es decir de la policía que los arrestó?

8.

Defense attorney: So if you told Manuel Antonio Gutiérrez that you only remained overnight in Juárez, that would be incorrect?
→ *Interpreter [addressing defense attorney]:* "That you remained only" what, sir?
Defense attorney [addressing interpreter]: Overnight in Juárez. That would be incorrect?
Defense attorney: And the first time you met him was in the desert on October fourteenth?
→ *Interpreter [addressing attorney]:* Was there another word after "desert," Mrs. Zolin? I did not translate anything after "desert."
Defense attorney [addressing interpreter]: No.

Interpreter [addressing attorney]: "The first time you saw him was in the desert."
Defense attorney [addressing interpreter]: In the desert.
Interpreter: Y la primera vez que Ud. lo conoció fue en el desierto.
Witness: Sí.
Interpreter [addressing attorney]: And he answered "yes."

Whereas many of these clarification procedures are relatively brief, as are the cases of 5 and 6, some involve more extensive verbal participation on the part of the interpreter, as can be seen in sequences 7 and 8. In sequence 7 the interpreter initiates two kinds of clarification routines, one in which she is not sure of the word that had been uttered by the attorney and the other whereby she informs the attorney that the witness may not have understood that particular word ("interview"). The two types of clarification procedures do not come together by chance. What appears to be happening, in effect, is that the interpreter is indirectly criticizing the attorney for choosing a word whose Spanish equivalent is unfamiliar to the witness. The interpreter, probably having had previous experiences of witnesses being unable to understand the word *entrevista*, "interview," is subtly influencing the attorney to change his choice of words. She does so via a two-step clarification procedure.

In sequence 8, in contrast to 7, the interpreter is genuinely trying to obtain a complete, accurate version of the attorney's question. This interpreter does all her consecutive interpreting by noting down questions in shorthand, a rare skill among interpreters. Most interpreters use a variety of notetaking methods that incorporate only the key concepts of a speaker's utterance and rely on memory to provide the rest of the utterance. Because this interpreter takes notes in shorthand, she is able to read back a question or an answer in the source language in its entirety. This makes for potentially remarkable accuracy in interpreting, and in fact this particular interpreter is exceptionally skilled at rendering accurate interpretations. She does so, however, at a cost to the proceeding. As can be seen in 8, she first makes a statement to the examining attorney about the way she interpreted the question; she then reads aloud the attorney's question as she has taken it down in shorthand; and finally for the clarity of the court record, she refers to the witness in the third person ("And he answered 'yes'"), something that violates the guidelines of court interpreting.[11] At this point in the sequence, however, the interpreter is correct in assessing the need for third-person reference, for if she had simply

[11] This sequence is taken from a deposition of a material witness before a federal magistrate in federal court. Whereas the witness himself has done something illegal, namely entering the United States without papers authorizing such entry, the case in which he is testifying is that of the person accused of smuggling him and other undocumented aliens into the United States. Thus the testimony of this witness becomes part of the court record of the upcoming trial. The magistrate who presided over this and most of the other depositions of illegal aliens usually allowed the aliens to return to Mexico, their point of entry, and prosecuted only those who had been habitual offenders of the crime of illegal entry.

said, "yes," the attorney might well have repeated the question, in order to make sure that the "yes" response was in fact a reply to his last question. In reality, what has happened during this segment of witness examination is a separation of attorney question from witness answer over time, and the additional element of lapsed time is due to the clarification attempts by the interpreter.

A situation that commonly results in an interpreter's request for the attorney to repeat a question is that following a ruling on an objection. Because of the time lag between the uttering of an attorney's question and the ultimate ruling by the judge after an objection has been raised, interpreters relying on memory for consecutive interpretation will have to ask that the question be repeated. This can be done either by having the court reporter read back the question or by asking the attorney to repeat it himself. In the next sequence the interpreter chooses the latter tactic. What is interesting in her request for a repetition is the metacommentary on interpreting as a skill ("Would you repeat the question, sir, so I can do it justice please?").

10.
> *Defense attorney:* You don't believe things will be better for you if you cooperate with the officials?
> *Interpreter:* ¿Pero está Ud. atestiguando, señor, porque Ud. cree que las cosas le van a salir mejor si Ud. atestigua?
> *Witness:* No no, yo no sé, yo, yo no más estoy diciendo lo que sé. (Oh no, I don't know, I'm only saying what I know.)[12]
> *Prosecuting attorney:* Pardon me, your honor; objection. Hasn't answered.
> *Interpreter [addressing witness]:* Está, este, está objetando el Señor Licenciado a la pregunta. [The attorney is, uh, is objecting to the question.]
> *Judge:* Well, I, I'll overrule the objection, but I, I think the witness is having some difficulty in understanding what you're getting at, Mr. McGee.
> *Defense attorney:* I'll try to take a different tactic, sir.
> *Judge:* Well, uh.
> → *Interpreter [addressing attorney]:* Would you repeat the question, sir, so I can do it justice please?
> *Defense attorney:* Do you believe that things might go better for you if you cooperate with the officials?

A second way in which the interpreter enters into dialogue with the attorney is by informing him of the interpretation that she has just made. This appears to be a tacit way of asking the attorney for approval of an interpretation that the interpreter senses may be somewhat off the mark in its wording. The following examples typify this type of interpreter attempt at clarification:

---

[12] English translations are provided in parentheses by this writer whenever either Spanish witness testimony or interpreter side comments are not interpreted into English for the benefit of the court.

11.

Prosecuting attorney: Do you feel that you could follow the path if you would go through it during the day? Is that the problem, that it was dark and you could not pick out landmarks?

→ *Interpreter [addressing attorney]:* Sir, the way I put the question is, "It is your answer, then, that if it were during the day you could follow that road. But it was because it was at night that you cannot follow that road." And his answer was, "Yes."

12.

Prosecuting attorney: When you got to the motel did you get a room?

Interpreter: Cuando Uds. llegaron al, al motel, ah ¿se registraron Uds. para que les dieran un cuarto?

Witness: No, no fui yo, no hablo inglés.

→ *Interpreter [addressing attorney]:* I, I asked the question, "Did you register so that a room would be given to you?" and he said, "It wasn't I; I don't speak English."

13.

Prosecuting attorney: Had you expected that you would have to pay another eight-hundred dollars?

Interpreter: Esperaba Ud. tener que pagar ochocientos dólares adicionales, señora?

Witness: ¿Adicionales, cómo?

→ *Interpreter:* Uh, I said, "Were you ups—, were you, uh, did you expect to pay, uh, eight hundred additional dollars?" and she doesn't understand the word "additional" in Spanish that I used.

Prosecuting attorney: Eight-hundred more dollars?

Interpreter: Ah, ¿esperaba Ud. tener que pagar ochocientos dólares más, además de lo que ya había pagado?

In sequence 13, rather than interpreting for the attorney the witness' answer, an answer that reveals the witness' failure to comprehend the question, the interpreter gives an accounting of her interpretation of the question and reports to the attorney what she perceives to be the difficulty that the witness is experiencing. In this case, then, a report on her interpretation is intended to speed up the question/answer sequence at a point where there is a comprehension gap on the part of the witness. If the interpreter had followed the guidelines of court interpreting, at such a problematical point she would have interpreted the witness' query, "¿Adicionales, cómo?" ("Additional ones? How's that?") An interpretation of the witness' response would have entailed the attorney's rephrasing of the question and the subsequent interpretation of that question into Spanish. By not following the guidelines, the interpreter has cut short the length of the interchange, thereby making the examination process more efficient. She has also, however, taken on a role not intended by the courts.

Some of the dialogues initiated by interpreters for the purpose of clarifying attorney questions become quite lengthy. In sequence 14, the interpreter addresses the attorney three times, once to inform him of the interpretation she has just completed, once to clarify what he meant by his question, and once to inform him about the revised interpretation she is about to make. Thus, the interpreter becomes much more prominent than is customary in the examination process.

14.

Defense attorney: What about the man that you've, that you describe or that you know by the name "Calvo"? Was he in the truck or did he get out of the truck?

Interpreter: Eh, y si nos referimos al hombre que Ud. describe al cual se refiere Ud. como "el calvo", ¿dijo él algo? La persona que Ud. identificó al que Ud. se refiere como "el calvo", ¿se quedó él adentro del troque o se bajó del troque?[13]

Witness: Se quedó en él. [He stayed in it.]

→ *Interpreter [addressing attorney]:* Excuse me. I thought I made the sentence, sir, in the sense that—did he say anything—because I thought that you were continuing the other question.

Defense attorney [addressing interpreter]: Okay, yes.

→ *Interpreter [addressing attorney]:* What you mean is, "Did Calvo stay in the truck or did he get out of the truck?" Is that the question?

Defense attorney [addressing interpreter]: Yes.

→ *Interpreter [addressing attorney]:* Excuse me, I'm gonna make it now, then, "He remained in the truck."

Experienced court interpreters are constantly aware of the court record and are conscious of the fact that their interpretations are being reported as they speak. The prefatory phrase of the interpreter in sequence 14 ("I'm gonna make it now. . .") reflects the fact that she is very much addressing the court record, more so perhaps than she is addressing the attorney. Sometimes, fidelity to the record leads interpreters to challenge or correct an attorney during his examining routine. Sequences 15 and 16 exemplify the ways in which interpreters can challenge an attorney and demonstrate the ways in which attorneys react to the challenge.

15.

Defense attorney: What was his destination?

→ *Interpreter [addressing attorney]:* I translated that, sir.

Defense attorney [addressing attorney]: Try again.

16.

Defense attorney: All right. When he came back with the other man.

→ *Interpreter [addressing attorney]:* Uh. . .Excuse me, sir. Excuse me, he said, "With a friend."

Defense attorney [addressing interpreter]: Okay, okay. When he came back with the other person, did you go any place with the person you've identified in the court and that other person?

---

[13] It should be noted that any discrepancies between an utterance in the source language and its interpretation will not be dealt with in this chapter.

In both 15 and 16, the attorney is irritated by the interpreter's attempt to correct him. In sequence 15, his reply is a verbal "put-down" of the interpreter: He sticks to his guns. In sequence 16 the attorney accedes to the interpreter's indirect request for a correction but does so through a compromise term. Thus, although the interpreter reminds him that the witness had used the word "friend," and the attorney is referring to "the other man," the attorney comes up with the neutral noun, "person." This is a concession to the interpreter but not a complete buckling to her will. His tone of annoyance is reflected in the prefatory, "Okay, okay."

Sometimes an interpreter will try to correct, or alter, the phrasing of an attorney's question on some syntactic basis. An interpreter's explicit attempt to achieve such an alteration produced the following dialogue:

17.
Defense attorney: So, are you saying that you wouldn't have told the border patrol officer.
Interpreter: Excuse me, sir. I have to tell you that you're using the negative all the time and his answer really doesn't mean much when you're using the negative form of questioning because when he answers "no" it actually comes out "yes." If you say, "Wouldn't do this," or "Wouldn't do that, yes I wouldn't." You see what I mean? You're using the negative and it's confusing him tremendously.

What the interpreter is trying to explain to the attorney is a difference between the linguistic habits of English speakers and Spanish speakers. When an English speaker answers "No" to a negatively worded question, as in 17a, the speaker is responding in the negative. A Spanish speaker, however, can answer either "Sí" or "No" to the same question and still be answering the question negatively, as 17a demonstrates.

17a.
A: So she wasn't at the bar that night?
B: (American) No [= no, she wasn't]
C: (Latin American) Yes [= yes, you're right: she wasn't there]
No [= no, she wasn't]

The interpreter in sequence 17 was trying to explain this point to the attorney but failed to do so adequately.

In other instances, when something in the wording of a question seems ambiguous to the interpreter, or a case of polysemy[14] occurs, she will realize that by choosing one sense of a word rather than the other she runs the risk of incorrectly interpreting the question. At such a moment, a well-trained interpreter is supposed to request a clarification of the attorney. In the case of sequence 18 however, the interpreter's feeling that the phrase "hit with a gun" is ambiguous would seem to be off the mark. Thus, although it is the intention

[14] Polysemy is a term used in semantics to refer to a word having more than one sense, or meaning.

of the interpreter to clarify what she perceived to be an ambiguity, the net result is a clarification procedure that need not have occurred had the interpreter had a native speaker's command of English.

18.
   Prosecuting attorney: Okay, now after he tried to hit you with the gun, what happened after that?
→ *Interpreter [addressing attorney]:* Excuse me, I have to clarify something. When you say "hit with a gun," do you mean "shoot with a gun," or actually "hit him with a gun"?
   Prosecuting attorney [addressing interpreter]: No, I mean, strike with the gun, not shoot.
→ *Interpreter [addressing attorney]:* Okay, I'm sorry, I, that wasn't clear.
   Prosecuting attorney [addressing interpreter]: Okay.

The interpreter is wrong in intuiting an ambiguity in the phrase, "hit with a gun." Whereas an expression such as, "He was hit," is in fact ambiguous in the sense of being shot, on the one hand, and of being given a blow, on the other, "hit you with a gun" is much more likely—given the context—to have only the latter meaning. It is probably the nonnative intuition of the Spanish-dominant interpreter that finds ambiguity in the phrase. Furthermore, if one notices that the interpreter's second example ("actually, 'hit him with a gun'") is virtually a repetition of the original phrase with the addition of the pronoun "him" and a shift from a definite article ("the") to an indefinite one ("a"), it becomes apparent that the interpreter's attempts to verbalize a clarification were defective because of her inability to elucidate the matter adequately on the spur of the moment. Similarly, the interpreter's attempt to explain via illustration the problematical aspects of interpreting negatively worded questions also failed, as she was unable to state her case with sufficient clarity. The net result is further confusion for the examining attorney and resentment on the interpreter's part. In some small way such clarification attempts must make the attorney feel that his questioning procedure is being challenged and by someone whom he considers not to be professionally his equal.[15]

---

[15] Ethnographic observation of court interpreters in the variety of courthouses that were visited by this investigator has revealed that the interpreter is considered to hold an occupational status on a par with court reporters, that is, persons whose status falls well below that of a lawyer or judge, yet is somewhat higher than that of a clerk or bailiff. Evidence of this occupational standing is the fact that interpreters' offices are generally placed within or alongside of offices of court clerks and that socialization on the part of interpreters is overwhelmingly with clerks, bailiffs, and law enforcement officers, rather than with lawyers or judges. Thus, court interpreters tend to eat lunch, share birthday celebrations, and even hold lunch-hour Tupperware parties with court clerks, reporters, and other secretarial-type staff. One reason for the relatively low occupational categorization that interpreters are placed into is the fact that many court interpreters are former clerks themselves. Through their bilingual capacity they often find a more specialized niche in the courthouse occupational structure.

5.3. Clarifying the Witness' Answer

Interpreters often halt the examination process because of a problem related to the witness' answer. This may concern the linguistic problems posed in translating a specific word (see examples 19–23), a grammatical construction that differs from language to language (see 24–25), the apparent inadequacy of the witness' response (examples 26–27), the failure of the answer to be heard or to be produced (examples 28–30), the tendency of witnesses to make comments to the interpreter on the side (see 32–35). Each of these categories is considered in the discussion below.

One very common type of problem that leads interpreters to clarify a witness' answer is the difficulty of translating words that vary dialectally in the Spanish-speaking world. Sequence 19 typifies the interpreter's attempts to clarify the meaning of a Spanish word that has different referents in different countries. The fact that the interpreter is aware of the variance in meaning speaks well of her, and her need to stop the examination process is motivated by her keen desire for accuracy.

19.

→ *Interpreter [addressing attorney]:* Excuse me, he used a term that's, *buso*, that I'm not familiar with, sir. May I clarify if he means a sweater or a shirt?
Interpreter: ¿Qué quiere decir "buso" señor?
Witness: Es una especie de chaqueta saco.
Interpreter [addressing attorney]: Oh, it's something like a jacket, he says.

In the examination of a witness that is cited next, the issue revolves around the multiple meanings of the verb *cancelar*. It should be noted that the attorney is irritated by the interpreter's interruption, considering her commentary to be something to which the jury should not have access.

20.

Prosecuting attorney: All right, what else was said, if anything?
Interpreter: ¿Qué más se ha. . . [What else was. . .]
Witness: No es no más, o sea que era la segunda parte que le daba, era la parte del trato.
Interpreter: That is, that this was the second portion, uhm, of the money, and the last installment. And this would cancel the deal . . . would *complete* the deal.
→ *Interpreter [addressing attorney]:* Excuse me, sir, the South Americans, I believe, and . . . and I would like to pursue this, but I. . . In my past experience they use the verb *cancelar*, "cancel," as "to complete." May I pursue if this is what he means?
Prosecuting attorney: Your honor, can, can we discuss this, uh, off the record? I . . . I don't think it's proper for the jury to
Judge: Very well.

Sometimes the interpreter halts the examination process because she has heard a Spanish word that she is totally unfamiliar with. Most codes of ethics for court interpreters specify that whenever such a linguistic problem arises, it is the interpreter's duty to inquire as to the meaning of the word, so that she may interpret it correctly. It is usually only the most competent interpreters who do so, however, because it requires a great deal of self-confidence to admit to a lack of knowledge in public, and on the record. In the following example, the word that the interpreter must inquire about, *pani*, turns out to be a Spanish-speaker's mispronunciation of the English word "Spanish."

21.

> *Witness:* Donde llegamos, llegamos a al Hotel Pani nada más, pero no sé cómo ha, ha llegado todo esto.
> *Interpreter:* Well, he arrived to where the *pani* is.
> → *Interpreter [addressing the judge]:* He uses a term I'm not acquainted with. May I pursue what he means by *pani*, sir?
> *Judge:* Yes.
> *Interpreter:* ¿Qué quiere decir "pani" señor?
> *Witness:* Es el Hotel Spanish.

Some lawyers are not very interested in what seem to them to be overly fine semantic distinctions. Rather than cooperate with the interpreter's attempt to clarify the meaning of a word uttered by the witness, they will override the interpreter's request and use a different lexical item instead. In the next example the interpreter tries to point out that the word *troque* could possibly mean "station wagon" or "truck." Skirting the issue of how to refer to it in English, in his next question the attorney avoids both choices and uses a third, more general term, "vehicle." By doing, so, however, he is minimizing the significance of the possibility that the noun *troque* may have two different meanings. Thus, the efforts of the interpreter to achieve semantic precision are often construed by attorneys as hairsplitting or nitpicking.

22.

> *Prosecuting attorney:* Where was Mr. Sandoval at that time?
> *Interpreter:* ¿Dónde estaba el señor Sandoval en ese tiempo?
> *Witness:* Fue por el troque.
> *Interpreter:* He had gone to get the, uh, truck.
> *Prosecuting attorney:* Did he say that⌐
> → *Interpreter [addressing attorney]:*   ⌐It could also, excuse me, it could also mean "station wagon," because "camioneta" means both things.
> *Prosecuting attorney:* Before he left, did he tell you he was going to get the vehicle?

An interesting case involving polysemy is 23, in which what is at issue for the interpreter is her inability to recall how she interpreted a polysemous word the previous day during the examination of a witness. The word in question is *moreno*, which can mean either "dark" or "black," and the same witness is testifying for the second day. It is clear from observing these interpreters that once an interpreter has decided on a particular target language equivalent for a given word in the source language, she will try to stick to that lexical item each time it occurs. Thus, in 23, the interpreter would like to continue using the English equivalent of *moreno*, but cannot remember which meaning she had been using the day before.

23.
Interpreter [addressing judge]: Um, your honor, I have, uh, uh, a little uh, worry of when she said, "a fat, a fat black man" or "a fat dark man." I'm not sure if I translated it "dark" or, or "black" and I would like to determine if this,—Oh, that was objected to. Excuse me. All right, thank you. All right, okay.

Problems of grammar seem to involve the lengthiest type of interpreter-initiated interruptions. In episode 24, the judge is clearly annoyed by the interchange between interpreter and attorney. Interestingly, the interpreter reaches a compromise solution to the problem of choosing between the pronouns "I" and "he": She uses the impersonal term "somebody." The irritation of the judge is expressed in his reaction, "All right, all right. All right, let's just,—."

24.
Defense attorney: Would you relate that conversation?
Interpreter: ¿Puede Ud. relatarnos esa conversación?
Witness: No, si podía acompañarlo a los Esta, a Estados Unidos. Si yo no conozco, y no hablo inglés.
Interpreter: Uh, could I accompany him.
→ *Interpreter [addressing attorney]:* I really don't know because he's using a pronoun that could—can be "I asked if he could, uh, or, if I could accompany him." It could apply to both, so it's a very ambiguous answer. Somebody asked if he could accompany him to the United States. It could be "he." It could be "I."
Defense attorney: Your honor, I don't think that's the entire answer. I think the answer was, "I asked to accompany him to the U- United States because I don't speak English."
→ *Interpreter [addressing attorney]:* Well, I was going to translate the other part, "I don't speak English," but the thing is that he didn't use a pronoun, sir.
Judge: All right, all right. All right, let's just,—we understand that. You state the, the complete answer then.
Interpreter [addressing judge]: Yes.
Interpreter [addressing the record]: Somebody accompanied him to the United States. Uh, I don't speak English.

The interpreter is quite correct in noting the ambiguity of the verb *podía*. All verbs of the -ir infinitive class in Spanish are semantically ambiguous among the first, second, and third person singular (i.e., *podía* could mean either "I could," or "you could," or "he/she could"). What is interesting in this case is that the defense attorney is bilingual and thus feels competent to dispute the interpreter's interpretation. The pairing of Spanish-speaking attorneys with Spanish-speaking defendants is quite common in courthouses located in the Southwest. Both prosecutors offices and public defenders offices make a conscious effort to assign Spanish-speaking lawyers to Spanish-speaking clients. Thus there often are occasions when bilingual attorneys quarrel with interpreters over the interpretation of statements made by witnesses or defendants.

In their attempts at clarifying some grammatical aspect of witness testimony, interpreters can engage attorneys in lengthy interchanges. In 25, the interpreter's explanation of the witness' answer is more of an indirect criticism of the attorney's phrasing of the question. From her tone she is clearly vexed with him, perhaps because she knows that she has made this point before, and the attorney has not altered the wording of his questions in accordance with her suggestion. It should be noted that the dialogue occurs in the middle of the attorney's examination of a witness, and becomes, in effect, a conversation in its own right. Throughout the discussion neither one addresses the witness.

25.

> *Attorney:* Has he said that he didn't, that he crossed the border 100 meters from the port of entry?
>
> → *Interpreter:* That's, that's what I understand that he said, that he crossed 100 meters from the port of entry, yes.
>
> *Attorney:* He didn't say Brownsville, Texas?
>
> → *Interpreter:* That's what I take it he said, yes.
>
> *Attorney:* And on the issue of the time, that he did not tell the border patrol agent "7:30"?
>
> → *Interpreter:* Uh, sir, the la—, the question that I was referring to that was mixed up was, "You wouldn't have told the border patrol agent something different from what you're telling us here?"
>
> *Attorney:* Uh, okay.
>
> → *Interpreter:* And he said, "No." You see, that doesn't mean anything. "Wouldn't," "No I wouldn't have" or "Yes, I would not have," it, it could mean either, and it's very ambiguous, so this is why I would appreciate it if you would make the questions in the affirmative.
>
> *Attorney:* I'll go along to the next question and answer. I'm going to ask him about Mr. Chavarría. I'm going to quote again to you from the question and answer that I have on this piece of paper, which says: Question from the border patrol agent: "Did you approach the men?"

In her subtle admonition of the attorney, the interpreter is not completely clear herself on the grammatical point that is troubling from the point of view of interpreting. Her claim is that the witness' answer of "No" to the question "You wouldn't have told the border patrol agent. . ." is ambiguous, meaning either that he wouldn't have told the agent or that he would have told the agent something different. She is, however, mistaken in finding ambiguity in the negative response, for it can only be taken to mean that he would not have told the agent. What she is confusing here is the response "No" with the alternative response "Yes" to the negatively worded question. A response of "Yes" could in fact be interpreted in two ways: as "Yes, I would have" or "Yes, it is the case that I wouldn't have," although the second sense of "Yes" is a far less likely one in spoken American English. In effect, then, the interpreter is touching upon a question format that is indeed problematical for her as an interpreter, although the particular answer that the witness gave was in fact not ambiguous. Thus the outcome of the dialogue for the attorney was a persisting confusion. He could not see any ambiguity in the witness' answer, and rightfully so. The outcome for the interpreter was a sense of frustration, as she saw that she had not gotten through to the attorney, whom she considered to be grammatically dense for not grasping her point.

Even though interpreters ideally should add nothing of their own words to explain or clarify a witness' or defendant's answer, even when the answer seems meaningless, interpreters often do offer unsolicited explanations at such moments. It should be kept in mind, as has been pointed out, that a nonsensical answer on the part of the witness or defendant casts doubt on the quality of the interpreter's interpretation. It may occur to those in the courtroom that the interpreter either has interpreted the question poorly into Spanish or else has interpreted the answer incorrectly into English. In sequence 26 the witness' answer clearly bears no relation to the attorney's question, and the interpreter decides to clear the confusion immediately.

26.
> *Attorney:* Can you describe for us what he looked like, ah, from your memory of that night?
> *Interpreter:* ¿Puede Ud. describir la apariencia del chofer según recuerda Ud., según su memoria de esa noche?
> *Witness:* ¿Escribir? No, pos no sé escribir.
> *Interpreter:* You mean "write"?
> → *Interpreter [addressing attorney]:* Descri, escribir, eh, eh, in Spanish "describe" and "write" are very similar. Um, he says, "I don't know how to write."
> *Attorney:* Can you tell us about his appearance on that night?

The attorney accepts the interpreter's explanation and takes it into consideration in rephrasing his question. He drops the word "describe" and refers instead to the "appearance" of the man in question.

The answers of Spanish-speaking witnesses or defendants may not necessarily be as completely off the mark as in 26. In the case of 27 the witness misunderstands the attorney's question, confusing point of departure for a job with location of the job.

27.
> *Defense attorney:* And where was he going to take you to work from, from what point was he going to take you to work?
> *Interpreter:* ¿Y de qué punto los iba él a llevar a trabajar?

Witness: Donde hubiera trabajo.
Interpreter: Wherever there would be work.
→ *Interpreter [addressing attorney]:* Sir, excuse me, I asked "From what point would he take you to work?" and he answered, "Wherever there was work."

Interestingly, the sort of misunderstanding demonstrated by this witness is something that could just as easily have happened to a native speaker of English who had been asked the same question. A native English speaker testifying on the stand might have misunderstood the question for a variety of reasons: nervousness, lack of sufficient attention, deficiencies in the manner in which the attorney conveyed the question (e.g., mumbling, speaking in too low a volume), or incompetence on his own part (e.g., low level of intelligence, unfamiliarity with formal English-speaking style). Finally, a native English speaker might have answered as did the Mexican illegal alien in 27, if he had been deliberately trying to conceal information from the court. In other words, a native English speaker's tangential answer might have made him appear either incompetent or deliberately evasive. The Mexican witness in this case might also have appeared incompetent or evasive to those in the courtroom. The interpreter's clarifying intervention, however, seems to be an accounting for his reply. Certainly in Case 26, where the interpreter clearly does account for the witness' defective answer with an explanation of the sound similarity between *describir* and *escribir*, the interpreter achieves a certain degree of mitigation for the witness' defective reply. To some extent, because of the interpreter's interrupting, he comes off appearing less incompetent, less evasive.

There are times when the interpreter must make herself heard in order to add to a witness' testimony that either has not been heard aloud or has not been given clearance by the judge. In the case of the former, it is often a matter of the witness having added something to an answer, while the attorneys are engaged in the next verbal activity (e.g., formulating the next question, addressing the judge), or else while the interpreter is finishing rendering her interpretation. The three sequences, 28, 29, and 30, illustrate this type of interpreter clarification of a witness' or defendant's testimony.

28.
   Defense attorney: So you and Mr. White were the only two people in the car?
   Interpreter: De manera que Ud. y el señor White eran las únicas dos personas que venían en el carro?
   Witness: Sí, porque él entró por donde se debe pasar, ¿no?
   Interpreter: Yes, because you see, he entered through where one should cross.
→ *Interpreter [addressing attorney]:* Excuse me. He added something I didn't hear.
   Interpreter [addressing witness]: ¿A través de dónde?
   Witness: O sea, por donde se pasa legal.
   Interpreter: Through where you, one crosses legally.

29.

Witness: No, no acordamos nada porque íbamos ya a arreglarnos acá ya llegando a la casa.

Interpreter: We did not agree on a specific amount, because we were going to agree on the amount once we arrived at our home.

Witness: A nuestra casa acá.

Interpreter [addressing attorney]: Excuse me, she added, "At our home over here."

30.

Prosecuting attorney: And do you recall meeting her once before in Juárez.

Interpreter: ¿Se acuerda Ud. de haberse encontrado Ud. con ella una vez antes en Juárez?

Witness: Mm, no.

Prosecuting attorney: The first time you met her.

Interpreter: ¿La primera vez que la conoció? ¿La primera vez que la conoció?

Witness: Fue en Juárez.

→ *Interpreter [addressing attorney]:* She answered "No" to the first part of your question and then she hasn't answered anything to the last part of the question. I repeated the last part of your question, "The first time you met her," and she answers, "It was in Juárez."

Sequence 30 is a rather complicated explanation and rather difficult for a listener to follow. The reason the interpreter is able to refer to the "first part of your question" and "the last part of the question" is that she has noted down the entire question verbatim. Certainly a juror, and perhaps even a judge, who does not have the attorney's question written before him, would be confused by the interpreter's clarifying remarks.

In cases in which a question/answer sequence is halted by the opposing attorney's objection and the interpreter either prevents the witness from answering or else refrains from interpreting the witness' answer until the objection has been overruled, the interpreter will speak for the witness in the third person. As soon as she refers to the witness as "he" or "the defendant," she is speaking as herself, the interpreter, and is no longer carrying out the interpreting role in the prescribed fashion. Thus it is not the witness who is speaking into the court record but the interpreter. A case in point, 31, is that of an objection that has been overruled.

31.

Defense attorney: And she has been living in San Diego for about six years?

Interpreter: Y ella ha estado viviendo en San Diego como seis años?

Prosecuting attorney: I object your honor.

Interpreter [addressing witness]: Momentito, objetó la licenciada Ellsworth. [Just a moment, Miss Ellsworth has objected.]

Judge: The objection's overruled.

Interpreter: Overruled, sir?
Judge: Yes.
→ *Interpreter [addressing the attorney]:* Uh, the defendant answered "yes," sir.

During this objection sequence, because of the overlapping of attorney and interpreter speech, the witness' barely audible affirmative response, "Sí," is lost amid the loud objection and the concurrent Spanish interpreting that is going on. Thus, rather than wait for the question to be repeated to the witness, the interpreter speaks on her behalf, reporting to the court the answer that had been given.

5.4. Accounting for the Side Comments of Witnesses and Defendants

There are many occasions on which a witness or defendant who is testifying speaks on the side to the interpreter or begins addressing her personally and stops directing his answers to the examining attorney. It is the interpreter's obligation to inform the judge of any such comments when they occur. She must also account for any remarks that she herself may be making to the witness in return. For this reason, the interpreter must inform the judge, for the record, of any side conversations that may have occurred in the course of the examination procedure. It is an accounting of her own verbal behavior and a clarification of the witness' speech as well. Examples 32, 33, 34, and 35 illustrate this type of clarifying procedure.

32.
Witness: ¿Puede Ud. repetir la pregunta?
Interpreter: Could you repeat the question please?
Interpreter [addressing witness]: Yo no puedo repetirla sin que la repita la licenciada. [I can't repeat it without the attorney's repeating it.]
→ *Interpreter [addressing judge]:* She means for me to repeat the question, your honor. And I advised her I cannot repeat it unless I'm given permission to do so and the attorney will do so.

33.
Interpreter [addressing judge]: Uh, I, I just advised her that I had just translated what she had said.

34.
Defense attorney: All right. If they weren't questions do, were ya, were ya asked just to tell what had happened as far as what you could remember as far as entering the country?
Witness [addressing interpreter]: Ud. es la que estaba explicando. (You're the one who was doing the explaining.)
Interpreter [addressing witness]: O sea la intérprete, o sea yo estaba presente? (You mean the interpreter, you mean I was present?)
Witness [addressing interpreter]: Mhm.
Interpreter: Well, you see, you were the one,

→ *Interpreter [addressing attorney]:* Excuse me, sir, he's referring to me, the interpreter. "You were the one who was asking what had happened."

Defense attorney: Okay. There was an interpreter present, is that right?

35.

Prosecuting attorney: Did you know you were entering the country illegally?

Interpreter: Cuando Ud. entró a este país, señora, ¿sabía Ud. que estaba entrando ilegalmente?

Witness: Sí, señorita.

Interpreter: Yes, sir.

→ *Interpreter [addressing attorney]:* Excuse me. I'm advising her not to answer "Yes, ma'am" or "No, ma'am" because I'm just the interpreter. Excuse me.

Sequences 34 and 35 not only demonstrate how witnesses' comments to the interpreter cause the interpreter to halt the proceeding in order to make an accounting, but beyond that, they show that some witnesses in fact talk to the interpreter rather than to the attorney, during the examination process. Case 34 also is illustrative of the interpreter's need to disentangle a confused situation. When she begins interpreting the answer with, "Well, you see, you were the one. . .," she realizes that those in the courtroom might assume that the pronoun "you" refers to the attorney who has asked the question. The interpreter, knowing that to untangle this misunderstanding would take several question/answer sequences and would possibly produce irritation in the attorney and judge, forecloses such a possibility. She does so by setting matters straight immediately, before even completing the interpreting of the witness' answer. She thereby saves the court time and helps make the proceeding go more smoothly and with less frustration for the official partici-pants. She also, however, has intruded into the proceeding, and in so doing, has saved the witness from an examination sequence that may have made him appear foolish.

There are times when the interpreter's interpreting of side comments are not welcomed by the court, however. For example, in the next episode, in which a magistrate is warning material witnesses in a case not to discuss their testimony with anyone, one of the witnesses begins adding to his testimony. The interpreter, in the course of accounting for his additional remarks, is rather abruptly cut off by the judge. This is unsolicited commentary from the witness, and the judge apparently is not interested in hearing it.

36.

Judge: Mr. Campos, I want you to remember the warning of the court not to discuss this case or your testimony with anyone today, other than when you may be alone with any of the four attorneys in the case. You may step down.

Witness: Mi declaración es que he llegado, y he llegado solo y estoy diciendo,

→ *Interpreter [addressing judge]:* He says, sir, that he has made his statement that he arrived alone and that was all, and I am telling

Judge:
⎡
⎣There's no question con. . .

Interpreter [addressing judge]: No, I mean,
Judge [addressing witness]:   You may step down. We may have Juan
   Espinoza Fernández.

Thus, the willingness of judges to hear the explanatory remarks of interpreters is not limitless. Judges, as opposed to attorneys, have the power to
curtail interpreters in midstream.

6. CONTROLLING THE FLOW OF TESTIMONY

In all the cases that have been discussed in the preceding sections of this
chapter, the intrusiveness of the court interpreter has been seen to derive from
speech produced by her in reaction to problems she perceives as existing in
the questions of lawyers and in the answers of witnesses and defendants.
They constitute various sorts of clarification procedures. All of the comments
of the interpreter ought to be noted in the court record. Yet the interpreter
exerts her influence in the courtroom in another way as well, a way that may
appear far less obtrusive than the preceding cases to the attorneys and to the
judge, both of whom are sensitive primarily to the court record. This type of
verbal intervention does not enter the record because it is carried out in
Spanish.
     The interpreter often plays a decisive role in controlling the speech of
witnesses or defendants who are testifying on the stand. This additional and
potentially decisive role is one of controlling the flow of testimony. The
interpreter may achieve her own kind of pressure on witnesses or defendants
in one of two ways: She can urge or prompt them to speak, and she can get
them to be silent. Because the verbal mechanisms that the interpreter uses are
in Spanish, the other court officials may be only dimly aware of them. In any
event, judges and attorneys may not be very concerned about them because
they do not form part of the official record, and they do seem to be aimed at
aiding the smooth flow of judicial process. To what extent these controlling
mechanisms affect jurors' perceptions of the witness or defendant is an open
question. How they affect the psyche of the person who is testifying is yet
another.

6.1. Prompting the Witness or Defendant to Speak

Up to now the focus has been on intrusive effects on courtroom procedure resulting from the court interpreter's interpreting of witnesses' and
defendants' speech. However, the interpreter also performs another function,
one that is not intended to be part of her job description: managing the

witnesses' or defendants' speech. This management can take the form of prompting the witness to speak, or alternatively, urging him to silence.

As can be seen in the following examples, interpreters use certain prompting mechanisms to speed up a witness' reply to an attorney's question or to accelerate a response to the routine "Do-you-understand?"-type of question used by judges to address defendants during arraignments, changes of plea, and sentencings. The principal method that interpreters use to prompt witnesses or defendants to answer an attorney's or judge's question is to order them to answer. Interpreters generally accomplish this by using the imperative mood of the verb *contestar*, "answer." It can be used by itself, *¡Conteste!* or, for a more polite, less commanding tone, it is followed by the phrase *por favor*, "please." The sequences 37 through 39 illustrate the use of the more polite, less forceful, *Conteste, por favor*, and the commanding, *¡Conteste!*

37.

Judge: You and Mr. Martin would be entitled to have at least thirty days. [pause] Do you understand?

Interpreter: Ud. y el Licenciado Martin, o sea abogado, tendrían derecho a que se les concediere por lo menos treinta días. ¿Entiende Ud. señor?

→ *Interpreter [addressing defendant]:* Conteste por favor. (Please answer.)

Defendant: Sí.

Interpreter: Yes.

The desire on the part of the interpreter to prompt a response from someone being questioned by a judge is probably greater in the case of multiple witnesses or defendants. Perhaps because often no one defendant is singled out, but instead all are asked the same question at the same moment, defendants become reticent. In the following case, 38, the defendants are illegal aliens who are to serve as witnesses in the case against the "coyote," or smuggler, who was purportedly paid to bring them illegally into the United States.

38.

Judge: As witnesses each of you is entitled to be represented by an attorney. Do any of you have an attorney?

Interpreter: Como testigos que son, tienen Uds. el derecho de ser representados por un abogado. Alguno de Uds. tiene abogado que los represente?

→ *Interpreter [addressing defendants]:* Contesten por favor. (Please answer.)

Defendants: No.

Interpreter [addressing judge]: All answered "No," sir.

In sequence 39, the interpreter prompts the witness to answer the question of the examining attorney, even though the witness has in fact responded to the question with an affirmative "Mhm." What she is doing, in effect, is taking on the role typically played by the judge, who normally would admonish the witness to "answer 'yes' or 'no'" for the record because "parasegmental" types of answers such as "mhm" are not acceptable for the court record.[16]

39.
   Prosecuting attorney: And you had no papers or documents allowing you to come in lawfully, is that correct?
   Interpreter: Y Ud. no tenía documentos o papeles que lo autorizaran a entrar legalmente a los Estados Unidos? ¿Es esto correcto?
   Witness: Mhm.
→ *Interpreter [addressing witness]:* ¡Conteste! (Answer!)
   Witness: ¿Que no tenía papeles yo de migración de este lado?
   Interpreter: You mean I didn't have any immigration papers from this side?
   Prosecuting attorney: Right.
   Interpreter: Sí.

The question that one must ask is how observers in the courtroom view the person who is being prompted. Does the witness look hesitant, unsure, or does he or she seem unwilling to answer? Does the interpreter's prompting give the judge, jury, or attorneys the impression that the witness is uncooperative? In the case of a defendant who is being asked a formalized set of questions by a judge, does he or she appear to the judge to be uncooperative? In reality, if a witness or defendant does not answer a question quickly, such hesitancy can often be a symptom of a failure to comprehend the question. A frightened witness or defendant may not feel confident enough to say, "I don't understand." Does the witness or defendant feel pressured by the interpreter into a premature response, when in fact he or she does not understand the question but is afraid to say so? These are areas of inquiry that need to be pursued.

A second way in which the interpreter prompts a witness or defendant to speak is to request a repetition of something he or she has already said. Apparently, most of the time this is done because the interpreter has forgotten part of the witness' testimony and needs to have it repeated so that she may give a complete interpretation. Sometimes the interpreter claims not to have heard the testimony well, but because she is physically very close to the witness on such occasions, the claim to not having heard may in fact often be a way of having the statement repeated when in reality she has forgotten a part of it. It should be kept in mind that consecutive interpreting, the mode of interpreting recommended for use with witnesses who are testifying, is perhaps the most difficult of the modes of interpreting. Memory plays a vital role in accurate consecutive interpreting, as do good note-taking skills. When an interpreter has not developed her note-taking ability to a sufficient degree, her need to have testimony repeated for her will be greater.

[16] The term "parasegmental," coined by Walker (1985:123), refers to "any feature of *speech* which either (1) coexists with (para) a word (segment) or stretch of words; or (2) takes the place of a word, or both."

Interpreters use several verbal tactics for getting a witness or defendant to repeat an answer for her. Nearly all of them involve a query directly to the person testifying, in Spanish, rather than a formal request to the judge for a repetition. One common prompt is the term *¿Cómo?* "What?" This is perhaps the bluntest, most direct way of getting the speaker to repeat his utterance. Another basic technique, the claim of not having heard well, can be accomplished by phrases such as, *No lo oí,* "I didn't hear you," or *No oí, no oí,* "I didn't hear." Variations on this type of mechanism involve additional explanatory statements, such as, *No puedo oírlo, ¿no puede hablar más alto?* "I can't hear you, can't you speak more loudly?" or *No lo oí, habla muy despacio y hay mucho que no lo oigo,* "I don't hear you; speak more slowly, there's a lot I don't hear from you." Finally, interpreters often use the expression, *Por favor, repita* "Please repeat." Often the request that the witness repeat the answer is done without consulting the judge or attorney. However, interpreters who are conscious of court protocol will inform the judge and attorney that they are asking for a repetition. The very act of informing them constitutes an indirect means of obtaining approval for such a verbal action. A typical way of handling this type of a request for a repetition is presented in 40.

40.
> *Prosecuting attorney:* Where in Guatemala were you born?
> *Interpreter:* ¿En dónde en Guatemala nació Ud.?
> *Witness:* Santa Cruz de Solalá Quetzaltenango.
> → *Interpreter [addressing witness]:* Por favor, repita.
> *Interpreter [addressing attorney]:* I'm asking her to repeat. It's quite long sir.

It should be noted that even in a case such as 40, where the interpreter does inform the court officials of her desire for a repetition, the request to the witness is made before the act of informing the judge, rather than the other way around. Thus, by the time the interpreter has informed the judge and attorney of her need to have the testimony repeated, the request is a *fait accompli.*

6.2. Silencing the Witness or Defendant: The Problem of Handling Objections

There are occasions in the courtroom when a witness or defendant is either interrupted midstream in a statement or is prevented from beginning his statement altogether. The interruption of a defendant commonly occurs at the initial appearance (or arraignment, in courts where the initial appearance is not a separate proceeding). There defendants frequently begin discursive explanations of why they are wrongfully being accused of the particular crime that they believe they are charged with. As soon as defendants begin such speeches, judges will tend to cut them off, advising them not to say anything further at that time and to wait until they have spoken to their defense counsel. In addition, judges warn defendants that anything they say at that time could be held against them in subsequent proceedings. When such admonitions come from judges, it is the interpreter's task both to interpret them and to successfully stop the defendant's stream of speech. In fact, judges typically instruct interpreters to get defendants to be quiet right away, before they incriminate themselves. Interpreters successfully stop the defendant's speech by interrupting with an interjection such as, *Señor, señor*, "Sir, sir," which serves to get the defendant's attention.

The second most common context in which a witness or defendant must be kept from speaking is during the course of an objection. From the vantage point of the court record, objections by nature are "messy" verbal exchanges: They usually involve an interruption of a speaker's speech and thereby result in overlapping speech. The overlap occurs when the attorney who is objecting speaks simultaneously with either the opposing attorney—during the formation of a question—or simultaneously with the witness on the stand. When the witness is aided by an interpreter, an additional vocal element is added to the equation. Objections that occur while an interpreter-assisted witness is testifying are highly confusing events for the spectator. Everyone seems to be speaking at once, and it is difficult for a moment to grasp what is being said or even to know who is saying it. Unless the observer himself can tune in to two or three different soundtracks simultaneously, he will not understand all the speech that is going on when one attorney is asking a question, the other is raising an objection, the interpreter is finishing interpreting the question of the examining attorney, and the judge is beginning to verbalize his decision to either sustain or overrule the objection.

Guidelines do exist on how interpreters should handle objections. In general, interpreters are expected to stop interpreting when an attorney makes an objection. The guidelines of the Judiciary Interpreters Association of Texas (Texas Judiciary, n.d.:2) state explicitly that,

> If counsel objects to a question, the interpreter must await the judge's ruling, even if the non-English speaking person has already given the answer. If the objection is sustained, the interpreter does NOT give the answer: if the objection is overruled, then the interpreter can give the answer, or ask to have the question and answer repeated by the court reporter or counsel.

The intent behind this guideline, which is consistent with the intent of attorneys who raise an objection during an all-English examination, is to prevent the witness from answering. However, even in all-English proceedings, witnesses often complete their answer as the objection is being made, before the judge has had a chance to make a ruling. In such cases, if the objection is sustained, the court reporter is told to strike the answer from the record, and the jury, if there is one, is instructed to ignore the answer that it may have heard. However, lawyers are well aware that an answer that has been heard is not automatically erased from the minds of jurors, simply because the judge has instructed the jurors to disregard it. A damaging bit of testimony can still leave its impact.

Despite the guidelines, however, observations of interpreter-assisted testifying show that there is a great deal of variation in the way that interpreters handle objections. Some interpreters stop interpreting the question in midcourse, at the moment at which the objection is made. Other interpreters not only complete the interpreting of the question but also go on to interpret the Spanish-speaking witness' answer. Completing the interpreting of the question leaves the door open to the possibility of the witness' answering it, and even if that answer is not interpreted into English, it will be heard. In the case of yes/no answers, which can form a sizable proportion of witness testimony, even non-Spanish-speaking jurors will be able to understand the meaning of Spanish *sí* and *no*. In the U.S. Southwest, where Hispanics make up a large part of the population, on any given jury several members may have a comprehension of Spanish, thereby having access even to narrative types of answers as well. In small towns on the U.S.–Mexico border, the Hispanic population can constitute a large majority of the total number of residents, and juries are aimed at reflecting the demographic character of the locale. Thus in most border towns, a majority of the members of a given jury could well understand Spanish testimony.

Nevertheless, there is a built-in factor limiting the likelihood of a non-English-speaking witness' answering a question to which an objection is being raised. The fact that the question must be interpreted first—and this ideally in consecutive mode, so that the interpreter does not begin interpreting until the attorney has finished uttering his question—results in a lag time in which the judge can make his ruling. Such a lag can prevent the witness from answering. When proceedings are carried out as usual, entirely in English, there is no such lag time, and so the possibility of a witness' answering a question that has been objected to is far greater than in situations where an interpreter is working with a witness. If the attorney who has posed the objectionable question hopes for an answer before the judge's ruling, the presence of the interpreter can interfere with his strategy, in that the interpreter inadvertently can prevent the witness from answering his question. Thus the interpreter unwittingly becomes an obstacle to one type of technique that attorneys employ in their questioning of witnesses.

Another element of variation introduced by the interpreter that can affect the outcome of an objection sequence is the use of simultaneous interpreting at the witness stand. Many interpreters have not mastered the skill of consecutive interpreting and therefore use simultaneous interpreting even when the consecutive mode is called for. Some interpreters use modified forms of consecutive interpreting. That is, they might allow half of a witness' utterance to be heard in Spanish and then begin interpreting while the witness is finishing, thus overlapping onto the second part of his utterance. Others do the entire testimony in simultaneous mode, including the attorney's questions as well. When an interpreter is using the simultaneous mode for an attorney's question, it means that she will complete her interpretation within a few seconds of the moment when the attorney stops speaking. This technique, then, will put the Spanish-speaking witness in a position that is virtually identical to that of an English speaker: He will be ready to answer at virtually the same moment, minus a few seconds. Thus, from the point of view of the attorney who has asked an objectionable question, the use of the simultaneous mode by the interpreter increases the likelihood of the witness' answering before the judge has made his ruling. Ironically, therefore, the interpreter who is unable to conform to the expected norm of using consecutive interpreting at the witness stand, ends up as a potential asset to the examining attorney: She opens up the possibility of the witness answering the lawyer's question.

Interpreters use a number of verbal means to prevent a witness from answering once an objection has been raised. Often they are successful, but sometimes they are not. In 42 and 43, the interpreter succeeds in keeping the witness from speaking. In 41, however, the monosyllabic answer, "No," is uttered before the interpreter can exercise her control over the speaker. Probably the most effective technique that an interpreter can use is the command, *¡No conteste!*, as in 42. Interpreters often preface the command with a brief explanation to the witness of what is occurring, as in 41, *Hay una objeción, no conteste*, "There's an objection, don't answer." At other times interpreters will halt the witness with an expression such as *Un momentito*, "Just a moment," as in 43. This last type of control mechanism is probably just as effective as the command, *¡No conteste!*, but it is more polite.

In Spanish, direct commands would not normally be given to people whom one does not know. They are restricted to use between persons who are in a socially asymmetrical relationship to each other and between whom power plays a significant role (e.g., parents/children, employers/employees). When Spanish-speaking persons use a direct command with someone they do not know, the social implication of this usage is that the person giving the command has authority over the addressee, as in the case of a policeman speaking to a motorist whom he has pulled over to the side of the road. Thus the interpreter who uses a plain direct command, without a prefatory explanation, is presenting herself as having authority over the witness. This type of verbal behavior exemplifies the highest form of linguistic coerciveness available to a Spanish speaker. Consequently, when the interpreter says to a witness, "Conteste," or "No conteste," the witness interprets the command as such and probably assumes that there is some degree of authority behind such an order.

Examples 41 through 43 demonstrate how the interpreter controls the speech of witnesses in the course of objections by attorneys. Essentially, the interpreter orders the witness not to answer the question, and later, after receiving clearance from the judge, gives the witness permission to speak.

41.
Judge [addressing defense attorney]: Mr. Langley.
Defense attorney: Thank you your honor. (pause) Mrs. Cordero, (pause) this individual that you mentioned earlier, uh, Felipe Guzmán, did, was he the one that told you and your husband to come to the United States?
Interpreter: Señora Cordero, este individuo que Ud. mencionó anteriormente, este Felipe Guzmán, fue la, la persona que les mencionó a Ud. y a su marido que viniera acá a Estados Unidos?
Prosecuting attorney: ⌈Objection,⌉ your honor. I believe it calls for hearsay.
Witness: ⌊No.⌋
→ *Interpreter [addressing witness]:* Hay una objeción, no conteste. (There's an objection; don't answer.)
Judge: The objection's overruled.
→ *Interpreter [addressing witness]:* Puede Ud. contestar. (You may answer.)
Witness: No.
Interpreter: No.

42.
Defense attorney: Have you ever been arrested, uh, by immigration or the border patrol in the United States?
Prosecuting attorney: I object, your honor.
Interpreter: ¿Alguna, en alguna ocasión la ha arrestado a Ud., la han arrestado a Ud. los oficiales de immigración o la patrulla de la frontera de los Estados Unidos?
→ ¡No conteste!
Judge: The objection is overruled.
→ *Interpreter [addressing witness]:* Hay una objeción, la denegaron, Ud. puede contestar. (There's an objection, it was dismissed, you may answer.)
Interpreter: ¿En alguna ocasión la han arrestado a Ud. oficiales de immigración u oficiales de patrulleros de la frontera en los Estados Unidos?
Witness: Sí.
Interpreter: Yes.

43.
Prosecuting attorney: I want you to look all around the courtroom and look closely at everybody in the courtroom and tell me if the pilot's in this courtroom, okay?
Interpreter: Quiero que busque Ud. cuidadosamente, y que busque si es que, si es que está el piloto aquí.
Defense attorney: Your honor, I object to this, uh, procedure. Uh, the witness *has* testified.
→ *Interpreter [addressing witness]:* Un momentito. (Just a moment.)
Judge: The objection's overruled.
→ *Interpreter [addressing witness]:* Oké, puede Ud. contestar. (Okay, you may answer.)

In trying to prevent a witness from answering a question that has been objected to, interpreters do not restrict themselves to verbal techniques. They often combine the linguistic mechanism with a nonverbal signal. That signal can be a raised hand motion, of the type used by traffic policemen to indicate a red light, or "STOP!" Another gesture used by some interpreters is putting their arm in front of the face of the witness, physically almost blocking his or her face from view. This is a very forceful technique and proves to be effective in both preventing a witness from speaking and stopping a witness who has already begun to speak. One wonders, however, how jurors perceive a witness whose speech must be blocked by another person's bodily intervention. Do such interventions cast a disparaging light on the witness? Do they make him appear timid and submissive, and consequently less competent than a monolingual English-speaking witness who would normally be cut off only verbally?

During an objection sequence, once the judge has overruled an objection, rather than to wait for the examining attorney to repeat his or her question, many interpreters take the initiative of prompting the witness to answer. This is done with the command, ¡Conteste!, or the more polite, Ud. puede contestar. It should be kept in mind, however, that whether the interpreter is prompting a defendant or a witness to answer, or preventing the individual from answering, in either case she is exercising a measure of linguistic coercion over that person. From her point of view and probably from the standpoint of the court, she is helping the proceeding run more smoothly and efficiently, and this is actually true. However, she is also to an extent controlling the speech of the testifying witness or defendant, and this is a role not intended for her by the judicial system.

7. CONCLUSION

This chapter has tried to demonstrate that the court interpreter is a new variable in the ecology of the American courtroom. She is an intrusive element, far from being the unobtrusive figure that judges and attorneys would like her to be. Her intrusiveness is manifested in multiple ways: from the introduction of the interpreter to the jury by the judge, to the common practice resorted to by judges and attorneys of addressing the interpreter rather than the witness when they ask their questions, to the need on the part of interpreters to clarify attorneys' questions and witnesses' answers. Included as well are the tangential side-sequence conversations engaged in by interpreters and testifying witnesses, interpreter silencing of witnesses who have begun to verbalize their answers, and interpreter prodding of witnesses when they are not responding appropriately to a question. Together, these intrusions make for judicial proceedings of a different nature.

One might ask whether these intrusions make a difference in the total scheme of things, that is, to what extent are they noticeable or do they count? A heightened awareness of the active role of the court interpreter is becoming more readily apparent with every new appeal that is made on grounds related to the interpreting process, and such appeals are multiplying at an increasingly rapid rate with every passing year (Berk-Seligson, 1990). Appeals are being made not merely on the basis of poor quality of interpreting, that is, lack of accuracy, but also on such grounds as interpreters holding private conversations with witnesses while at the stand and attorneys addressing the interpreter rather than the witness.[17] Thus it is becoming increasingly apparent to lawyers that the present state of court interpreting leaves some cause for concern. Fortunately, most of the problems that have been pointed out in this chapter are remediable. The first step toward remedying them is to bring them to the attention of court administrators, judges, and lawyers, for thought as to how to solve them.

Perhaps the most important finding of this study is that the interpreter affects whatever power an interrogating attorney may have over a testifying witness or defendant. Through her interruptions, many of which may be subsumed under what have been called here "clarification procedures," the interpreter unwittingly usurps some of the power of the interrogating attorney. Finally, it has been shown that the interpreter brings to the judicial proceeding her own measure of coercion; whereas sometimes her coercion works in consonance with the efforts of examining attorneys, many times it works against them.

The findings of this study inform us as to what goes on when the speech of attorneys, judges, witnesses, and defendants is mediated through the filter of a court interpreter. They do not reveal whether such a linguistic filtering leaves any impact on the perceptions of jurors listening to such bilingually conducted proceedings. New research by this investigator (Berk-Seligson, 1988, 1989, 1990) indicates that the court interpreter does indeed make a significant impact on the perceptions of persons asked to listen to interpreted

---

[17] Appeals on the basis of problematical interpreting are possible because there do exist baseline criteria for what constitutes good court interpreting. This baseline is derived from a number of different sources, all of which have one element in common: reliance on the expertise of professional interpreters. Essentially, baseline knowledge of ideal court interpreting practices comes from (1) the written guidelines of the various regional court interpreting associations (e.g., California Court Interpreters Association; Court Interpreters and Translators Association, an Eastern-seaboard-based organization; the Texas Judiciary Interpreters Association); (2) the standards set by federal and state certificate-granting institutions (e.g., at the federal level, the Office of U.S. Courts Administration); (3) courses in court interpreting, both full-blown certificate programs such as that provided by San Diego State University and intensive summer training programs such as that given by the Monterrey Institute of International Studies, the University of California at Berkeley, and the University of Arizona; and (4) workshops and lectures provided periodically at conferences held by the various court interpreting associations.

legal proceedings and that her impact is not only on monolingual English speakers but on bilingual Hispanics as well.[18] The court interpreter, therefore, must be viewed as an important new variable in the configuration of verbal participants in the American courtroom.

8. REFERENCES

Atkinson, J. M., & Drew, P. (1979). *Order in court: The organization of verbal behavior in judicial settings.* London: Macmillan.

Berk-Seligson, S. (1987). The intersection of testimony styles in interpreted judicial proceedings: Pragmatic alterations in Spanish testimony. *Linguistics, 25,* 1087–1125.

Berk-Seligson, S. (1988). The impact of politeness in witness testimony: The influence of the court interpreter. *Multilingua, 7*(4).

Berk-Seligson, S. (1989). The role of register in the bilingual courtroom: Evaluative reactions to interpreted testimony. *International Journal of the Sociology of Language, 79,* 79–91.

Berk-Seligson, S. (1990). *The bilingual courtroom: Court interpreters in the judicial process.* Chicago: University of Chicago Press.

Berreby, D. (1982). How Polish gypsies get justice in the U.S., and other court tales. *The National Law Journal,* December, 20, 1, 24–25.

Conley, J. M., O'Barr, W. M., & Lind, E. A. (1978). The power of language: Presentational style in the courtroom. *Duke Law Journal, 78,* 1375–1399.

Danet, B., & Bogoch B. (1980). Fixed fight or free-for-all? An empirical study of combativeness in the adversary system of justice. *British Journal of Law and Society, 7,* 36–60.

Danet, B., & Kermish, N. C. (1978). Courtroom questioning: A sociolinguistic perspective. In L. N. Massery II (Ed.), *Psychology and persuasion in advocacy* (pp. 413–441). Washington, DC: Association of Trial Lawyers of America, National College of Advocacy.

Danet, B., Hoffman, K. B., Kermish, N. K., Rafn, H. J., & Stayman, D. G. (1980). An ethnography of questioning. In R. Shuy & A. Schnukal (Eds.), *Language use and the uses of language: Papers from the Fifth Annual Colloquium on New Ways of Analyzing Variation* (pp. 222–234). Washington, DC: Georgetown University Press.

Dustan, R. (1980). Contexts for coercion: Analyzing properties of courtroom 'questions'. *British Journal of Law and Society, 7,* 61–77.

Erickson, B., Lind, E. A., Johnson, B. C., & O'Barr, W. (1978). Speech style and impression formation in a court setting: The effects of 'powerful' and 'powerless' speech. *Journal of Experimental Social Psychology, 14,* 266–279.

Grice, H. P. (1975). Logic and conversation. In P. Cole & J. L. Morgan (Eds.), *Syntax and semantics, Volume 3: Speech acts* (pp. 41–58). New York: Academic Press.

Hymes, D. (1962). The ethnography of speaking. In T. Gladwin & W. C. Sturtevant (Eds.), *Anthropology and human behavior* (pp. 13–53). Washington, DC: Anthropological Society of Washington.

Hymes, D. (1972). Models of the interaction of language and social life. In J. J. Gumperz and D. Hymes (Eds.), *Directions in sociolinguistics* (pp. 35–71). New York: Holt, Rinehart & Winston.

---

[18] This investigator has studied the impact of a number of different types of interpreter-induced alterations in witness testimony (Berk-Seligson, 1990). Supported by a grant from the National Science Foundation (#RII-8516746), the project has investigated the extent to which the behavior of the court interpreter has an impact on jurors' social/psychological evaluations of both testifying witnesses and examining attorneys.

Lakoff, R. (1975). Language and woman's place. New York: Harper & Row.
Lind, E. A., Erickson, B., Conley, J. M., & O'Barr, W. M. (1978). Social attributions and conversational style in trial testimony. Journal of Personality and Social Psychology 36, 1558–1567.
Linda, E. A., & O'Barr, W. M. (1979). The social significance of speech in the courtroom. In H. Giles & R. St. Clair (Eds.), Language and social psychology (pp. 66–87). College Park, MD: University Press.
O'Barr, W. M. (1982). Linguistic evidence: Language, power, and strategy in the courtroom. New York: Academic Press.
O'Barr, W. M., & Atkins, B. K. (1980). 'Women's language' or 'powerless language'? Women and language in literature and society. In S. McConnell-Ginet, R. Borker, & N. Furman (Eds.), Women and language in literature and society (pp. 93–110). New York: Praeger.
O'Barr, W. M., & Conley, J. M. (1976). When a juror watches a lawyer. Barrister 3, 8–11, 33.
O'Barr, W. M., & Lind, E. A. (1981). Ethnography and experimentation—partners in legal research. In B. D. Sales (Ed.), The trial process. New York: Plenum Press.
O'Barr, W. M., Walker, L., Conley, J. M., Erickson, B., & Johnson, B. R. (1976). Political aspects of speech styles in American trial courtrooms. Working Papers in Culture and Communication 1, 27–40. Philadelphia: Temple University Department of Anthropology.
Philips, S. U. (1979). Syntactic variation in judges' uses of language in the courtroom. Paper presented at the International Conference on Language and Social Psychology, University of Bristol, July 16–20.
Reese, B. P., & Reese, A. J. (1984). Case comment. Polyglot, June–July, 1.
Sacks, H., Schegloff, E., & Jefferson, G. (1974). A simplest systematics for the organization of turn-taking in conversation. Language, 50, 696–735.
Texas Judiciary Interpreters Association guidelines for interpreters. (No date). Unpublished manuscript.
Walker, A. G. (1986). From oral to written: The 'verbatim' transcription of legal proceedings. (Doctoral dissertation, Georgetown University, 1985). Dissertation Abstracts International, 47/01A, 169A.

9. CASES CITED

Mercure v. A. G. Saskatchewan, Supreme Court of Canada (1988). Appeal responds to Sask. Prov. Ct.: (1981), 44 Sask. R. 43, [1981] 4 W.W.R. 435; and Sask. C.A.: (1985), 44 Sask. R. 22, 24 D.L.R. (4th) 193, 23 C.C.C. (3d) 140, [1986] 2 W.W.R. 1.
State v. Vasquez, 101 Utah 444, 121 P. 2d 903 (1942).

Chapter 7

LANGUAGE AT WORK IN THE LAW
The Customs, Conventions, and Appellate Consequences of Court Reporting

ANNE GRAFFAM WALKER

1. INTRODUCTION

Court reporters are charged by law with the duty of making verbatim transcriptions of legal proceedings. The necessary presumption behind this task is that an accurate record of an oral/acted event can be made by writing down exactly what was said. But in any movement from the oral to the written, certain discrepancies between the original event and its written representation are bound to occur, discrepancies which are traceable not merely to inherent differences between spoken and written language, but in the case of court reporting, to the cultural and professional climates in which reporters do their jobs. Perhaps most particularly, discrepancies occur because of the intersection of beliefs which reporters hold about language and about their profession.

Traditionally, discrepancies in a verbatim record have been regarded by the legal profession pragmatically, their concern being reserved for discrepancies of an obvious sort: a misidentified speaker, a garbled stretch of speech, something missing, something added. These errors are usually handled on the local level, with the lawyers and judge involved negotiating any necessary

ANNE GRAFFAM WALKER • Forensic Linguistics Associates, 6404 Cavalier Corridor, Falls Church, Virginia 22044.

changes to the written record. There are other discrepancies, however, of a much more interesting and potentially much more influential type which, because they are not obvious, escape either concern or correction. These deviances from reality take the form, for example, of grammar that is "cleaned up" for one speaker but not another; dialect that is sanitized so that speakers from Boston, the Bronx, Iowa, India, and South America all "sound" alike on paper; and mm-hmms and unh–unhs that for the sake of "correctness" appear in print as Yes, and No. Because discrepancies of these and other types are unrecognized, they continue unabated, unstudied, and unregulated in the court reporting profession, and thus the written record of trials continues to be something more and something less than what happened.

It is the thesis of this chapter that this sort of transformation of events from spoken/acted to written form is an important and interesting phenomenon which deserves exploration in both its legal and linguistic aspects. Court reporters produce a document which is virtually indispensable in the functioning of the American trial process, and the methods by which they produce that document—the verbatim transcript—provide a window into the functioning of linguistic processes in a practical world. What follows, then, is an abbreviated look through that window, first at the task which reporters perform and the obstacles they face; next at the linguistic tools of their trade and the effects these tools have on the event being represented; and finally at the implications of the conduct of this profession both for linguistic study and legal processes. The data on which this discussion relies are taken primarily from Walker (1985)—a comprehensive study of the court reporting profession undertaken while I as the author was myself a practicing reporter.

The exploration begins with a look at the court reporter's task.

2. THE TASK

2.1. The Importance of the Task

In a 1953 article entitled "The Significance of Verbatim Recording of Proceedings in American Adjudication," law professors David Louisell and Maynard E. Pirsig took as their premise an assertion that the verbatim recording of trial proceedings exerts a profound influence on the administration of justice in the United States, with its sphere of influence extending over the conduct of the trial itself, the relationship between court and counsel, in-trial planning and review, and appellate practice. During the 8 years I spent as a reporter, I saw their premise proved true: the need to make a record does force a certain order on the proceedings, and the knowledge that "every word is being taken down" both tempers observations which might otherwise be made to or by court and counsel and underscores the formality of the event.

Verbatim transcripts of prior and ongoing proceedings are often used in trial strategy. But as Louisell and Pirsig pointed out, verbatim reporting is important for reasons far more significant than its symbolic or moderating effect on trial participants and its use as a tool in advocacy: it is important because its product—the verbatim record—is the *sine qua non* of the appellate process.

One of the acknowledged foundations of American jurisprudence is a litigant's right of access to an appellate hearing following an unfavorable lower court decision, and this right of access is routinely connected by the courts to the maintenance of a complete and accurate record of trial proceedings.[1] The responsibility for producing this record of the trial was placed originally in the hands of court reporters[2] by title 28, section 753(b) of the United States Code—otherwise known as the Court Reporter Act—a statute which embodies the belief that having a record made contemporaneously by a trained and objective observer would "provide a safeguard to which not only the court but also the defendant is entitled in the preservation of his rights" (*United States v. Taylor*, 303 F.2d 165 at 169 [4th Cir. 1962]). The statute also crystallizes the confidence that both bench and bar have in the competence of reporters by granting to their product a prima facie presumption of correctness which assumes that the official certified transcript is correct unless it is *proven* wrong.[3] This position of confidence which reporters hold is further enhanced by the fact that in a conflict between the court and the reporter over what should enter the official record, the reporter, in principle, prevails. As Louisell and Pirsig note,

[1] One expression of this connection is found in *United States v. Workcuff*, 422 F.2d 700 (D.C. 1970, at 701-2): "There can be little doubt that the absence of a complete and accurate transcript impairs the ability of appellate counsel to protect his client's basic rights."

[2] With the advent of electronic recording and with the 1982 revision of the Court Reporter Act, some jurisdictions have replaced stenotype court reporters with court "recorders" (*Manual*, 1981) who monitor the tape recording of a proceeding, caring for the machine(s), and keeping an information log on times, speakers, etc. At the time of this writing, videotape records are also being used in 19 Kentucky courtrooms as the official record and are being used experimentally in California, Florida, Michigan, Mississippi, North Carolina, and Washington trial courts, with, according to National Center for State Courts estimates, "at least nine other state court systems . . . giving active consideration to the use of videotape systems" ("Video-Recording Evaluation," 1988:1). (See the Implications section of this chapter for discussion of videotaping.) But all audio- and most of the videotapes are turned into transcripts anyway, so the problems, solutions, and effects discussed herein still apply.

[3] No one seriously believes that court reporters' records are infallible: "Even the strictest standards cannot guarantee against the error of the reporter" (*United States v. Perkins*, 498 F.2d 1054 at 1058, n.4 [D.C. Cir. 1974]). For this reason, the Federal Rules of Appellate Procedure, in paragraph 10(3), provide for corrections to the record (1975). Reporters have, however, established an impressive record of reliability, as reflected by the following language of an appellate opinion: "lawyers and judges of experience know that [the court reporter's] notes contain, with few exceptions, the testimony of witnesses as it was given, and are thoroughly reliable" (*State v. Perkins*, 120 N.W. 62 at 73 [1909]). Although dated some 80 years earlier, this view continues to be typical of the legal profession at large. (See Louisell & Pirsig, 1953:30; Waltz & Kaplan, 1983:31.)

> While the reporter as one of the officers of the tribunal is subject generally to the
> direction of the court, the performance of his essential duties cannot be curtailed by
> the court. Thus, a trial court has no authority to direct the court reporter ". . . to
> disregard his sworn statutory duty to take down all rulings and exceptions"
> [citations omitted]. In other words, *the right of each party to have made a word for word
> record of everything said cannot be negated by the trial court.* (Louisell & Pirsig, 1953:31,
> emphasis added)

The effect of this prima facie presumption of correctness, then, is to confer on reporters a kind of localized power to determine what a word-for-word record really is, and the linguistic and legal aspects of the task which reporters perform provide, often unconsciously, the bases upon which that determination is made.

2.2. The Linguistic Task

The central task performed by court reporters—a task periodically shared by linguists and other social scientists who study language in action—is to transform an event from its spoken manifestation into a written one, thus performing what some scholars say flatly is an impossible operation: providing an equivalence in two different media (Catford, 1965:53). The reasons for such a negative assertion lie in the problem of preserving meaning from one medium to another and arise out of the essential differences between the characteristics of, and our expectations about, speech and writing. There is a considerable body of literature on this oral/literate dichotomy—or continuum, depending on the scholar involved (see, for example, collected works in Tannen, 1982, 1984), and some of the features studied in the literature are particularly pertinent to the taking, shaping, and appellate use of transcripts. Those features are *word shapes, cohesion and thought processes, contextual meaning,* and *negotiation of meaning.* Because our expectations about written language in general are best exemplified by printed expository prose, and our expectations about spoken language by conversation, those two genres will form the basis for this brief discussion.

2.2.1. Word Shapes

When we read, our eyes are capable of scanning several words, sentences, and even lines with one glance, but we have been trained by the writing conventions of English to expect that each of those words and sentences will be discrete. In written English, the boundaries of each independent linguistic element—letter, word, sentence, paragraph—are expected to be clearly delineated. Thus the phrase, "coming around the mountain," is written just that way, despite the fact that when spoken in conversation, the sounds appear not as short, separate, staccato bursts, but as a smooth, undifferentiated stream: cuminuhrounthuhmoun'n. Furthermore, in conversation, we *expect* the sounds to merge smoothly. If they do not, if a speaker carefully enunciates every syllable and separates each word from its neighbors, it becomes remarkable, and we as hearers make inferences about the speech that have little to do with its content. "Siddown, and "Sit—Down" carry two very distinct messages—or so the normal hearer would infer.

But readers are limited by the written forms that appear on the page as to the inferences they can make. Because by convention, written words are already separate, the import of careful enunciation is lost (unless noted editorially), as is any message that might (misleadingly) be sent by writing words in an unbroken string across the page.

2.2.2. Cohesion and Thought Processes

Our expectations concerning discrete word shapes in written language have a philosophical cousin in what we expect about the internal organization of the text that we read. Boundaries imply order; phrases, clauses, sentences, paragraphs imply a step-by-step progression from the particular to the general, and readers of English expect that written language will be orderly in both shape and content. Written ideas, we believe, should be presented in logical order, be smoothly connected, and form a cohesive whole. And although as readers we do not want to be aware of how the author has contrived this smoothness, as writers we struggle to find just the right connective, subordinating conjunction, or embedded phrase that will achieve the coherence we desire. Yet while our thoughts must be clear to the reader, the process by which we organized them must not be.[4]

In conversational speech, however, the process of thinking is often very much in evidence. We start an idea, change our minds, hesitate, go back, start over, shift in midstream to another idea entirely. We use far fewer integrative devices: nominalizations, participles, complements, and relative clauses (Chafe, 1982); and for the relevance of one thought to another, or to the conversation itself, we often rely not on words but on the comfortable assumption that our hearers know enough about the subject, or about us, to fill in the blanks. Spontaneity and the lack of cohesion that frequently accompanies it are accepted. But although disorganized, unplanned speech in conversation

---

[4] There are times when even in speech the organizing process gets explicit comment. Karen Schoeve, a reporter in Texas, reports the following exchange between an exasperated attorney and his witness:

Mr. Piro: Do you see how easy it would have been if you just said "stock"?
The Witness: Bob, I have to process these things through my mind.
Mr. Piro: But the processing doesn't have to be coming out of your mouth ("Witness Encouraged," 1989, p. 116).

does our images no particular harm, and well-organized, planned writing can enhance them, disorganized speech when written down has a quite different, deleterious effect. This odd dissonance in our expectations about language is one of the linguistic facts that influence the production of transcripts and exert an effect upon their eventual appellate readers.

2.2.3. Contextual Meaning

Of all of the features that distinguish writing from speech, the one which is potentially the most significant in transcription, is the inability of our writing conventions to express some of the para- and extralinguistic signals that speakers rely on to get their meaning across. In conversation, the sense of what is said is often supplied not simply by *content*—the words and the order of the words—but also by the *context*: here very narrowly defined as the "how" of the saying. Paralinguistic features such as intonation, breathiness, emphasis, high and low pitch, long, drawn-out sounds, among others, all are part of a spoken message. Extralinguistic features like raised eyebrows, outflung arms, nods, sneers, and smiles can convey meaning on their own or alter the significance of the words they accompany. Silent pauses and hesitations of all sorts are particularly meaningful in conversation because in our culture they are often perceived negatively (Tannen & Saville-Troike, 1985). However, given that the printed medium is one-dimensional, none of these meaning-bearing contextual components of speech can be represented by using English orthography alone. Although we do have a few orthographic devices at our disposal—punctuation, capitalization, underlining—for suggesting intonation or emphasis (you. you? You! YOU, you), writers must often rely on creative spelling (yoooooou), editorial comment ([sarcastically]), or authorial description ([raises eyebrow], [nods head]) to convey more fully to readers what viewers/hearers of an event have experienced. Without the freedom to go beyond orthography, a sometimes-critical component of communication can fail to be passed along in written form.

2.2.4. Negotiation of Meaning

Besides being one-dimensional, the printed medium is also a one-way modality which does not allow questions to be asked of the author if the text is somehow incomplete or unclear, nor does it allow authors to check with their readers for misunderstandings. In speech, meaning can be negotiated through give-and-take as the conversation progresses, but writers get one chance only to make their intentions plain. Once the words are frozen on the page, they become fair game for the reader's interpretation, and clarification of what they mean is out of the author's hands.

2.2.5. Scripts

In the discussion of four of the dimensions along which speech and writing differ, expository prose has served as the model for understanding our expectations about written language. But transcripts are a very special form of written language, and another kind of model that can contribute to understanding the significance of what court reporters do when they turn talk into type is provided by scripts: the shape taken by dialogue in stories, movies, and plays. Although there has been some movement toward attempting conversational "reality" in fiction (Tom Wolfe's *The Right Stuff*, for instance), most story dialogues are constructed in order to move along some plot, so authors waste little time in having the characters stumble, stammer, make false starts or grammatical slips, or otherwise replicate conversation "in the flesh." When authors do depart from the dictionary norms for written words (He's jis' roamin' aroun') or have their characters abandon smoothness of delivery (Uh, I thi– I think—I mean, uh), it's taken to be planned and therefore meaningful. We *notice* these scripted written deviations from the norm (although we might very well not notice them in our own conversations), and as we are intended to, we make inferences from them about the characters. As Robin Lakoff noted in her discussion of the way *The New York Times* reported something former Alabama Governor George Wallace said (Lakoff, 1982), a "should've" in conversation and a "should of" in print, although the two sound the same to the ear, do not send the same message.

But sending—or more precisely, preserving—the same message is, after all, the ultimate purpose of any transcript of an event. The first requirement, therefore, is to be aware beforehand what the "message" is, that is, to have a working concept of what counts as information. Whatever the field of inquiry, the task provides that definition, and for verbatim reporters, the legal community sets the task.

2.3. The Legal Task

2.3.1. The Cultural Climate

The legal community is at heart a literate one, offering perhaps the purest example of a culture in which, as one scholar of literacy suggests (Ong, 1979:2), its citizens "are so stubbornly literate in principle as to believe that what makes a word a real word is not its meaningful use in vocal exchange, but rather its presence on the pages of a dictionary." The lawyers and judges who constitute the community are educated members of a literate culture in which knowledge is equated with "facts and information [which are] preserved in written records" (Tannen, 1980:1). In such a culture, reverence for facts, the written word, precision, and an impersonalized notion of "literal" meaning is inculcated early in the education process. It is this background in which the institution of law in the United States is embedded.

From infancy on, lawyers, like the rest of us, are products of a schooling process in which language use progresses steadily from mere speech which "wells up out of the unconscious" (Ong, 1979:2) to writing—a form in which the structure of language becomes a matter of conscious thought. To borrow Olson's phrase, we as students move "from utterance to text" (Olson, 1977). In traditional law schools, the process is magnified: the law which students there learn is essentially law as literature: that is, law is taught not as a living, spoken, acted entity but as something that resides in the pages of a book. Students study and learn to emulate the formal language of statutes, and essays, and appellate opinions, in which the values of the literate tradition for structure, logic, precision, and reverence for words are strong. The Socratic question and answer process in the classes they attend relies heavily on the recitation of facts memorized from written opinions and briefs (Philips, 1982:182). Attention is directed away from the human emotions surrounding the causes of action which bring litigants into court and is directed toward the facts and the principles of law which apply. For the vast majority of lawyers, most of whom do not end up in trial courts, not only their education but the practice of law is firmly attached to a written tradition and the beliefs about language that accompany it.

Even the litigators who move into the courts, where law assumes its spoken form, take with them threads of attachment to literate values. In trial courts, the business of law is persuasion—a linguistic art which relies heavily on strategies associated with ancient oral cultures in which absorption and retention of ideas were accomplished in part by the listener identifying emotionally with the speaker and situation. In such cultures, "the listener had to become engaged . . . to the point of total emotional involvement" (Ong, 1967:209), and that kind of emotional engagement with the listener remains the aim of adept trial attorneys. As one eminent lawyer wrote some 35 years ago:

> Whatever means you employ, you must lift your jury from mere logic to the springs of action that transcend cold reasoning, to the feelings and the emotions that govern, inspire, and produce the verdict. Never for an instant forget that it is a favorable verdict you are seeking. (Stryker, 1954:128)

Although trial lawyers use such stratagems to temper the literate approach to reasoning with the oral appeal to emotion, however, their language reflects an accompanying awareness that what is being carried on in court as a spoken exercise in immediate persuasion is also being transformed into a written record designed to be read later as information. Phrases such as "For the record [please give us your name]," "Off the record, . . .," "Back on the record, . . .," "Let the record reflect . . .," all acknowledge explicitly the documentary nature of the proceedings. Subtler clues appear when the deictic expressions normally used in conversation—"Look at this," "He hit me right here"—give way to named items and places: "I hand you Exhibit A and ask you to look at paragraph 6"; "John hit me in the face, right over my left eye." Silent nods and shakes of the head get translated by lawyer or reporter into words that can be written: "Is that a 'yes' answer?" "Please say 'yes' or 'no' out loud."

Not everything is turned into words for the record, however. Sighs, sarcasm, curled lips (whether those of the witness[5] or the questioning attorney), and even laughter or tears are rarely if ever acknowledged explicitly, and this too is in keeping with the literate tradition: emotions are not generally regarded as information to be recorded.

The literate tradition, then, has the last word in the courts of record, supplying the beliefs that guide the making of the record of the proceedings: that the primary function of language is to transmit information; that information is equated with the content of language, and content is best preserved in written form; and most particularly, as Ong phrased the belief, "if one has the exact words someone else has uttered, one has . . . his exact meaning" (1967:32). These assumptions, which all focus on the "what" and not the "how" of language, lead naturally to a related assumption which is presumed to be statutorily attached to transcripts: that they can be, and must be, verbatim (28 U.S.C. §753[b]), or "word for word." The relationship of this assumption both to the creation of a record and to the entire transcription process is fundamental, for the attempt to render a complex spoken event into writing, to capture its meaning word-for-word, is what transcription of court proceedings is all about. That is the task set by the legal community for its guardians of the record, and in its execution, the literate tradition and the verbatim concept play pivotal roles.

2.3.2. The Verbatim Transcript

2.3.2a. Statutory Requirement. The assumption referred to that there is a statutory requirement for a verbatim transcript is widespread in the legal world. Case law is full of reference to "verbatim transcriptions" (e.g., *Williams v. United States*, 338 F.2d 286 [D.C. 1964]), "verbatim recitations" (e.g., *United States v. Hodges*, 556 F.2d 1283 [7th Cir. 1977]), and the exact phrase, "verbatim transcripts" (e.g., *United States v. Cabra*, 662 F.2d 182 [5th Cir. 1980]). The connection between the statute's force and the transcript is made clear by the language of *United States v. Perkins*, 498 F.2d 1054 (D.C. Cir. 1974), which states

---

[5] The term "witness" is used here and throughout this chapter to mean anyone "whose declaration under oath (or affirmation) is received as evidence for any purpose" (*Black's Law Dictionary*). That would include plaintiff, defendant, lay or expert witness.

that it is the court reporter's "obligation to provide a verbatim transcript." Yet the statute—the Court Reporter Act—does not mention a verbatim transcript at all.

What the statute does say is that the court reporter "shall record verbatim" the designated proceedings and shall then "transcribe" that "record of proceedings" and "attach to the [resultant] transcript his official certificate" (which swears that the record is true, complete, and objective). The statute goes on to state that the official certified transcript "shall be deemed prima facie a correct statement of the testimony taken and the proceedings had."

This chain of language, by linking a verbatim recording with a correct transcript, apparently serves as the basis for the belief which is routinely accepted and acted upon, that a verbatim transcript is mandated. It also, however, hides a troublesome ambiguity: it fails to specify what "verbatim" means.

2.3.2b. Verbatim? The ambiguity is not immediately apparent. When asked what the word "verbatim" means, lawyers, judges, and court reporters all respond with some version of "in exact words" or "word-for-word." Although most law dictionaries do not list the term at all, Ballentine's mirrors Webster's by saying it means "In the very same words. Word for word." Those few courts who have had to address the question agree. A South Dakota judge wrote:

> A verbatim record means the taking of the record word for word; all the dictionaries so define it. (*In re DLF,* 176 N.W.2d 486 at 488 [S.D. 1970])

And the ruling of a Washington court suggested that slightly exasperated overtone with which people often respond when asked to define the obvious: "Verbatim in this rule means *verbatim*" (*Caffrey v. Chem-Ionics Corp.*, 419 P.2d 809, 811 [1966]).

The problem, then, does not lie with the perceived clarity of the term or sureness about its definition. Everyone in the legal world "knows" that verbatim means word for word. Not everyone, however, agrees on *which* words come under the verbatim umbrella, or *whose* words, or even on *what* a word is. This uncertainty leads to considerable slippage between the definition of "verbatim" and its application. The resulting equivocation between what the standard for transcription is said to be and what it actually is is demonstrable on all levels of court practice, from appellate judges who find it possible to make a distinction between "substantially verbatim" and "precisely verbatim" (e.g., *Williams v. United States*, 338 F.2d 286 [D.C. 1964]), to "verbatim" court reporters who edit transcripts as a matter of course (Walker, 1981).

Because it is ill-defined, the verbatim concept is continually in conflict with the recording and transcribing process, as will become increasingly evident as this discussion progresses. On a level of practice by attorneys, the conflict is generally considered *de minimus*: it is unimportant until it becomes a tool for appeal. Even then, the issue is one of broad application of the concept—that is, considering the verbatim standard in relation to the trial as a whole. Here, the ambiguity as to what "verbatim" means arises over *which blocks* of words are to be covered by the statutory requirement, that is, which portions of the proceedings.

Under a strict interpretation of the statute, *all* portions of the proceedings—everything uttered from beginning to end—are to be recorded (*United States v. Piasik*, 559 F.2d 545 [9th Cir. 1977]). But the fact is that in many jurisdictions, the practice is otherwise, with, for example, the voir dire (preliminary examination of the jurors) and opening and closing arguments of counsel often going unreported. This practice necessarily results in a less than complete, therefore less verbatim, record (and transcript) of the proceedings, which then leaves the door open for appeals based on a claim that federal law (the Court Reporter Act) was violated and that this in and of itself mandates a new trial (*United States v. Robinson*, 459 F.2d 1164 [D.C. 1972] remanded on other grounds).

This aspect of verbatimness, then, when applied to blocks of words—portions of proceedings—is one with which the legal world is familiar, and which in fact they can turn to as a possible basis for an appeal to an unfavorable trial court decision. As an issue, it is available and arguable on a conscious level. And its implications are very well understood.

But when application of a verbatim standard moves from "which words" to "whose words" (which speakers) or focuses on what actually constitutes a "word" (Is a nod a word? Is "uh" a word? Is a stammer, a stutter, a false start a word?), the issue of its definition is much less available for discussion or argument. For the lawyers and judges whose speech and acts ":nake" the record, these aspects of verbatimness, if recognized at all, are connected more with the readability of a record than with any potential appellate significance. For the court reporters, who "take" the record, verbatimness is a daily ad hoc problem that must be coped with, rather than an issue with roots and consequences to be understood. Because they must deal with it on a moment-to-moment basis, their concern with verbatimness is more apt to focus consciously on the difficulty of accurately segmenting a stream of sound into discrete words and phrases, of translating foreign accents into dictionary shapes, of balancing the requirement for "exactness" with the necessity to have the resultant record both readable and acceptable in the eyes of the professionals for whom they work. But even while they endeavor consciously to cope with the inherent conflicts involved in trying to mold an oral process into a written product, they, like the judges and attorneys with whom they work, appear to be essentially unaware of either the extent of or foundations for the legal profession's indeterminate approach to what constitutes a "verbatim" record. Consequently, the implications remain unexplored.

Court reporters are perhaps even more wedded to the literate tradition than are the members of the courts whom they serve. Their primary business is language, not law, and as professionals they are taught that their product reflects not only the content of the event they reported but their own literate skills. Their expectations about those skills, about language in general, and about the people who speak it, not only serve as the critical influence on their work but create, paradoxically, the most significant of the many obstacles they face in their attempt to achieve the realization of their putative goal, a verbatim record.

3. OBSTACLES

Expectations about language influence both how people understand what is said and how they report it. Each of those operations carries its own set of obstacles to accurate communication; in the courtroom they assume a special significance.

3.1. Obstacles to Understanding Speech in the Courtroom Setting

3.1.1. Segmenting the Stream

"You start with spoken words and phrases which, in popular modern speech, are slurred, mumbled, transposed and butchered," writes the author of "How to be a Court Reporter" (Morphy, 1959:11) and from this "slovenly speech" (Swem, 1984:45), the court reporter is expected to "separate words or groups of words so that the reader may readily understand the meaning that the speaker intended to convey" (Weiss, 1971:1). Doing this correctly, of course, depends on the interaction of a number of linguistic and sociolinguistic operations, but first it requires that the reporter be able to distinguish what constitutes a word.

That this can be done is obvious, and the expectation that it can be done correctly is implicit in the very existence of the word-for-word standard under which reporters work. But experimental evidence suggests that it is not as uncomplicated an operation as it would seem. Writing on characteristics of the process of understanding speech, linguist Woods (1980:62) discusses this problem:

> A naive view of speech understanding might consider it as a process of successively recognizing speech sounds (called phonemes), grouping phonemes into words, parsing word sequences into sentences, and finally interpreting the meanings of those sentences. However, considerable experience now indicates that the acoustic evidence present in the original speech signal is not sufficient to support such a process.

In other words, we do not normally understand language as bits of clearly differentiated, *meaningful* single sounds or words which can be instantly "heard," recognized, and processed in isolation. Rather, we understand language in chunks, disassembling the chunks into words whose individual identities come clear only when there is sufficient context surrounding them. "The listener does not fully determine the status of each linguistic item as it is received," reports Lieberman (1963, p. 174) in a study of intelligibility of speech; "he may delay many decisions until later items are received and the general structure of the sentence is determined." If such structure is absent, if there is not adequate semantic and syntactic information to help segment the sounds, understanding is problematic. Linguistic context of this kind is crucial to comprehension; without it, any listening task becomes markedly more difficult, as the following anecdote from a noted reporter illustrates:

> Reporting just words, with no real context, can be a jarring experience. One of the hardest assignments of my career was a two-day deposition in which a witness read into the record terse entries in a longhand diary. The words were simple, and the witness wasn't fast; but there was absolutely no context to the entries. I almost went out of my mind. (Gilman, 1982:31)

Not even context can save the reporter, however, if she is unable to hear in the first place; yet given the fact that courtrooms and other legal settings are rarely built with the reporter in mind, that is not always possible. Poor room design, poor acoustics, and environmental noise from air conditioning, traffic, and doors opening and closing often interfere. Participants contribute by coughing and sneezing, covering their mouths with their hands, lowering their voices, turning away, rustling papers, and talking among themselves while the reporter is supposed to be getting the testimony.

The problem is pervasive, and in its extreme form, the simple inability to hear can result in an incomplete record. But when the second requirement for correct segmentation—thorough knowledge of one's own linguistic code and professional jargon, together with sufficient background knowledge—is not met, the result is not incomplete but inaccurate transcripts. Because as noted, we speak in clusters, many of which sound alike (consider the closeness of "euthanasia" and "youth in Asia"), and because we as cooperative listeners attempt to use what we already know in order to make sense of whatever we hear, errors of understanding can easily occur. Poor knowledge of idiomatic English, for instance, can (and did) result in "by and large" being transcribed on a test as "be enlarge" (Gilman, 1982, p. 31); lack of familiarity with legal jargon can and did put a "some re-judgment" into a transcript where "summary judgment" ought to have appeared ("Bloopers," 1984:56). And it is easy to connect lack of familiarity with the subject matter of testimony with the sometimes humorous errors of the "foramen ovale/ foreman of the valley" variety (Whitford, 1898:47) which are made when reporters and transcribers, like the rest of us, reach for familiar shapes in the stream of sound.

3.1.2.   Putting It Back Together

Usually, of course, for both the ordinary listener and the court reporter, it is not necessary to pay conscious attention to the segmentation and identification of particular sounds: Conversational processing takes place "below the level of introspection" (Woods, 1980:63). Even in court, where every word is supposed to count, it is the gist of the speech that is attended to by the participants, and holes, if any, in the fabric of the message can be mended by each hearer's unconscious knowledge of the structure of language and the characteristics of subject and situation.

Reporters too carry out this same patching process for much of what they record, but in general they are denied the luxury afforded to others of *relying* on those linguistic expectations. Whereas the "trained reporter follows the sense of all that he records . . .[tracking] the thread of argument, his mental faculties constantly alert to the necessities and requirements of an accurate record" (*Making the Record*, 1976:14), it is not sense but words that must be written down. In particular, reporters must write the individual words that others lose.

That can be difficult. Besides the problem of simply getting the acoustic signal, that is, hearing it, reporters frequently must dissect a garbled or "dialectal" delivery and reconstruct it into an understandable whole. If ordinary listeners are faced with such a problem, they can wait until the utterance is well underway and then say, Huh?, but reporters not only are charged with the duty of instantaneous "understanding" and recording, they are discouraged by custom (however illogical) from interrupting speakers for any reason. This sometimes results in the necessity, as one professional phrased it, of taking a "leap of faith," in which the attempt to make sense is abandoned and reporters "wind up taking down the sounds in the (sometimes slim) hope that when we read it back the sounds will signify something more than nothing" (Ramshaw, 1977:7).

3.2.   Obstacles to Accurate Representation of Speech

Leaps of faith are often necessary when reporters are confronted, as they increasingly are, with the accented speech of foreign witnesses. When put in context, the phonetic representation in stenographic notes of heavy accents ("eets"; "wit joo 'n choo") can usually be puzzled out and put into meaningful Standard English forms ("its"; "with you and you"), but the result, paradoxically, is *in*accurate representation of speech which is perceived in its written form as accurate. The paradox which attends the representation of "deviant" sounds and forms in fact illustrates all three types of obstacles to actual verbatim reporting—mechanical, cultural, and conventional, each of which will be discussed briefly below.

3.2.1. Mechanical Obstacles

Aside from the fact already noted that English orthography cannot handle paralinguistic cues like intonation, it is also unable to represent some of the odd noises we humans make. Although a few of the common ones have acquired an agreed-upon spelling of sorts (hmmph, psst, tsk-tsk), more have not (a sudden intake of breath, whistles, any phonetic testimony by a linguist) and thus cause problems for both the shorthand writer and the transcriber. Whether a spelling of such nonwords is "correct" or not matters little to most typed records; the obstacle comes in the challenge these sounds present to automaticity of writing for the reporter on the scene: Each split second of figuring out how to write some sound is an eternity in which to fall behind the speaker.

A more serious drawback of any standard writing system, however, is its very linearity: without special conventions, words (devoid of intonation) can only follow one another, one at a time, in a straight line on a page. Speech is linear, too, of course, but in conversation, the linearity of speech is confounded by plurality: more than one person can talk at a time, a fact which presents a challenge to both the writing system and the reporter. Overlapping, or cospeech, is far from a rare occurrence in court, and the methods by which reporters represent this phenomenon, along with the possible implications for the appellate process, will be discussed later.

3.2.2. Cultural Obstacles

3.2.2a. Educated Speakers Use Good Grammar. Literate cultures, whose language can be made visible, socialize their members through schooling to meet standards of acceptability or correctness for their language in both its spoken and written forms. Perhaps the most linguistically interesting and possibly unique aspect of the court-reporting profession is that it requires that two models of language—the spoken and the written—be applied simultaneously to overheard discourse. In most cases in which a third party is passively listening to two others talk, the model of language that the listener uses is the one earliest acquired: a model for speech in which the "grammar" is a set of unconsciously derived rules which govern both the perception and production of language. Because language is a matter of norms as well as of convention, the listener may also judge incoming speech against a culturally acquired standard of correctness—or "grammar" in the prescriptive sense. However, with the possible exception of novelists on the lookout for realistic-sounding conversation or journalists who seek a sensational quotation, most listeners do not also measure incoming speech by what it will look like when it is written down. Or, as in the case of reporters, what it *should* look like.

One of the beliefs which stem naturally from our literate society is that "education" (not mere school attendance) and command of Standard English are synonymous—or at least should be synonymous—past the high-school level. And because education and social class are also correlated on a perceptual level (Labov, 1966; Laver & Trudgill, 1979) members of the professions are expected to employ grammatically correct speech, with all that implies (e.g., correct pronunciation, skilled word choice, error-free syntax). The opposite is also true: Members of the "working class" and below not only are expected to use but are often detected through their "ungrammatical" speech (Laver & Trudgill, 1979:22).

Being members of a literate culture, reporters share these expectations. What language should look like when it is written down varies, in reporters' eyes, depending on the speaker: Educated citizens use good grammar and should be "seen" to do so; uneducated ones do not. As the English textbook of the NSRA (National Shorthand Reporters Association) phrases it: "Presumably all judges and most if not all lawyers are men of education, and they will resent having attributed to them in stenographic reports ungrammatical and carelessly-phrased remarks" (English, 1983:4). On the other hand, the text continues, "Witnesses are often illiterate, and as a rule they do not see the reports of their testimony." Of these witnesses they note, "It goes without saying that the testimony of ignorant or illiterate witnesses should be literally rendered" (1983, p. 5). This dichotomy of belief is the norm in the profession, and it finds realization in practice: According to the nationwide survey which I conducted of court reporting practices, most reporters do admit to editing the grammar of judges and lawyers (who are educated speakers), and few claim to edit grammar of lay witnesses (who may or may not be educated). Expert witnesses—again, presumably "men of education"—had their speech edited by more than a third of the respondents (Walker, 1985).

Two of the corollary issues raised by this quotation from the NSRA text— the use of editing in conjunction with a verbatim record and the classification and hierarchy of courtroom speakers—will be taken up in sections ahead. The point here, as in the discussion of dialect that follows, is to notice the force with which the literate tradition operates as it lays a foundation for practices that interfere with the accurate representation of speech in court transcripts: differential editing and verbatim records are not, after all, compatible concepts.

3.2.2b. *Transcripts Are Documents, Not Novels.* Consistent with the literate orientation of the law toward language is the notion that the function of language as it occurs in legal settings is primarily referential, or fact-oriented. That does not mean that the expressive, or emotional, function of language is ignored. Emotion is not only acknowledged but relied upon and regularly manipulated by lawyers in order to carry out their persuasive tasks.

But in spite of the important function of emotion in court, emotional or expressive language in transcripts is frowned upon. No matter what the provocation, a certain decorum is supposed to be maintained during legal proceedings, and the same decorum is expected to be reflected in the transcripts. As illogical as it may seem, transcripts are expected somehow to preserve the essence of the event without any (or very much) reference to the paralinguistic features which give it flavor—including the use of dialect. Says the NSRA text in suggesting that witnesses' language be treated literally (i.e., "verbatim–ly"), "[such] literalness should not extend to the point of dialect if the language has a reasonable equivalent in ordinary English words. After all, the shorthand reporter is not a novelist" (Budlong, 1983:5).

The shorthand reporter is, however, creating a document, and our literate culture's notions about documents include the expectation that the information in them will be readily accessible. It is the general belief among reporters, therefore, that literal rendering of speech on the phonological level is not only uninformative but disruptive. It may also be interpretive. As an official reporter commented in response to my questionnaire on reporter practices: "No one attempts to reproduce dialect. What may sound like dialect to one is normal pronunciation to another" (Walker, 1985:216).

Whatever the rationale, however, there is a professionwide reluctance to put into a transcript any of the features of speech that might mark a person's origins. The same paradoxical reluctance to be "accurate" extends to representing in written form the casual linguistic forms found in almost everyone's speech: dunno (don't know), doin', dju (did you). This written sanitation of spoken speech variation stems from the legal profession's literate approach to language, an approach which dictates for transcripts the twin but mutually contradictory requirements for readability (thus acceptability) and verbatimness. But to satisfy one requirement means to compromise the other, and the tension between the two sets up the greatest single obstacle to accurate representation in transcript form of a spoken/acted legal proceeding.

3.2.3. Conventional Obstacles

Mechanical limitations of the written modality make it impossible to provide a truly accurate representation in a transcript of a spoken event; cultural assumptions about language, its function, its speakers, and its documents set up another series of obstacles; and the conventional belief of both reporting and legal professions that reporters should be objective, noninterpretive conduits of language paradoxically provides the third and final set of obstacles to be taken up here.

Why should such a belief be an obstacle? The answer lies in the fact that there is no clear definition of what it means to *be* objective. Historically, reporters have served without serious challenge as distanced and impartial observers of trials who have no personal stake in the adjudications recorded, so there is no particular problem defining "objective" in relation to reporters and the outcome of the proceedings. But when applied to the kind of details touched on earlier—details of dialect, intonation, and nonverbal features such as gesture and pausing—the line becomes blurred between what is objective, that is, what constitutes an observable, objective "fact" of speech that should properly become part of the record, and what constitutes an "interpretation" which should therefore not be included. This blurring presents an obstacle in the form of proscriptions, uncertainty, and variability.

Interestingly, considering how deeply ingrained the proscription against reporter interpretation is, there is very little in legal or reporting literature directed explicitly at the subject; rather, interpretation is generally touched upon tangentially as part of a discussion on editing. When mentioned, it centers primarily on those expressive aspects of conversation which writing cannot capture, such as intonation, silent pauses, and gestures, and on speech dysfluencies (e.g., hesitation sounds, false starts). Reduced to its colloquial expression in the court-reporting field, the admonition states, "It is the reporter's job to *take* the record, not *make* it." Unfortunately, this uncodified directive is frequently at odds with a companion directive, supported this time by case law, that it is the reporter's job to make a "correct and authentic" (*United States v. Taylor*, 303 F.2d 165, at 169 [4th Cir. (1962)]) and "complete" (*Hardy v. United States*, 375 U.S. 277, at 288 [1964]) record, the implication being that the appellate court, within the limitations of a written record, should "see" the same trial that the lower court saw.

The obstacle which this discord between two directives presents to creating an accurate record can be illustrated by a simple, very common example: the nonverbal answer delivered by moving the head in some direction or another. What should the reporter do? The reporter who takes the first directive literally ("Take, don't make the record") may write simply [No audible response] because there was nothing to hear, or may even go as far as writing [No response]. One who "interpretively" follows the second directive (Make a correct and authentic record) and thus attempts to convey the speaker's intention writes [Witness nods head affirmatively] (or negatively). And one who attempts to follow both directives by giving as many objective clues as possible to what went on, writes some variation of [Witness nods head up and down]. All three descriptions, along with other variations, are in sanctioned present-day use, each one giving the reader a slightly different view of the event (and in the case of [No response], a false one). Which version is "accurate" is open to question.

Significantly, in most jurisdictions, the form used to indicate these wordless answers is ultimately within the discretion of the reporter. In fact, the Federal Judicial Center's Revised Guidelines for the Preparation of Transcripts, in discussing nonverbal behavior and pauses, states

> It is the responsibility of the attorneys, as well as the judge in some instances, to note for the record any significant non-verbal behavior, i.e., physical gestures, and lengthy pauses on the part of a witness. . . . Ultimately, however, the inclusion of parentheticals to indicate any type of non-verbal behavior or pauses is solely at the

discretion of the audio operator/court reporter. (Greenwood, Horney, Jacoubovitch, Lowenstein, & Wheeler, 1983:147)

In theory, then, according to the admittedly equivocal FJC guidelines, the reporter *may* do some interpretive reporting. (Note the judgment required for anyone to determine what "significant" behavior and "lengthy" pauses are.) And even some judges (85% of the respondents in the Judges Survey reported in Walker, 1985) agree that reporters should indicate, for instance, pauses in the record if they are "prolonged beyond the speaker's style" (Walker, 1985:281)—an opinion which clearly calls for interpretation. Interestingly, the same percentage of judges also thought that reporters should indicate laughter, crying, shouting, whispering, and sighing—although these paralinguistic features are rarely "spoken" into the record by attorneys or judges themselves.

But reporters see their responsibility differently. Their responses to the Court Reporter Survey showed that overwhelmingly (90%) they would not indicate silent pauses in anyone's speech, and a similar percentage (89%) would "never" show laughter or tears. (Those who would show such features would do so for witnesses but not for lawyers and judges.) The reasons they gave in the survey for not indicating these or other expressive aspects of speech explicitly by use of parentheticals ([shouting]), or implicitly through orthography (No!, NO, No), reflect the underlying everyday beliefs which guide a reporter's work. "That would be interpretation," one wrote, "and it is not allowed." Others noted, "It is the reporter's job to write what is said, not interpret it"; "It is up to the lawyer to note any of the above for the record."

There is no doubt that phenomena such as silent pauses are subjectively perceived. But while the same argument might be made for laughter and tears, however weakly, it would fail completely when applied to filled pauses (those hesitations in speech marked by sounds such as "uh," and "er,") and false starts. These are objectively observable facts of speech, yet one of the grounds given by judges in the Judges Survey for their *ex*clusion from the record is that *in*clusion would "interject the reporter's subjective judgment." It is a curious position but understandable, considering that equivocation over exactly what constitutes reporter interpretation is the norm and not the exception in both reporting and legal communities. Dealing with that equivocation is another of the obstacles reporters face in attempting to produce an accurate representation of the legal events they cover.

4. TOOLS OF THE TRADE: MEANS AND DEVICES

The work of transcription—taking an often disorderly mass of speech and turning it into an orderly written account—gets done through two means: instrumental and linguistic. Instrumental means—which will not be discussed here—are the movable tools of the trade, so to speak: pen shorthand, stenomasks, tape recorders, stenotypy, and Computer-Aided Transcription, otherwise known as CAT. The linguistic means consist of the tools and techniques of editing: the mechanical devices of punctuation, paragraphing, and parentheticals, and the artistic devices by which what is said in court gets corrected, rearranged, eliminated, or restored to its underlying full form. Before taking up selected aspects of these editorial devices, however, it is worth looking separately at the rationale behind the apparently self-contradictory notion of correcting, rearranging, or otherwise editing what is putatively a "word for word" record.

4.1. Editing: The Rationale

> edit . . . tr.v. . . . 1.a. To make (written material) suitable for publication or presentation. (*The American Heritage Dictionary*, 1975)

If it were possible to speak of editing in simple terms of commas, periods, and paragraphs distributed through a text according to some mechanically applied, value-free formula, there would be nothing to discuss here. The treasured notion that court reporters are mere conduits of language would be safe; the issue of interpretation and subjectivity would never arise. But editing is not value-free. To "make suitable for publication" requires a judgment of what "suitable" means, and what is suitable depends a lot on who is doing the judging, and eventually, who will be doing the reading. In the case of court transcripts, the initial judges are the reporters; the readers are the professionals who hired them; and suitability—being a matter not of mechanics, but of human judgment, background, and training—is necessarily variable.

Variability in the production, form, and content of transcripts is not a topic for discussion as such in the court-reporting profession, but editing, which is its most immediate cause, is. It is a universal practice: "To edit or not to edit is not the question; every reporter does it in greater or less degree," notes the National Shorthand Reporters Association (*English*, 1983:26)—and because no written record is useful unless it is readable, the primary aim of editing is always to improve clarity of meaning without altering the content. The second, perhaps equally powerful aim, is self-protection: a reporter's reputation and employability can be affected by editing skills.

Just what constitutes editing is little agreed upon, but opinions abound. Lawyers and judges express themselves on the topic in terms that range from "shocked indignation at 'tampering' " to "serious expressions of 'a reporter's *obligation and duty* to correct obvious errors, patent misstatements and oversights' " (Bieber, 1976:27, emphasis added). Reporters themselves carry on a spirited debate, their opinions frequently featured in their national magazine, the *NSR, National Shorthand Reporter*.

One of those articles, entitled "Why the record MUST BE Verbatim" (Aurelio, 1988), is typical both in its honest expression of concern over the intricacies and proprieties of editing and in its apparent lack of awareness of the profession's self-contradictory views on editing practices. The author, arguing accurately that both the reporter's day-to-day reputation and the integrity of the appellate process are jeopardized if obvious editing occurs, states the following underlying condition for reporters *as guardians of the record*: "Verbatim reporters do not make up synopses of the testimony; we report every word spoken." But several paragraphs later, and without any apparent shift in point of view, he acknowledges the facts of life for reporters *as employees*, writing of his own experiences,

> "When certain attorneys ordered me to clean up their false starts or bad grammar, I did so, but very sparingly. . . . I'd leave out about one third of their false starts, only if those false starts were not germane." (Aurelio, 1988:36–37)

In making known his practice, this reporter reveals two of the essential characteristics of reporting: (1) the reporter's de facto, ad hoc autonomy as to the form of the record (in Aurelio's example, his arbitrary choice as to how much of a speech dysfunction was to be left in the record), and (2) the unspoken acceptance of the exercise of a reporter's individual judgment as an integral part of the job ("only if [they] were not germane").

The fact that the object of Aurelio's editing is false starts is not accidental: False starts are a natural source of the controversy and confusion caused by the essential underlying conflict between the demands of a literate society for both a "verbatim" and a "readable" document. The position of false starts in this crossfire of purpose is not surprising; the federal government itself not only considers them to be generally extraneous bits of speech but consigns to reporters the responsibility of making that determination. In their guidelines for reporters in federal district courts, under "Editing of Speech," they declare, "The transcript should provide an accurate record of words spoken in the course of proceedings" (i.e., be verbatim). But then they add, "In the interest of readability, however, false starts, stutters, uhms and ahs, and other verbal tics are not normally included in transcripts" (Greenwood *et al.*, 1983:143). Finally, in what is an apparently unconscious ratification of the reporter's *duty* to interpret (i.e., edit), they continue: "But such verbalizations *must* be transcribed whenever their exclusion *could change a statement's meaning* (1983:143, emphasis added).

The most liberal view of editing does not stop at a level of promoting mere readability, however, and interestingly, this is the view presently espoused by the National Shorthand Reporters Association. This organization, which guides court reporter activities and gives accreditation to schools, takes as its "approach and objectives . . . making, as far as the requirements of our work permit, *grammatically perfect records*" (*English*, 1983:1, emphasis added). This statement, found in the preface to their textbook on English, not only demonstrates again the literate, prescriptive language standards set for reporters but goes a long way toward explaining the mind set that permits, even requires, editing in the first place. "Editing," they note, "is the elimination from the

transcript of the recognizable language errors of speakers" (*English*, 1983:2).[6]
"Speakers," however, is not used as an all-inclusive term, and witnesses
are generally excluded from the class of speaker to whom editing is applied.
This exclusion is apparently influenced by the status of witness speech as
"sworn testimony" which, because it is evidence, must not be altered. "[A]
reporter who in any way changes sworn testimony is living dangerously and
behaving unprofessionally," points out an official federal reporter (Gustafson,
1977:167), who continues: "In judicial proceedings [editing] is confined to
utterances of counsel, the court, and those who are not sworn or under
examination."

But even on this point there is no unanimity within the profession, as in
some cases the supposedly sacred verbatim status of sworn testimony itself
gives way to the literate tradition. When it comes to those features mentioned
earlier that are considered by the reporter to be noninformation (e.g., false
starts, uh's, and in the "well-educated," even ungrammaticality), the general
attitude is expressed in an article included in the NSRA English text:

> The correction of such lapses can have no possible bearing on the force or credibility
> of the [well-educated or expert] witness' testimony, any more than does the inser-
> tion of the proper punctuation marks. (Budlong, 1983:5)

That there should be the divergencies of approach represented and that
internally inconsistent views on editing should exist in an atmosphere of
controversy is hardly surprising, given the fact that a reporter's task is itself
inherently contradictory. To naturally occurring, spoken/acted events, reporters are expected to apply, simultaneously, the mutually exclusive standards of verbatimness and readability, all the while maintaining the integrity
both of the event and of speaker meaning. Further, they must attempt this task
by selecting from a limited pool of resources: their mechanical and artistic
transcription conventions. Chief among these devices for producing the desired "accurate, readable, written-English record" (Rodebaugh, quoted in
Morphy, 1959:140) is punctuation, the essential tool in any transcriptionist's
arsenal.

4.2. Linguistic Means of Producing the Transcript

4.2.1. *Mechanical Devices: Punctuation, Paragraphing, and Parentheticals*

4.2.1a. Punctuation and Paragraphing.[7]   Perhaps as a legacy of the days when
punctuation was a "stepchild of the writing process" (Mellinkoff, 1963:245)

---

[6] The NSRA text on English (which includes all references to Budlong) underwent review of the
National Shorthand Reporters Association Books and Tapes Committee in the summer of 1989.
The committee, of which I am a member, recommended that the text be neither reprinted nor
endorsed in the future.

[7] For a full discussion of reporters' use of punctuation and all other transcription conventions, see
Walker (1985).

and was considered by the legal profession to be "no part of the statute" (*Cushing v. Worrick*, 75 Mass. 382 at 385 (1857)) and "essentially feminine" (Lavery, 1923:225), reporters are expected to reach toward clarity, sense, and verbatimness in their transcripts with less than a full inventory of the already meager number of punctuation marks available in English. As in virtually every other aspect of reporting, agreement is lacking even on what constitutes this inventory, but in general, because reporters are enjoined over and over to remain impartial, impassive, and objective and are told to avoid being interpretive or injecting themselves or their opinions into the record, punctuation marks which are associated with emphasis, such as the exclamation point and underscore, are avoided.

Good reporters punctuate their notes as they go along because they cannot rely on the words alone to supply meaning, and they cannot rely on their memories later on as to where a sentence started or stopped. When in my surveys of reporter practices (Walker, 1985), I asked reporters how they knew where to put their punctuation—for instance, a period—they all answered with some form of vague "knowing": They "just knew," based on "intonation," "breathing," "inflection, context, and pauses."

These kinds of intuitive guides usually suffice but not always. Intonational cues often are missing from naturally occurring talk and contextual ones as well. Neither one of those cues, for instance, can help a reporter know which answer to the following question is correct—

Q. When the officer asked him how much he had to drink, what did he say?
A. Nothing.
A. "Nothing."

—yet the punctuation is crucial to the testimony.

The difference punctuation can make to the meaning of a stretch of speech is obvious. Not so obvious is the fact that punctuation can on occasion hide rather than illuminate what goes on at trial. In the transcripts of a reporter who follows Standard English rules rather than the evidence of her ears by writing, for instance, "Could I see that?" with a question mark instead of with a period ("Could I see that."), intonational cues as to speaker attitude (politely requesting versus ordering) could well be missed, and the record seen by a potential appellate court would not correspond to what had actually happened. Because attitude is an important component of witness demeanor and can also provide grounds for appeal against a presiding judge, such seemingly innocuous choices about punctuation can have significant legal effects.[8]

---

[8] On the subject of punctuation, politeness, and appellate courts, one respondent in the Judges Survey gave an interesting account of the practical implications of the difficulty of representing inflection and its attendant clues to the speaker's intention. He wrote,

4.2.1b.   Paragraphing and the Dash.   Although speaker attitude can be masked by punctuation, so can interruptive behavior, which has been shown to be an important influence on how jurors perceive lawyers and witnesses (O'Barr & Conley, 1976). The habit some speakers have of talking at the same time, whether by design or by accident, presents reporters with one of the toughest challenges to accuracy in the record that they face, and it is usually handled, if it is recognized in the transcript at all, by a combination of paragraphing and the dash.

A typical example from my own early files of simultaneous talk, or as I refer to it, cospeech (Walker, 1982), shows this convention as it is most commonly employed:[9]

Q. So it's the corner of Fourth and some other street that--
A. I'm vague--
Q. --you're not aware of.
A. I'm vague on the name.

An obvious problem with this convention is that it does not indicate whether both speakers were in fact talking at once, or whether one of them yielded the conversational floor while the other continued talking.

Although both the court reporting literature and the returns from my survey show that the dash and paragraphing are used fairly consistently throughout the field to indicate cospeech, there is disagreement as to whether it is to be shown at all. The strict verbatim approach represented by the example given attempts to show all incidences of cospeech in as nearly an exact fashion as possible. A more moderate view, one representative of most of the reporters whom I knew during my court-reporting years, takes into consideration the length of the exchange: If it is short, it is written as if there were two sequential utterances; if it is long, interruptions are shown. Transcribed in that style, the example given above would read:

Q. So it's the corner of Fourth and some other street that you're not aware of.
A. I'm vague on the name.

Yes [features of how something is said should be included in a transcript] but I don't know how to accomplish this. Court of Appeals once accused me of being rude based upon [the] transcript when indeed, I was not rude. I was, however, insistent.

[9] During my reporting career, I made several tries at representing cospeech more accurately, and the system I finally settled on—made possible because of the electronic backup I always used—looked like this:

Q. You've never visited the site--
    Q. --since the accident?
[Together]
    A. I had no reason to.

Note that in this style, some of what was said is missing, with the result that what really happened gets lost. It is, however, unarguably more "readable." The third view of cospeech emphasizes the need for readability over exact representation even in the case of long stretches of interruptive talk, and to this approach, one lawyer author takes strong exception.

> If we are to have a *verbatim* record, as the law requires, we must recognize that the trial court or the jury saw and heard the testimony as it was given. The accurate transcript, therefore, should be the same. . . . [A] record that shows constant interruptions or is replete with evidence of the witness's anticipation of counsel's questions is very meaningful, and may, perhaps, even be of some ultimate probative value. (Bieber, 1976:29)

It is rather interesting to note that in his objection to a transcript that does not attempt to show cospeech accurately, Bieber places a questionable and empirically unsupported responsibility for the interruptions ("anticipation of counsel's questions") on the witness, rather than distributing it equally among both speakers or acknowledging simultaneous talk as a fact of natural language. However, there is evidence (Conley, O'Barr, & Lind, 1978; Walker, 1985) that interruptions—even when seen on paper—are in fact "meaningful" and may very well have some "ultimate probative value" for appellate practice and review (Walker, 1986).

4.2.1c. Parentheticals. A bracketed notation in a transcript which reads [bench conference], or [recess taken] is simply descriptive. The parenthetical [interrupting] is more interpretive than the merely redundant [continuing], and one that reads [shouting] is more objective than one that reads [angrily]. [No response] as a substitute for the nonverbal [nods head] is manifestly misleading, and what may or may not be a [pause] is problematic. If court or counsel requests the reporter to read back some testimony and the transcript shows [The last question and answer were read], an accurate read-back is implied. If the transcript reflects "Q. And what did he do then?" followed only by "A. [Indicating]," when what the witness did was to draw his finger slowly across his neck, demonstrative evidence does not make it into the record.

Parentheticals represent the frankest exercise of editorial power that a reporter has, the most easily noted and therefore most easily controlled form of "interpretation." Yet curiously, although the Federal Judicial Center, which one would expect to take the most conservative view, grants reporters the ultimate discretion over their insertion into the record, the general view in the profession itself is that parentheticals "should be used sparingly and only to avoid confusion" (*Court Reporter's Manual*, 1981:24).

If the argument *for* parentheticals goes to clarity, the most pressing argument *against* them concerns interpretation and the need for reporters to avoid "testifying" by putting their own words (parentheticals) into the transcript, particularly because such "testimony" is secret. In arguing in favor of

bare-bones parentheticals (e.g., a minimal entry like [indicating] to signify
nonverbal answers and gestures), Weiss, an authority on reporter punctuation, addresses this secrecy, and thereby supplies what may in fact be the
underlying logic for the pervasive position against reporter interpretation. He
writes:

> The reporter should never take it upon himself in a parenthetical remark to specify
> any height or distance a witness may have indicated, . . . [or otherwise] set himself
> up as an estimator, whether of distances or of anything else. An error on his part
> might help one side or the other, *with no way of correcting the error. By contrast, when
> one of the participants estimates something for the record, the others can hear him and
> contradict him on the spot*, with the subject of discussion still before them. (Weiss,
> 1971:65, emphasis added)

Punctuation, paragraphing, parentheticals—all are visible in their presence on the page. Although some of their editorial effects may be more
obvious than others, more consequential than others, they are at least observable by the reader, and therefore, for the most part, challengeable. Punctuation is acknowledged by case law to be an interpretive device (*Mondani v.
Cuneo*, 1 C.A.3d 1008 [1969]), and it is well litigated.[10] As an editing device, its
vagaries are at least known.

But there is a more subtle, subjective kind of editing that is *not* observable
in the transcript, a kind of editing that alters in a different way the form in
which the content of the trial is transmitted. It is, as far as I can discover, not a
cause of litigation, for its effects are not yet well known. It employs what I call
the artistic devices of correction, elimination, rearranging, and restoration.

4.2.2. Artistic Devices: Correction, Elimination, Rearranging, and Restoration

4.2.2a. Correction. The artistic editing device of correction is triggered by a
sensitivity to grammar that stems from reporters' membership in a literate
society in which "well-educated" and "well-spoken" are expected to be synonymous. This bias continues as they enter reporting schools, whose curricula
reinforce the expectation that the written word be the grammatical word: well-
organized and error-free.

The speech which passes through reporters' hands, however, falls far
short of the refinements expected of language as it is taught in school, and this
gap between their expectations and reality presents reporters with an eternal
conflict. As the normative view of one of their texts expresses it:

---

[10] For examples of cases which include litigation on the subject of mechanical editorial devices
see: period: *Am. Fruit v. Avis*, 118 Ga.App. 840 (1968); comma: *State v. Carter*, 182 P.2d 90 (S.C.
Ariz 1947); semicolon: *State v. Milwaukee County*, 222 N.W. 2d 592 (S.C. WI 1974); colon: *Palmer v.
State*, 312 So. 2d 399 (C.C.A. Ala 1975); question mark: *Sanders v. State*, 344 So.2d 1243 (C.C.A.
Ala 1977); dash: *State v. Carter*, 182 P.2d 90 (S.C. Ariz 1947).

Correct English we may find in a book, and correct speech we may find in the
theatre or on the air. We do not often hear it in the courtroom, and from the witness
stand—practically never.

We spend our days in court reporting testimony the bulk of which is given in
English which, like the initial product of the Oklahoma oil wells, is crude and
unrefined. This customary, everyday lingo grates on our delicate ears and we have
an inner urge to improve it in transcription. (*English*, 1983:88)

Reporters deal with this "inner urge" in a number of ways. Some resist it,
claiming not to edit grammar for anyone. For them, GIGO is the policy:
Garbage In, Garbage Out (Walker, 1985:117). Others allow themselves to be
influenced by the status of the speaker, and the urge is permitted to operate on
the utterances of judges, lawyers, and in some cases, expert witnesses. Their
rationale is the one advanced by the text just quoted:

> It is well settled that the reporter should make every effort to eliminate obviously
> bad grammar from his transcript. The only questions are—whose utterances shall
> enjoy the privilege of being edited? and how bad must grammar be to warrant the
> reporter's departing from a strictly verbatim report?
>
> The general rule advanced by the advocates of liberal editing by the reporter is
> that the utterances of the lay witness should be recorded strictly verbatim but that
> those of judges, lawyers, and expert witnesses (usually professional men, entitled
> by presumption to a certain elegance of expression) should be polished by the
> skillful grammarian-reporter. (*English*, 1983:26–27)

According to the 1984 nationwide survey of court reporters, (Walker, 1985),[11]
82% follow this practice, editing judges and lawyers some or all of the time,
whereas 36% clean up the grammar for the better educated expert witnesses.
Lay witnesses rarely are accorded this "privilege." The figures from the
survey are shown in Table 1.

4.2.2b. Elimination. In keeping with reporters' belief that like children,
they should be seen but not heard, their own spoken words rarely appear in a

TABLE 1. Differential Editing of Courtroom Speakers' Grammar

Speaker	Edit		
	Always	Sometimes	Never
Judge/lawyer	27%	55%	18%
Expert witness	9%	27%	64%
Lay witness	0%	18%	82%

[11] I conducted two surveys of reporter practices over a period of 3 years. The first was a 1981
telephone survey of 20 reporting firms in the Washington Metropolitan Area, representing
approximately 100 reporters. Of these responses, 60% claimed to edit no one; 40% said they
cleaned up the speech of lawyers and judges only. The second nationwide survey was done in
1984 by mail, and the results are summarized in this text. Both are discussed in detail in Walker
(1985).

transcript, and some feel as well that it is the better part of valor not to memorialize an untoward remark of a judge. But the kind of speech which is most often eliminated from the written record is the false start, the very mention of which guarantees argument in the court-reporting field.

The policymakers—the National Shorthand Reporters Association and the federal government—both take the (implicit) position that in most cases, false starts can safely be left out of a transcript. Each, in consonance with the literate/legal appreciation of "getting to the point," apparently regards false starts as generally meaningless bits of language which interfere with the readability of a transcript, and accordingly, as with parenthetical remarks, reporters are allowed discretion in including or excluding them from the transcript. Although it is not stated clearly, the federal guidelines imply that even the testimony of witnesses falls within this discretion (Greenwood *et al.*, 1983:143); the National Shorthand Reporters Association texts appear to take a more cautious view that restricts this policy to the "well-educated or expert witness" (e.g., Budlong, 1983:5). The view (not policy) reflected in the national magazine is usually consistent with the literate approach to documents: If it has no meaning, omit it; if it does, include it. Left unaddressed by any authoritative source to date is the paradox presented by this kind of standard, which requires an objective, noninterpretive reporter to determine what does and does not carry meaning.

In actual practice, status or class membership of the speaker is a prime consideration for about one-third of those who responded to my surveys— that is, 33% claimed to eliminate false starts from the speech of lawyers and judges, while retaining them in that of the witnesses. Another 24% said that it depends on the circumstances, and the circumstances include too much clutter in the record (out), a need for sense (in), and the length of the false start (*out* if short, *in* if long). Of the remaining group, 24% claimed to include all false starts no matter who the speaker is because they are "verbatim reporters"; and the final 19% reported that they leave them out for everyone.

4.2.2c. Rearrangement. In their efforts to create a readable and acceptable record, reporters utilize two types of rearranging of speech: One kind involves document design and is illustrated by their treatment of cospeech in which decisions are made about how interruptive behavior is to be shown, if at all; the second sort is more closely related to grammatical training. This second kind of rearranging focuses solely on single sentences and involves moving a word, phrase, or clause from one point to another. Typically, rearrangement is not regarded by the authorities as appropriate for witness speech, and the examples given in Weiss's book on punctuation (Weiss, 1971) and in the NSRA text (*English*, 1983) are confined to utterances of lawyers and judges.

Whether or not a reporter employs the artistic device of rearrangement during colloquy (exchanges between counsel) is probably not only inconsequential but immaterial. It is hard to see any significance in changing, for instance, "I wonder if we could avoid the expansion of this record *by stipulation*" to "I wonder if *by stipulation* we could avoid the expansion of this record" (Weiss, 1971:10, emphasis added). But changes of any sort in a judge's charge to the jury are not taken lightly by appellate courts, yet the NSRA text adds to the confusion reporters must deal with by recommending them on the familiar grounds that

> Judges are supposed to be men of education and culture; and it is quite unfair to them to have appellate courts presented with crude and blundering expressions when the change or transposition of a few words will remedy the matter *without in the slightest degree affecting the sense of what was said*. (Budlong, 1983:7, original italics)

This is dangerous advice to give a verbatim reporter, whether or not the "sense" will be affected; appellate courts expect a written record of what was said, not of what should have been said. Further, any suggestion to rearrange or otherwise tamper with a charge to the jury sits very oddly next to the observation made earlier in the same chapter of that text that "Accurate reporting of judges' charges and rulings is of the greatest importance, because most reversals by appellate courts are founded upon them" (Budlong, 1983:7).

4.2.2d. Restoration. No speech style is free of some kind of dialectal features, and whether the features are noticed or not depends on the listener. In print, however, variances from the standard become noticeable to everyone, which is why it matters what reporters do with dialects and their cousins, the casual forms such as *gonna, havta,* and *comin'.*

In general, reporters believe that features like these do not belong in transcripts, and by a 2 to 1 margin, the respondents in the survey reported that they restore these variant phonological renditions to their standard dictionary shapes. One telephone respondent, asked if she used forms like "idear" and "wif" (with) said, "No, I put the right—I feel funny saying 'right'—but I put the right word down" (Walker, 1985:123).

One of the most interesting forms of restoration, however, has to do with lax tokens—those familiar "uh-huh," "mm-hmm," and "huh-uh" substitutes for "yes" and "no" which are widely used in conversation. The universal advice to reporters on these tokens is to try to convert the response to a clear yes or no by breaking into the exchange with some version of "Is your answer yes, or no?" Because that tactic is singularly ineffective in changing a speaker's style,[12] reporters are left with two options. One is to try to write the affirmative or negative sound (there are no standardized spellings); the other is to

---

[12] The following anecdote, illustrating the futility of such exhortations, appeared in a recent edition of the NSR:

A. Uh-huh.
Q. You have to say yes or no so the court reporter can get it down. Is that a yes? You said uh-huh.
A. Uh-huh. ("One Reporter's Favorites," 1989:79)

restore the lax token to whatever they perceive its intended full form to be: "yes" or "no." Those who advise this course see no particular problem with it. In their view, as expressed in one reporting text, "The customer reading the transcript [simply] wants to know if the answer to the question was yes or no" (Morphy, 1959:106), and these are the forms in which the answer should appear.

A transcript on which a reporter has exercised this kind of editorial artistry—one in which grammar has also been corrected, false starts removed, and syntax rearranged—is undeniably more readable than its verbatim version. It is also a transcript in which reality has undeniably been transformed. This is the dilemma which reporters face. In the practice of their profession, the tug toward verbatimness vies with readability, objectivity with interpretation, statutes with common sense. Reporters must constantly choose one direction or the other, and the choices they make and the tools they use affect both the representation of the event itself, and, my research suggests, appellate practice and review.

5.   EFFECTS OF VARIABLE REPORTER CHOICES

5.1.   Effects on the Event

5.1.1.   Discrepancies

In speaking of the Court Reporter Act, the appellate court in *United States v. Taylor*, 303 F.2d 165, at 169 (4th Cir. 1962) describes it as having been "designed to preserve a correct and authentic record . . . free from the infirmities of human error." But in spite of this optimistic view, the most obvious effect of asking an imperfect human being to perform an impossible linguistic task is not that error is prevented but rather that it is guaranteed. Considering the staggering possibility for discrepancies between event and representation presented by the kinds of mechanical, cultural, and conventional obstacles discussed earlier, however, transcription errors which are of *recognized* potential legal significance appear to be minimal. The Federal Judicial Center's study of alternative methods of court reporting (Greenwood *et al.*, 1983) reported that of the discrepancies which they identified in the transcripts generated by both court reporters and transcribers of electronic records, 89% were of no legal importance; and my own independent analysis of the discrepancies which the FJC's panel of raters found to be serious, or "functionally relevant" (11%) showed that many of these errors were easily resolved if judged with adequate context.

5.1.2.   Speaker Categories

The Federal Judicial Center study was essentially concerned with the familiar kinds of language errors whose effects on the legal process might

reasonably be predicted. It focused on individual details of language variation—what was omitted, added, substituted—rather than on the overall
patterns reflected by these individual "errors." It mattered in the FJC study,
for instance, that false starts were omitted (although no discrepancy of this
type was judged to be legally significant), but not whether false starts were
omitted systematically for one kind of speaker and not for another.

It would not be surprising to find that they were, given the evidence
already gathered. There are, in fact, at least seven *de facto* categories of
courtroom speakers, created through a variable application of the verbatim
standard. This categorization has a particularly powerful effect on the record
of the event because how a speaker is categorized fairly well predicts how
exact a copy of his or her speech will be made (Walker, 1985).

The seven categories, several of which have already been alluded to, are
(1) sworn/unsworn, (2) educated/uneducated, (3) expert/lay witness, (4) ins/
outs, (5) employer/nonemployer, (6) liked/disliked, and (7) sees transcript/
doesn't see transcript. The classification which has the most impact on how
and whether speech is edited is the sworn/unsworn category, and all speakers
belong to this and to at least one other category.

The *sworn/unsworn* classification is related directly to questions of evidence; sworn speakers are those and only those who are giving testimony
under oath from the stand. Because testimony is the primary source of
evidence in a trial, those who are giving it are the least likely to have their
speech edited, even for form. All other speakers are classified as unsworn and
may or may not be edited, depending on how they fit into in one or more of the
remaining categories.

The classification which has the second greatest impact on editing is
educated/uneducated. As noted earlier, the known or perceived education of a
speaker has considerable influence on reporter practice; educated speakers
are significantly more likely than uneducated speakers to be edited. As sworn
speakers, witnesses may be either educated or not and fall as well into one of
two divisions of the third category, *expert/lay witness*. The distinction here,
although still acknowledging a hierarchy of education, is a legal one which
separates those witnesses who by virtue of their training, experience, and
knowledge are formally granted the right to express an opinion from those
who are not. Experts, of course, are expected to reach a higher standard of
English than lay ("often illiterate") witnesses, and reporters treat their speech
accordingly.

The fourth speaker category, the *ins/outs*, reflects a speaker's status as a
member of the bar. The lawyer and judges who constitute the *ins* form the
power nucleus of the legal community, are presumed to be educated and to
have access to transcripts, and are either actual or theoretically potential
employers of reporters.

Reporters are employed by lawyers or judges in one of two ways. They
can be "official" reporters for a court system, or they can be independent

contractors whose services are negotiated for, either through a reporting firm or by themselves individually. Technically speaking, official reporters are governmental employees, being hired by a state or federal agency, but they *work* for judges, a fact which sometimes sets up a personal relationship that is influential in how the judge's speech is both perceived and treated. The same relationship can occur between a reporter and a lawyer, but reporters are not, and *may not* be in-house employees of law firms. They are hired by lawyers on a case-by-case basis. The connection between this *employer/nonemployer* category and the reporters' treatment of speech is fairly self-evident. Whatever other of the reporter's beliefs about speakers are in operation, they are reinforced by a natural caution connected with keeping their jobs.

But part of the decision about how to treat the customer is also affected by whether or not the speaker belongs to yet another category: *liked/disliked*. Verbatim reporters are expected to be impartial, but the fact is that both reporters and those who use their services quietly acknowledge that likes and dislikes for speakers can be reflected in degrees of verbatimness in a record. Says one judge,

> [T]he worst thing a reporter can do to a judge, *if he doesn't like that judge*, is to record him strictly verbatim. If he records the judge word for word and doesn't get the spirit of what is said, that judge is in a lot of trouble. (Goldfluss, 1981:21)

The final speaker category is *sees transcript/doesn't see transcript*. This category comprises only those speakers who see *their own* speech transcribed, and as such, it excludes anyone not directly involved in the original legal proceeding. Witnesses, however, who are involved by giving testimony in a legal proceeding, rarely become members of this class. They are most likely to be included if they have given a deposition (pretrial interview under oath) and if they have not waived their attendant right to read their testimony before signing it to verify the accuracy of the transcription. There is no such right connected with trial testimony, and consequently, most trial witnesses never "see" themselves on paper. Lawyers and judges, of course, as members of the *in* class, also belong to the *Sees transcript* half of the category, and reporters are well aware that these professionals, even though they are experienced readers of transcripts, share a cultural belief that their status is partially affirmed by the language they are seen to use. Despite the fact that they "know" that the speech they read is extemporaneous and prone to error and that the record is supposed to be word for word, they still carry with them a normative model for written speech, and they tend—lip service notwithstanding—to feel that their "erudition is in doubt" (Gustafson, 1977:17) if their written words are not in order. The fact that reporters share this literate orientation toward language is what makes the operation of these speaker classes possible, thereby contributing to the variability with which speakers are represented in the written versions of legal proceedings.

5.2. Effects on Appellate Review

Popular legal wisdom has it that appellate courts, being deciders of law and not fact, seldom have occasion to read transcripts because transcripts are embodiments of facts which have been decided upon by a lower court. In that case, any discussion of an appellate effect from court reporter customs and conventions would be moot: no matter how influential some of their variable transcription features might be in creating a climate of belief or disbelief, there would be no significant audience to be swayed. Popular legal wisdom, however, is mistaken, according to the Judges Survey reported in Walker (1985). There is in fact a significant audience of jurists who read transcripts for purposes that include to become acquainted with the issues before trial (50%), to consider as evidence during lower court proceedings (82%), and, significantly, *to make decisions during the appeal process* (62%). The frequency with which these transcripts are read—a minimum of 677,646 times per year—was based on figures available as of 1982. Because the roster of judges keeps growing, that number could be expected to be considerably greater now.[13]

The size of the available juristic audience is not the only surprise turned up by the Judges Survey. Contrary to the opinion expressed by reporters in their texts and practice, these judicial readers appear to be less committed as a group to the notions of what written language should look like (grammatical, orderly, free of dysfluencies) than they are to the desire to learn as much as possible about the speaker, and most particularly about the witness. Expressing a need to gauge such attributes as the "character, intelligence and credibility of the witness," the majority of these judges cited as important many of the features which reporters edit out (false starts and "ungrammatical" speech for *any* speaker) as well as some that reporters traditionally consider too interpretive to put in (parentheticals such as [laughs]).[14] It seems clear from these results that judges who are performing appellate functions, then, are actively engaged in forming impressions of the trial participants and are using those impressions in reaching their decisions.

According to a companion survey reported in Walker (1985), the features that are influential in forming impressions are politeness, confidence, cooper-

---

[13] Judges are not the only influential readers of transcripts, as a lawyer friend who works for an investigative branch of the government recently pointed out to me. There are "batteries" of lawyers who read transcripts of testimony given in depositions, trials, and before congressional hearings to search out "wrongdoing" of various kinds, and although they are concerned with content, they also, according to my friend, weigh the credibility of the testimony, using what they see in the transcript as a guide.

[14] With this as with all self-report data, it should be kept in mind that what respondents *say* they feel/think/do is not necessarily what they *in fact* feel/think/do. The instruments I used in this (and the Readers' Impression Survey) were relatively unsophisticated, and it is left for later studies to get at the evidence of how these readers actually would react to, say, seeing their natural speech accurately represented.

TABLE 2. Variables for Transcript Study

Variables of impression	Variables of conventions
About the attorney	Punctuation: period/question mark
Politeness	Interruption by attorney
Competence	Interruption by witness
Control	Use of [laughs] (witness)
	[Pause] (witness)
About the witness	Attorney use of "uh"
Politeness	Witness use of "uh"
Confidence	"Mm-hmm" (witness)
Cooperativeness	Casual forms
Credibility	Underline

ativeness, and credibility of the witness, and the competence, degree of control, and politeness of the questioning attorney. Shown in Table 2, they represent only those transcription conventions which court reporters actually can and will use in a transcript and which are solely within their discretion.

The results of the Readers Impression Survey were startling. Of the 10 transcription conventions tested in the survey, *every one* was found to have an effect on readers' impressions at a level greater than chance, with 7 of the 10 shown in Table 2 correlating at levels of confidence of $p < .05$ or better. The attorney who both interrupted and was interrupted by the witness was seen as lacking in control. The interrupting witness was perceived, unsurprisingly, as impolite. Pausing, whether filled ("Uh") or silent ([Pause]), correlated with negative opinions about witness self-confidence, cooperativeness, and credibility. "Uh" in attorney speech led to perceptions of lack of competence and control and in witness speech with a lack of self-confidence. The correlations of these reporter-controlled features with the impression formation are shown in Table 3.

Although a full discussion of these results is beyond the scope of this chapter, it might be worth commenting briefly on two aspects of the data: first, that they support the findings of the Duke study that a lawyer who either interrupts *or is interrupted* is at risk of being perceived negatively by a jury (O'Barr & Conley, 1976), and second, that they suggest that witnesses would be well advised to avoid using "mm-hmm" instead of "yes" in answering questions. Not only can an mm-hmm (uh-huh, huh-uh, etc.) in a transcript be considered ambiguous and thereby provide grounds for appeal (e.g., *Commonwealth of Pennsylvania v. Stufflet*, 419 A.2d 184 [1980]; *State v. Martinez*, 644 P.2d 541 [1982]), but the perceptions of a witness who routinely uses those forms are, these data suggest, uniformly negative as to politeness, cooperativeness, self-confidence, and credibility. Because "mm-hmm" in a transcript

TABLE 3. Correlation of Impression with Transcription Convention[a]

Feature	Lawyer Compe-tent	Control	Polite (L)	Witness Polite (W)	Confi-dent	Cooper-ative	Credible
Interruption by							
Lawyer (L)	—						
Witness (W)	—*			—	—		
[Pause] (W)					—*	—*	—
Lawyer "Uh"	—*	—*					
Witness "Uh"					—*		
"Mm-hmm" (W)				—*	—	—*	—

[a]+ = Impression is positive for that feature; − = Impression is negative for that feature.
* = Significant at $p \leq .001$.
All other factors significant at levels of confidence from $p \leq .05$ to $p \leq .01$.

represents an informal expression being used in a very formal environment, the findings of this study might be interpreted as yet another bit of evidence that the expectations about language in court settings are very strong and nontrivial in their consequences when violated. The strength of the consequences also suggests that reporters' decisions about how to represent these and other personal features of speech are nontrivial as well.

6. IMPLICATIONS FOR LINGUISTIC STUDY AND LEGAL PROCESSES

A court transcript is a unique example of written language representing a unique case of spoken language. It has no author, but has an editor, and on its pages it represents planned yet unscripted task-oriented talk, carried on in a group whose most important participant, the person on the stand, has the least linguistic power and the most to gain or lose. Because it is the product of a human being who carries constraining notions about language, the world, and the speakers in it, both the transcript and the process by which it is produced provide the opportunity for the study of linguistic processes, while suggesting implications for appellate practice.

From the linguistic point of view, because of its unique mingling of language and situation, task, and output, court reporting offers a fertile field for study in the areas of the spoken–written continuum, language attitudes, and the impact of the literate tradition on what constitutes information, to name a few. Because as I have claimed elsewhere (Walker, 1988), court reporting is another kind of interpretation, it might even be that a study of this task could contribute to a broader theory of translation, one which would account not only for *inter*linguistic moves across codes but which would also give an account of (1) *intra*linguistic moves from one code to another (i.e., spoken language to machine shorthand) and (2) moves from one modality to another (speech to writing). The development of such a theory of transcription/translation might well be facilitated by comparing in a formal way the processes, task, and output of simultaneous interpreters for both non-English speakers and the deaf (especially within court situations) with the processes, tasks, and output of court reporters as they have been outlined here and in Walker (1985).

But perhaps the most salient linguistic "lesson" here concerns the well-recognized fact that a scholar's theoretical approach to a problem constrains the findings. Spoken data are increasingly utilized as a source for social science research, and the transcript which is made from these data often becomes the *de facto* object of investigation. The heavy involvement of interpretive processes connected with transcription poses a problem both for the integrity of the original sample and for the validity of inferences that are drawn. That is not to say that interpretation *per se* and selectivity among all possible representable features in a block of data are wrong. On the contrary, as Ochs notes (1979:44), a transcript should not attempt to display every possible detail, so directed selectivity is often necessary. But it is also necessary that the original transcriber *be aware* of the fact that choices are being made and be aware as well (insofar as is possible) of the biases that lead to those choices. Furthermore, because transcripts are used not only by the original investigator but also by others who, with perhaps different aims, work from the same data, it is even more important that these distanced users understand the theoretical and personal bases upon which the documents were constructed.

The legal implications of court reporting begin with a linguistic fact—that language alters its message in subtle ways by changing its form. The change in linguistic form involved in transcription is, however, far from subtle, and the transformation of a message from its spoken to its written state creates an apparently unending opportunity for discrepancy between the truth of the instant and the truth of perpetuation. The consequences of discrepancy can be considerable. In the world of the courts, a discrepant record can set off a chain of events that increases an already notable expenditure of time, attention, and emotion by the participants, and the money of everyone: "Justice" is expensive, and all citizens pay the bill. The question then becomes, what can be done about it?

The answer depends on the source of the discrepancy: whether it is *inherent* in the task or is overlaid by *institutional* pressure. Two of the inherent problems, which are in fact difficult to separate, concern modality and bias. As the system of reporting in the courts now stands, there is little that can be done about the first. As long as spoken proceedings are reduced by any means into writing (whether from stenotapes, electronic recordings, or video-tapes), not only will there be leakage of life in the form of losing the contextual features of communication, but the message, simply by being filtered through human perception, may be altered. Legal practitioners are of course aware of part of this problem, and the growing experiment with videotaping is one attempt at a solution (see footnote 2).

But videotaping, despite is perceived advantages, is not without its drawbacks. Bias is still possible because the viewer is restricted to whatever the camera saw and how the camera saw it. Even when the filming is done under optimal conditions with high technology, it is still possible not to know what was being said or who was saying it, as my own experience in reviewing videotaped hearings has verified. Furthermore, there is a growing body of evidence to the effect that videotaped records are time-consuming and diffi-cult to handle, catalog, and review (Sanders, 1988; "*Unhappiness Grows*," 1989). Unlike a written record of a trial, which can be flipped through quickly, review of a videotape requires not just the expenditure of an hour of review for every hour of the proceeding but also requires an enormous amount of time to play and replay sections in order to pinpoint the important issues—a task about which appellate attorneys are particularly unhappy.

When it is well done, videotaping comes as close as our technology now permits to preserving the record whole. By retaining the "how" of speech along with the "what," it fills in those holes in "meaning" that a transcript cannot fill, but this attribute also raises what may be the most consequential question of all: Can an appellate court avoid making its *own* judgment—traditionally reserved to the trial courts—of the credibility of the witnesses, or sufficiency of the evidence, or competence of the attorney if it sees a videotape of the trial (or portions of the trial) itself? It is an intriguing question, not as yet researched, with possible far-reaching consequences because it involves the potential compromise of the deference traditionally accorded by appellate courts to the trial court's appraisal of demeanor evidence.[15]

But at present, the written record is in no real danger of being replaced by videotape. Transcripts continue to be the vehicle of record in by far the majority of trial courts, and in their representation of depositions as well. Thus in the transcripts of most legal proceedings, there is really no practical way to redress the loss of context and the record discrepancies which result.

The problem of bias, which is another of the inherent sources of discrep-ancy in transcripts, is somewhat more complicated. All transcription as we know it now begins with human perception, and perception, while resting on a purely biological basis, itself both shapes and is shaped by life experiences. Bias, therefore, is an inherent, individual, and often unconscious force which

---

[15] Some of these questions are now being studied by the National Center for State Courts in a project for which I am a consultant. For a good summary of the problems, see Sanders (1988).

is difficult to combat and redress. But transcription does not exist in a vacuum: the institution in which it occurs has goals, needs, desires, and biases of its own, and these institutional influences on the transcription process are more easily discovered and redressed. Because redress requires informed recognition, the first step in reducing institution-originated discrepancies in legal records, therefore, is to create awareness.

The need for awareness begins at the top, where the problem is the juristic equivocation over what constitutes a verbatim record. Although claiming to adopt the dictionary definition of "word for word" as the standard for verbatimness, the members of the legal profession exhibit through their behavior that in fact something more and something less is required. The need for readability, the desire to look on paper as educated as they know they are, the preference not to pay for pages filled with the *er's*, *ah's*, and other extraneous and "meaningless" bits of language all illustrate their literate bias and mitigate against a document in which natural speech is naturally, that is, "verbatim–ly," represented. This equivocal (and unexamined) attitude has resulted in the present-day state in which, to quote the Federal Judicial Center report once more,

> [E]ach official court reporter has established personal discretionary guidelines as to what should be included in, and what should be transcribed from, the official record of the proceedings, and thus what is "verbatim." (Greenwood *et al.*, 1983:211)

In view of the fact that reporters are constantly enjoined simply to take down what they hear, never to interpret and never to exercise personal discretion, this *de facto* definition of verbatimness is more than a little ironic.

The juristic attitude toward reporter interpretation in creating a verbatim record is a second source of both equivocation and discrepancy. Here the distinction between linguistic competence to understand language and its accompanying gestures, and legal competence to assign significance to the same has simply been confused. No one would ever suggest putting the parenthetical [sarcastically] into a transcript because (1) it would represent an inference which even if accurate was made by someone without decision-making power in the judicial process (thus separating reporters who infer from jurors and judges who infer) and (2) being written silently as opposed to being spoken aloud, the inference would not be made explicit and thereby negotiable at the time of its occurrence. All of this is understandable.

It is somewhat more difficult, however, to understand or defend the traditional position that an observable, public, describable phenomenon such as [laughs] or [crying] is interpretation if noted by a reporter but not if noted by a lawyer or judge. Denying equal communicative competence to reporters in cases like these is particularly odd when the competence is returned to them by those judicial readers who, for instance, want reporters to put [pause] in a record "when significant" and to retain false starts only "when meaningful." There seems in fact to be no well-reasoned ground behind the various stands taken, and as long as such inconsistency and equivocation remain—particularly when ratified formally although no doubt unconsciously by the federal guidelines for production of transcripts—so will related discrepancies in "verbatim" records. Reporters have idiosyncratic notions of verbatimness in part because the *professionals* for whom they work have idiosyncratic standards for verbatimness.

The application of these idiosyncratic standards will, of course, result in discrepancies between the event and its representation, some of which, *because they are known*, provide possible (albeit rarely successful) avenues of appeal to attorneys whose "trained fingers and eyes" roam through the transcript searching for ways to carry the adjudication process past the unfavorable outcome of a trial. The very fact that appeals are based on these kinds of discrepancies points up their obviousness, and that such appeals can and do take place is well known by both readers and producers of transcripts. These and the several other categories of "error" earlier described can be laid to problems with court custom, English training, manual skills, and systems of reporting. Any resultant transcript discrepancies are negotiable and can either be ignored when discovered, corrected by agreement, or pressed into service as grounds of appeal. Their consequences are thus fairly straightforward.

But there are other kinds of discrepancies between the proceedings and their transcripts which are not so available for observation and discovery, and whose impact on the appellate system is less knowable and therefore more troubling. These are discrepancies that enter the record as the result of reporters' cultural and conventional beliefs, and they involve the language "shoulds" (how language should sound and look, who should speak what kind of language) and the "shouldn'ts" (reporters should not interpret, reporters should not interrupt, reporters should not let court and counsel look like "dummies"). Exacerbated by the continual conflict between the verbatim and readability standards under which reporters work, these discrepancies take such forms as rendering dialect heard in the courtroom into "the right English forms" seen in the transcript, of correcting grammar for the unsworn but not for the sworn speakers, of smoothing out speech dysfluencies for the professional "ins" of the scene but not for the "outs." Because of the conscious and unconscious operation of reporters' beliefs about their jobs, about what constitutes information, about their language, and about its speakers, both language and speaker are treated inconsistently. Not all words (false starts, repetitions, lax tokens), not all speech (the reporter's own talk, whispered but audible asides), not all speakers (lay witness, expert witness, judge) get equal treatment in the transcript. And although every reporter knows all of this (or should) and court and counsel may or may not know some of it, witnesses— the speakers who have the most to lose and the most to gain—know none of it. The consequences of such discrepancies between a legal proceeding and its representation are much harder to know.

The Readers' Impression Survey and the Judges Survey, taken together, strongly suggest that reporters' choices in these matters are in fact consequential. According to these data, perceptions of competence, credibility, and intelligence are unfavorably affected by seeing in print such features as pauses, *ers*, *uhs*, casual forms, and ungrammaticality. Given the validity of those perceptions, it follows that there are inevitable social—and legal— implications when those features are variably edited out or left in transcripts. The issue has not been studied sufficiently; the work reported on in this chapter is only a start. But it seems plain that there is something here worth investigating. Without awareness, and without inquiry, institution-based discrepancies will continue to be irregularly characteristic of verbatim transcripts, and the customs and conventions of court reporters will continue to carry unknown consequences for the appellate process and those who enter into it.

7. REFERENCES

Aurelio, S. J. (1988). Why the record must be verbatim. *National Shorthand Reporter, 49*(4), 34–37.

Ballentine's Law Dictionary (3d ed.). (1969). Rochester, NY: The Lawyers Cooperative Publishing Company.

Bieber, S. (1976). Let verbatim be your guide. *National Shorthand Reporter, 37*(7), 27–29.

Black's Law Dictionary (Revised 4th ed.). St. Paul, MN: West Publishing Company.

"Bloopers of the month (Tape Division)." (1984). *National Shorthand Reporter, 45*(10), 56.

Budlong, P. E. (1983). Editing court proceedings and speeches. In *English* (pp. 4–14). Vienna, VA: National Shorthand Reporters Association.

Catford, J. C. (1965). *A linguistic theory of translation*. London: Oxford University Press.

Chafe, W. L. (1982). Integration and involvement in speaking, writing, and oral literature. In D. Tannen (Ed.), *Spoken and written language* (pp. 35–53). Norwood, NJ: Ablex.

Conley, J. M., O'Barr, W. M., & Lind, E. A. (1978). The power of language: Presentational style in the courtroom. *Duke Law Journal, 6*, 1375–1399.

Court Reporters Manual. (1981). North Dakota Supreme Court.

English. Professional Education Series. (1983). Vienna, VA: National Shorthand Reporters Association.

Federal Rules of Appellate Procedure. (1975). Mineola, NY: The Foundation Press, Inc.

Gilman, M. L. (1982). Our native idiom. *National Shorthand Reporter, 43*(6), 31.

Goldfluss, H. E. (1981). The judicious partnership. *National Shorthand Reporter, 42*(4), 21–23.

Greenwood, J. M., Horney, J., Jacoubovitch, M.–D., Lowenstein, F. B., & Wheeler, R. R. (1983). *A comparative evaluation of stenographic and audiotape methods for U.S. District Court Reporting*. Washington, DC: Federal Judicial Center.

Gustafson, C. (1977). Between Scylla and Charybdis. *National Shorthand Reporter, 38*(5), 16–17.

Labov, W. (1966). *The social stratification of English in New York City*. Washington, DC: Center for Applied Linguistics.

Lakoff, R. T. (1982). Some of my favorite writers are literate: The mingling of oral and literate strategies in written communication. In D. Tannen (Ed.), *Spoken and written language: Exploring orality and literacy* (pp. 239–260). Norwood, NJ: Ablex.

Laver, J., & Trudgill, P. (1979). Phonetic and linguistic markers in speech. In K. R. Scherer & H. Giles (Eds.), *Social markers in speech* (pp. 1–32). New York: Cambridge University Press.

Lavery, U. A. (1923). Punctuation in the law. *American Bar Association Journal, 9*, 225–228.

Lieberman, P. (1963). Some effects of semantic and grammatical context on the production and perception of speech. *Language and Speech, 6*, 172–187.

Louisell, D. W., & Pirsig, M. E. (1953). The significance of verbatim recording of proceedings in American adjudication. *Minnesota Law Review, 38*(1), 29–45.

Making the record. (1976). National Shorthand Reporters Association.

Manual for court reporters/recorders. (1981). State Court Administrative Office. Lansing, MI: Author.

Mellinkoff, D. (1963). *The language of the law.* Boston: Little, Brown.

Morphy, A. N. (1959). *How to be a court reporter.* Bayonne, NJ: Pengad Companies.

O'Barr, W. M., & Conley, J. (1976). When a juror watches a lawyer. *Barrister 3*(3), 8–11, 33.

Ochs, E. (1979). Transcription as theory. In E. Ochs & B. B. Schiefflin (Eds.), *Developmental pragmatics* (pp. 43–71). New York: Academic Press.

Olson, D. R. (1977). From utterance to text: The bias of language in speech and writing. *Harvard Educational Review, 47*, 257–281.

"One reporter's favorites." (1989). *National Shorthand Reporter, 50*(3), 79.

Ong, W. J. (1967). *The presence of the word.* New Haven: Yale University Press.

Ong, W. J. (1979). Literacy and orality in our times. *Profession, 79*, 1–7.

Philips, S. U. (1982). The language socialization of lawyers: Acquiring the "cant." In G. Spindler (Ed.), *Doing the ethnography of schooling* (pp. 176–209). New York: Holt, Rinehart & Winston.

Ramshaw, P. (1977). "Auditory Discrimination": A tough subject—even for reporters. *Caligrams,* November 6–7.

Sanders, R. (1988). Technology and the politics of change. *Oregon State Bar Bulletin, 48*(10), 5–14.

Stryker, L. P. (1954). *The art of advocacy.* New York: Simon & Schuster.

Swem, C. L. (1984). Stopping the Witness. *National Shorthand Reporter, 45*(4), 66–68.

Tannen, D. (1980). Implications of the oral/literate continuum for cross-cultural communication. *Georgetown University Round Table on Languages and Linguistics 1980.* Washington, DC: Georgetown University Press.

Tannen, D. (Ed.). (1982). *Spoken and written language: Exploring orality and literacy.* Norwood, NJ: Ablex.

Tannen, D. (Ed.). (1984). *Coherence in spoken and written discourse.* Norwood, NJ: Ablex.

Tannen, D., & Saville-Troike, M. (Eds.). (1985). *Perspectives on silence.* Norwood, NJ: Ablex.

The American Heritage Dictionary, College Edition. (1975). New York: American Heritage Publishing Co., Inc. & Houghton Mifflin Company.

"Unhappiness grows with videotape for the record." (1989). *National Shorthand Reporter, 50*(8), 18.

"Video-recording evaluation and guidebook development." (1988). National Center for State Courts Application, February 4, 1988. Williamsburg, VA.

Walker, A. G. (1981). *Transcription conventions: Do they matter? A sociolinguistic study of a legal process.* Unpublished master's thesis, Georgetown University.

Walker, A. G. (1982). Patterns and implications of cospeech in a legal setting. In R. J. DiPietro (Ed.), *Linguistics and the professions* (pp. 101–112). Norwood, NJ: Ablex.

Walker, A. G. (1985). *From oral to written: The "verbatim" transcription of legal proceedings.* (Doctoral dissertation, Georgetown University).

Walker, A. G. (1986). Context, transcripts and appellate readers. *JQ, 3*(4), 409–427.

Walker, A. G. (1988). *Court reporting: Another kind of interpretation.* Paper presented at the International Conference for Translators & Interpreters, May 28–29, 1988, Arlington, VA.

Waltz, J. R., & Kaplan, D. (1983). *Evidence: Making the record.* Mineola, NY: Foundation Press, Inc.

Weiss, N. (1971). *Punctuation for shorthand reporters.* Vienna, VA: National Shorthand Reporters Association.

Whitford, W. (1898). Defective hearing or mishearing in its relation to shorthand writing. *The Phonographic Magazine.* Reprinted in *National Shorthand Reporter* (1982), *43*(3), 46–49.

"Witness encouraged to edit." (1989). *National Shorthand Reporter, 50*(3), 116.

Wolfe, Tom. (1979) *The right stuff.* New York: Bantam.

Woods, W. A. (1980). Multiple theory formation in speech and reading. In R. J. Spiro, B. C. Bruce, & W. F. Brewer (Eds.), *Theoretical issues in reading and comprehension* (pp. 59–82). Hillsdale, NJ: Lawrence Erlbaum Associates.

8. CASES CITED

Am. Fruit v. Avis, 118 Ga. App. 840 (1968).

Caffrey v. Chem-lonics Corp., 419 P.2d 809 (1966).

Commonwealth of Pennsylvania v. Stufflet, 419 A.2d 184 (1980).

Cushing v. Worrick, 75 Mass. 382 (1857).

Hardy v. United States, 375 U.S. 277 (1964).

In re D.L.F., 176 N.W.2d 486 (S.D. 1970).

Mondani v. Cuneo, 1 C.A. 3d 1008 (1969).

Palmer v. State, 312 So. 2d 399 (C.C.A Ala 1975).

Sanders v. State, 344 So.2d 1243 (C.C.A Ala 1977).

State v. Carter, 182 P.2d 90 (S.C. Ariz 1947).

State v. Martinez, 644 P.2d 541 (1982).

State v. Milwaukee County, 222 N.W. 2d 592 (S.C. WI 1974).

State v. Perkins, 120 N.W. 62 (1909).

United States v. Cabra, 622 F.2d 182 (5th Cir. 1980).

United States v. Hodges, 556 F.2d 1283 (7th Cir. 1977).

United States v. Perkins, 498 F.2d 1054 (D.C. Cir. 1974).

United States v. Piasik, 559 F.2d 545 (9th Cir. 1977).

United States v. Robinson, 459 F.2d 1164 (D.C. 1972).

United States v. Taylor, 303 F.2d 165 (4th Cir. 1962).

United States v. Workcuff, 422 F.2d 700 (D.C. 1970).

Williams v. United States, 338 F.2d 286 (D.C. 1964).

9. STATUTES CITED

28 U.S.C. § 753(b) (1976). Revised under the Federal Courts Improvement Act of 1982, Public Law 970-164, § 401, 96 Stat. 25, 56–57 (1982).

Part IV

CONSTRUING LANGUAGE FOR LEGAL PURPOSES

Chapter 8

LINGUISTIC ANALYSIS OF CONVERSATION AS EVIDENCE REGARDING THE INTERPRETATION OF SPEECH EVENTS

GEORGIA M. GREEN

1. INTRODUCTION

The phenomenon of an academic linguist[1] testifying in court as an expert witness is relatively recent. Linguists' testimony has concerned many aspects of language, but one which has arisen with increasing frequency is the analysis of conversation. Most frequently, this has involved conversations recorded surreptitiously and used as evidence to support charges of such criminal activity as bribery, conspiracy, racketeering, and sale of controlled substances, among others. Both laymen and judges commonly assume that expert testimony is not needed to analyze conversations because conversations are so familiar a part of our daily lives. Consequently, linguistic testimony about conversations is often excluded.[2] Because the opposition to

---

[1] By linguists, I mean of course, scholars with professional training and academic degrees in linguistics, as opposed to polyglots or experts in particular languages.
[2] Cf. Wallace (1986) for an extensive review of the legal issues involved.

GEORGIA M. GREEN • Department of Linguistics, University of Illinois, Urbana, Illinois 61801.

admitting expert testimony by linguists concerning the analysis of conversation is often based on incomplete understanding of that sort of analysis,[3] it is the purpose of this chapter to describe what linguistic analysis of conversation comprises and to propose that linguistic analysis of conversation does in fact qualify as a proper subject of expert testimony.

In the following sections, I describe and illustrate linguistic analysis of conversation and then detail its relevance in a particular criminal case. After a brief review of the status of such analysis as an academic discipline and its history as the subject of expert testimony, I conclude with a discussion of why the linguistic analysis of conversation should be considered a proper subject of expert testimony in accordance with the Federal Rules of Evidence.

2. LINGUISTIC ANALYSIS OF CONVERSATION

What is linguistic analysis of conversation, and why should an officer of the court care? Linguistic analysis of conversation is the application of techniques derived from principles of conversational interaction to records of conversation or other discourse (including written statements, letters, and official documents). Linguistic analysis of conversation encompasses, among other things, the examination of the forms and content of discourse to determine what kinds of questions are asked by whom, and at what point in a conversation, to whom they are addressed, how they are responded to, who introduces new topics, who resolves or disposes of topics, and what sorts of politeness and power phenomena are displayed by each speaker to each other speaker.

By virtue of being grounded in these principles, the techniques of linguistic analysis of conversation allow inferences to be drawn about the likely attitudes of participants toward one another and toward the topics of their discourse. Interpretation of data derived by the techniques referred to can illuminate, for example:

- *Relationships*: Whether A and B speak to each other like friends and equals, strangers but equals, employer and employee, seller and client, etc.
- *Purposes*: Whether A and B are engaged in casual conversation, or whether one or both have goals that are not purely social which they are trying to accomplish by means of the conversation
- *Commitments*: To what extent a speaker has participated in an alleged transaction; whether a speaker has proposed or accepted an arrangement or course of action

---

[3] As documented in Wallace (1986).

In a legal context, linguistic analysis of conversation can contribute to correctly understanding conversations introduced in evidence in cases involving such charges as conspiracy, bribery, sale of controlled substances, extortion, entrapment, hiring someone to commit a felony—probably any case where the claim of the existence of an oral agreement is in question.

In recent years, academic linguists have participated in the defense of individuals accused in such cases; the prosecution has also used expert witnesses (typically not linguists) to interpret conversations introduced into evidence. In addition, linguists have testified in civil trials concerning the potential or likely interpretation of language in written documents (e.g., official forms, written contracts). Although I shall be addressing mainly the use of linguists as expert witnesses to interpret conversation, many of the points I make will be equally applicable to expert testimony by linguists about written language.

Linguistic analysis of conversation is known among linguists by a number of names: conversational analysis, discourse analysis, text analysis, natural language understanding, and linguistic pragmatics, though all of these terms have been used in narrower senses as well (cf. Levinson, 1983; Green, 1982). It takes as its domain all the ways in which the use of a linguistic form reflects the attitudes and beliefs of a speaker. Linguistic analysis of conversation is thus the study of the structure of discourse and the interaction of participants in a conversation as evidenced by what they say, how they say it, and how it is responded to.

As a field of theoretical inquiry, the purpose of discourse analysis is to discover what makes one utterance coherent, effective, forceful, or successful, and another one incoherent, ineffective, or bizarre, and to discover how people use language to further personal and social and other kinds of goals (cf. Green, 1982, 1988).

Applications of discourse analysis include, among other things, evaluating the appropriateness of both oral speech (such as jury instructions) and written documents (such as product-recall notices, truth-in-lending documents, and notices sent by government agencies to affected citizens, (e.g., Medicare recipients)). They may involve evaluations of text or speech for particular audiences (e.g., third-graders, "average" adults, mechanical technicians), or they may involve making testable inferences about the assumptions, interpretations, and conversational goals of participants in a discourse.

The discourse behavior of individuals (that is, how they put what they say) is particularly revealing because it is especially resistant to conscious manipulation, as any lawyer who has tried to prepare witnesses before trial can testify. It is very difficult, for example, to get people to refrain from hedging their testimony with expressions like *I think* and *probably*. As unconsciously governed behavior, discourse behavior reflects, beyond conscious control, the attitudes, beliefs, and agendas of the speaker. Even linguists who study this sort of behavior are pretty much unable to control it in themselves.[4]

To carry out linguistic analysis of recorded conversation, a researcher begins by listening to the relevant conversation(s) from beginning to end. Then, prior to analysis, the conversations must be carefully transcribed and annotated to indicate not just the words each speaker uttered but also their intonation, and all the pauses, hesitations, overlaps, and interruptions that occurred. This typically involves listening to the tape, segment by segment, several more times. The analysis itself proceeds via application of the scientific method (hypothetico-deductive reasoning)[5] to the speech acts observed in the conversation as raw data. In other words, the foundation of linguistic analysis of conversation consists of the same principles as have constituted the foundation of research in the natural sciences (e.g., physics and chemistry) for centuries.

There are two major kinds of analysis: content analysis and interaction analysis.

2.1. Content Analysis

Content analysis includes, among other things, analysis of lexical choice and topic analysis.

2.1.1. Lexical Choice

Lexical choice analysis involves close textual analysis of each individual's speech for what the choice of words reveals about the speaker's attitude toward her conversational partner(s) and toward what she is referring to. For example, there are unstated, untaught conventions governing the use of many of the little "function" words we use, words such as conjunctions like

---

[4] The following true story illustrates the difficulty of consciously controlling discourse behavior. A linguist was in labor with her first child. Her husband and Lamaze coach, also a linguist, needed to know when she was having contractions. She did not want to talk during contractions, even to answer yes–no questions. Therefore, between contractions, they agreed that if he wanted to know if she was having a contraction, he should STATE that she was having a contraction; then if she was not, she could happily contradict him, and if she was, she would not have to answer. Both were (and are) skilled discourse analysts, but the husband nonetheless softened his assertions with "tag questions," in accordance with the compelling social convention against telling people about their feelings, and said things like "You're having a contraction now, aren't you?"—which, being a question, defeated the whole purpose. The woman felt just as compelled to answer it, with predictable consequences.

[5] Hypothetico-deductive reasoning consists of forming hypotheses, deducing what they predict about the subject of scrutiny, and testing the hypotheses by observing whether the circumstances they predict will be present are in fact present, and then revising and retesting as needed, until no more revisions are necessary.

but, though, and *since* and interjections like *well, why,* and *oh*—. These little words are often overlooked because they do not refer to observable properties or events, but in their own way, they may speak volumes about the person who uses them. The conventions governing the use of these words are such that speakers will only use one when they hold a certain attitude toward the referent or content of their speech. Everyone who speaks the language in a normal and natural fashion abides by these conventions (or rules) in using and understanding these words, though hardly anyone is ever aware of them. For example, the conjunction *though* is used to adjoin a subordinate clause B to a main clause A if and only if the speaker believes that the addressee would not expect the proposition in B to be true when A is true. Thus, I used *though* in the sentence just before the last one because I expect people to assume (counter-factually) that if you regularly and unfailingly act in accordance with a rule, you must (consciously) know the rule,[6] or at least to assume that other people assume this (see Nunberg, 1978:107–117). Consider what would be inferred if I said, "Though it's June, the maples are in full leaf." One would have to assume from my use of *though* that I thought it unreasonable to expect the maples to be in full leaf in June, and therefore either that I had strange and false beliefs, or that I was referring to maples in the southern hemisphere or some other place where such a belief ought to be quite reasonable.

To take another case, the conjunction *since* is used to attach to a main clause A, a subordinate clause B which refers to a proposition that the speaker assumes not only is true but is generally assumed to be true. Thus a person who says "Since John got a raise, he won't have to live on pork and beans anymore" assumes that John got a raise and that his audience knows that. The use of "since" would be inconsiderate (or extremely florentine) if the speaker believed her addressee did not know about John's raise, and the addressee would be justified in interrupting to clarify whether John did get a raise ("John got a raise?"). If the speaker was merely mistaken about the addressee's beliefs about John, the addressee's question would inform her of this.

Speakers sometimes exploit this property of *since* and *though* when they do not expect their audience to hold the requisite assumption. A speaker

---

[6] Indeed, Bach and Harnish (1979) base numerous criticisms (e.g., pp. 12, 137, 193–194) of various accounts of communication on the implicit assumption that it is inconceivable that people could regularly act in accordance with a convention without being consciously aware of the convention. The assumption that people cannot act according to a convention if they are not consciously aware of it is common enough, but it is demonstrably false. The rules of syntax are conventional in that there are no logical or biological reasons to explain when adjectives precede the words they modify and when they follow, or why the rules are different for French and English, yet both French and English speakers abide by these various conventions without apparent difficulty. But speakers of English are generally not aware of these conventions and are unprepared to articulate them and explain why we say *the tall one* and *someone tall,* but not **the one tall* or **tall someone.*

might do this to flatter the audience (by conveying an impression that the speaker believes that the audience knows more than they do in fact know, as in 1, or it might be done to sneak important assumptions into the context of the conversation as in 2 (see Horn, 1986).

1. Since passage of Senator Eks's amendment would seriously jeopardize first amendment rights, we urge you to write your senator and ask him to oppose it.
2. Since we cannot provide any more funds, you will have to choose between smaller paychecks and larger classes.

Similarly, a person who says "Since John McEnroe has never lost at Wimbledon, he must be pretty good" must either believe that McEnroe has never lost at Wimbledon, or at least want his audience to believe he believes that.[7]

Sentences with interjections like *well* and *why* also illustrate the significance of lexical choices. As pointed out by R. Lakoff (1973b), the use of *well* in a response to a question indicates that the response, although true, is not complete. Thus if A asks B what time it is, B might say "Two-thirty," suggesting certainty, or "Well, my watch says 2:30," implying that the watch may not be completely accurate, but not "Well, 2:30"—unless B has reason to believe that the answer "Two-thirty" would be misleading to A. This might be the case, for example, if what A really wanted to know was what time it was in a nearby city which, unbeknown to him, happened to be in a different time zone.

Similarly, if A is asked, "Did you kill Mrs. Wayne?," and answers "Well, yes," A is indicating a belief that more is relevant than just "Yes." Maybe A thought at the time of the killing that he was killing someone else; maybe A did not intend his act to have a fatal effect; maybe A did not even know at the time that anyone was injured as a result of his act. If A is asked who is buried in Grant's tomb, and answers, "Well, General Grant," his answer indicates there is something more to be said. (For example, that someone else is in there, too.) When "well" prefaces a question, as Lakoff points out (1973b:463), it indicates dissatisfaction with the sufficiency of a previous utterance or action (cf. the usual uses of "Well, why not?" vs. a simple "Why not?").

On the other hand, the use of *why* to preface a question or a direct response to a question implies that the previous utterance contradicts some assumption of the speaker's (Lakoff, 1973b:461–464). Thus if *why* prefaces an answer, it implies that the answerer believes that the asker ought to know the answer, but does not. Accordingly, when a teacher absentmindedly asks a

---

[7] Or want his audience to believe that he wants them to believe that he believes it. There is no principled limit to the depth of potential deception of this sort, though it gets exponentially more unlikely with each step.

student where the hats and coats are, the student can answer, "Why, in the closet," without committing a breach of etiquette, but the student risks being censured as a smart aleck if the question is when Abraham Lincoln was born, and he answers, "Why, in 1809."

An account cited by Clarence Darrow's biographer Irving Stone (1941) succinctly illustrates this use of "why." Darrow had written an article defending the socialists, referred to as anarchists in the press, who were accused of conspiring to throw the bomb which incited the Haymarket Riot in 1886. According to Stone, Darrow "demonstrated that the eight men had been railroaded in a corrupt and illegal trial" (Stone, 1941:96). Stone then quotes the following story as told to him:

> Clarence was invited by H. H. Waldo, a bookseller, to come to Rockford and read this paper before a select audience of twenty-five people, among whom was the editor of the *Morning Star*. At the conclusion of the reading there was a moment of silence, broken by Mr Browne, the editor, who declared:
> "Don't you think it was necessary, in order that society should be protected, that these men be hanged as an example, even if they were innocent?"
> "Why, Mr Browne," retorted Darrow, "that would be anarchy."

2.1.2. Topics

Topic analysis, as described in more detail by Shuy (1981a, 1986, 1987) involves noting what topics a speaker brings up, and how that speaker responds to topics brought up by others. If a speaker brings up a topic, that indicates he wants to talk about it. If his interlocutor changes the topic in response, or is silent, or says very little by way of answer, that can indicate that the interlocutor does not want to talk about that topic. Tracking the introduction of topics and responses to them can provide relevant information in cases involving such issues as bribery, conspiracy, and entrapment.

In addition to engaging in topic manipulation to attempt to control a conversation, speakers sometimes manipulate the *way* they refer to introduced topics in an attempt to constrain the moves of their conversational partners: They may ask leading questions, or they may use loaded speech—speech which purports to do something straightforward but actually also injects a new idea into the conversation as if it were one which participants already accepted, as in expressions like "Since John got a raise," discussed before. To take another example, if someone asks you, "Have you stopped swiping tips?," she purports to be asking a straightforward information question, but she is acting as if you and she both assume that you have been swiping tips. If you do not want to disrupt the conversation, out of politeness you will refrain from objecting to this kind of unfair move, and it will look as if you agree with this implication, whether you really do or not. Because politeness (see 2.2.3) is a significant variable in normal conversation, this is one way (among many others) in which taking a conversation at face value and failing to consider covert intentional manipulation may lead an untrained listener to an incorrect inference.

2.2. Interaction Analysis

Interaction analysis includes, among other things, the analysis of questions, cooperativeness, turn-taking behavior, and politeness. Both content analysis and interaction analysis contribute to illuminating the nature of a speaker's contributions to a conversation. For example, if a person asks a lot of sincere, information-seeking questions, that can indicate that he is trying to influence the course the conversation will take, for two reasons. First, asking such a question is a reliable way to establish a discourse topic. Second, given normal assumptions about cooperative behavior (Grice, 1975), questions demand relevant answers (Sperber & Wilson, 1986). Likewise, the proportion of a speaker's utterances that are questions of this type may indicate how important controlling the conversation is to that speaker. As an example, consider the very different inferences that will be drawn about the participants in a job interview depending on which one asks most of the questions. If it is the personnel director, we see her as in charge of the conversation, finding out what she wants to know. If it's the applicant, we see him as interviewing the company, taking charge and finding out whether *it* will suit *him*, perhaps telling the personnel director what he wants her to know but not concerned enough about the company's needs to let her ask the questions.

2.2.1. Question Analysis

Question analysis involves determining who asks questions of whom, and what kinds of questions they are. There is a wide range of question types, whose identification is relevant to understanding participants' interactions. Straightforward sincere questions, like "What time is the Smiths' party?" or "Is your blue suit at the cleaners?," indicate that the speaker wants some information (the information that would answer those questions) and also indicates that the speaker believes that the addressee has that information. However, not all questions are like that. Questions of clarification, like "Huh?" or "What?" or "He did what?" indicate that the speaker knows he has been spoken to, but is not certain exactly what was said to him. (With more stress or pitch variation, they can indicate surprise, shock, indignation and the like, in addition.) Confirmatory questions like "Really?" or "University is south of Church St., right?," or "You did put the mayonnaise back, didn't you?" indicate that the speaker believes some statement is true, but is not sure and believes that the addressee does know for sure. Sometimes a person A asks a question to which he knows the answer and knows that the addressee B knows that A knows the answer. Examples would be questions like "Boy, we really beat them good, didn't we?" or "Remember when we played baseball on the Midway without a ball or bat?" Questions like this are commonly used to evoke a feeling and display of agreement and solidarity with the speaker. Questions with the same structures (e.g., "You were late again, weren't you?," "Remember what I told you about being late?") can also be used to badger an addressee into admitting something relevant to the speaker's conversational goals. In addition, sometimes people use very minimal, noncommittal questions like "Is that so?" or "Yeah?" or "Is he?" to encourage the addressee to keep talking and say more about the subject of the conversation.

Information retrievable from tabulation and comparison of each participant's use of various question types may be relevant to determining their respective roles in any enterprise in which they appear to be engaged—for example, who is trying to get whom to do what. But analysis of this sort requires a trained analyst who has hours to pore over transcripts and listen and relisten to tapes. It is not something that can be done by intuition on one hearing of a tape.

2.2.2. Cooperativeness

Conversation among rational members of a society depends on participants conforming to what Grice (1975:45) has called the cooperative principle:

> Make your conversational contribution such as is required, at the stage at which it occurs, by the accepted purpose or direction of the talk exchange in which you are engaged.

Accepted conversational purposes may, of course, be assumed or inferred rather than being explicitly agreed upon, and may exist at more than one level. Being cooperative, as Grice explained, involves saying as much as is required for the understood purpose, saying no more than is required, telling the truth, and being relevant, orderly, and clear (i.e., avoiding both vagueness and ambiguity).

How cooperative the participants in a conversation are with each other can shed light on their social relationship. If a Speaker A cooperates with Speaker B, then it indicates that A is interested in helping B attain whatever goal A perceives B to be pursuing in that portion of the conversation, or at least that A wants to give the impression that he is interested. If A does not conform to the cooperative principle—does not answer questions or answers them with just one or two words [does not say enough] or changes the subject [is irrelevant] or takes every opportunity to monopolize the conversation [says too much], then that indicates either that A is not rational or that A is not interested in helping B to accomplish the goals that B appears to be trying to accomplish by his talk or perhaps even that A wants B not to accomplish these goals. If B's speech is consistently vague or ambiguous, B may not be genuinely cooperating with A. B's true goals may be somewhat different from what

B would like A to believe they are, and if B purports to be supporting A's apparent goals, this suggests B may be a false friend ("white man speak with forked tongue"). Analysis of this sort of conversational behavior can be used in showing whether two conversants act like they are working together on a common goal, or separately, with individual purposes.

2.2.3. Politeness

Finally, a conversational analyst can look at which politeness conventions the participants appear to be observing in their interaction with each other, since politeness behavior reflects the kind of relationship speakers believe they have with other participants, or want to have (Brown & Levinson, 1978). I am following the usage standard among linguists here and using "politeness" to refer to whatever means are employed to display consideration for one's addressee's feelings (or "face"), regardless of the social distance between speaker and addressee.

Participants in a conversation can choose to be actively polite in a way appropriate to their relationship and intentions regarding it; they can withdraw from the conversation and participate only to the extent necessary to avoid being rude, or they can choose to do as they please conversationally with utter disregard for others' feelings and wishes. In the terms of Lakoff's (1973a) analysis, there are three distinct politeness principles, each appropriate to different situations.[8]

The principle governing formal situations where there is an acknowledged difference in power and status between the participants, such as between a student and a dean, or between a factory worker and a vice-president in charge of personnel, is DON'T IMPOSE. Not imposing means not giving or seeking personal opinions, avoiding personal reference (therefore using titles or titles and last names), avoiding references to family, personal problems, habits, and the like—in short, upholding a pretense that participants have no personhood or shared experience.

In informal situations, where the participants have approximately equal status and power, but are not close acquaintances as in, for example, the relationship between a businessperson and a new client, or the relationship between two strangers sharing a semiprivate room in a hospital, the governing principle is OFFER OPTIONS. Offering options means expressing oneself in such a way that one's opinion or request can be ignored without being contradicted or rejected: for example, saying "I wonder if it would help to get a perm" or "Maybe you should get a perm" instead of "you should get a perm."

The principle for friendly or intimate situations, ENCOURAGE FEELINGS OF CAMARADERIE, is appropriate to interactions among intimates and close

---

[8] A more detailed analysis essentially consistent with Lakoff's is presented in Brown and Levinson (1978).

friends.[9] Encouraging feelings of camaraderie includes showing interest in the addressee by asking personal questions or revealing personal details about oneself. In general, it involves conspicuously displaying evidence that the participants are important to each other as individuals and that they have many common bonds. Intimate politeness tactics are also sometimes used to try to make a new acquaintance feel like an old and treasured friend.

The principles for the more formal situations hold in less formal interactions as well, except when following them would violate the principles specifically for informal or intimate situations. Thus the formal politeness rule "Don't Impose" is in principle consistent with "Offer Options" and "Encourage Good Feelings." Imposing on a stranger by making personal conversation may be just as much a social faux pas as doing it with a social superior, and it is just as bad to impose by putting a friend on the spot by baldly offering a strong opinion he is likely to disagree with, as it is to burden your boss with the details of your home life that caused you to be late. But asking personal questions is often polite in intimate situations because it indicates an interest in the addressee, even though it is considered to be an imposition in formal and informal situations.

It is important to note that the relationship between politeness tactics and social relationships is not always direct or obvious. People apply the various politeness strategies in different ways according to such variables as

1. Their personal style
2. Their estimate of their relationship to the addressee
3. Their desire to change that relationship
4. Their estimate of what kind of situation a certain behavior is appropriate to
5. Their sensitivity to the effect of various behaviors

As an example of personal style differences, some people believe that asking personal questions like "What were you in the hospital for? or "How much did your TV cost?" is a good way to show interest and thus conform to the conventions for intimate politeness. But their conversational partners may feel that they are not in an intimate situation, that they do not know each other well enough, and so may take the questions as implying a greater intimacy than exists or is desirable. Similarly, some people believe that interrupting with relevant remarks shows interest in what the other person is talking about; other people feel that it shows utter disregard for the interrupted speaker (Tannen, 1984).

Given the conditioned variability in application of politeness principles,

---

[9] Even lovers have to be polite to each other at the appropriate level, or their relationship will come unstuck. If a woman's spouse or boyfriend or best friend should choose to display formal politeness behavior toward her, she may interpret it as giving her the cold shoulder and wonder what had caused the relationship to change.

how does a linguist interpret speakers' politeness behavior in a conversation? The mere fact that some linguistic form was used at some point in a conversation cannot be taken as evidence that a particular social relationship holds between the participants. Rather, with interpersonal behavior of this sort, use of a particular form on a particular occasion does not invariably indicate a particular attitude or intention on the part of the speaker. Inferences about speakers' attitudes and intentions must be based on the preponderance of behavioral tokens, interpreted in context, not isolated tokens taken out of context. As with question analysis, politeness analysis is a complex task, requiring multiple, fine-grained examinations of a conversation. It is not the sort of thing that an untrained observer can do on one exposure to a conversation, where it is difficult to tell one voice from another and keep track of who said what and what it sounded like. Furthermore, one must look for patterns in politeness behavior and how they are affected by the dynamics of the conversation; what A says to B may affect (i.e., alter) B's relationship to A, her perception of it, and/or her intentions regarding it.

As an example of what might be reasonably inferred from politeness behavior, suppose that in addressing someone, a speaker S displays primarily formal politeness behaviors (such as the use of titles like *Mr.* or *Professor*, terms of address like *sir* and *ma'am*, use of technical terms like *deceased* and *micturate*, or language that makes the speaker appear humble (cf. Lakoff, 1972). Then it is reasonable to conclude that S believes (or wishes to give the impression that he believes) that he is in a formal politeness situation, talking to someone with greater status and power whom he wishes not to offend, or to someone with lesser status and power, with whom he wishes not to be more intimate.

If S uses primarily informal politeness behaviors, hedging his assertions with expressions like *probably, I think*, using euphemisms like *pass away, use the powder room, sleep with someone* (polite ways of referring to topics that are not discussed in polite company), and going out of his way to be cooperative and agreeable, then, all other things being equal, it is reasonable to conclude that he believes he is in an informal politeness situation and wishes to be polite and cooperative.

If S uses primarily intimate politeness behaviors, asking personal questions and confiding personal details about himself, using nicknames and pronouns without expressed referents (and in certain groups, using slang and four-letter words freely and without anger or sexual interest), it is reasonable to conclude that, all things being equal, he believes he is talking to a friend or intimate, as an equal, and is interested in maintaining the relationship.

I have discussed a sampling of techniques that a linguist may employ in the analysis of conversation and the kinds of inferences that may be drawn from it and mentioned ways in which these inferences could be used in a judicial setting to determine such relevant facts as A's attitude (e.g., belief) toward some proposition or A's relationship with an interlocutor B. In the following section, I describe what linguistic analysis was able to contribute to the presentations in court in an actual case.

3. LINGUISTIC ANALYSIS OF CONVERSATION IN COURT: A CASE STUDY

3.1. Background

The case to be discussed involved a young man accused of being involved in a conspiracy to distribute cocaine. The defense attorney asked me to provide an analysis of a recording which the prosecution would introduce as incriminating the defendant. The recording, made covertly by a federal drug agent, was of a conversation involving the agent, the defendant, and a drug dealer. The defendant was a college athlete who was invited to the dealer's apartment to autograph an athletic event program for "a friend"—the agent. The defendant was supposed to have been involved in a conspiracy with the dealer, who became a witness for the prosecution at the last minute. I analyzed the questions asked by these three participants, the topics each introduced, and the politeness and cooperativity each one exhibited with respect to each of the others. The results of these analyses enabled revealing contrasts to be drawn among the participants and their roles in the recorded interactions.

3.2. Analysis

Analysis of the questions asked by the three participants showed that the agent's speech contained two times as many questions as any of the other participants' (44 in all, 30% of his utterances). About three-quarters of these appeared to be sincere information-seeking questions or questions of clarification or confirmation. The rest were social questions, questions whose purpose was to keep his conversational partner talking or to express solidarity with him. The agent was polite to both other participants, mostly exhibiting marks of intimate politeness (personal questions and free use of gutter language to express mild emotion).

Analysis of topic introductions showed that the dealer initiated at least two-thirds of the conversations about drugs, half of the conversations about sports, and most of the conversations about himself. Whenever he talked about dealing drugs, he used the pronoun *I*, not *we*, indicating he considered himself to be acting alone. He was scrupulously polite to the agent, about two-fifths of the time using informal politeness, making efforts to be helpful and a good host, even two or three times offering the agent a marijuana cigarette.

The rest of the time he was polite at the level of intimate politeness, confiding personal details, asking solidarity questions, and using more gutter language than any other participant. But he was less than polite to the accused, ordering him about, not giving him options, reproaching him in the company of others.

By contrast, the accused spoke only when spoken to. He did not participate in any conversations about drugs. The dealer did not even offer him a marijuana cigarette. The accused asked only three questions, all three to find out exactly what had just been said to him. I observed only one instance of an effort on his part to be polite: at one point, he volunteered personal information to add to a story the dealer was telling. The defendant did not participate with the others in the use of profane language to show solidarity, not even in response to the agent's "Seems like a lot of it's bullshit, really." In fact, he conspicuously failed to observe the conventions of conversational politeness in that, in the recorded conversation:

- He is conversationally uncooperative:
  He gives brief, minimally informative answers to the questions asked him (e.g., "Yeah").
  He avoids answering questions, responding to the dealer's asking him "How long you been home?" with "How long have I been home?" (meaning "Are you really asking me how long I've been home?")
  He changes the topic to avoid answering questions.
- His clarification questions indicate that he hasn't been attending to the conversation.
- He interrupts three discussions concerning sports or athletes to correct or contradict the dealer or the agent.

3.3. Conclusions

Based on these observations, I concluded that the dealer was concerned to keep his customer the agent happy and had no idea that the latter might be an undercover narcotics agent. (I never imagined that the selling of drugs could be accomplished with as much gentility as the agent and the dealer manage.) The dealer's utterances also indicate that he was concerned to make the agent believe that he knew a lot of important people, was close friends with a lot of athletes, and could arrange for the agent to meet them at a moment's notice. Because he never used the pronoun *we* in discussing current or future drug deals, I concluded that he considered himself to be acting alone, independently, and autonomously in selling marijuana and cocaine.

I was prepared to testify that on the basis of my analysis of this conversation, the defendant went to the dealer's apartment for the express purpose of signing an autograph. As soon as the agent was introduced to him, the defendant was asked to sign an autograph, and he seemed neither surprised nor particularly pleased by this, as if he expected it and had come to the dealer's precisely for that purpose.

The agent and the dealer both used the defendant's name when speaking to him, to get his attention, and at least once, his first response to them was "Huh?" These two facts, plus the fact that his speech was barely audible (and sometimes was inaudible) on the tape, compared to the agent's and the dealer's, indicate that he was not paying much attention to what they were saying or doing and may have been physically removed from them. There was no evidence in the taped conversation to suggest why he stayed at the dealer's after he had done what he had apparently come to do: sign the autograph.

Significantly, there was no linguistic evidence that the defendant possessed or was responsible for the sale of any drugs. No one asked him for any drugs, he never said "Here it is," no one ever said "Thanks" or "You brought it" to him. One would expect utterances of this sort if he had come to deliver drugs. There is also no linguistic evidence of his getting or expecting any money for his trouble in coming to the dealer's. He did not participate in any discussion relating to the ongoing sale of a couple of thousand dollars worth of cocaine, or to any future drug transactions, nor was he referred to in any of those conversations. Furthermore, the absence of positive politeness behavior by the defendant, his general inattention to both the dealer and the agent, and his conversational uncooperativeness described above are inconsistent with the dealer's claim that the defendant was his partner in the drug deals discussed. Thus there was a good deal of linguistic evidence, both in what was said, and in what was not said, in favor of the defendant's innocence.

I testified in an offer of proof before the judge, with the jury absent, but the judge declined to admit the testimony.[10] The analysis I had prepared was still useful to the attorney, however, in preparing direct and cross-examination of witnesses and in summation. The defendant was acquitted. Thus expert linguistic analysis can be valuable even when not admitted as evidence.

4. LEGAL ISSUES

Although the foregoing discussion makes it clear what linguistic analysis of conversation can offer to the individuals responsible for determining discourse facts in cases recording conversation, legal professionals are often unaware of its existence and scientific status. Judges have sometimes been

---

[10] I was not asked for my opinion on the ultimate issues of whether the defendant had delivered controlled substances or been part of a conspiracy to distribute them.

reluctant to admit testimony by linguists about conversation (Wallace, 1986), and many trial lawyers do not realize that there is a body of scientific knowledge about conversation, on the basis of which expert testimony might be offered. Because an attorney offering testimony as expert testimony must be prepared to show that it is based on a body of knowledge that has achieved general acceptance in its field, it is worthwhile to review some of the relevant facts about the status of linguistic analysis of conversation which could be used to support the claim that it meets this criterion. Thus the following section briefly discusses the status of linguistic analysis of conversation as an academic discipline and the history of linguists' testimony about conversation in the courts and then turns to the logical and empirical questions involved in determining its admissibility.

4.1. Discourse Analysis as an Academic Discipline

Although linguistic analysis of conversation goes by a variety of names and is the concern of researchers who concentrate on different aspects of it, its scholarly foundations are beyond dispute. That the field is based on seminal works by Grice (1975), Searle (1969), Austin (1962), Sacks, Schegloff, and Jefferson (1974), Cohen and Perrault (1979), R. Lakoff (1973a), Brown and Levinson (1978), and Bransford and Johnson (1973) is not controversial. It is important to note that for the most part, these works are not directed to analysis of conversation *per se* but rather constitute major advances in older disciplines (such as philosophy, psychology, and sociology, as well as linguistics and artificial intelligence), which facilitated the development of techniques for the linguistic analysis of conversation.

Courses in linguistic pragmatics (also known as discourse analysis, or conversational analysis, and text analysis) are taught in the linguistics departments of at least 32 universities. Articles in these fields appear in the major general linguistics journals such as *Language* and *Linguistics and Philosophy*. In addition, the International Pragmatics Association and several scholarly series or journals are dedicated to pragmatics, language use, and analysis of discourse (including *Discourse Processes, Language in Society, Advances in Discourse Processes, Journal of Pragmatics, Pragmatics and Beyond*). The Linguistic Society of America sponsors sections devoted to discourse at its annual meetings, sometimes constituting as much as 20% of the delivered papers. Research in discourse analysis is funded by the National Science Foundation, the National Endowment for the Humanities, the National Institute of Mental Health, and the National Institute of Education. Finally, there are at least seven textbooks for graduate and undergraduate instruction in discourse analysis (under one name or another), and more in the works.

This is not to say that all linguists are experts in linguistic analysis of conversation, any more than all physicians are experts in reading X-rays, or performing abdominal surgery. But there is a considerable number of linguists who are qualified by background and interest to do this sort of analysis, and a smaller number who have actually done so in legal cases.

4.2. Admitted Testimony about Conversation

Although linguists' testimony about conversation is not routinely admitted by the courts, in a number of criminal cases the appellate court has upheld the trial court in admitting testimony concerning recorded conversations by various government agents (see Wallace, 1986:95–97 for references). Although prosecution witnesses have tended to be FBI or DEA experts in particular kinds of crime,[11] rather than linguists, their testimony has involved inferences of exactly the same sort that an expert linguist is qualified to make, and furthermore, to articulate and explain (see 4.3 for details). What is particularly relevant about these cases is that it is evident that the government agents were not limited in their testimony to information grounded in their expertise about particular criminal activities. In addition to explaining the meaning of referential terms (that is, nouns and verbs) which have specialized senses in the cant of thieves, bookies, or drug dealers, they were allowed to testify as to the intended referents of ordinary expressions that belong to the common language and are used in standard ways. For example, in *United States v. Hajal* (555 F.2d 558 [1977]), a federal drug enforcement agent was allowed to testify that "four of 'em" meant 'four pounds of something.' In *United States v. Bailey* (607 F.2d 237 [1979]), another DEA agent was allowed to testify that the words "the same thing" meant that the terms of a previous purchase would apply to the purchase or sale being negotiated.

Testimony about the referents a speaker could rationally have intended a pronoun to have in a particular context is exactly the sort of testimony that a linguist is prepared by training and experience to provide. Although the agents were testifying as expert witnesses, the basis for their testimony appears not to be their expertise but their participation in the event they testified about. Unless expressions like *four of 'em* and *the same thing* are demonstrably idioms or code, it seems highly unlikely that a case agent has anything more to go on in deciding what the referent of *them* or *he* is in a certain conversation than his participation in the conversation, in which case, the testimony as to the referent of the pronoun is not expert testimony admissible under Fed. R. Evid 702.[12] In any case, such a witness is without linguistic training and would be unprepared to explain or justify his conclusion explicitly. In contrast, a linguist could explain under what circumstances

---

[11] For example, in *United States v. Milton*, 555 F.2d 1198 (1977); *United States v. McCoy*, 539 F.2d 1063 (1976); *United States v. Alfonso*, 552 F.2d 605 (1977); *United States v. Barletta*, 565 F.2d 985 (1977); *United States v. Cirillo*, 499 F.2d 872 (1974); *United States v. Bailey*, 607 F.2d 237 (1979); and *United States v. Hajal*, 555 F.2d 558 (1977).

[12] See 4.3 in text.

it would be rational for the speaker to have intended, say, Smith rather than Jones (or vice versa) as the referent of some pronoun (see Prince, 1984).

Furthermore, the linguistic testimony of the government agents extended to inferences from the recorded conversation about the roles and relationships of the participants vis-à-vis each other. In a number of decisions upholding admission of "linguistic testimony" by case agents, appellate courts have used language which would seem to sanction the use of linguists to testify about conversations. Thus, in *United States v. Milton* (555 F.2d 1198), expert witnesses for the prosecution, working from transcripts of conversations, were introduced to testify about the interpretation of certain bets as "lay-offs." The appellate court held that their testimony concerning each defendant's role in an alleged bookmaking organization was consistent with the rules of evidence regarding expert witnesses. The court in *United States v. McCoy* (539 F.2d 1050 [5th Cir. 1976]) characterized the FBI special agent who testified as an expert witness as "able to analyze these conversations in a way that the average juror or layman could not" and stated that "in characterizing certain transactions as lay-offs the expert was correctly 'drawing inferences from the facts which a jury would not be competent to draw'" (McCormick, 1954:Sec. 13). This is exactly the sort of expert testimony that a linguist trained in linguistic analysis of conversation can offer.

4.3. Legal and Empirical Issues

Rule 702 of the Federal Rules of Evidence provides that "if scientific, technical, or other specialized knowledge will assist the trier of fact to understand the evidence or to determine a fact in issue, a witness qualified by knowledge, skill, experience, training, or education may testify thereto in the form of an opinion or otherwise," while Rule 403 provides that relevant evidence may be excluded "if its probative value is substantially outweighed by the danger of unfair prejudice, confusion of the issues, or misleading the jury, or by considerations of undue delay, waste of time, or needless presentation of cumulative evidence." In a few cases, expert testimony about conversation has been rejected as unreliable,[13] or potentially confusing,[14] although it is important to note that the appellate courts upholding these exclusions did so only for the particular cases being appealed and do not represent precedent for generally excluding linguists' expert testimony about the analysis of conversation. Rule 704 says that "testimony in the form of an opinion or inference otherwise admissible is not objectionable because it embraces an ultimate issue to be decided by the trier of fact." Thus the relevant questions for the admissibility of expert testimony about conversational evidence are:

[13] *State v. Conway*, 472 A.2d 588 (N.J. Super.A.D. 1984).
[14] *United States v. Deluna*, 763 F.2d 897 (1985); *United States v. Schmidt*, 711 F.2d 595 (1983).

- Will expert testimony about the linguistic analysis of conversation assist the trier of fact (the jury, or the judge, when there is no jury), and therefore be admissible according to Rule 702?
- Or is it unnecessary (and therefore not admissible under 702)?
- Or is it a waste of time, or misleading, and therefore excludable according to Rule 403?

In terms of the sorts of questions courts ask about the admissibility of expert testimony, these questions may be particularized to:

1. *Reliability*: Is linguistic analysis of conversation sufficiently reliable to qualify as a proper subject of expert testimony?
2. *Scientificism*: Is linguistic analysis of conversation so technical as to risk prejudicing the trier of fact by sheer force of technology?
3. *Necessity*: Does expert testimony by a linguist provide analysis and interpretation, or tools for analysis and interpretation, which the jury cannot reasonably be expected to come up with on its own, or is such expert testimony an invasion of the province of the jury?

The following sections respond to these questions, and demonstrate that testimony by linguists about conversational events can indeed aid the trier of fact in understanding conversations placed in evidence. A conversation is more than the sum of utterances it encompasses, and its structure is such that an eavesdropper cannot be counted on to interpret the conversational interchanges as they were intended to be understood. Consequently, expert testimony about the analysis of conversation does not (as is often claimed) constitute a waste of time, nor is it needless presentation of cumulative evidence, and so need not be excluded by Fed. R. Evid 403.

4.3.1. Reliability

In *Frye v. United States* (293 F. 1013 [1923]), the court admitted the difficulty of defining "just when a scientific principle or discovery crosses the line between experimental and demonstrable stages" but established as a criterion for admissibility that "the thing from which the deduction is made must be sufficiently established to have gained general acceptance in the particular field to which it belongs." The fact that discourse analysis is an established part of the linguistics curriculum at over 30 major universities, the fact that meetings of the Linguistic Society of America regularly devote sessions to it, and the fact that research in discourse analysis is regularly published in the major general linguistics journals as well as in specialized journals indicate that discourse analysis (by whatever name) has achieved general acceptance as a subfield of linguistics.

Nevertheless, the court in *United States v. Williams* (583 F.2d 1194 [1978]) rejected the "Frye test" as inapplicable. Appellants had argued that because there was considerable disagreement among experts about the validity of spectrographic comparisons to identify voices, such spectrographic evidence should not have been admitted. But in rejecting the applicability of the Frye test, the court upheld its admission, citing five specific criteria for reliability (potential rate of error, existence of standards, abusability, analogy to routinely admitted handwriting and ballistics identification, and consequences of defective equipment), which it said spectrographic evidence met. Not all of these very particular criteria are relevant to the admission of expert linguistic testimony because it does not depend on sophisticated technology and does not necessarily involve questions of disputed speaker identification,[15] but responsible practitioners maintain the same standards of accountability for linguistic analysis of conversation as for other subdisciplines of linguistics: claims are not to be made unless they can be backed up with evidence or reasonable inferences.[16] The reliability of this sort of analysis can be tested empirically by comparing analyses of the same material by different analysts (a standard technique in experimental behavioral sciences), and research is underway which does just this for linguistic analysis of conversation (Green & Di Paolo, forthcoming).

4.3.2. Scientificism

It is clear from the description of linguistic analysis of conversation in 2 that it is not a technological analysis, based on complicated machinery or abstruse calculation, but a rational one, based on demonstrable behavioral conventions. This attenuates any danger of overwhelming the jury with impressive machinery. Nonetheless, some opinions sanctioning the exclusion of expert testimony do so on the related grounds that admission raises the specter of a "battle of the experts" (*United States v. Fosher* 590 F.2d 381, 384 [1979]), where one side's expert witness will be rebutted by the other's, and both experts will be cross-examined at length to discredit their testimony. This is seen as wasting time and having a potential to mislead the jury. In the case of expert testimony about linguistic analysis of conversation, however, a limited "battle" might contribute more to the jury's being able to evaluate the expert testimony (and the conversation itself) than it risks in confusion. The

---

[15] In principle it could. Testimony by nonlinguists using various aspects of recorded language to identify the author of a disputed text has been offered, but has not met with much acceptance (*United States v. Hearst*, 412 F.Supp 893, 895 [N.D. Cal 1976], aff'd 563 F.2d 1331 [9th Cir. 1977], *cert. denied* 435 U.S. 1000 [1978]; *United States v. Clifford*, 704 F.2d 86, 88–91 [1983], 543 F. Supp. 424 [W.D. Pa. 1982]).

[16] Preparing to present research to a knowledgeable and hostile or competitive audience at scholarly conferences is not much different from what is necessary to prepare testimony that might be cross-examined.

reason for this is that responsible linguistic analysis can be supported by argument from explicitly stated (and independently motivated) premises and observations, and so, while laypersons are not generally experts in the analysis of their own language, they are often in a position to evaluate the observations and dependent arguments that a linguist could present to support an analysis. I expect, however, that "battles" at that level of detail would be unlikely to be allowed to develop. In any case, expert testimony about the data and the analysis of it can sometimes be as effective by providing the jury with the background to interpret the evidence on their own as it would be by providing an opinion on an ultimate issue (as allowed by rule 704).

4.3.3. Necessity

The other major issue that remains to be discussed is whether linguistic analysis of conversation might be necessary to assist the trier of fact in understanding conversational evidence or determining a discourse fact in issue. There are at least two sorts of cases where one could expect that linguistic analysis might be required for an accurate determination of conversational facts. The first involves cases where it is not clear what has been said. Sometimes both sides will agree on a transcription of a recorded conversation, but this is not always the case. Ordinarily, the conditions under which covert recordings are made are not ideal: the microphone is hidden and covered by layers of clothing and may be masked or obstructed by the positioning of participants or the incidental placement of objects. In addition, there is often considerable background noise. Consequently, there may be legitimate disagreement over what words were actually uttered, or by whom they were uttered.[17] The potential for mishearing speech recorded under such conditions should not be underestimated; Mack and Gold (1985) showed that in a condition where context provided no clues for decoding, over a third of noisy speech was misheard, whereas only 3% of clear speech was misheard. A linguist's analysis of the dynamics of a conversation could provide evidence for particular versions or attributions, and against others.

The second sort of circumstance where linguistic analysis of conversation could be expected to help the trier of fact determine the relevant facts involves cases where there is agreement on what words were uttered, but no agreement on what they signify. Here again, the linguist's discussion of how various interpretations would fit into the demonstrable conversational patterns could provide an informed expert opinion as to whether, when Y uttered

---

[17] Cf. Prince (Chapter 9 this volume) for a discussion of this issue, which is of crucial importance in the preparation of transcripts used in trials. Walker (Chapter 7 this volume) also discusses this and a number of other relevant aspects of conversation that may become obscured by transcription.

the words "kill her," and X responded with "yeah," that constituted a request on Y's part and an agreement to comply on X's part, given the context in which it was uttered. Perhaps X's "yeah" only meant "I hear you; keep on talking," or maybe it was meant ironically—equivalent to "that's ridiculous."

From the court's point of view, the relevant question is: Could the trier of fact determine all of this without expert help, or would a judge who admitted expert testimony on linguistic analysis of conversation be invading the province of the jury?

Admitting expert testimony which "could not add to common sense evaluation" (*Fosher*, at 383) because it concerns a subject which is not both "beyond the ken of the ordinary juror" (*Fosher*, at 383) and "reliably analyzed by modern science" would violate the rules of evidence. So, the question boils down to

1. Can linguistic expert testimony about conversation add to common-sense evaluation?
2. Can jurors be expected to independently intuit the conclusions which expert linguistic analysis could provide evidence for, and if so, would they trust those intuitions, or reject them as prejudice?
3. Is conversation reliably analyzable by modern science?

These are, of course, empirical issues also, and question 3 has been addressed (Section 3.2.1). As for questions 1 and 2, Di Paolo and Green (1988) compare interpretations by excused jurors of the conversation described in Section 3 with interpretations arrived at by trained linguists, and show that the volunteer participants drew different conclusions from the linguists about the speakers' involvement in the tape-recorded events, and came to different conclusions about the defendant's innocence, the linguists' conclusions more closely matching those of the actual jury.

On the face of it, it is unreasonable to expect that untrained jurors would come to the same conclusions about a conversation as a trained analyst. There are several reasons why this is so.

4.3.3a. Common or Uncommon Sense. Jurists who object to expert testimony by conversational analysts on the grounds that it invades the province of the jury apparently do so in the belief that all it takes to reach the same conclusions as an expert is common knowledge, regardless of whether the average juror could articulate its application. Apparently the assumption is that since common law assumes that jurors can evaluate the demeanor of a testifying witness in order to judge whether the witness is lying (apparently on the presumption that they rely on such an ability to conduct their daily lives), then jurors must be able to evaluate *recorded* conversation for sincerity, politeness, friendliness, hidden agendas, and the like, because (presumably) they must make such judgments in their own daily conversations.

The two tasks, however, are not comparable. When evaluating the demeanor of a testifying witness on the stand, the juror is considering linguistic behavior to determine one thing only: is the witness credible? In contrast, when the trier of fact is evaluating covertly recorded conversations as evidence, what is at issue is not limited to whether the speaker is knowledgeable about what he is talking about and is telling the truth. Any number of things might be at issue—for example, the speaker's beliefs about some alleged fact, or his attitude toward some person(s) or propositions, or what he might be trying to get others to do, or what, if anything, he is committing himself to, and other questions of this sort. In many cases, what is to be considered may not be explicitly identified by counsel before the trier of fact hears the conversation, which makes it much less likely that a juror will attend to the relevant phenomena. Furthermore, jurors listening to a covertly recorded private conversation may have no information about any participants who have not been introduced as witnesses before the tape is heard; similarly, there is no guarantee that jurors will have access to social, dialectal, or contextual background against which to judge the conversational behavior of a taped speaker, as they do when a foundation is laid for the testimony of a sworn witness. (See DiPaolo and Green (1989) for more discussion.)

Finally, the rules for acceptable testimony in court suspend the rules for normal conversation (Lakoff, 1985; Walker, 1982). Court discourse demands a high level of formal politeness and imposes the unnatural constraints of formal interrogation (for example, the witness must speak only when spoken to and must give direct answers to all questions, even where the witness knows that a direct answer would be misleading). Above all, in-court testimony calls for abiding by the oath to tell the truth, the whole truth, and nothing but the truth. In this formal environment, with its special written and unwritten rules, a witness is cut off from many normal conversational devices, and the clues to speaker attitudes which these provide are fewer and weaker. Thus in considering the demeanor of a witness giving sworn testimony, not only is the trier of fact supposed to be evaluating it for one property only, namely credibility, there is not much else in the way of interpersonal interaction to evaluate.

In contrast, in social conversation, propositions may be implicated without being asserted—or even explicitly mentioned (cf. Grice, 1975; Green & Morgan, 1981; Green, 1987, 1988), levels of politeness may be deliberately manipulated by either participant to accomplish social goals, speakers are free to interrupt each other and to be unresponsive, and especially important, telling untruths is tolerated and even expected, if not encouraged, in the course of making excuses, making other participants feel better, and offering entertaining narratives (jokes and personal anecdotes). These elements of social conversation are rarely consciously analyzed. Indeed, a person who routinely did so could be considered paranoid or otherwise self-obsessed. On the rare occasions that they are consciously analyzed in the course of natural conversation, analysis is unlikely to be systematic because systematic analysis requires multiple reviews of the conversation (see Sections 4.3.3b and 4.3.3d below).

Thus, although many ordinary speakers are excellent evaluators of speech directed at them in a context they are familiar with, they are generally not prepared to make inferences from interruption patterns, politeness manipulations, and the like in a conversation they are not part of. There are two reasons for this. First, such patterns are not observable from a single hearing, even if one is looking for them. Second, making valid inferences from such behavior requires that the patterns be interpreted in the context of the individual speaker's style (see Section 2.2.3). In contrast, the expert who spends hours cataloging, classifying, and comparing such patterns can point them out and put the trier of fact in a position to come to a conclusion from them.

4.3.3b.   Timing and Time Constraints.   In criminal cases, expert testimony about conversation may also serve to avoid obstacles to interpretation that are inherent in the way trials are conducted. The trier of fact ordinarily hears about the charges before evidence is presented which provides a context for the allegedly criminal acts. In cases involving covert recordings as evidence, the recordings are often part of the prosecution's case, and as such are presented before the defense counsel has an opportunity to explain to the jury the elements of the conversation that are relevant to issues that will form the crux of the defense arguments. Much of a recorded conversation which is relevant to the issues the defense may raise, issues which have to do with the participants' personal relationships with each other and their plans vis-à-vis each other and which are ultimately relevant to the facts at issue, may not be directly relevant to the charges. For example, the prosecution may be interested in showing from (1) A's speech to B about C before C arrives on the scene and (2) the consummation of a drug deal after C arrived, that A and C conspired to distribute controlled substances. The defense may wish to show from C's *non*-participation in social or business conversation with A that C was merely an unwitting courier and an embarrassed guest. In cases like this, the crucial elements may not be attended to when the recording is presented by the prosecution. When the defense requires an expert witness to explain these properties, the explanation may be too involved to be given in opening arguments.

In addition, what is relevant to defense issues may involve the way something is said as much as the content of what is said. An example would be the circumstances where the defendant's clearly audible "yeah" could express enthusiastic agreement, encouragement to keep talking, a request for confirmation, or sarcastic dismissal of an interlocutor's idea. Furthermore, conversational content which is relevant to the defense may not be the same as what is relevant to the charges. Moreover, even when the trier of fact can be advised of what to look for, it is humanly impossible to attend to the content and the form of a conversation simultaneously. (If you are not convinced of this, try attending to the discourse particles *well, uh, oh*, which your interlocutor uses and understanding what is being said at the same time.) In these circumstances, expert testimony about conversation can compensate for such completely human constraints on attention.

It can similarly compensate for similar constraints on memory. Ordinarily, in a case involving recorded conversation, the jury is afforded only one opportunity to hear the tape. In some cases, only parts of the conversations are entered into evidence. This may be sufficient to verify that the parties uttered the expressions which are claimed to incriminate them, but it is in no way sufficient for the jury to evaluate the context in which they are uttered and interpret the intent of the speaker in uttering them. According to one sociolinguist, just hearing a defendant's voice in a recording of a conversation where some illegal activity is discussed is enough to persuade some jurors of the defendant's guilt (Shuy, 1986). The jury may have the right to rehear a tape or reexamine a transcript, but they do not necessarily have both, or even the time to listen carefully enough to notice relevant linguistic behavior. A linguist working with the same materials is likely to want to hear the tape in its entirety at least five or six times to determine and note the way in which things were said—the intonation, pauses, interruptions and overlaps, and how the various remarks fit into the structure of the conversation. This takes hours and hours for a skilled linguist; it is unreasonable to expect an untrained listener to reach an accurate assessment in the time afforded in a trial setting.

4.3.3c. Unnatural Conversation. Even if ordinary people using intuition alone could reliably evaluate natural conversation on the fly, for the sincerity, personal attitudes, beliefs, and intentions of the participants, much legally recorded conversation differs significantly from natural conversation in that at least one party knows that the conversation is being recorded, and furthermore knows why it is being recorded, namely to preserve incriminating utterances to be used in prosecuting a suspect. In fact, it is often the responsibility of this person to get the other participants to incriminate themselves with their words. The temptation is therefore great for the recording agent to use more or less sophisticated means to manipulate the target into agreeing to some proposition not originally on his agenda or to cut him off when he begins to act like he wants to clarify or reduce his role, especially in "sting" operations like Abscam (see Shuy, 1987, for a detailed description of manipulative strategies in making covert recordings). It is again unlikely that an untrained juror could observe how this manipulation and entrapment is accomplished because in entrapment case it fools the equally untrained victim, but brief testimony by an expert in conversational interaction can make the deployment of manipulative techniques manifest.

4.3.3d.   Unconscious, Inaccessible, and Unreliable "Knowledge."   A case can also
be made that expert testimony about conversation is necessary "to assist the
trier of fact to understand the evidence, or to determine a fact in issue" (Fed.
R. Evid. 702) because much of what ordinary people know about language is
unconscious, tacit knowledge—like knowing how to ride a bicycle—and their
conscious beliefs about language use may be false. Even though in conducting their daily lives, ordinary people do make inferences from each other's
speech behavior, they are not always aware of making them, and when made
aware, may be disinclined to trust them. As an example of unconscious
inferences, it is well known that people regularly make (incorrect) inferences
from the conversational behavior of speakers from different cultures (e.g., the
black or Hispanic who, out of deference, avoids eye contact in conversation
with superiors in a formal situation and suffers for acting "guilty" or "shifty";
or the Anglo who politely looks directly at a superior in a formal situation in a
Hispanic or Japanese culture and cannot understand why he is taken to be
arrogant or defiant (Hall, 1959, 1966; Labov, 1969). I am concerned here,
however, with inferences made by members of the same culture as the
participants whose speech is observed. In these cases, the inferences may be
correct, but incorrectly disregarded as untrustworthy, or reflecting prejudice
(even though an expert could show that they are valid and rational) because
the inferrer cannot articulate the basis for them. For instance, it is clear that
ordinary people can make correct inferences from speech behavior addressed
to them or to someone else for them to see: They react to rudeness, politeness,
obsequiousness, tentativeness (cf. Erickson, Lind, Johnson, & O'Barr, 1978;
O'Barr & Lind, 1981), solicitude, familiarity, and the like. All of this is reflected
in identifiable speech behaviors. But people also often misinterpret each
other's behavior when they make the "seat of the pants" judgments that are
required to carry on normal discourse, and many people cannot articulate
what particular behavior makes them feel that a speaker is rude, polite,
obsequious, overly familiar, or the like.[18]

So even if the trier of fact has the ability to correctly interpret aspects of

---

[18] An example may be helpful. A few years ago, my sister told me that after 15 years, she had a
revelation about what irritated her when she was talking with my brother. She said, "The way he
talks it sounds like he's trying to show you how much he knows about stuff," and went on to
give an example, saying, "Yesterday, when I drove him to the airport, and we noticed all the
flattened skunks, he said, 'Don't you think that's because the high water has forced them out of
their normal environment?'" I suggested that he was probably trying not to show off and was
avoiding saying "That's because. . . ." I added that saying "Do you think that's because. . ?"
would have served his purpose better than "Don't you think. . .?" because "Don't you
think. . .?" implies that he thinks it and you probably don't, whereas "Do you think. . .?"
implies that he doesn't know for sure but thinks that maybe you do. When my sister expressed
astonishment at the insightfulness of this analysis, I explained that it was part of my business as
a linguist to be sensitive to such things, just as it is a doctor's business to be sensitive to reflex
responses in patients.

speech behavior beyond the literal meaning of what is said, the knowledge that accounts for this ability is almost entirely subconscious and thus not subject to conscious control. This is evident in the fact that jurors (and even judges [Conley, 1982]) will make inferences from the in-court behavior of parties and counsel despite explicit pretrial instruction not to. It is perhaps even clearer in some striking results of research by O'Barr and his colleagues (Erickson *et al.*, 1978; O'Barr & Lind, 1981). Erickson *et al.* (1978) showed that subjects in a jury simulation made inferences about the competence and credibility of witnesses from various properties of their speech style—specifically, from their use of hedges like *I think* and *sort of*, hesitation phenomena like *uh, um,* intensifiers like *very, definitely, really,* and question intonation in making declarative statements. At first glance, this seems to support the thesis that jurors can do without expert testimony to interpret conversational events. However, O'Barr and Lind (1981) also showed that when subjects in the same conditions were informed (via special jury instructions) that speech style might not reflect competence and truthfulness, but merely idiosyncratic style, they made exactly the same judgments. That is, they were unwilling or unable to exclude certain sorts of evidence. Quite likely this is because they did not, perhaps could not, recognize such evidence as such in the course of listening to testimony. This is exactly what one should expect from individuals who are not accustomed to analyzing and discussing such evidence explicitly. A trained linguist, on the other hand, has a rich classificatory system and a corresponding vocabulary for describing various aspects of speech style and can readily pick out instances of various distinctive, empirically identifiable styles of speech, and show whether, and if so how, they follow a consistent pattern, and what inferences might be validly made from that pattern, under what circumstances. The average person can easily follow a well-organized discussion of the principles for this sort of analysis but does not come to a trial equipped with the framework or vocabulary for consciously identifying the relevant instances. Consequently, it is hardly surprising that O'Barr and Lind's subjects failed to come to different conclusions about the participants whose speech they considered when told to ignore certain data in their possession.

The juror's position is analogous to that of the layperson who, serving as a witness, may sense that opposing counsel has done something unfair, but may be utterly unable to articulate that feeling, and say what was unfair and why. One reason for this, of course, is that the ordinary person is utterly unfamiliar with the rules of civil and criminal procedure and the rules of evidence.

It is also possible that some speakers who *can* identify aspects of a witness' or conversant's speech which they interpret as indicating particular attitudes or intentions may believe that those interpretations are irrelevant or prejudicial and not within the scope of what they have been charged with judging. Research reported by Di Paolo and Green (1989) indicates that jurors would be uncomfortable drawing inferences in a trial situation from the manner of speaking of individuals relatively unlike them in socially significant ways.

4.4. Conclusions

The preceding section described a number of circumstances where the testimony of a linguistic expert might be necessary to enable the trier of fact to draw valid inferences from conversation introduced as evidence. These included cases where conversational patterns would be relevant but would not be evident to someone not trained to look for them. In any case, such patterns often require many hours and considerable bookkeeping to demonstrate. The circumstances discussed also included instances where the timing and structure of the presentation of evidence might pose a serious obstacle to attending to all relevant aspects of conversation introduced as evidence. I also discussed the real possibility that triers of fact may reject correct inferences, mistakenly believing them to be the result of prejudice rather than valid evidence.

In all of these circumstances, expert testimony which speaks to these issues, brings them out in the open, and demonstrates how contextual factors limit valid inferences is surely more likely to result in enlightenment than in confusion.

It is instructive at this juncture to characterize the kind of information a linguistic expert can supply about conversation by comparing it to the sort of testimony that some other kinds of experts could provide. The analogy made earlier comparing experts on linguistic analysis of conversation to radiologists is perhaps not quite apt. What a radiologist knows concerns representations ordinary people never see (X-rays) of objects that ordinary people never see (skeletal structures and internal organs). A linguist's expert knowledge concerns the interpretation of behavior that ordinary people interpret every day. The knowledge that an untrained observer has about conversation compared to the knowledge that an expert has is more like the knowledge of football that the fan in the street has compared to the knowledge that an NFL coach has. A fan can see that a receiver caught or missed a pass that the quarterback threw, but he usually cannot see how the defense tried to prevent all the receivers from catching the ball, and how the offense foiled them, or tried to, because he is not accustomed to attending to so much at once, or to conceiving of the plays as involving so many individual, interacting parts. A coach can look at a play, or a videotape of one, and see all these things, even when the play involves teams he is unfamiliar with, and explicate them.

An untrained observer listening to a conversation may notice that one of the participants talks a lot less than the others but may not observe that he speaks only when spoken to; may see that lots of topics are discussed but may not notice that a certain participant only speaks on one topic; may see that both Smith and Jones are polite but may not see that Smith is polite formally and Jones informally. In any case, an untrained listener may well not know what to make of any such observation. It is testimony on exactly these sorts of issues that a linguistic expert in conversational analysis can supply in legal proceedings.

5. REFERENCES

Austin, John. (1962). *How to do things with words.* Cambridge, MA: Harvard University Press.
Bach, Kent, & Harnish, R. (1979). *Linguistic communication and speech acts.* Cambridge, MA: MIT Press.
Bransford, John D., & Johnson, M. K. (1973). Consideration of some problems in comprehension. In W. G. Chase (Ed.), *Visual processing.* New York: Academic Press.
Brown, Penelope, & Levinson, S. (1978). Universals in language usage: Politeness phenomena. In Esther Goody (Ed.), *Questions and politeness: Strategies in social interaction* (pp. 56–311). Cambridge, England: Cambridge University Press.
Cohen, Philip R., & Perrault, C. R. (1979). Elements of a plan-based theory of speech acts. *Cognitive Science, 3,* 177–212.
Conley, John. (1982). The law. In William O'Barr (Ed.), *Linguistic evidence: Language, power, and strategy in the courtroom* (pp. 41–47). New York: Academic Press.
Di Paolo, Marianna, & Green, G. M. (1988). The interpretation of conversational evidence by laypersons.
Di Paolo, Marianna, & Green, G. M. (1989). Juror beliefs about the interpretation of speaking style.
Erickson, Bonnie, Lind, E. A., Johnson, B. C., & O'Barr, W. M. (1978). Speech style and impression formation in a court setting: The effects of powerful and powerless speech. *Journal of Experimental Social Psychology, 14,* 266–279.
Green, Georgia M. (1982). Linguistics and the pragmatics of language use. *Poetics, 11,* 45–76.
Green, Georgia M. (1987). Some remarks on why there is implicature. *Studies in the Linguistic Sciences, 17*(2), 77–92.
Green, Georgia M. (1988). *Pragmatics and natural language understanding.* Hillsdale, N. J.: L. Erlbaum Associates.
Green, Georgia M., & Di Paolo, M. (forthcoming). Inter-rater reliability in analysis of conversational interaction.
Green, Georgia M., & Morgan, J. L. (1981). Pragmatics, grammar, and discourse. In P. Cole (Ed.), *Radical pragmatics* (pp. 167–181). New York: Academic Press.
Grice, H. Paul (1975). Logic and conversation. In P. Cole & J. L. Morgan (Eds.), *Syntax and semantics, Vol. 3: Speech acts* (pp. 41–58). New York: Academic Press.
Hall, Edward T. (1959). *The silent language.* Garden City: Doubleday.
Hall, Edward T. (1966). *The hidden dimension.* Garden City: Doubleday.
Horn, Laurence. (1986). Presupposition: Variations on a theme. In A. Farley, P. Farley, & K.-E. McCullough (Eds.), *Papers from the parasession on pragmatics and grammatical theory* (pp. 168–192). Chicago: Chicago Linguistic Society.
Labov, William. (1969). The logic of nonstandard English. Reprinted in W. Labov, *Language in the inner city* (pp. 201–240). Philadelphia: University of Pennsylvania Press (1972).
Lakoff, Robin. (1972). Language in context. *Language, 48,* 907–927.

Lakoff, Robin. (1973a). The logic of politeness, or minding your p's and q's. In C. Corum, T. C. Smith-Stark, & A. Weiser (Eds.), *Papers from the 9th regional meeting, Chicago Linguistic Society* (pp. 292–305). Chicago: Chicago Linguistic Society.

Lakoff, Robin (1973b). Questionable answers and answerable questions. In Braj B. Kachru, Robert B. Lees, Yakov Malkiel, Angelina Pietrangeli, & Sol Saporta (Eds.), *Issues in linguistics: Papers in linguistics in honor of Henry and Renee Kahane* (pp. 453–567). Urbana: University of Illinois Press.

Lakoff, Robin. (1985). My life in court. *Georgetown University Roundtable on Languages and Linguistics 1985*, pp. 171–179. Washington, DC: Georgetown University Press.

Levinson, Stephen, (1983). *Pragmatics.* Cambridge, England: Cambridge University Press.

Mack, Molly A., & Gold, B. (1985). *The intelligibility of non-vocoded and vocoded semantically anomalous sentences.* Tech. Rep. 703. Lincoln Laboratory. Cambridge, MA: MIT Press.

McCormick, Charles T. (1954). *Handbook of the law of evidence.* St. Paul, MN: West Publishing Company.

Nunberg, Geoffrey. (1978). The pragmatics of reference. Ph.D. dissertation, CUNY.

O'Barr, William M., & Lind, E. A. (1981). Ethnography and experimentation; partners in legal research. In Bruce D. Sales (Ed.), *The trial process* (pp. 181–207). New York: Plenum Press.

Prince, Ellen. (1984). Language and the law: Reference, stress, and context. *Georgetown University Roundtable on Languages and Linguistics 1984*, pp. 240–250. Washington, DC: Georgetown University Press.

Sacks, Harvey, M., Schegloff, E. A., & Jefferson, G. (1974). A simplest systematics for the organization of turn-taking in conversation. *Language, 50*, 696–735.

Searle, John. (1969). *Speech acts.* Cambridge, England: Cambridge University Press.

Shuy, Roger. (1981a). Can linguistic evidence build a defense theory in a criminal case? .*Studia linguistica 35*(1–2), 33–49.

Shuy, Roger. (1981b). Topic as the unit of analysis in a criminal law case. In Deborah Tannen (Ed.) *Analyzing discourse: text and talk* (pp. 113–126). Washington, DC: Georgetown University Press.

Shuy, Roger. (1986). Some linguistic contributions to a criminal court case. In Susan Fisher & A. Todd (Eds.), *Discourse and institutional authority: Medicine, education, and law* (pp. 234–249). Norwood, NJ: Ablex.

Shuy, Roger. (1987). Conversational power in FBI covert tape recordings. In Leah Kedar (Ed.), *Power through discourse* (pp. 43–56) Norwood, NJ: Ablex.

Sperber, Dan, & Wilson, Deirdre. (1986). *Relevance.* Cambridge: Harvard University Press.

Stone, Irving. (1941). *Clarence Darrow for the defense.* New York: New American Library.

Tannen, Deborah. (1984). *Analyzing talk among friends.* Norwood, NJ: Ablex.

Walker, Anne G. (1982). *Discourse rights of witnesses: Their circumscription in trial.* Sociolinguistic Working Paper 95. Austin, Texas: Southwest Educational Development Laboratory.

Wallace, William D. (1986). The admissibility of expert testimony on the discourse analysis of recorded conversations. *University of Florida Law Review, 38*, 69–115.

6. CASES CITED

Frye v. United States, 293 F. 1013 (1923)
State v. Conway, 472 A.2d 588 (N.J. Super.A.D. 1984)
United States v. Alfonso, 552 F.2d 605 (1977)
United States v. Bailey, 607 F.2d 237 (1979)
United States v. Barletta, 565 F.2d 985 (1977)
United States v. Cirillo, 499 F.2d 872 (1974)

United States v. Clifford, 704 F.2d 86, 88–91 (1983), 543 F.Supp. 424 (W.D. Pa. 1982)
United States v. Deluna, 763 F.2d 897 (1985)
United States v. Fosher, 590 F.2d 381 (1979)
United States v. Hajal, 555 F.2d 558 (1977)
United States v. Hearst, 412 F. Supp. 893, 895 (N.D. Cal 1976), *aff'd* 563 F.2d 1331 (9th Cir. 1977), *cert. denied* 435 U.S. 1000 (1978)
United States v. McCoy, 539 F.2d 1063 (1976)
United States v. Milton, 555 F.2d 1198 (1977)
United States v. Schmidt, 711 F.2d 595 (1983)
United States v. Williams, 583 F.2d 1194 (1978)

7. STATUTES CITED

Fed. R. Evid. 403, 702, 704.

Chapter 9

ON THE USE OF SOCIAL
CONVERSATION AS EVIDENCE
IN A COURT OF LAW

ELLEN F. PRINCE

1. INTRODUCTION

In this chapter, I shall discuss two issues which have come up in my work as a
linguistic consultant and expert witness and which I feel are serious and in
need of attention: first, what I take to be a misguided and dangerous use of
covertly taped social conversation as courtroom evidence, and, second, the
shockingly poor quality of FBI transcriptions of these tapes. I shall first
describe the data on which my statements are based and then discuss the two
issues, in reverse order.

2. THE DATA

As a linguist, I have been professionally involved in one way or another in
10 or so court cases in which the federal government was prosecuting some
individual or individuals. My specific role was that of linguistic consultant for
the defense lawyer. In addition, in two of the cases, I served as an expert

ELLEN F. PRINCE • Department of Linguistics, University of Pennsylvania, Philadelphia,
Pennsylvania 19104.

witness and testified in court. The cases involved a diverse set of charges, including conspiracy to murder, drug dealing, perjury, mail fraud, and graft.

In all but one case, one, if not the, major source of evidence presented by the government consisted of utterances made by the defendant in private social conversations, covertly taped by the defendant's interlocutor in the service of the FBI. The one case not involving social conversation made use instead of covertly taped service encounters. That case, however, will not be relevant in this chapter, as what I shall say pertains only to the more common practice of using social conversation.

In all the relevant cases, the interlocutor, wearing a hidden tape recorder, was an FBI agent posing as a peer (e.g., as a friend of a friend) or, more often, was an actual peer who was convicted of or was liable to be convicted of some related crime and was conducting the taping as part of a deal made with the federal government. In either case, it was of great interest to him that the defendant somehow incriminate himself/herself. (All the interlocutors in these cases were male; two of the defendants were female.)

3. THE USE OF SOCIAL CONVERSATION AS LEGAL EVIDENCE

In the cases in which I have been involved, the use of social conversation as legal evidence is grounded on an assumption that the government seems to make that there is a necessary and direct relationship between utterances and knowledge/beliefs. This is reflected primarily in two ways. In the simpler situation, the government acts as though the defendant's uttering of a statement conveying proposition P entails that that defendant knows/believes P (see section 4.2.1 for discussion and examples). In the more complex situation, the government acts as though the defendant's assenting to, or simply not contradicting, a proposition P conveyed by the interlocutor's utterance entails that the defendant either already knows/believes P or else comes to know/believe P (see section 4.2.2 for discussion and examples). Thus something the defendant says or appears to assent to in private social conversation is construed as a reflection of a piece of his/her belief state. This assumption and the inferences that are made on the basis of it become relevant, of course, when proposition P is in some way incriminating.

4. PROBLEMS WITH THE ASSUMPTION

I shall not here even touch upon the enormously problematic phenomenon of the interlocutor manipulating the conversation in order to get the defendant to say apparently self-incriminating things or otherwise to put himself/herself in an apparently self-incriminating position, as Roger Shuy has discussed this elegantly and in detail, both in court and in linguistic contexts (see Shuy, 1981a,b, 1982, 1987, inter alia).

The two problems I shall discuss are, in my opinion, equally pervasive and pernicious: (1) the government's understanding of what was actually said and (2) the importance of "truth" in social conversation. Let us consider each separately.

4.1. Understanding What Was Said

The main problem I have come up against in the use of social conversation as legal evidence is, in my opinion, outrageously inexcusable: In the cases I have worked on (and they are not unique; cf. Walker, 1986), the government has on occasion simply misunderstood what was said, often to the detriment of the defendant. This comes about basically in two ways: (1) the government mishears and mistranscribes the tapes and (2) the government hears correctly what was said but proceeds to misunderstand it.

4.1.1. Mishearing/Mistranscribing

Mishearing and mistranscribing is rampant in the FBI work I have seen, where, working with a Sanyo transcriber, I have found an average of 14 substantive errors per typewritten page of transcript. Here I am not including the very large numbers of errors of punctuation and spelling, including "eye dialect," which may themselves have a pernicious effect. (Eye dialect is the spelling of words in such a way as to represent the standard pronunciation, where that spelling differs from the conventional, for example, "sez" for "says," "wimmin" for "women"; it is typically used in comic strips to suggest that the character is less than literate.)

First, whole words, phrases, and even sentences may be omitted, as in examples 1–3, where the a versions are from the FBI transcripts, and the b versions are what I clearly heard on the tapes. In all the examples, T is the individual wearing the tape recorder, that is, the informer, and D is the individual being taped without his knowledge, that is, the subsequent defendant. (In the transcriptions presented in this chapter, upper-case words indicate heavy stress, time periods, for example, 4 sec, in brackets indicates length of silences, double slashes, that is, //, indicate simultaneity of the following segment with the segment following the next set of double slashes, and underlining indicates the part of the utterance particularly relevant to the linguistic analysis.)

(1)a   T: . . .I don't know whether he said he followed him or they followed him when he left there. I don't know.

b   *T:* . . .I don't know whether he said HE followed THEM or THEY followed HIM when he left there. [4 sec]
    D: <u>They can't HAVE anything</u>.
    T: I don't know.

(2)a   *T:* [Discussion of FBI investigation and own fears]
    D: Jesus Christ—that's a shame. I don't know what the hell to <u>do</u>.

b   *T:* [Discussion of FBI investigation and own fears] [4 sec]
    D: Jesus Christ. [5 sec] That's a shame. [3 sec] I don't know what the hell to <u>tell you</u>.

(3)a   *D:* Just watch them. Don't do, don't let them know too much of your business—believe me. They are treacherous motherfuckers, I tell you. And I know dealing with freight, they're no good, they'<u>ll</u> beat you to death. (Nonpertinent conversation.)

b   *D:* Just watch them. Don't do it, don't let them know too much of your business, believe me. They're treacherous motherfuckers, I'<u>ll</u> tell you. And I know <u>with</u> dealing with freight, they're no good, they beat you to death. <u>You give them fucking gold, they come back with the price of copper</u>.
    T: <u>Yeah. Right</u>.
    D: <u>I'm telling you, I KNOW what happens. You know, uh, we—</u>

Such poor transcriptions are pernicious not only when the mistranscription constitutes direct evidence against the defendant but also—perhaps even more so—when it simply adds an aura of shadiness or guilt to the defendant. The reason is as follows. Typically the tapes are played (once) for the members of the jury, who are also given transcripts to read along. Now, we as linguists know only too well the difficulty of hearing what is actually said on a tape of naturally occurring discourse between acquaintances. Moreover, FBI tapes are typically of very poor quality, understandably so, given how and where they are made—with the tape recorder concealed on the person of the taper and with the interaction often taking place in noisy public places. I would venture a very confident guess, therefore, that jurors rely entirely on the transcripts in front of them and would virtually never notice any discrepancy between the tape and the transcript. Therefore, for the jurors, the transcript is in fact what was said, but they have the mistaken belief that they have actually heard what they have read.

In 1, the omission on the transcript of "They can't HAVE anything" resulted in the jury's failing to be aware of one of the instances where D said something that would support his case.

In 2, the FBI version, "I don't know what the hell to do," makes D look as if he is personally involved and seeking his own plan of action, when in fact he said, "I don't know what the hell to tell you," simply responding to T's alleged fears.

In 3, where D is a fence, that is, a dealer in stolen goods, on trial for conspiracy to murder, the omission of his wonderful metaphor about gold and copper as "nonpertinent conversation" makes the preceding sentence, about beating to death, seem intended literally. In fact, D is clearly being metaphoric in both sentences, commenting only on prices paid for "freight."

I have even found one instance in which the original transcript given to the defense was correct but where a pernicious change was made in the transcript given to the jury. The relevant passage is shown in 4, where 4a is the original correct version, 4b the incorrect one shown to the jury:

(4)a   [. . .] Uh, [X] has called me. [Y] has called me. [Z] has called me. All them guys have been calling me here at the house since I've been home. Jesus, I mean, uh, they all of them asking, do you <u>need</u> anything, can we do anything? No, man, you can't do nothing for me.

   b   [. . .] Uh, [X] has called me. [Y] has called me. [Z] has called me. All them guys have been calling me here at the house since I've been home. Jesus, I mean, uh, they, all of them asking, "Do you <u>know</u> anything? Can we do anything?" "No, man, you can't do nothing for me."

The change in 4 from "Do you <u>need</u> anything?" to "Do you <u>know</u> anything?", quoted from [X,Y,Z], local gamblers, to D, the chief of police, inserts an implicature of collusion, of special "shared knowledge" between them. This tape and transcript were shown to the jury on the first day of the trial. In the evening paper, this passage was cited in a front-page article under the headline "Tape Ties [X] to Ex-Chief."

4.1.2. Misunderstanding

Even when some utterance is correctly transcribed, it can happen that it is grossly misunderstood by the government. The most extraordinary such instance I have found comes from a case involving an organized crime figure accused of conspiracy to murder. It is shown in 5, where 5a is the fragment as it was punctuated by the FBI, 5b the fragment as a linguist would have punctuated it:

(5)a   T: When we killed that [X].
         D: <u>Yeah</u>.
         T: He wanted to have me killed, you know.
         D: Yeah.
         T: Yeah, [Y]—You know?
         D: Yeah.
         T: And uh I still got that against him.
   b   T: When we killed that [X],
         D: <u>Yeah</u>.
         T: He wanted to have ME killed, you know.
         D: Yeah.

T: Yeah, [Y]—You know?
D: Yeah.
T: And uh I still got that against him.

Hard to believe, perhaps, but D's first "Yeah" in 5 was considered as evidence that D had a part in killing X! This was in fact the most incriminating utterance in all the tapes made in this case.

Even the defense lawyer thought that this "Yeah" was a problem—and that is why a linguist was called in. I explained to him the two problems with construing this monomorphemic utterance as an admission of conspiracy to murder. First, as linguists know well, such "yeahs" do NOT mean "Yes, I hereby inform you that I am committed to the truth of the last-uttered proposition" but are rather what Goffman (1967) calls "back-channel cues," that is, items like "yeah," "uh huh," "mm," "I see," "right," which communicate something like "I have processed, or purport to have processed, the preceding clause; you may now go on." Second, English "we" is ambiguous: It can be either inclusive "we," denoting minimally the speaker and hearer, or exclusive "we," denoting the speaker and some third party or parties but excluding the hearer. (Many languages, e.g., Sedang, a language of Vietnam, have one word for the inclusive sense and another for the exclusive.) Therefore, even if, in 5, D were in full agreement with T's proposition, we still would not know if D thought he himself had killed [X]. (Of course, had they been speaking Sedang or some other language that differentiates between inclusive and exclusive "we," this would have been disambiguated, but unfortunately for the defense they were speaking English.)

I could continue at length on the errors of hearing, transcribing, and understanding that the federal government makes in such tapes, but I believe I have made my point and shall turn now to the second large problem with using social conversation as legal evidence—the role of truth in social conversation.

4.2. Truth

The second problem simply boils down to a fact which is well known among linguists and no doubt laymen alike but apparently unknown to the federal government: "The truth, the whole truth, and nothing but the truth" is not one of the higher priorities of individuals engaged in social conversation, not as speakers and not as hearers. A crucial entailment of this is, therefore, that there is no necessary correlation between what one says or what one assents to in social conversation and what one in fact believes.

It has been argued (Keenan, 1976) that, at least in one society, truth is entirely irrelevant in social discourse. Although I am not convinced by her arguments, it seems relatively uncontroversial that people, hopefully all people, lie on a regular basis.

The government's apparent assumption that commitment to truth is of the highest priority in social conversation leads it to two conclusions: first, that one's statement reflects one's belief, and, second, that one's failure to contradict another's statement demonstrates that one shares with the other that belief.

4.2.1. D's Statement = D's Belief

Let us first consider the common situation, in which one's statement fails to reflect one's beliefs, that is, where people fail to tell the truth in social interaction. A number of possible reasons for this suggest themselves.

One reason has to do with matters of politeness and the general management of social interaction (see Brown & Levinson, 1978, inter alia). Consider the invented examples in 6:

(6)a   I just peeked in the nursery and saw him. What a sweet little baby. I think he has your mouth. [Re prunelike neonate that speaker finds hideous]

   b   Don't feel so bad—everybody goes through a red light once in a while. [To friend who has just totaled a car]

The type of polite lying in 6 is hopefully universal. However, what one is lying about will presumably vary from subculture to subculture: Cloistered monks, for example, will presumably have little need for 6a, and city dwellers whose circle of friends do not drive will not need 6b. Of course, they will simply have other things to make people feel better about.

One instance of this type of polite lying is very likely exemplified in a covertly taped conversation in the perjury case I worked on in which the defendant (D) is a chief of police just home from the hospital and is being visited by the assistant chief of police (T), wearing a concealed tape recorder in the service of the FBI. The assistant chief, following a prearranged scenario, has been expressing great concern for more than a half hour that he (T) will be prosecuted for taking bribes. And, for a half hour, the chief has been responding that T has nothing to worry about because T never took anything. Finally, D utters the incriminating lines in 7:

(7)   T: [long speech expressing his fears of prosecution] [8 sec]
       D: I'll tell you, they certainly have created a monster. . . [10 sec] You just uh. . . [4 sec] You didn't do anything else—anything wrong o—other than what: everybody else on the police force did at that time. At Christmas time, we accepted//
       T: //Oh man! Christmas time, it was like—I remember the days, Christmas time used to be like//
       D: //Damn right. Christmas time, everybody accepted money.

D's statements in 7 were considered highly significant by the government, even though D had stated under oath that he himself had received gifts
of money at Christmas. The issue was his knowledge of OTHERS receiving
money from specific donors. T's donor was not relevant. The government
claimed that this fragment showed that D knew that others (besides T)
received money and implicated (i.e., suggested) that he knew specifically
who they were and from whom the money had come.

In the trial, D testified with respect to this fragment that he did not
specifically know who received money and that he had said what he did in 7
merely to calm T. I quote from D's testimony: "I imagine some of the fellows
did receive Christmas gifts. I did. I received Christmas gifts. . . . When I
started telling him [T] about other fellows taking money, it seemed to relax
him. I thought that was what he wanted to hear." Given the preceding half-
hour of T's expression of fear, D's testimony seems plausible. Supporting this
are the (presumably manipulative) long periods of silence prior to D's utterances on the tape: Silence is painfully unacceptable in social conversation
and often inspires speakers to take desperate measures.

Before leaving the topic of socially acceptable lying, I should like to point
out that telling untruths occurs regularly in discourse also for affective
reasons, for example, humor, sentiment, beauty. Consider the examples of
sarcasm and hyperbole in 8a and the metaphors in 8b, c:

(8)a   You should see the geniuses I have in Ling. 101—My philodendron is more
        alert.
   b   Ich bin ein Berliner. [As uttered by John F. Kennedy]
   c   All the world's a stage.

In fact, Grice (1975) has pointed out that speakers do all kinds of creative
things with the Maxim of Quality, the abstract presumption of truth, to
produce a variety of indirect understandings, called "conversational implica-
tures," including those responsible for sarcasm, hyperbole, and metaphor.

Finally, people can simply lie. When one is engaged in social conversation in one's kitchen or in a neighborhood bar or on the telephone or wherever,
one can say what one feels like. Social lying, bullshitting, telling fish stories or
tall tales may or may not be admirable traits in a given subculture of our
society, but they are not yet illegal.

Furthermore, speakers and hearers, from a very early age, it seems to me,
take one another's utterances with a grain (or pound) of salt, but the government seems to believe that we are all under oath at all times, in all places. If, for
example, I am overheard in a bar saying that it was I who shot John Kennedy,
my statement could certainly prompt an investigation, but it cannot be taken
as proof of my guilt or even, I would maintain, as serious evidence. And,
presumably, no one would consider hiring me to remove their brain tumor
simply because they had heard me say in a South Philly bar that, before
becoming a teamster, I had been a brain surgeon.

So far, I have discussed situations in which the defendant's own utterance carries the supposedly incriminating proposition. I shall now turn to the closely related situation in which D's appearing to assent to someone else's utterance is assumed to reflect D's belief.

4.2.2. D's Assent = D's Belief

Let us reconsider the fragment in 5, this time imagining that the "we" in T's utterance is unambiguously inclusive, that is, that T has just uttered a proposition that would be false if both he and D had not killed [X].

The government would like to believe that, if it were the case that T and D had jointly killed [X], then D's failure to contradict T by stating explicitly that the proposition "D and T killed [X]" is false demonstrates that D is committed to the truth of that proposition.

Clearly, as is well known, that is simply not true: People fail to contradict others for a variety of reasons having to do with social interaction, cultural mores, power roles, and so forth, and no conclusion can be validly drawn about one's beliefs from one's failure to contradict. Moreover, in the case of 5, the social facts of the situation are such that it is particularly unlikely that D would contradict T, no matter what T said. T is an organized crime hitman—a hired killer. He is very large, strong, known to carry a gun and to use it. He is also known to be not too bright and basically illiterate. On the other hand, D is a small, nonphysical type in his 60s, a dealer in stolen goods, a man who has lived by his wits and who has been one of the quietest, least noticeable members of the area's organized crime operation. Their conversation is taking place in a neighborhood bar. Thus it seems most unlikely that D would contradict T, regardless of what D said or what T believed about what he said.

In fact, in the same set of tapes, we have direct evidence of D's disinclination to contradict or correct T, in an innocuous exchange where D has told a narrative that T has misunderstood. This exchange, omitted from the FBI transcript as "nonpertinent conversation," is presented in 9:

(9)
[Several people at bar have recounted humorous narratives about crime.]
D: That guy in Chicago is the best one.
T: What, the uh—//The [. . .]?
D: //Did you read that, the [. . .]? No? Did you read that, [X]? That guy in Chicago? Every anniversary they write [the] story about it. He worked in a bank, OK? Now in this bank, they worked on a Saturday. Now he was a trustee, but he had NO right to go into the vault. You know, he wasn't one to go into the vault. On Saturday, they left the vault open, because they were closed, they did accountings and all that. He went in and stole over a million dollars, OK? They KNOW he did it. He's the only one, he resigned his job and all, rather than take a lie detector test. Every anniversary, they write it up in the paper. It's three years. It says, he now has four years. If he hits the four years, he keeps the money.

T: That's all in the paper?

D: They—It says the FBI are constantly [. . .] the Treasury Department; he has not changed his style of living; they don't know how he did it; they said he carried eighty pound of money out of that fucking bank, eighty pound, and they don't know how he did it. And//

T: //[. . .]

D: You know, they locked the bank up at night. [. . .] for three years. [. . .] his anniversary. And it says, and they—they're giving odds in Chicago that he'll go fo—four more years and wind up with that money.

T: Huh!

D: And he hasn't changed his style of living. Did you read that? It was in the paper about—about two months ago, his anniversary.

T: I didn't see it.

D: Yeah! Did you see it? A million and some dollars! Eighty pound of money! They—that's what baffled them: HOW did he get OUT of the building with eighty pound of money? They said that he couldn't put it in his clothes, you know, he had to have—and there was guards, security, like going out of the bank, in and out. And they searched everywhere, they can't find it. So when they asked him to take a lie detector test, he says nope, he says, "I'll resign my job [if that's what you want]."//

*T: //Let me tell you something. We used to get four dollars a fucking bag for sugar. I could pick up three fucking bags and heave them motherfuckers in a truck. And at sixty pound a bag, that's sixty: hundred and twenty:::

$D: But walking out with—Yeah, but walking out of a BANK—

T: When you're stealing, man, you can take it.

%D: Oh, I agree with you. There's a way, there's always a way. [6 sec]

T: Especially money, man, that don't weigh nothing.

D: They checked everything, they checked the [. . .] and all. He [. . .] where he put that fucking money. [8 sec] [Someone else begins another narrative. T heard in background talking about "three fucking bags."]

In 9, we see that T has missed the point of D's narrative: D is speaking of the money in terms of its weight, but listeners are expected to infer the *volume*: The interesting point of the narrative is that someone has walked out of a bank with a parcel that is as *large* as 80 pounds of money must be. T misses this inference entirely and thinks the point is that it is amazing that the robber could have carried out such a *heavy* parcel. (See turn marked *.) D most discreetly tries to give T another chance to draw the weight-to-volume infer- ence (turn marked $), T fails again, and D gives up (turn marked %) and *explicitly asserts agreement with T's misunderstanding!*

Thus we find compelling evidence that, even if, in 5, T's "we" meant "you and I," which it does not necessarily mean, and even if D's "yeah" meant "I hereby commit myself to the truth of the proposition just expressed," which it certainly does not mean, we still could not conclude from this that D in fact believed that he had any part in killing [X].

5. CONCLUSION

In this chapter, I have tried to bring attention to two areas that I feel are highly problematic for the use of social conversation as legal evidence: the inaccuracy that is found in the government's hearing, transcribing, and understanding what was said and the assumption that the participants are primarily concerned about getting the truth on the hidden tape.

How serious a problem is this? In point of fact, most of the defendants for whom I have worked are not terribly attractive people, and they may well have been guilty of all sorts of crimes, including those for which they were indicted. However, it seems very clear to me that, if such careless and uninformed work on the part of the federal government can incarcerate undesirables, the rest of us may be at risk as well because, given sufficiently imaginative charges and enough mishandled covert taping, anyone can be made to look guilty of a crime.

As is usually the case, the problem is easier to find than the solution. One solution, of course, would be to stop surreptitious taping of social conversations by the government. However, this is not likely to occur, as the practice seems to be constantly on the rise and the trend shows no signs of changing. Perhaps the best we can hope for is a more knowledgeable government, one that knows how to listen to speech, how to transcribe it, and how to interpret it, one that is informed by basic linguistic and sociolinguistic principles of how social conversations work and of how individuals interact verbally. In short, maybe it's time for Big Brother to learn some linguistics.

6. REFERENCES

Brown, P., & Levinson, S. C. (1978). Universals in language usage: Politeness phenomena. In E. Goody, (Ed.), *Questions and politeness: strategies in social interaction* (pp. 56–310). Cambridge: Cambridge University Press.

Goffman, E. (1967). *Interaction ritual.* Garden City, NY: Anchor.

Grice, H. P. (1975). Logic and conversation. In P. Cole & J. L. Morgan (Eds.), *Syntax and semantics III. Speech acts* (pp. 41–58). New York: Academic Press.

Keenan, E. O. (1976). The universality of conversational postulates. *Language in Society, 5,* 67–80.

Shuy, R. (1981a). Can linguistic evidence build a defense theory in a criminal case? *Studia Linguistica, 35*(1–2), 33–49.

Shuy, R. (1981b). Topic as the unit of analysis in a criminal law case. In D. Tannen (Ed.), *Analyzing discourse: Text and talk [Georgetown University Round Table on Languages and Linguistics 1981]* (pp. 113–126). Washington, DC: Georgetown University Press.

Shuy, R. (1982). *Entrapment and the linguistic analysis of tapes.* Unpublished manuscript.

Shuy, R. (1987). Conversational power in FBI covert tape recordings. In L. Kadar (Ed.), *Power through discourse* (pp. 43–56). Norwood, NJ: Ablex.

Walker, A. G. (1986). The verbatim record: The myth and the reality. In S. Fisher & A. D. Todd (Eds.), *Discourse and institutional authority: Medicine, education, and law* (pp. 205–222). Norwood, NJ: Ablex.

Chapter 10

LANGUAGE AND COGNITION IN PRODUCTS LIABILITY

1. INTRODUCTION

It is no secret that the last several years have seen a marked increase in the
degree of interest and involvement in the legal process on the part of cognitive
psychologists. This change is reflected in the creation of a new division of the
American Psychological Association devoted entirely to the interface of psychology and law, in an increase in publication of relevant books and articles,
and in the appearance of the one clear sign that a subdiscipline has *arrived*:
competition among publishers in soliciting and marketing textbooks designed specifically for courses in psychology and the law. I think it is safe to
say, although I am quite sure that the legal profession is not yet entirely
comfortable with the prospect, that the mutual influence of the psychological
and legal professions upon each other can only grow. In this chapter, I would
like to consider some ways in which practitioners of one "psychology and. . ."
hybrid (psychology and language) might contribute to the growth and development of another (psychology and law).

Most of the contributions which cognitive psychologists, including those
interested in language, have made (or have offered to make) in the legal
domain have been concentrated in areas involving either criminal procedure
or the trial process generally. There has been comparatively little work done on

---

MICHAEL G. JOHNSON • Department of Psychology, University of Tennessee, Knoxville,
Tennessee 37996-0900.

the civil side, even though there are several areas that seem to present obvious opportunities. I would like to explore one of these, namely the rapidly (though perhaps temporarily, given the intense lobbying efforts of the insurance industry) growing body of law known as products liability.

Attorneys who participate in products liability cases are finding with increasing frequency that they are facing issues surrounding the linguistic and cognitive aspects of such actions (Noel & Phillips, 1981). As the world, and specifically the world of manufacturing and technology, becomes more complex, it is harder and harder to keep up with the many hazards that the man-made environment has to offer. This places an increasing burden on the producers and sellers of goods to provide knowledge which the general public cannot, as a matter of course, be expected to possess—and to do so in a manner which effectively communicates what needs to be known. Questions concerning language and communication are the central issue in many products liability actions: A manufacturer or seller can be liable for injury or damage if it fails to provide adequate warnings concerning knowable safety hazards or if it fails to provide adequate directions required to use a product safely. It can be similarly liable if it misrepresents, whether innocently or knowingly, the product in such a way that injury or damage results. It is not my purpose to provide a detailed survey of all of the ways in which language issues arise in products liability law but rather to consider these issues generally in the context of a theory, or perhaps more accurately a description, of communication and the role that a psycholinguistic expert might play in informing the judicial process in this important civil arena.

The issues that I address in this chapter first became salient for me about 6 years ago when I received a letter from an attorney who had appeared as a guest in one of my classes. The letter contained an outline of the facts of a rather simple products liability case: An elderly lady, while walking through the central corridor of a modern shopping mall (all of which are essentially similar), approached an area where new automobiles were being displayed by various dealers. In an effort to make their automobiles more attractive, the representatives setting up the various displays had followed what is apparently common practice in such situations and had sprayed their wares with an aerosol silicone spray product. This is designed to make their products appear more shiny and new. As the plaintiff walked through the display area, she suddenly slipped and fell, incurring personal injuries. The silicone spray that escaped (or accidentally oversprayed) onto the terrazzo floor of the corridor had apparently produced a slippery spot.

The attorney representing the plaintiff (my contact) had joined as co-defendants the automobile dealers and the silicone spray manufacturer in a personal injury suit and was interested in whether or not I could help his case against the manufacturer—the dealers were willing to offer a favorable settlement. In his letter, he enclosed a copy of the label on the silicone spray product. The label contained the usual information extolling its virtues, along with few specific warnings: to avoid inhalation; to use in ventilated area; to avoid incinerating the spent spray can; a caution concerning the flammability of the spray itself; and finally the admonition to *avoid spraying on tile floors."* The manufacturer contended that this constituted sufficient warning to reasonable users of the product to avoid the conditions that occurred in this case.

Because this was the first case I had ever been asked to participate in and it arose before I had any acquaintance with the substance of the law and judicial process (conditions which have since changed considerably), I was not sure what I could contribute, but I agreed to try. In doing so, I found that I not only had to come to grips with the assumptions and theories of my own discipline but also had to deal with some jurisprudential and evidentiary issues as well. In the sections that follow I will describe the results of my own education on these matters, beginning with a cognitive account of the communication process.

2. AN OUTLINE OF A COGNITIVE THEORY OF COMMUNICATION

In order to explore how a psycholinguist might function as an expert in the area of products liability, it will be useful to first examine in a general way what we *know* or (where controversy exists) what we can assert in a *principled* manner, concerning the nature of language, communication, and meaning. I will briefly consider three interrelated topics which I consider to be central to an analysis of the communication process in products liability. These are first, the role of context in communication and comprehension; second, the primacy of knowledge in understanding the communication process; and, finally, the probabilistic character of human communication.

2.1. Contextual Factors in Communication and Comprehension

It is by this time, certainly, the consensus among language scientists that the meaning a language user attaches to a word or larger linguistic unit is in significant part a function of the context in which it is embedded, taken in conjunction with the knowledge of the rules of the "language game" that a human language user possesses (Johnson & Henley, 1988; Lakoff, 1987; Wittgenstein, 1953). It was not that long ago that many cognitive psychologists were in hot pursuit of the structure of a subjective lexicon thought to be somehow independent of context, but that chase has been largely abandoned. It was replaced first by a series of compelling demonstrations designed to highlight the importance of context in comprehension (e.g., Barclay *et al.*, 1974; Bransford & Johnson, 1972) which usually ended up being negative demonstrations (in the Wittgensteinian tradition) of what meaning and language are *not*, rather than offering a new and comfortable theory.

Some of these demonstrations are based upon observations that contex-

tual support is critical to the interpretation of a large part of linguistic communication. Take for example the common complaint that one's words "were
taken out of context," or Fillmore's (1976) comparison of the meaning of the
word "breakfast" in the phrases "the Wongs eat chicken soup for breakfast"
and "breakfast served any time." Fillmore's argument is that words are typically associated with more than one background knowledge "frame" from
which we derive their meanings in various contexts. The context in which the
word "breakfast" appears helps select the appropriate frame (the first meal of
the day, or foods typically consumed by Americans during the morning) for
interpreting the word in that context.

Some of my favorite examples of the importance of context in comprehension are a series of demonstration experiments by Bransford and Johnson
(1972) in which they provided subjects with paragraphs, made up of simple
sentences which (taken together) are confusing and difficult to interpret until
a context is provided—sometimes in the form of a cartoon which explicates
the paragraph, sometimes in the form of a simple title for the paragraph—
after which they seem perfectly clear and straightforward. The following
paragraph is one of those used in the Bransford and Johnson study:

> If the balloons popped, the sound wouldn't be able to carry since everything would
> be too far away from the correct floor. A closed window would also prevent the
> sound from carrying, since most buildings tend to be well insulated. Since the
> whole operation depends on a steady flow of electricity, a break in the middle of the
> wire would also cause problems. Of course the fellow could shout, but the human
> voice is not loud enough to carry that far. An additional problem is that a string
> could break on the instrument. Then there could be no accompaniment to the
> message. It is clear that the best situation would involve less distance. Then there
> could be fewer potential problems. With face to face contact, the least number of
> things could go wrong. (Bransford & Johnson, 1972, p. 719)

The first impression that people have, after hearing or reading passages such
as this, is a feeling of vagueness and confusion. All of the words are familiar,
and the words are arranged in perfectly grammatical sentences, but the
passage doesn't seem to have any coherence. When a bit of context is provided, however, the situation is much different. If the reader or listener is
presented with a cartoon, showing a woman on a high balcony of an apartment building being serenaded by a man on the ground who is projecting his
voice and guitar through a microphone and speaker (the speaker suspended
from a cluster of helium-filled balloons hovering outside the balcony, the
passage makes sense and can be recalled reasonably accurately. Demonstrations such as this are quite compelling, and I have found them quite useful
both in the classroom and in legal settings.

Another demonstration of the role of context in communication comes
from observations Robert Malgady and I have made in a series of studies
involving randomly generated language materials in the spirit of Chomsky's

famous colorless-green-ideas-sleep-furiously example (Chomsky, 1957). In these studies, we present such materials, which range from randomly generated metaphors (e.g., "people are doors") to randomly constructed but grammatical sentences (e.g., "total coffee loses eternal spots") and ask people to interpret them in some way—the actual instructions vary from study to study (Johnson & Malgady, 1980). Beyond the fact that we have found it virtually impossible to invent materials that cannot be meaningfully interpreted, we also find that people almost always reach their interpretations by inventing contexts in which otherwise anomalous materials somehow make sense.

In the past few years demonstrations concerning the *fact* of the contextual or situational determinants of language comprehension have given way to attempts to explore the parameters of context that are most important. This shift has led to a somewhat depressing state of affairs for many psychologists because it now begins to appear that psychologically significant contexts are virtually unlimited. This became clear to me personally when a colleague and I did a literature search using several databases in preparation for a jointly taught graduate seminar on the general topic of context in psychology. Exhaustion limited our bibliography to approximately 1,000 entries, but we estimated that there were at least several thousand more pertinent studies demonstrating the importance of some aspect of context, and this list is growing rapidly since it has become a popular topic in the field.

If it is true (as it may well be) that everything in human experience has the potential for influencing the character of human experience (including the comprehension of language), then this is a complication that we must deal with in our consideration of the nature of language (Johnson & Malgady, 1980; Rommetveit, 1974). Before sketching some of the implications of this kind of thinking for a model of communication, it will be useful to consider a related topic: the role of knowledge in language and communication.

2.2. The Primacy of Knowledge in the Communication Process

One theme that has dominated cognitive psychology over the past few years, and especially the computer-oriented branch of the discipline that has become known as cognitive science, is the idea that the key to understanding human cognition can only come from understanding what we know, rather than (as cognitive psychologists used to believe) from understanding the mechanics of how we process information (Neisser, 1976). Many years ago, linguistic philosophers Katz and Fodor (1963) made the assertion that a semantic theory would be impossible if it had to include one's knowledge of the world. They may have been right, depending upon the goals of one's semantic theory. The problem of course is that, beginning with Bolinger's (1965) interesting review of Katz and Fodor (1963) and culminating in recent attempts to deal with natural language problems in artificial intelligence

(Winograd, 1981; Winograd & Flores, 1986), it seems that knowledge of the world is inseparable from any attempt to deal meaningfully with meaning. Every facet of cognition requires some kind of internal representation of experience—that is, knowledge. Cognitive theorists have become unanimous in acknowledging that perceiving, remembering, thinking, and acting are both knowledge dependent and knowledge driven and have postulated a variety of constructs to account for this fact in their theories, including: frames (Fillmore, 1976; Minsky, 1987); schemata (Neisser, 1976); plans (Schank & Abelson, 1977); scripts (Schank & Abelson, 1977); and rules (Harré & Secord, 1972). Theories of language comprehension make use of these constructs, as well as others such as presupposition (Johnson, Bransford, & Solomon, 1973), speech acts (Searle, 1969), background (Searle, 1983), and image schemata (Lakoff, 1987). All of these suggest the same answer to the central question in understanding the communication process: When an individual is participating in the act of comprehending some language segment, where do the raw materials for that comprehension come from? The obvious answer is that the message to be comprehended (of which context is an inextricable part) stimulates, triggers, or otherwise engages something that is already a part of the message receiver—that is, the comprehender's knowledge. As several scholars have suggested, words do not *have* meanings, they *invite* them (Bransford & McCarrell, 1974; Johnson & Henley, 1988; Lakoff, 1987; Verbrugge & McCarrell, 1977; Wittgenstein, 1953). From the point of view of understanding communication, the most interesting fact is that the same message can invite a variety of interpretations, and this leads us next to a consideration of the probabilistic nature of comprehension.

2.3. The Probabilistic Character of Human Communication

Psychologists have been studying the characteristics of language comprehension in aggregated populations of people ever since the word association test was invented by Sir Francis Galton in the late nineteenth century. In all of the thousands of studies that have been conducted since that time, there is one common (and usually overlooked) fact: No matter what measure of the content of comprehension is employed, people differ in their responses. This fact can be demonstrated in a number of ways. One of my favorite classroom demonstrations is to give my students a few language segments (words, phrases, or sentences) and ask them to write phenomenological accounts of what they experienced immediately upon hearing whatever was used as the stimulus item. These accounts are then compared in class and demonstrate that to a greater or lesser degree (depending upon the nature of the materials presented), people have different comprehension experiences.

Another demonstration of variability in comprehension comes from a study (previously mentioned) Robert Malgady and I conducted a few years ago (Johnson & Malgady, 1980) in which we gave a group of 75 experimental subjects a series of 20 randomly generated metaphors, which the subjects were to interpret by completing a sentence in the following form:

People are doors, _____ (subject's response).

The 75 subjects gave 27 *different* completion responses for this metaphor, some of which are as follows:

- They can be either open or closed
- You have to go through them to get what you want
- They move back and forth without ever going anywhere
- They squeak unless oiled
- They are rigid
- You find them most often in houses
- They work best when they are in good condition
- They come in a variety of colors and sizes

Although it is true that most of the messages we encounter in everyday life do not have as many interpretive possibilities as this example, it does illustrate the proposition that we must be careful about individual differences when talking about comprehension. A similar study with similar findings was conducted by Fraser (1979). Responses to all language comprehension tasks in which data is collected from groups of people form distributions of responses, and reflect diversity rather than unanimity in interpretation. These distributions allow us to talk about the probabilities associated with different interpretations, but do not allow us to say in any definitive way that interpretation will be given by a single individual.

2.4. A Cognitive View of Comprehension

It might be useful at this juncture to make explicit some assumptions about what happens when an individual encounters a linguistic message, both as a means of summarizing what has been said thus far and to make a transition to the practical implications of a cognitive approach to comprehension in products liability cases.

Without committing to any particular view of what really happens when an individual comprehends a message—for example, whether imagery is involved, or some kind of computational process occurs, because these issues are unresolved in philosophical and psychological debates—we can nevertheless assemble a general model of communication using the principles outlined so far. When an individual encounters a message, an interpretive process occurs which results in the "whatever" an individual experiences when comprehension occurs. When one tries to understand this process it is extremely important to be clear about whether one is focusing on comprehension from the hearer's perspective (that is, adopting a first-person perspective) or on the perspective of an outside observer (or third-person perspective). From the point of view of the recipient of the message, or from a first-person perspective, the interpretation of that message will be determined by many factors, all of which come under the headings of knowledge and context. These include the hearer's knowledge of the concepts embodied in the words which make up the message; the current concerns of the individual (whatever is currently occupying the thoughts of the hearer on either a temporary or long-term basis such as an impending divorce, writing a paper for a conference, the weather, work, or almost anything); the recipient's perception of the intentionality of the author of the message; the recipient's sense of knowledge shared by the author and recipient; the recipient's intentionality in interpreting the message; whether the recipient is alert or tired or drunk; or an almost unlimited number of other factors (Rommetveit, 1974). All of these will be effortlessly integrated and factored into an interpretive process which ordinarily takes place without any conscious awareness on the part of the message recipient. Language is, in Heidegger's (1962) terminology, a tool which is "ready to hand" and which only becomes figural or part of our conscious awareness when something breaks down. Comprehension occurs, and from the point of view of the recipient of the message, it almost always occurs without any awareness of alternative interpretive possibilities. Most people most of the time do not self-consciously analyze their interpretations of the messages they receive—with the possible exception of language scientists, and then only some of the time. This fact has some important implications for products liability cases, which I will consider presently.

On the other hand, if we take the point of view of an observer of the linguistic interaction, what the message recipient actually comprehends is more problematical. Because we have no direct access to another individual's knowledge or phenomenological (perceived) context, we cannot know precisely how a given message will be (or has been) interpreted by a given individual. It is important to realize, however, that the operative word in the previous sentence is "precisely." As linguists, psycholinguists, or everyday communicators we are, in fact, capable of making some predictions about the comprehension of a message; if we could not, communication would be impossible.

There are many factors which make it possible for us to make some predictions about others' interpretations: shared contexts, shared knowledge, knowledge about shared knowledge, a sense of the probabilistic characteristics of word meaning and usage, and linguistic competence however defined (Rommetveit, 1968, 1974). All of these factors are utilized automatically and (usually) effortlessly when we communicate. We can group them all together and talk about communicative competence, or describe them by saying that human communicators are, in effect, capable of functioning as analog models of other human beings. It is the degree of precision in our predictions that is at issue, and this leaves room for the potential introduction of communication or comprehension expertise into the products liability forum because the degree of precision is an empirical issue and therefore amenable to study by language researchers.

It is probably the case that communication is seldom precise in the sense that, or to the degree that, what the sender of a message wishes to convey is what the receiver actually comprehends (Reddy, 1979). However imprecise our ordinary communication may be, it is nevertheless adequate for most purposes. Where the necessary degree of precision is not achieved and where this is recognized by speakers, matters can be corrected via feedback when the opportunity for feedback exists. For purposes of the present discussion, it is important to note that one of the major obstacles to precise-enough communication via product warnings and instructions is that this opportunity is ordinarily not present.

One phenomenon that provides at least anecdotal evidence for communicative imprecision is one that I have come to call "the 'click' of communication." It is the feeling that many of us experience on those rare occasions in which you suddenly feel that the person or persons you are communicating with are on exactly the same wavelength. This phenomenon has been noted by others (Tannen, 1984). Although there is no clear-cut answer to the question of why this happens, I suspect that the feeling is brought about by a complete consistency in the feedback received—something that provides evidence that precision has been achieved. It is the rarity of this experience which suggests that under ordinary circumstances, we are content with something less than this precision: Communication that is "good enough" to achieve whatever purpose we wish or need to serve.

Along with the proposition that communication is seldom perfectly precise, I suggest that most people most of the time engage in a kind of linguistic egocentricism. Unless there is some reason to question the assumption, we tend to assume that what we intend to communicate is in fact comprehended by the message recipient and that what we comprehend as the recipient is in fact what the sender intended to communicate. Most adults are capable of transcending this egocentricism when the occasion demands, although there are, it seems obvious, rather large individual differences in both the willingness (or tendency) and ability to do so (see Brown, 1965, for a review of the authoritarian personality in this regard). This egocentric assumption is probably adaptive in most ordinary communication because it allows us to make communication something other than a reflective intellectual exercise, but it is also maladaptive in contexts where miscommunication can have serious consequences—as when failure to adequately warn (or failure to appreciate a warning) results in a product causing personal injury.

The points that I have raised with respect to the cognitive character of communication represent a useful set of constructs for the analysis of the communication process in a products liability lawsuit, and they determine much of the methodology to be used in such an analysis.

3. LANGUAGE COMPREHENSION IN PRODUCTS LIABILITY CASES

In any products liability action, a number of threshold legal issues (issues which must be resolved if a case can go forward) have to be considered before any linguistic issues even arise (Noel & Phillips, 1981). For purposes of this discussion, the most important of these is the foreseeability of the particular use of the product by the injured plaintiff, which is presumed to be the proximate (or effective) cause of the plaintiff's injury. It is foreseeability that gives rise to a duty to provide adequate warnings and/or directions to prevent a potential consumer from using the product in a dangerous manner. Assuming that this issue has been dealt with and that the case does involve a potential communication problem—that is, involves questions concerning the labeling, instructional materials, or representations (advertising or otherwise) concerning the product—then we immediately pass into a rather confusing area in products liability law: the standard of care against which to measure the conduct of the actors in the case. As I indicated earlier, it is not my intent to deal with substantive products liability law, but this one question has important practical and theoretical implications for a language scientist interested in this aspect of the judicial process.

3.1. The Legal Standard in Warnings and Directions Cases

In most products liability cases in which warnings or directions are at issue, one of two questions is involved: first, did someone misuse the product; or second, were foreseeable and unavoidable risks made clear enough so that a consumer (usually the plaintiff) could rationally decide whether or how to use the product. Regardless of which of these questions is involved, the linguistic issues are similar and center on the *adequacy* of the labeling message itself. In cases where liability turns on the adequacy of the warning, the standard of care seems to be based upon negligence concepts, no matter whether the theory pled by the plaintiff is one of negligence, warranty, or strict liability in tort (Noel & Phillips, 1981:188). In negligence, the test is whether an actor (usually the defendant) exercised reasonable care under the circumstances.

The concept of "reasonable care under the circumstances" involves one of the most fascinating inventions of common law jurisprudence: the ordinary reasonable person. This fictional entity, apparently born in eighteenth-century Britain (Prosser, 1971) and now living happily in America, is important because it is the psycholinguistic entity which must be dealt with in analyzing communication in products liability cases. The ordinary reasonable person is at the same time an "everyperson" and a "noperson." As the noted torts scholar Prosser (1971:150) puts it:

> The courts have gone to unusual pains to emphasize the abstract and hypothetical character of this mythical person. He is not to be identified with any ordinary individual. . . . Nor is it proper to identify him even with any member of the very jury who are to apply the standard. . . . It is sometimes difficult to escape the conviction that the refinements which have been developed in instructing the jury, in the effort to avoid the application of any personal standard which one of them might be tempted to apply, are artificial and unreal, and quite beyond the comprehension of the average man in the box. The only possible justification lies in a basis of experience justifying considerable uneasiness about what any jury may conceivably do, which has led to an excess of precaution in the effort to give them proper guidance.

In language liability cases, the ordinary reasonable person standard is applied to both the plaintiff and the defendant. Under that standard the defendant is required, in effect, to serve as an objective ordinary reasonable communicator of a warning or direction and the plaintiff is required to be an objective ordinary reasonable recipient of the warning. What I find most interesting about this so-called objective standard of conduct is that it matches up rather nicely with what I have called the outside observer or third-person view of the communication process.

3.2. The Psychologist and the Ordinary Reasonable Person

One of the reasons that psychologists often feel uncomfortable in the courtroom is that they are asked to do what they do least well—that is, make statements about individuals. To compress an argument that I have made elsewhere (Johnson & Malgady, 1980), psychologists are almost by definition required to do research from the point of view of an outside observer—the third-person point of view. Research has traditionally involved the collection of data from a group of individuals, which is then aggregated in some form: means, regression lines, and the like. All too often this has led to the conceptual error of pushing these aggregated values back into the heads of each individual. Data common to the group do not generalize well to individuals. What group data do generalize well to is the group.

Because researchers must adopt the position of the outside observer, a psycholinguist will not be able to make a definitive statement about the actual interpretation of a given message by another individual. Unfortunately, all of the factors that make such a task difficult or impossible for a psycholinguist operate in other areas of forensic psychology as well. Psychologists and psychiatrists find it very difficult to make reasonable statements about the state of mind of a criminal defendant at the time of the criminal act, which they are required to do if they are to offer testimony germane to an insanity defense (Robinson, 1980). By the same token, a psychologist testifying on the issue of eyewitness identification cannot make a definitive statement about the real issue—whether or not the witness actually saw the defendant—but can only talk in general terms about factors that influence eyewitness accuracy (Loftus, 1979). This is not to suggest that testimony in such cases is not useful to the judicial process, although there is a lively internal debate on this subject (McCloskey & Egeth, 1983), but it does point up the fact that the questions and answers that are relevant to legal inquiry often do not mesh well with the questions asked and answers obtained in the social sciences.

There is an interesting parallel between the work done by those interested in eyewitness identification and the approach to products liability analysis that I am advocating here. In eyewitness identification, the inquiry focuses on the malleability and potential fallibility of perception and memory, whereas in cases involving language liability, the focus is on the potential fallibility of communication. Expert testimony in both areas essentially deals with the same underlying characteristics of human cognition. The difference between these areas is the nature of the focus of explanation: on the one hand a real human being (the eyewitness) and on the other an entity that never has existed and never will (the ordinary reasonable person). Paradoxically the latter entity comes closer to what cognitive psychologists actually study and can actually say something meaningful about. In order to make this point relevant to the present discussion, I will reconsider the probabilistic properties of language in the context of the ordinary reasonable person.

3.3. The Probabilistic Nature of Language and the Ordinary Reasonable Person

Although I suspect that most jurists would blanch at the assertion that the ordinary reasonable person is a probabilistic construct (probabilities are not popular in a discipline that has historically considered itself deterministic and deductively logical), I would argue that the concept of the ordinary reasonable person maps onto probabilistic thinking in a way that makes probabilistic data relevant to the evidentiary concerns of the courts in products liability cases.

I have suggested that unless as language experts we can somehow take the first-person point of view of a given recipient of a given message in a given context (something which is ordinarily *not* possible), we cannot say precisely what *the* interpretation of that message is. Because we are, however, normally limited to taking the point of view of the third-person outside observer, our expertise is limited to what the outside observer can know. What we may be able to make reasonable statements about is the *nature* of and the *range* of *possible* interpretations, which may be relatively circumscribed or open-ended depending upon the communication situation. The two most obvious questions now become: First, how can we come to be able to make such statements about the range of possible meanings or interpretations (as language experts)? And, second, how can such statements be made relevant in dealing with the question of the adequacy of warnings and directions? I will consider these questions in reverse order.

4. THE RELEVANCE OF PSYCHOLINGUISTIC DATA IN PRODUCTS LIABILITY LITIGATION

Let us assume that for any given message, there is a finite range of potential interpretations and that these are discoverable. Let us further assume that these potential interpretations vary in the probability that any one interpretation will be the actual interpretation produced by a given message recipient and that the probability value for any given interpretation can be specified within some acceptable range of accuracy. If we have this much information, do we have anything meaningful to say about liability in the context of the negligence standard we have articulated previously, given that from the outside-observer perspective we cannot know which interpretation will actually be arrived at by the recipient.? I think so.

In a products liability case, there are two actors whose negligence may be at issue. (In the following discussion, I will assume that a products liability case already exists, because this is the point at which language experts will become involved and will refer to "plaintiffs" and "defendants" rather than consumers, manufacturers, and sellers.) Looking at the defendant, who is the communicator of information in a products liability case, the duty is one of communicating information concerning known (or knowable) hazards in such a way that a reasonable plaintiff could have avoided or knowingly assumed risks involved in the use of the defendant's product. Ordinarily the standard of care required of a defendant in products liability is not that of the ordinary reasonable person *per se* but that of the ordinary reasonable person who is expert in the domain of the product in question (Prosser, 1971:644). Although this logically ought to include the duty to be, or consult with, an expert in the communication of product-labeling information, I am not aware of any cases in which the courts have adopted this position (although I have not yet made a definitive survey of the case law on this particular topic). The increased participation of language experts in products liability cases may be the agency required to achieve a much needed change here. If one takes the view that a products liability defendant should be held to a higher standard of communication expertise, namely, that of a communications expert, this duty can be cast in the terms of the communication model I am proposing.

If we go beyond the mere duty to warn and translate the duty to provide an adequate warning into probabilistic communication terms, we might come up with the following formulation: It is the defendant's duty to encode and send a warning message in such a way that the required information (the information the defendant has a duty to convey) is *a probable enough* interpretation to be arrived at by a foreseeable message recipient. The term "probable enough" refers simultaneously to the absolute probability that the intended interpretation itself will be comprehended by the recipient and to the relative probability of the intended interpretation within the range of alternative possibilities (that is, relative to the commonality of the interpretation within the overall distribution). What constitutes "probable enough" is the ultimate question of fact in a language liability case and is therefore a question left to the jury. Putting a value on the probability and providing that information for the use of the jury can, however, provide a role for a language expert.

Looking at the situation from the other side, we also need to take a third-person view of the plaintiff's duty, because what is at issue is not what the plaintiff actually comprehends (except in the case where the defendant raises assumption of the risk as an affirmative defense (Prosser, 1971:441)—an issue beyond the scope of the present discussion)—but rather what the ordinary reasonable person would comprehend. The duty of the plaintiff, as an ordinary reasonable person, is to comprehend and heed a warning message communicated by the defendant if the comprehension of the warning is a *probable enough* interpretation of the message from the vantage of an outside observer. "Probable enough" has the same meaning here as that stated previously.

According to the foregoing analysis, information concerning the range and distribution of alternative interpretations of a message is (or should be) relevant to a products liability forum where language liability is at issue. It is time to turn to the question of how one might go about obtaining such information.

5. TOWARD A METHODOLOGY FOR COMMUNICATION ANALYSIS IN PRODUCTS LIABILITY LITIGATION

According to the analysis I am proposing in this chapter, the primary task of a language expert in a products liability case is to acquire distributional information about the range and relative probabilities of possible interpretations of a warning or instructional message. In order to do this, three requirements must be met. First, one must identify and obtain the voluntary cooperation of a population of people reasonably representative of the foreseeable users of the product in question. Second, one must present these people with a sample of the product information message in question in a way that is reasonably comparable to the situation in which a foreseeable user might encounter the message. Third, one must probe individual interpretations of the message in such a way that a probability distribution index of interpretations can be determined. These requirements are obvious to anyone familiar with tenets of good experimental design. None are trivial, but language experts have the means of meeting all three. Without going into great detail, some observations are in order.

Finding a suitable (and representative) population depends upon the requirements of a particular case and the ingenuity of the language investigator. For cases that I have been consulted on, I have used evening-school students, shopping mall patrons, university maintenance personnel, farmers, firemen (an exceptionally receptive population), church congregations, neighbors, and college sophomores. As a result of my experiences, collecting comprehension-based frequency distributions from a variety of populations over a number of years, two facts stand out: First, for *most* purposes (not all), the distributional responses do not vary significantly from population to population; second, a large number of subjects is rarely needed to get a reasonable estimate of distribution parameters for language comprehension. Thirty is usually enough, and very little additional information is gained after 50. Unlike opinion surveys which are subject to large sampling errors, interpretation distributions stabilize relatively quickly.

The second requirement falls under the general heading of what many psychologists call "ecological validity" (Neisser, 1976). The essence of the concept is that researchers should try to duplicate as much as possible the psychologically important characteristics of the setting in which the phenomenon under scrutiny occurs normally. This is not always easy to do; for example because it is usually not possible to collect data from actual consumers of a product because in most cases a record of the identity of consumers is not available, and where available is very costly to use. (It might be possible if it could be economically justified in the context of a particular case.) In general, the most important objective is to make the context in which data are collected nonbiasing (interpretively neutral), and to try to get subjects to play the role of a consumer—a role which most of them find quite familiar.

A number of different probe questions can be asked which will generate distributional information concerning people's interpretations. One can ask directly for a verbal interpretation of a warning or direction, or indirectly ask for a listing of possible hazards suggested by a set of warnings or directions. It is also possible to use a series of objective-type questions to test comprehension or to generate rating scales or indexes of agreement (like those used in personality tests and opinion surveys). Open-ended interviews generating verbal protocols which can be content-analyzed represent another possibility. All of these techniques have a body of methodological literature associated with them. One of the strategies that I have found helpful is to use more than one type of probe (using different subjects for each probe) in an effort to find corroboration for the findings through a kind of convergent validity.

One aspect of this sort of case-specific research that is worth noting is that it does not follow the traditional model of pure versus applied research. The usual assumption in the sciences has been that pure research builds a body of cumulative fact and theory, which is then at the service of various applied branches of the science. Several commentators have noted recently that this model does not seem to be appropriate for the psychological sciences because a half-century or more of laboratory research has failed to build a cumulative body of knowledge (Newell, 1973), and there is little evidence that laboratory findings generalize well to other laboratory settings, let alone to the real world (Jenkins, 1980). The one advantage of the approach I am suggesting is that it minimizes the problems of generalizing from the data to the situation at issue in the courtroom.

The kind of research needed to answer questions of fact in products liability cases is not very costly and can generally be conducted in a relatively short period of time. Given the usual long delay between the filing of a complaint and the trial, case-specific research is not only helpful, but quite feasible. As an example, I would like to return to the silicone spray example that began this chapter.

The reader will recall that the plaintiff's injury was due to slippery footing caused by the presence of silicone on the shopping mall floor. The manufacturer did not deny that such an injury was foreseeable but contended that the phrase "do not spray on tile floors" was warning enough to put an ordinary reasonable user on notice that such a hazard existed. I and my research assistant presented cans of the silicone spray to two randomly selected groups of adults we encountered in a shopping mall similar to the one in which the incident occurred and asked them questions about the can label. Embedded in a series of questions were two that we were particularly interested in.

One group of respondents were simply asked what they thought the phrase "do not spray on tile floors" meant. In our sample, fewer than 20% of the subjects thought that it had something to do with making the surface slippery, whereas most of the respondents (53%) thought that it meant that the spray might somehow damage the finish on tile flooring. They evidently assimilated the meaning of the direction on the label with similar statements on a variety of other products that they were familiar with—for example, "do not spill on automobile finish."

A second group of subjects was asked to list what they thought were the possible safety hazards associated with the use of the product. Only 2 out of 34 people surveyed mentioned possible slippery conditions.

This example illustrates quite clearly the existence of communicative egocentricism (if not incompetence) on the part of the author of the warning material on the label. Why, for instance, does the label specify only tile floors, when the hazard applies equally well to linoleum, marble, hardwood, or terrazzo? To prepare an answer to an anticipated question ("What would be an adequate warning?"), we composed a label identical to the one on the product spray can, except that we substituted the word "floors" for "tile floors." The result was that the responses having to do with slippery conditions were approximately equivalent in frequency to those mentioning problems with finish. Of course, a simple phrase such as "to avoid the danger of slipping, do not allow spray to get on floors" eliminates the ambiguity on its face. (It is worth noting that in the time between the injury in this case and the scheduled trial date—the case was settled—the manufacturer changed the label to incorporate this language.)

The reported products liability cases in which language questions arise are fairly consistent in making questions concerning the adequacy of labels and directions matter of fact, for the jury, and not something to be decided as a matter of law. In deciding these adequacy questions, what information can the jury rely on? There is no authoritative source to help in deciding the wide range of language issues that arise in these cases. Moreover, as Judge Learned Hand said, "It is one of the surest indexes of a mature and developed jurisprudence not to make a fortress out of a dictionary" (*Cabel v. Markham*, 1945, at 739). In matters of language it is difficult for people who are not sophisticated in the study of language to transcend their own subjectivity, which is what jurors are asked to do. Once pointed out, a possible interpretation of a message is clear (very much like the hidden picture puzzles given children), but it is difficult afterward to return to the innocent state that existed before and to make an estimate of what the "ordinary reasonable person" might have seen (or understood) unaided. The kind of data support that I have suggested here might in fact be just what the jury needs to apply this elusive concept of an objective standard for human understanding. As more and more language scientists become involved in the judicial process, especially in the civil arena, let us hope that the acceptance of linguistic and psycholinguistic evidence will increase.

6. REFERENCES

Barclay, J., Bransford, J., Franks, J., McCarrell, N., & Nitch, K. (1974). Comprehension and semantic flexibility. *Journal of Verbal Learning and Verbal Behavior, 13*, 471–487.

Bolinger, D. (1965). The atomization of meaning. *Language, 39*, 170–210.

Bransford, J., & Johnson, M. (1972). Contextual prerequisites for understanding: Some investigations of comprehension and recall. *Journal of Verbal Learning and Verbal Behavior, 11*, 717–726.

Bransford, J., & McCarrell, N. (1974). A sketch of a cognitive approach to comprehension: Some thoughts about understanding what it means to comprehend. In W. Weimer & D. Palermo (Eds.), *Cognition and the symbolic process* (pp. 189–229). Hillsdale, NJ: Erlbaum.

Brown, R. (1965). *Social psychology*. New York: Free Press.

Chomsky, N. (1957). *Syntactic structures*. The Hague: Mouton.

Fillmore, C. (1976). Frame semantics and the nature of language. In S. Harnad, H. Steklis, & J. Lancaster (Eds.), *Origins and evolution of language and speech* (pp. 20–32). New York: New York Academy of Sciences.

Fraser, B. (1979). The interpretation of novel metaphors. In A. Ortony (Ed.), *Metaphor and thought* (pp. 172–185). Cambridge, England: Cambridge University Press.

Harré, R., & Secord, P. (1972). *The explanation of social behavior.* London: Basil Blackwell & Mott.

Heidegger, M. (1962). *Being and time* (J. Macquarrie & E. Robinson trans.). New York: Harper & Row. (Original work published 1927)

Jenkins, J. (1980). Can we have a fruitful cognitive psychology? *Nebraska Symposium on Motivation, 28,* 211–238.

Johnson, M., & Henley, T. (1988). Something old, something new, something borrowed, something true. *Metaphor and Symbolic Activity, 3,* 233–252.

Johnson, M., & Malgady, R. (1980). Toward a perceptual theory of metaphoric comprehension. In R. Honeck & R. Hoffman (Eds.), *Cognition and figurative language* (pp. 259–282). Hillsdale, NJ: Erlbaum.

Johnson, M., Bransford, J., & Solomon, S. (1973). Memory for tacit implications of sentences. *Journal of Experimental Psychology, 98,* 203–205.

Katz, J., & Fodor, J. (1963). The structure of a semantic theory. *Language, 39,* 170–210.

Lakoff, G. (1987). *Women, fire, and dangerous things.* Chicago: University of Chicago Press.

Loftus, E. (1979). *Eyewitness testimony.* Cambridge: Harvard University Press.

McCloskey, M., & Egeth, H. (1983). Eyewitness identification: What can a psychologist tell a jury? *American Psychologist, 38,* 550–563.

Minsky, M. (1987). *The society of mind.* New York: Simon and Schuster.

Neisser, U. (1976). *Cognition and reality.* San Francisco: Freeman.

Newell, A. (1973). You can't play twenty questions with nature and win. In W. Chase (Ed.), *Visual information processing* (pp. 283–308). New York: Academic Press.

Noel, D., & Phillips, J. (1981). *Products liability* (2nd ed.). St. Paul: West.

Prosser, W. (1971). *Handbook of the law of torts* (4th ed.). St. Paul: West.

Reddy, M. (1979). The conduit metaphor—A case of frame conflict in our language about language. In Ortony, A. (Ed.), *Metaphor and thought* (pp. 284–324). Cambridge, England: Cambridge University Press.

Robinson, D. (1980). *Psychology and law.* Oxford: Oxford University Press.

Rommetveit, R. (1968). *Words, meanings and messages.* New York: Academic Press.

Rommetveit, R. (1974). *On message structure.* New York: Wiley.

Schank, R., & Abelson, R. (1977). *Scripts, plans, goals and understanding.* Hillsdale, NJ: Erlbaum.

Searle, J. (1969). *Speech acts.* Cambridge, England: Cambridge University Press.

Searle, J. (1983). *Intentionality.* Cambridge, England: Cambridge University Press.

Tannen, D. (1984). *Conversational style: Analyzing talk among friends.* Norwood, NJ: Ablex.

Verbrugge, R., & McCarrell, N. (1977). Metaphoric comprehension: Studies in reminding and resembling. *Cognitive Psychology, 9,* 494–533.

Winograd, T. (1981). What does it mean to understand language? In D. Norman (Ed.), *Perspectives on cognitive science* (pp. 231–264). Norwood, NJ: Ablex.

Winograd, T., & Flores, F. (1986). *Understanding computers and cognition.* Norwood, NJ: Ablex.

Wittgenstein, L. (1953). *Philosophical investigations* (2nd ed.). New York: Macmillan.

7. CASES CITED

Cabel v. Markham, 148 F.2d 737 (2d Cir. 1945).

Chapter 11

ADEQUACY OF CIGARETTE PACKAGE WARNINGS
An Analysis of the Adequacy of Federally Mandated Cigarette Package Warnings

BETHANY K. DUMAS

1. INTRODUCTION[1]

The recent rise of interest in health warnings has coincided with federal legislation mandating new, rotating warnings on cigarette packages (Comprehensive Smoking Education Act of 1984); the warning requirement has also been extended to smokeless tobacco products, including snuff and chewing

[1] I want to express my gratitude to my editors, Judith N. Levi and Anne Graffam Walker, for the uncompromising rigor of their standards and for their tireless encouragement and assistance. Both made important substantive as well as stylistic contributions to this chapter. I am particularly grateful to Professor Levi for suggesting to me the role of space limitations in the wording of the cigarette package warnings. I also want to acknowledge the assistance of colleagues at the University of Tennessee in performing statistical analysis and planning and preparing displays of the data treated herein. Special thanks are due to Ralph G. O'Brien, of the Department of Statistics and the Computing Center, who prepared Figures 1–3; thanks are also due to Donald R. Ploch, of the Department of Sociology and Milton D. Broach and Michael O'Neil of the Computing Center. Finally, I want to express my gratitude to John Karnes, who provided prescription drug labels, and to all those persons who assisted in the research by responding to questions posed during Experiments 1, 2, and 3.

BETHANY K. DUMAS • Department of English, University of Tennessee, Knoxville, Tennessee 37996-0430.

tobacco (Comprehensive Smokeless Tobacco Health Education Act of 1986). The new warning requirements stem from the increased awareness on the part of the public health advocates of possible health risks (Blasi & Monaghan, 1986) and also from increased efforts by lobbying groups to further restrict both cigarette advertising (Abramson, 1986:1) and permissible smoking in public areas.

There has also been a new round of litigation in which cigarette smokers or survivors of deceased cigarette smokers have attempted to recover damages from cigarette manufacturers on the theory that addictive smoking of cigarettes is responsible for maladies and conditions such as (1) lung cancer, (2) emphysema, and (3) limb amputation resulting from cardiovascular problems. Most of the lawsuits against tobacco companies in recent years have been wrongful death cases in which plaintiffs have charged that tobacco manufacturers are responsible for deaths or illnesses resulting from these maladies and conditions.

From the point of view of some of plaintiffs' litigators, the current cases constitute Phase 2 of an ongoing cigarette litigation saga (Lee, 1986). Phase 1 occurred between 1954 and the late 1970s. Although the tobacco manufacturers lost no cases during Phase 1, cases brought during that period sometimes resulted in findings by juries that smoking cigarettes causes lung cancer, but that tobacco manufacturers could not have known that prior to the issuance of the Surgeon General's first report on smoking and lung cancer in 1964 (Office of Smoking and Health, U.S. Department of Health, Education and Welfare, *Smoking and Health: A Report of the Surgeon General* [1964]) and so were not liable. After a several-year lull in litigation, Phase 2 "got into full swing in published opinions in 1984" (Lee, 1986:21); Phase 2 cases differ from Phase 1 cases in part because of the existence of federally mandated warnings from 1965 to the present (Federal Cigarette Labeling and Advertising Act of 1965, Public Health Cigarette Smoking Act of 1969). Some litigators predict that Phase 3 will involve mass litigation and ultimate success for plaintiffs (Gidmark, 1986:8–9; Lee, 1986:23).

These factors—the general rise of interest in health warnings, the new federal legislation mandating warnings on tobacco products, and renewed litigation involving claims against tobacco product manufacturers—suggest the need for research into the adequacy of warnings on cigarette packages. The concern of this chapter is the adequacy of past and present federally mandated warnings on cigarette packages.

This chapter begins by identifying the legal issues implicated in cigarette warning litigation, after which it identifies some issues of adequacy from the point of view of linguistics and human factors analysis. It then discusses what is known about the structure and function of warnings and describes strategies for exploring how individuals interpret warnings in general, then warnings on cigarette packages in particular. The chapter concludes that there is strong evidence for the existence of objective criteria by means of which the relative adequacy of warnings on cigarette packages can be assessed and that those objective criteria are for the most part not characteristic of present or past cigarette package warnings. Suggestions are offered for strengthening existing warnings, and additional research is proposed.

It should be understood by the reader at the outset that it is controversial whether written or graphic warnings ever constitute effective forms of safety information. The presence of written or graphic warnings on products seems mandated primarily by *common sense*, on the basis that explicit information will, in fact, be heeded by consumers (Lehto & Miller, 1988:5). However, some researchers have argued that warning labels play only a small role in the propensity of consumers to heed or disregard information found on them.[2]

It should also be understood that the warnings on cigarette packages have a different history and perform a different function from warnings on consumer products that must be used in order to accomplish specific tasks and also from warnings on pharmaceutical products whose prescribed use is beneficial to the consumer, though perhaps associated with certain health hazards or negative side effects. There is no reported long-term benign or therapeutic physical effect of the daily cigarette smoking habits that characterize most American smokers.[3] Thus the task of the tobacco industry in promoting its products is to sell, on the basis of short-term satisfaction, products with severe long-term negative consequences for both consumers and others. In drafting cigarette warnings, Congress has had to walk a tightrope between warning the public of health hazards associated with use of the product and avoiding angering the tobacco industry, a powerful economic force that is still heavily subsidized by our government.

The smoking of cigarettes is still legal in our society, yet there is strong

---

[2] One researcher (Breznitz, 1984) has explored the psychology of false alarms in early warning systems and has demonstrated that the effectiveness of warnings may be reduced by the *false alarm effect*, which operates to reduce (1) the credibility of the warnings and (2) the willingness of individuals to engage in protective behavior. On the basis of that research, Breznitz has suggested that consumers eventually ignore health and safety information because they engage in a continuous process of self-shaping based on false alarms: "Consider, for instance, the case of smoking. In spite of all the information to the contrary, one smokes a cigarette and nothing happens. One smokes another cigarette and still nothing happens. Thus, in the absence of any clear signals that may indicate the danger involved, these turn out subjectively to be false alarms" (p. 232). (The alert reader will note that Breznitz has used *threats* as a synonym for *warnings*. The similarities between *threats* and *warnings* are discussed later in this chapter.) (See also Weinstein *et al.*, 1978:63.)

One design engineer, Roger L. McCarthy, has had great success on the witness stand as a defendant's expert claiming that "the presence or absence of a warning absolutely makes no measurable effect on safety-related behavior, period." To the best of my knowledge, McCarthy has not substantiated that claim with empirical evidence (Deposition, 1987:156).

[3] The *psychological satisfaction* reported by such smokers is generally regarded by the medical profession as constituting "relief of the nicotine withdrawal syndrome by the self-administration of the drug in the form of tobacco" ("A Glossary of Tobacco Terms," 1985, citing Samfield, 1980:102, 151).

evidence that smoking is both addictive and deadly. In fact, there is mounting evidence that there is no safe use of cigarettes. So long, however, as cigarette smoking remains legal, it may be impossible to persuade consumers that smoking is deadly. At the very least, the decision to smoke cigarettes may be the result of such a complex rationalization process that there is no reasonable way to affect it. Alternatively, it may be that in the case of such a product there are more effective ways of providing safety information to consumers than by placing warning labels on packages. However, under present law, the requirement that cigarette packages carry warning labels is a major way of providing safety information to consumers. It is, therefore, highly appropriate to analyze these warnings in order to assess their adequacy and effectiveness.

1.1. The Legal Issues

Two legal issues are basic to all contemporary tobacco product cases: causality and failure to warn. In law, causality is what is known as a threshold issue: It must be proved before the issue of failure to warn can become important. Because causality is a matter for medical expertise, it will not be discussed here; it is worthy of note, however, that the issue of causality presents problems to medical researchers because of the complexity of the interrelationship between environmental factors and individual human heredity.

Failure to warn is also a potentially crucial legal issue. Manufacturers of dangerous products can be held liable for failure to warn consumers of the dangers of using such products and can become liable for enormous sums of money. In our society, we have three mechanisms for controlling dangerous products. Some products are controlled by decisions of federal agencies such as the Food and Drug Administration. Other products, like cigarettes, can be manufactured and sold only if they carry warnings that are mandated by Congress. Finally, there is the control provided through common law, which is case law evolved not from legislation but from judicial opinion based on precedents in our legal system.

An examination of case law demonstrates that there are three general guidelines for consumer product warnings:

1. Safety warnings must be displayed on products if such products would be *unreasonably dangerous* without such warnings (Restatement [Second] of Torts § 402A, Comment j [1965]).[4]

---

[4] This section of the Restatement also contains a widely-accepted definition of *unreasonably dangerous*, under which an article is held to be unreasonably dangerous only if it is "dangerous to an extent beyond that which would be contemplated by the ordinary consumer who purchases it, with the ordinary knowledge common to the community as to its characteristics." The section goes on to give examples of dangerous products whose characteristics are sufficiently well known that they are not deemed unreasonably dangerous. Tobacco is given as an example of such a product: "Good tobacco is not unreasonably dangerous merely because the effects of smoking may be harmful; but tobacco containing something like marijuana may be unreasonably dangerous."

2. Warnings should be directed to the ultimate users of the product or to any individuals who might be expected to come into contact with the product. (Restatement [Second] of Torts § 388, Comment a [1965].)

3. To be adequate, a warning should (1) catch the attention of a reasonably prudent person in the circumstances of its use, (2) be understandable, and (3) convey a fair indication of the nature and extent of the potential danger to the individual (*Ford Motor Co. v. Nowak*, 1982).

The requirement of adequacy is the vaguest of the guidelines. Some of the reasons the courts have found manufacturers in violation of the requirement of adequacy have been (1) failure to communicate the level of the danger (*Bituminous Casualty Corp. v. Black and Decker Corp.*, 1974), (2) failure to display the warning in a reasonable location (*Griggs v. Firestone Tire and Rubber*, 1975), (3) failure to give sufficient information about how to avoid the danger (*Wallinger v. Martin Stamping and Stove Co.*, 1968), and (4) failure to preserve the integrity of the warning by including statements that nullify its impact (*American Optical v. Weiderhamer*, 1980).

Because, in the case of cigarette package warnings, the precise wording is mandated by Congress, the question arises: Is mere literal compliance with the statutory requirements sufficient to constitute adequacy of warning? That is, has Congress preempted the common-law guideline requiring that warnings, to be adequate, must (1) catch the attention of a reasonably prudent person in the circumstances of its use, (2) be understandable, and (3) convey a fair indication of the nature and extent of the potential danger to the individual? In one legal interpretation of the required warnings (*Roysdon v. R. J. Reynolds Tobacco Company*, 1986, discussed later), such literal compliance with statutory law constitutes adequacy as a matter of law. The question is important both to lawyers, on the one hand, and forensic linguists and human factors analysts, on the other, because matters of law are decided by the court (in the person of the judge); only matters of fact are the province of the jury. Thus once a judge rules that the warnings are adequate as a matter of law—as some have so ruled—then that issue cannot go to the jury, and no expert testimony on the subject can be offered during trial. Given such a circumstance, a linguistic or human factors analysis of warning adequacy would be rendered moot.

If, however, a cigarette manufacturer's responsibility is held to go beyond mere literal compliance with the statutory law, then the legal issue does become a potentially interesting one to researchers in linguistics and human factors. To forensic linguists, the issue presents the opportunity to study and render an opinion on a number of syntactic, semantic, and pragmatic factors. To human factors researchers, the issue presents the opportunity to study and render an opinion on such factors as size, placement, and visibility of warnings. These factors, each of which plays a part in the effectiveness of warnings as perceived by the public, will be featured in the discussion to follow.

The research reported in this chapter was conducted in the context of a trial in which plaintiff's lawyers anticipated that the adequacy of warnings on cigarette packages would be at issue. In the course of conducting that research, I reached some conclusions about the relative adequacy of past and present cigarette package warnings. The reader should note that the research was carried out during a relatively brief period of time and that it should thus be regarded as a pilot study. In my final section, I describe additional research, which I plan to carry out in the future.

1.2. The Adequacy Issues

In order to address the issue of adequacy of warning, we must first of all know when someone has been warned. The first question for the researcher is then: What constitutes a warning? In this chapter, I shall be concerned only with written statements whose wording explicitly identifies them as warnings. Further, I shall approach the question primarily from the point of view of the recipient, rather than the sender. Whichever point of view is adopted, it is generally acknowledged by philosophers (e.g., Searle, 1969), linguists (e.g., Fraser, 1975), and others (e.g., Lehto & Miller, 1986) who have studied warnings that the formalization of the semantic and syntactic rules for warnings is difficult.[5]

Formalizing the rules for warnings is difficult for two reasons. First, no discipline recognizes a clear, unambiguous definition of *warning*. Cross-discipline uncertainty about the precise meaning of the term is even greater than that within discrete disciplines (e.g., linguistics). Second, warnings may be either direct or indirect and either literal or nonliteral. That is, many warnings are highly context-dependent, and their interpretation may depend upon lesser or greater amounts of inferencing.

The uncertainty of the definition of the term "warning" derives largely from (1) its being confused with such activities as *instructing, persuading,* and *advising* and (2) its being associated with a wide variety of functions, different ones of which are stressed by different sectors of society (Lehto & Miller, 1986:15).

Dictionaries recognize the uncertainty of definition, partly by acknowledging that the activity of *warning* includes one or more of, but not necessarily all of, such activities as *informing, telling, counseling,* and the like. They also typically recognize close similarities among such words as "warn," "forewarn," "admonish," and "caution." *Warn* is generally stipulated as being the most comprehensive of such words; the common element of meaning among them is generally regarded as *giving notice of either actual danger or the possibility of danger.*

[5] See Kreckel (1981a, b) for the suggestion that there may be differing cultural notions about what it is to be warned.

An examination of definitions of the term *warning* in various disciplines underscores the uncertainty reflected in dictionary definitions. This uncertainty will be discussed later with respect to linguistics and philosophy. Only in human factors engineering textbooks is great consistency of emphasis displayed with respect to warnings. There, *alerting to a necessity for action* (including negative action, e.g., refraining from smoking) seems to be the major component of a warning (Lehto & Miller, 1986:14, citing De Greene, 1970:313; McCormick, 1970:189; Murrell, 1969:156, 208; Robinson, 1977).

Consumer products often arrive with "[a] wide variety of literature . . . expected to perform several functions that are commonly viewed as being warning-related" (Lehto & Miller, 1986:15). Different segments of society stress different functions of warnings, depending upon the nature of their stake in the product under examination; thus, there are varying perspectives on warnings. "These perspectives can simplistically be divided into the views of society as a whole and the views of the directly affected parties, which include [,among others,] manufacturers . . . and consumers" (Lehto & Miller, 1986:15). The general societal view of warnings is that they function primarily to reduce accidents and health damage by informing people of risks associated with the use of consumer products (Weinstein, Twerski, Piehler, & Donaher, 1978).

From the perspective of manufacturers, warnings may function largely as a defense against litigation (Lehto & Miller, 1986:16). Using a warning for such a purpose may lead to its actually having an *antisafety* function, that is, warnings may be used as a replacement for careful design (Schwartz & Driver, 1983).

But what about the perspective of the consumer? It is from this perspective that issues of adequacy arise. In the absence of a clear and unambiguous definition of warning, some researchers have accepted as a working definition that of Searle, a language philosopher who described warnings as *statements about future events or states which are not in the hearer's best interest, and which are uttered in situations in which it is not obvious to both the hearer and the speaker that the event will occur or that the state will transpire* (1969, p. 67). I used that working definition as a starting point for the research described here.

In positing the illocutionary act rules for warnings, Searle suggested that warnings are either categorical or hypothetical (1969:67). His definition (given before) was of categorical warnings, which are, he suggested, "like advising, rather than requesting" (1969:67). Hypothetical warnings are explicitly predictive: They follow IF–THEN logical structure and are of the type "If X, then Y." Searle suggested that most warnings are probably in this "hypothetical" category. An example is "If you do not do X, then Y will occur" (1969:67).

Searle has not, so far as I know, offered any evidence for these generalizations. The research reported later explored the distinction between categorical and hypothetical warnings, partly to test subjects' sensitivity to the difference, partly to test the adequacy of the classification.

Fraser (1975) pointed out that it is difficult to isolate warnings. From a strictly linguistic point of view, it is difficult to distinguish them from threats and promises. Fraser analyzed warning acts in a speech act framework and concluded that threats are a special type of warning, one wherein "the speaker takes on the responsibility for bringing about the disadvantageous action" (Fraser, 1975:173), whereas a promise is a specification of a future act in which "the speaker intends the utterance to count as the undertaking of an obligation to carry out the action" (Fraser, 1975:175). The close similarity between warnings and promises is illustrated by the frequent occurrence in informal conversation of the joking rejoinder, "Is that a threat or a promise?"

According to Fraser, then, warnings are like both threats and promises in that, as noted, they refer exclusively to future actions. Warnings are like threats and unlike promises in that they refer to undesirable future events. Warnings are unlike both promises and threats in that the future action or nonaction referred to is in the control of the hearer, not the speaker. Warnings are also unlike threats and promises in that they are never absolute, being always conditional or contingent, even though categorical warnings are only implicatively conditional or contingent. Though both promises and threats can be contingent, they can also be absolute as in "I promise I'll never do that again" and "I'll get you for this."

Further, as noted, warnings, like other specific illocutionary acts, can be indirect as well as direct, nonliteral as well as literal. Fraser (1975) has pointed out that warnings can be either verbal or nonverbal and that no particular words are necessary to warn. A raised eyebrow may constitute a stern warning at a dinner party. The words "Look out!" in a physically dangerous situation can certainly constitute a warning. And, again as noted, there are differing notions of the functions of warnings.

I have said that I am concerned here only with written warnings identified by explicit wording as being warnings. With respect to warning labels, it is important to note that the *warning label*, as distinct from a *warning* per se, has functions other than that of introducing a sincere warning. One function appears to be a mere lip service compliance with the letter of the law. Note, for instance, the following two current rotating *warnings* on cigarette packages:

1. SURGEON GENERAL'S WARNING: Quitting Smoking Now Greatly Reduces Serious Risks to Your Health.
2. SURGEON GENERAL'S WARNING: Cigarette Smoke Contains Carbon Monoxide.

The first example can be read as a sincere warning only if one allows for a negative inference—"If I don't quit smoking now, I continue to sustain serious risks to my health." As phrased, the statement is actually more like an explicit promise or a forecast because explicitly positive results are mentioned.

The second example, on the other hand, mentions no results of any kind and thus appears to be merely informational. A consumer who is unaware of the effect of carbon monoxide on the human body could not, therefore, be relied upon to read the second example as a warning. In both cases, each of which will be discussed at greater length later, the intent seems to be merely to comply on a surface level with the statutory requirement. (The first example offers a further problem, that of the uncertainty triggered by the word "now." An addicted consumer may well be prompted to rationalize away the message of this warning by asking ask one of these questions: *Would my quitting smoking last year not have greatly reduced serious risks to my health? Would my quitting smoking next year not greatly reduce serious risks to my health?* This is surely nit-picking, but it is nit-picking that was engaged in by some of the subjects I interviewed in the research described later.)

Another function of the *warning label* is merely to direct attention to an item. Consider the legend on the cover of a Chinese restaurant menu in Knoxville, Tennessee:

WARNING!
Chinese Food Lovers
Eating Any Selection From The Enclosed MENU
Can Be Dangerously Habit Forming!

Clearly this tongue-in-cheek announcement is made not to warn away but to entice customers to try the food because no self-respecting restaurant owner would seriously suggest that his or her food is clinically addictive.

Difficult as it is to identify warnings and to distinguish them from warning labels, it is a great deal more difficult to know what constitutes an adequate or effective warning. One of the processes humans appear to be engaging in when they read warnings is that of risk assessment. Risk assessment is an extremely complex process, partly because of the inherent complexity of the process whereby consumers process and act on any information. On the basis of the research reported, it seems clear that some of the linguistic factors that affect the extent to which consumers heed warnings include those of syntax, semantics, and pragmatics. Others appear to be such variables as size, placement, and visibility of warnings. Without claiming to address the full scope of the adequacy of warning issue, in this chapter I will undertake to identify some objective criteria of warning messages reported effective or ranked high on an effectiveness scale; I will then assess past and present federally mandated cigarette package warnings with respect to whether they are characterized by those objective criteria.[6]

[6] Since completing the empirical research described in this chapter, I have become familiar with the books by Lehto and Miller (1986) and Miller and Lehto (1987) cited before. *Volume I, Warnings: Fundamentals, Design, and Evaluation Methodologies* (Lehto & Miller, 1986), focuses on safety information labels on products from the perspective of human factors and product design engineering. It contains a chapter, "Definitions and Modeling Techniques" and three chapters

1.3. Genesis of the Study

The research reported here had its genesis in a request by a plaintiff's lawyer in Knoxville, Tennessee, that I conduct research on the issue of the adequacy of past and present federally mandated cigarette package warnings. Between late October and early December of 1985, I carried out an empirical investigation in preparation for the submission of a report in the case styled as *Roysdon v. R. J. Reynolds Tobacco Company* (1986), a case in which plaintiff Roysdon claimed that his leg amputation (necessitated by cardiovascular disease) was the result of his having smoked cigarettes manufactured by R. J. Reynolds Tobacco Company for most of his life.

In planning my research, I focused primarily on the six warnings that either have been required to be printed on cigarette packages since 1965 or are required now. The plaintiff in the case had smoked since before 1965, so he had smoked when there were no required warnings, continued to smoke during the tenure of the 1965 and 1970 warnings, and on into the early months of the new rotating warnings. Statutes of limitations precluded his suing under the no-warning period or the time of the 1965 warning (1965–1970). However, I felt that comprehensive testing of all these warnings plus some fabricated ones was necessary for comparison of the effect of various linguistic and extralinguistic factors in warnings. The six federally mandated warnings I planned to test are given below in order of promulgation; 3 through 6 are the rotating warnings currently in force:

1. Caution: Cigarette Smoking May Be Hazardous to Your Health (1965)
2. Warning: The Surgeon General Has Determined That Cigarette Smoking Is Dangerous to Your Health (1970)
3. SURGEON GENERAL'S WARNING: Smoking Causes Lung Cancer, Heart Disease, Emphysema and May Complicate Pregnancy (1985)
4. SURGEON GENERAL'S WARNING: Quitting Smoking Now Greatly Reduces Serious Risks to Your Health (1985)

---

on the effectiveness of warnings. Lehto and Miller use a knowledge-based approach (in the sense used in artificial intelligence) to human performance and task analysis and advocate strongly the need to address risk rationally, rather than on the basis of *common sense*. Though the volume does not include the perspectives of linguistics and philosophy, it is an extremely important book for anyone seriously interested in issues involving consumer product warning formulation and adequacy. Volume II is an *Annotated Bibliography with Topical Index* (Miller & Lehto, 1987). A third volume, tentatively titled *Formalized Design Standards and Design Methods for Compliance* (Lehto, Miller, & Clark) has been announced for publication in late 1988 or early 1989. It will contain, among other things, a summary of the warnings required by the federal government; descriptions of warning/labeling standards as functions of products; identification of products required to have warnings; and the specific nature of the warnings that must be designed for the products. It is also to contain an illustrative expert system designed to assist in the design and layout of physical warning labels.

5. SURGEON GENERAL'S WARNING: Smoking by Pregnant Women May Result in Fetal Injury, Premature Birth, and Low Birth Weight (1985)

6. SURGEON GENERAL'S WARNING: Cigarette Smoke Contains Carbon Monoxide (1985)

The general legal issue in the context of which I was asked to conduct my research was whether past or present cigarette package warning labels are adequate to warn consumers of the possibly negative effects of cigarette smoking. Specifically, I was asked to give an opinion as to whether the 1970 warning is adequate to warn consumers of the potentially negative cardiovascular effects of cigarette smoking.

Shortly before trial, however, Judge Thomas G. Hull of the Eastern District of Tennessee, the presiding judge, rendered my testimony inadmissible by ruling that, as a matter of law, the federally mandated warnings on cigarette packages are adequate. This ruling had the effect of removing the issue from the jury's consideration of it. Further, at the end of the plaintiff's presentation of his evidence, Judge Hull dismissed the suit, ruling that the plaintiff had made no case. Judge Hull gave two reasons for doing so: (1) The federal statute on cigarette package labeling had preempted state common-law actions based on alleged inadequacies, and (2) common knowledge about tobacco was such that cigarettes are not *unreasonably dangerous*.[7] The plaintiff appealed, but the Sixth Circuit upheld the ruling of the trial court. No attempt will be made by the plaintiff to appeal to the Supreme Court of the United States, so defendant R. J. Reynolds won. Although my prepared testimony therefore did not play an important role at the trial, it did provide the impetus for further study of the issues in dispute.

As suggested, my overall goal in preparing for trial had been to conduct research designed to shed light on this general question: Are past or present federally mandated cigarette package warnings, particularly the 1970 warning, adequate to warn smokers of the harmful effects of smoking, particularly the potentially negative cardiovascular effects of cigarette smoking? In order to explore this general question, I addressed the following specific questions:

1. Can warnings be identified by the presence of specific semantic, lexical, syntactic, or other characteristics? If so, what are they?

2. Can warnings be meaningfully classified? If so, on what bases? Do consumers respond to or evaluate warnings on such bases?

3. Is it possible to state categorically how warnings are perceived by consumers? If so, how are warnings perceived?

4. Do warnings differ by degree? Do consumers classify warnings as strong versus weak?

[7] Judge Hull noted that Tennessee tort law has been held to incorporate the comment defining *unreasonably dangerous* in the Restatement (Second) of Torts, § 402A, discussed in footnote 4.

5. Are the federally mandated cigarette package warnings strong or weak? If they are weak, how could they be made strong?
6. Do the statements at issue here constitute warnings? If so, precisely what do the statements appear to warn against?
7. Are the warnings at issue adequate to warn consumers of possible negative effects of cigarette smoking, particularly with regard to the potentially negative cardiovascular effects of cigarette smoking? If they are not, could they have been?

In addition, I wanted to investigate the extent to which there is uniformity in how individuals understand warnings. Should there be a great uniformity in the effect of some of the factors I had identified earlier (and which I discuss later), such evidence might eventually suggest a theoretical model for the formalization of linguistic rules concerning adequate warnings. At a minimum, such evidence would suggest a general framework for analysis of the adequacy of many consumer products.

1.4. Initial Analysis of Warnings on Cigarette Packages

In my initial analysis of the warnings, I familiarized myself with the legislative history of the federal promulgation of the warning label requirements on cigarette packages and with the role of the Federal Trade Commission (FTC) in the history of that promulgation. After that, I examined some federally mandated warning labels used on prescription drugs. Finally, I analyzed the six cigarette warnings in order to identify potential problems with content and readability and to formulate hypotheses for research.

Legislative history is made up of legislative background documents and events, including committee reports, hearings, and floor debates; it is used by courts when they are required to determine the legislative intent of a particular statute. I read the legislative history of the warning label requirements on cigarette packages in order to isolate the factors identified as important by the drafters of these warnings. From it, I learned that the warnings that have actually been required have always been significantly weaker (as determined by criteria I report later in this chapter) than those initially proposed. For instance, legislation mandating use of the original (1965) warning "Caution: Cigarette Smoking May Be Hazardous to Your Health") actually had the effect of preempting a proposed FTC Trade Regulation Rule that would have required all cigarette packages and advertisements to disclose clearly and prominently that "Cigarette Smoking is dangerous to health and may cause death from cancer and other diseases." (The Trade Regulation Rule for the Prevention of Unfair or Deceptive Advertising and Labeling of Cigarettes in Relation to the Health Hazards of Smoking, 29 Fed. Reg. §§ 8324, 8325, 8356 [July 2, 1964] ["The 1964 Cigarette Rule"].) Had Congress not preempted the requirement of The 1964 Cigarette Rule, the very first federally mandated warning would have mentioned specific negative consequences of smoking cigarettes, namely specific diseases, and would have specified that smoking *is dangerous*, not merely that it *may be hazardous*.

Later, in 1969, shortly before the end of a congressionally mandated moratorium on requiring cigarette manufacturers to reveal tar and nicotine contents of cigarettes, the FTC proposed a modified version of The 1964 Cigarette Rule; had that modified version of the original proposal been adopted, it would have required all cigarette packages and advertisements to carry this message: "Warning: Cigarette Smoking Is Dangerous to Health and May Cause Death From Cancer, Coronary Heart Disease, Chronic Bronchitis, Pulmonary Emphysema, and Other Diseases." (34 Fed. Reg. § 7919 [1969]) Congress, however, amended the message on cigarette packages to read: "Warning: The Surgeon General Has Determined That Cigarette Smoking Is Dangerous To Your Health." (15 U.S.C. §§ 1331 *et seq.*, 1970).

Since then, the four rotational warnings in current use have been adopted. Again, the impetus for change seems to have come from the FTC. A May 1981 FTC Staff Report on the Cigarette Advertising Investigation ("Staff Report") sets out the reasons why that agency thought the 1970 warning was ineffective. The first factors, identified on the basis of *common sense*, were (1) overexposure (the warning was "worn out"), (2) lack of novelty (it contained no new information), (3) abstract and general nature of the wording, and (4) lack of personal relevance of the warning. Also, the unchanging size and shape of the 1970 warning were felt to contribute to its ineffectiveness. Later market research surveys reported by the FTC suggested additionally that (1) if warnings were to be effective, they should be short (one idea per warning), simple, and direct, and (2) disease-specific warnings, that is, those listing specific diseases as possible consequences of smoking, are far more effective than non-disease-specific warnings.

The proposal to use a rotational warning system evolved partly as a way to address the four problems cited before. The FTC recommended that the rotational warnings should be selected in accord with four criteria: (1) medical accuracy, (2) demonstrable filling of a gap in consumer knowledge about health hazards, (3) intelligibility, and (4) ability to "prompt consumers to think about the health hazards of smoking" (Staff Report pp. 5–33). Sample warnings prepared by the FTC meet all those criteria. Representative ones include the following:

1.	WARNING:	Smoking causes death from cancer, heart attacks and lung disease.
2.	CARBON MONOXIDE:	Cigarette smoke contains carbon monoxide and other poison gases.
3.	WARNING:	Smoking may be addictive.
4.	LIGHT SMOKING:	Even a few cigarettes a day are dangerous.

Again, we find the same pattern of FTC-proposed warnings mentioning specific negative consequences of smoking, followed by Congressionally promulgated warnings mentioning fewer or weaker specific negative consequences of smoking. The four rotating warnings currently required are a good deal weaker and certainly less comprehensive than the first ones proposed by the FTC.[8]

After having familiarized myself with the legislative background, I next examined some federally mandated warning labels used on prescription drugs. In order to do so, I obtained a large sampling from a Knoxville, Tennessee, pharmacist. In examining them, I noticed that the pharmaceutical labels appeared to observe the criteria listed here very well. Most of the warnings are brief; additionally, the labels appear to be medically accurate; and they certainly did fill gaps in my own knowledge about health hazards. They were generally intelligible, and, as a consumer, I felt that they generally would prompt me to think about the health hazards of any prescription drugs associated with them. The most striking aspect of the prescription warnings was the use of graphic symbols (such as automobiles and outlines of faces) and color contrast. On the basis of this examination, I decided that it was obviously possible for warning label designers to comply strongly with those four FTC-proposed criteria: The resulting warnings could be medically accurate; they could fill gaps in consumer knowledge about health hazards; they could be intelligible; and they could "prompt consumers to think about the health hazards of smoking."

The FTC seemed to expect that the introduction of rotational warnings would correct the prior problems of overexposure and lack of novelty, while recognizing that the problems of the abstract nature of the prior warnings, and the perceived lack of personal relevance, would have to be corrected by a judicious choice of wording for each of the rotating warnings. The choice of wording would in addition have to conform to the following criteria:

1. Medical accuracy
2. Demonstrable filling of a gap in consumer knowledge about health hazards
3. Intelligibility

---

[8] This chapter is not an appropriate forum for discussing the process whereby legislation is promulgated by our Congress. I would, however, like to note that one important difference between Congress and federal regulatory agencies like the FTC is that Congress is the target of systematic lobbying by private interest groups, often with interests at odds with those of the average consumer and often with enormous sums of money at their disposal. One such group is the Tobacco Institute, the lobbying arm of the tobacco industry. The wording of cigarette package warnings in this country has always been the result of a compromise between Congressional proposals and successful lobbying efforts of the Tobacco Institute and other private groups.

4. Ability to direct consumers' attention to health consequences of smoking (possibly by keeping warnings short (one idea per warning), simple, and direct, and by creating disease-specific warnings)
5. Specificity and concreteness
6. Personal relevance
7. Variation in format

Criterion 1 is an issue for medical research; it will not be discussed further here. Discussed here are criteria 2 through 7, particularly criteria 3 through 7. At issue are both the actual importance of all these criteria and also the extent to which current warnings comply with them.

1.5. Hypotheses

Using what I had learned from completing the steps discussed, I analyzed the six cigarette warnings for the purpose of identifying potential problems with content, readability, and format. I considered (1) vocabulary, (2) syntax, (3) warning type (using Searle's distinction between categorical and hypothetical warnings), and (4) identity of addressee. I also identified some potential problems with content (e.g., some labels not constituting warnings *per se*; others being too narrowly targeted to be personally relevant to most smokers; still others containing modal auxiliaries like "may" and "can") and with readability (e.g., use of technical vocabulary and unusual syntax). After that, I identified additional potential problems based on extra-linguistic factors such as size, placement, and visibility of warnings. At this stage, I formulated the following set of general hypotheses with respect to the warnings under consideration:

1. When asked, respondents rank-order warnings with great consistency.
2. Specific, identifiable factors are characteristic of those warnings selected as stronger.
3. Other things being equal, respondents rank hypothetical warnings as stronger than categorical warnings.
4. The modal auxiliaries "may" and "can" weaken warnings; further, the presence of one of these hedging modals anywhere in a warning has the effect of being taken to be generally applicable to all clauses in the warning.
5. The presence of either modal auxiliary "may" or "can" in a warning in a rotational series has the effect of being read into all the warnings in the series.
6. Disease-specific warnings are perceived as stronger than non-disease-specific warnings.

7. Unusual syntax, as in the *double -ing* construction (*Quitting Smoking Now . . .*), weakens warnings.

8. The presence of a nonwarning (*Quitting Smoking Now . . .*) instead of a warning in a statement labeled as a warning weakens the statement's potential for alerting to health risk.

9. The presence of a nonwarning in a rotational series of warnings has the effect of reducing the effectiveness of all the warnings in the series.

10. Technical or semitechnical terms, which may be misunderstood by some consumers, render warnings less effective. (One of my graduate students reported that some women in birth classes attended by lower socioeconomic families in Oak Ridge, Tennessee, read *Fetal Injury* as *Fatal Injury*. Other women in those classes thought that *Low Birth Weight* was a desirable result of smoking. It was unclear whether that was because they interpreted the statement to mean that *their* weight would be lower at birth or that having a baby weighing less would be desirable. It is difficult to propose a practical solution to the problem illustrated here because it results partly from the very restrictive space limitations imposed upon the cigarette package warnings. This issue is discussed in detail later.)

11. Warnings that are hard to read because of type size or color contrast are ignored.

12. Warnings that are placed so that they can be ignored (i.e., consumers opening a package of cigarettes or removing a cigarette from a package avoid looking at such a warning).

2. EXPERIMENT 1: CATEGORIZATION, RANK ORDERING, AND TRANSLATION OF WARNINGS

In Experiment 1, I explored primarily general hypotheses 1 and 3: (1) When asked, respondents rank order warnings with great consistency and (2) other things being equal, respondents rank hypothetical warnings as stronger than categorical warnings. Hypothesis 1 stemmed from my suspicion that consumers process public information in similar ways; Hypothesis 3 stemmed from my conviction that the IF–THEN logical structure of hypothetical warnings would trigger consistent classification; also, I expected that hypothetical warnings would be recognized as warnings *per se* more easily than categorical warnings and would for that reason also trigger more consistent classification. I also gathered some data with respect to all the other hypotheses (except for 10); because these data are not quantifiable, I defer further mention of them until the discussion section.

In order to test Hypothesis 1, I needed to know first of all whether there was a consistent pattern of rank ordering of warnings; then I needed to know whether the same characteristics showed up consistently in those warnings ranked strongest. In order to test Hypothesis 3, I needed to know initially whether the distinction between categorical and hypothetical warnings was susceptible to empirical testing, that is, whether respondents could distinguish between them consistently on the basis on brief instruction. I also wanted to know how respondents would translate warnings if asked to rewrite them in their own words.

I thus designed a questionnaire, "Reactions to Warnings," which asked respondents to perform four tasks: (1) identify warnings as either categorical or hypothetical, on the basis of brief instruction, (2) select the stronger warning of several pairs of warnings, (3) rank order a set of 10 warnings as to strength, and (4) translate the 1970 warning into their own words.

I administered the questionnaire to 27 students enrolled in two beginning linguistics classes (one undergraduate class, one class with both undergraduates and graduates) taught by me at the University of Tennessee during the fall quarter of 1985. I will discuss each task and responses to it separately.[9]

2.1. Task I: Categorization of Warnings

2.1.1. Methods

The 16 warnings that were provided to subjects in this experiment are shown here in the order of presentation in the experiment:

1. [DRAWING OF A SKULL AND CROSSBONES] POISON
2. Take heed, sweet soul.
3. You have a right to remain silent. If you choose not to remain silent anything you say or write can and will be used against you in a court of law. You have a right to consult a lawyer before any questioning and you have a right to have the attorney present with you during any questioning. You not only have a right to consult with a lawyer before any questioning but, if you lack the financial ability to retain a lawyer, a lawyer will be appointed to represent you before any questioning. If you choose not to remain silent and do not wish to consult with a lawyer or have the lawyer present, you still have the right to remain silent and you have a right to consult with a lawyer at anytime during the questioning.
4. Let me tell you something straight. When you go and snitch to anyone that we had anything to do with this, you'll find a snitch tattoo on your forehead.

[9] Readers interested in replicating the experiments described in this chapter may obtain copies of the warning labels tested by requesting them from the author (see also Figure 3).

5. [DRAWING OF AN AUTOMOBILE] Caution This Drug alone or with alcohol may impair your ability to drive
6. Komsing Causes Lung Cancer, Heart Disease, Emphysema, and May Complicate Pregnancy
7. Warning: The Surgeon General Has Determined That Komsing Is Hazardous to Your Health
8. This is the final warning. I have acted as a gentleman should, have given you ample time to consider my demands before an unfortunate incident occurs. You have twenty-four hours to introduce a bill in the Congress of the United States of America to return to me, as the rightful heir to James Smithson, the Smithsonian Institution and its belongings. Time has run out, sirs.
9. [DRAWING OF A PROFILE OF A FACE WITH AN OPEN MOUTH] FOR ORAL USE ONLY
10. SURGEON GENERAL'S WARNING: Quitting Komsing Now Greatly Reduces Serious Risks to Your Health.
11. The Surgeon General Has Determined That Komsing Is Dangerous to Your Health
12. [DRAWING OF A PROFILE OF A FACE WITH A HALF-CLOSED EYE] may cause DROWSINESS USE CARE when operating a car or other Dangerous machinery
13. SURGEON GENERAL'S WARNING: Etteragic Komse Contains Carbon Monoxide
14. Komsing by Pregnant Women May Result in Fetal Injury, Premature Birth and Low Birth Weight
15. Warning: Komsing is Dangerous to Health and May Cause Death from Cancer and Other Diseases
16. Etteragic Komsing May be Hazardous to your Health

All the examples provided for the respondents are "real" warnings—that is, they were collected from actual sources in the world, rather than being fabricated. Eight of the warnings are thinly disguised cigarette package warnings (warning No. 15 was once proposed but never implemented). Thus the base element "smok-" of the word "smoking" appears in reverse (as "koms-," hence "komsing") and the word "cigarette" is spelled in reverse ("etteragic") in every instance. (The disguising was done only in Task I, in which I was interested solely in whether respondents could distinguish the two types of warnings. In the remainder of the questionnaire the cigarette warning labels are reproduced without disguise.)

Four of the other warnings (Nos. 1, 5, 9, 12) are pharmaceutical labels in present or past use. Warning 3 is the familiar *Miranda* warning, the use of which is mandated in many arrest scenarios. Two warnings, 2 and 8, come from literature, the first from the final act of Shakespeare's *Othello*; I obtained it by asking the senior Shakespearean in the English Department at the

University of Tennessee to provide me with a statement from literature that he was positive was a warning, though it did not look like one. The latter, 8, is from Margaret Truman's novel, *Death at the Smithsonian*. The final warning, 4, I extracted from a surreptitiously tape-recorded conversation that I had analyzed for a Knoxville defense attorney in a solicitation/conspiracy to commit murder case.

The reader may be curious to know why I tested an assortment of both oral and written warnings at this stage when I have made it clear that my concern is with written warnings. In the earliest stages of my research, I was seeking common factors among effective warnings, regardless of whether they were oral or written. Thus in preparing the written questionnaire, I made no attempt to exclude oral warnings. Some of the warnings on the questionnaire are highly problematic, particularly (as I discuss later) the very long *Miranda* warning, with its embedded hypothetical warning and the highly decontextualized Shakespearean quotation.

In Task I, respondents were asked to categorize 16 warnings as either categorical or hypothetical. I provided the respondents with a brief categorization of the two types of warnings and then asked them to categorize the 16 warnings by labeling them with a "C" or an "H." The students were asked to categorize the warnings on the basis of the following instructions:[10]

> The English language allows two types of warnings. One type consists of what are called categorical warnings. Categorical warnings are generally felt to fulfill the function of advising, not requesting. Such warnings inform hearers or readers that certain results will follow certain modes of behavior, but the warnings do not attempt to get a given individual to modify his or her behavior. An example, tongue-in-cheek, is a statement on a menu that says, "Eating Any Selection From The Enclosed MENU Can Be Dangerously Habit Forming!"
>
> The other type consists of what are called hypothetical warnings. Hypothetical warnings are phrased in such a way that they fulfill the function of requesting. The basic logical structure for a hypothetical warning is *If X, then Y*, though the *if* and *then* may be implicit, rather than explicit. Thus an example might be *Give me your money or I'll shoot*, a statement which is generally regarded as a demand that the individual spoken to turn over money. (It is also a special type of warning, a threat.) There is occasionally a question as to which type of warning a particular statement is, so I would like to get your reactions to some warnings.

2.1.2. Data Analysis

In Experiment 1, I tested primarily the general hypotheses stating that (1) respondents rank order warnings with great consistency and (2) other things

---

[10] I now realize that the instructions for Task I were not as clear as they could have been. It is possible that some of the responses were equally divided in the way they were because of the way the instructions were worded, that is, students may have been sufficiently confused that they simply guessed at the answers. In future replications of this experiment, I shall word the instructions more carefully and also select clearer examples.

being equal, respondents rank hypothetical warnings as stronger than categorical warnings. In order to test them, I formulated the following sets of narrow hypotheses about the stimuli in the test instrument:

H1. Hypothetical warnings are recognized as such by a large majority of respondents.

H2. Categorical warnings are recognized as such by a smaller percentage of respondents.

H3. It is possible to identify characteristics that favor the identification of categorical warnings as categorical.

H4. Directions and incomplete statements are judged to be categorical by about half the respondents, as hypothetical by about half the respondents (because they will be guessing).

H5. Other things being equal, hypothetical warnings are judged to be stronger than categorical warnings.

Of the 16 warnings, I classified 2 (3, 4) as unambiguously hypothetical, one (8) less certainly so, and 10 (5, 6, 7, 9, 10, 11, 13, 14, 15, and 16) as categorical. Of the remainder, 1 (1) is a statement so incomplete that the respondent must supply information in order to be able to categorize it, and 2 (2, 12) are directions rather than warnings.

The responses, summarized in Figure 1, strongly confirm narrow hypotheses H1, H2, H3, and H4. As expected (according to Hypothesis H1), two hypothetical warnings, 4 and 8, were strongly recognized as such. Also as expected (according to Hypothesis H2), there was less agreement about the categorical warnings. Also as expected (according to Hypothesis H4), incomplete warnings and directions were interpreted about equally as categorical and as hypothetical. For example, the incomplete warning in 1 (*POISON*) was

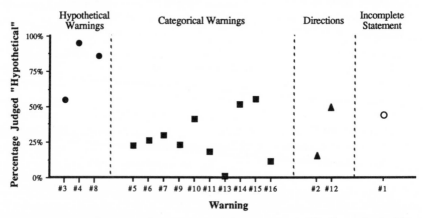

FIGURE 1.   Percentage of subjects judging warning to be "hypothetical."

identified as categorical by 15 respondents, as hypothetical by 12. Similarly, the informational statement in 13 ("SURGEON GENERAL'S WARNING: Etteragic Komse Contains Carbon Monoxide") was identified as categorical by 13 respondents, as hypothetical by 13.

Narrow Hypothesis H5 was not tested directly here; as far as it is concerned, Experiment 1 was a phase for the gathering of information for use in later experiments. I will offer some observations about them in the summary section.

2.1.3. Discussion

Respondents showed some sensitivity to the difference between hypothetical and categorical warnings. With relatively brief instruction, they were highly consistent in their identifications. Only one respondent failed to respond to a hypothetical warning, whereas five respondents failed to respond to other types of warnings.

It was of considerable interest to me that the familiar *Miranda* warning was misidentified as categorical by close to half the respondents. I had originally expected it to be classified as a hypothetical warning by many subjects (and half of them did so) because of the embedded IF–THEN proposition, "If you choose not to remain silent, anything you say or write can and will be used against you in a court of law."

I think the results can be explained by these two reasons. First, the entire statement is a syntactically complex and illocutionarily quite complex text; it would really be quite surprising had subjects interpreted a lengthy and complex example in the same way that they identified one-sentence, one-clause examples. Further, the text of the *Miranda* warning is often truncated in films and television shows to the first 14 or so words, which inform suspects of rights: "You have a right to remain silent. If you choose not to remain silent. . . ." In fact, the responses to the *Miranda* warning illustrate the important nature of such factors as length, syntactic complexity, and illocutionary force.

I now think of the *Miranda* warning as a "hidden hypothetical (HH)"; by calling it that I do not intend to suggest that it constitutes a cognitively significant subcategory; rather, I intend the term to suggest a failure of intent. One intent of the *Miranda* warning was to put suspects on notice that their future rights could be jeopardized by how they chose to conduct themselves at the time of arrest; a failure to recognize the *Miranda* warning as a hypothetical warning may mean that the warning fails to achieve this purpose.

Also, I note with interest that the directive statement in warning 2 ("Take heed, sweet soul.") was identified as categorical by 22 respondents, as hypothetical by only 4. The consistency may be due to respondents' response to the high degree of inferencing required by the passage and its extreme decontextualization. The line comes from the last act of Shakespeare's *Othello* and, in the context of the scene, clearly constitutes a warning with an implied consequence, for with it Othello continues his menacing questioning of Desdemona about the nature of her relationship with Cassio. However, I think it is possible that a modern equivalent statement, perhaps "Watch out, babe," would test differently, even out of context, simply because less inferencing would be required. I think that we probably more easily infer an implied consequence to "watch out" than we do to "take heed."

On the basis of responses to Task I, it appears that the following factors may favor the identification of warnings as categorical: (1) incompleteness, (2) decontextualization, and (3) the use of abstract and general terms as opposed to concrete and specific terms. Thus if it appears that hypothetical warnings are more effective than categorical warnings, it will be important to formulate them as complete statements, to avoid decontextualization, and to avoid couching them in abstract and general terms as opposed to concrete and specific ones. On the other hand, evidence will be offered below to the effect that the single word *POISON* is a very strong warning. Because it is arguably incomplete by almost any test, this issue needs further study.

2.2. Tasks II and III: Rank Ordering of Warnings

2.2.1. Methods

Uniformity of ranking and relative strength of warnings were tested further in Tasks II and III of the written questionnaire. In Task II, respondents were asked to select the stronger member in each of six pairs of warnings. In Task III respondents were asked to rank order ten warnings. Both Task II and Task III were described briefly in the final sentence of the general instructions for the entire questionnaire; immediately preceding Task II, the instruction to circle the stronger warning was given. The pairs are given below:

I. A. Cigarette Smoking May Be Hazardous to your Health
    B. The Surgeon General has Determined that Smoking Is Dangerous to Your Health
II. A. [Use whichever warning you found stronger in 1 and write its letter—A or B—here.]
    B. Smoking Causes Lung Cancer, Heart Disease, Emphysema, and May Complicate Pregnancy
III. A. Smoking Causes Lung Cancer, Heart Disease, Emphysema, and May Complicate Pregnancy
    B. [DRAWING OF A PROFILE OF A FACE WITH A HALF-CLOSED EYE] may cause DROWSINESS USE CARE when operating a car or other dangerous machinery

IV. A. Warning: Smoking Is Dangerous to Health and May Cause
Death from Cancer and Other Diseases
   B. [DRAWING OF A PROFILE OF A FACE WITH AN OPEN
MOUTH] FOR ORAL USE ONLY
V.   A. Smoking by Pregnant Women May Result in Fetal Injury,
Premature Birth, and Low Birth Weight
   B. [DRAWING OF AN AUTOMOBILE] Caution This Drug alone
or with alcohol may impair your ability to drive
VI. A. SURGEON GENERAL'S WARNING: Cigarette Smoke Con-
tains Carbon Monoxide
   B. [DRAWING OF A SKULL AND CROSSBONES] POISON

2.2.2. Data Analysis of Task II

The students' responses to Task II, summarized in Figure 2, confirm
general Hypothesis 1 that individuals rank order warnings with great consistency. On pairs I, II, and VI, almost all subjects (26/27, 24/24, and 26/26,
respectively) judged warning B to be stronger; on pair III, close to 90% (23/26)
judged warning A to be stronger. For pairs IV and V, subjects judged the
statements to be more similar: Approximately 60% (16/26 in both cases) said
warning A was stronger.

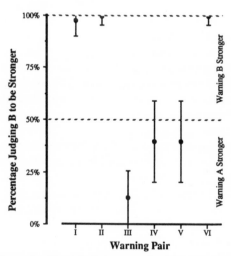

FIGURE 2.   Percentage of subjects judging warning B to be stronger than warning A.
Error bars represent approximately 95% confidence intervals for the population percentage. These intervals were obtained using $\%B \pm 2[s.e.(\%B)]$, where $\%B$ is the
sample percentage based on $N = 26$ subjects and s.e. $(\%B)$ is estimated using the larger
of $SQRT[(\%B)(100 - \%B)/N]$ or $SQRT[(99)(1)/N]$.

By their 26:1 choice, it is clear that respondents regard the 1970 cigarette package warning in I.B. as stronger than the original 1965 *Caution*, shown in I.A. It is at least equally clear (by a 24:0 margin) that the new disease-specific warning shown as II.B. is considered stronger than the 1970 warning. And, what is not surprising is that respondents chose the powerful *POISON* over a "warning" about carbon monoxide by a 26:0 margin. It is interesting that a disease-specific warning that says that "Smoking Is Dangerous to Health and May Cause Death from Cancer and Other Diseases" was rated weaker than one that said "For ORAL Use Only." Comments from respondents elsewhere on the questionnaire suggest that capital letters and drawings strengthen the impact of a warning. Respondents' comments also suggest that these two hypotheses would be well worth further investigation: (1) that listing a series of unpleasant consequences strengthens a warning and (2) that inclusion of modal auxiliaries that hedge an assertion, such as *may* or *could*, weaken warnings. Another possibility is that nonparallel structure (as in IV.A.) weakens a potentially strong warning because the weaker of two clauses may "contaminate" the stronger.

2.2.3. Data Analysis of Task III

In Task III, respondents were asked to rank order 10 warnings as to relative strength:

1. [DRAWING OF A PROFILE OF A FACE WITH AN OPEN MOUTH] FOR ORAL USE ONLY
2. Take heed, sweet soul.
3. You have a right to remain silent. If you choose not to remain silent anything you say or write can and will be used against you in a court of law. You have a right to consult a lawyer before any questioning, and you have a right to have the attorney present with you during any questioning. You not only have a right to consult with a lawyer before any questioning but, if you lack the financial ability to retain a lawyer, a lawyer will be appointed to represent you before any questioning. If you choose not to remain silent and do not wish to consult with a lawyer or have the lawyer present, you still have the right to remain silent and you have a right to consult with a lawyer at anytime during the questioning.
4. Let me tell you something straight. When you go and snitch to anyone that we had anything to do with this you'll find a snitch tattoo on your forehead.
5. [SKULL AND CROSSBONES] POISON
6. The Surgeon General has Determined that Smoking Is Hazardous to Your Health
7. This is the final warning. I have acted as a gentleman should, have

given you ample time to consider my demands before an unfortunate incident occurs. You have twenty-four hours to introduce a bill
in the Congress of the United States of America to return to me, as
the rightful heir to James Smithson, the Smithsonian Institution
and its belongings. Time has run out, sirs.

8. The Surgeon General has Determined that Smoking is Dangerous to
    Your Health
9. Warning: Smoking Is Dangerous to Health and May Cause Death
    from Cancer and Other Diseases
10. Cigarette Smoking May be Hazardous to your health.

The responses, reflected in Figure 3, further address the issues of uniformity of ranking and relative strength of warnings and tend to confirm specific
hypothesis one about consistency of ranking.

Though there was a wide distribution of rankings across the respondents, a pattern of uniformity emerged from an examination of the mean
ranks and modes of the 10 warnings in Task III.[11] The uniformity of these
rankings suggested that, although not everyone evaluates the strength of the
warnings the same, there is enough of a tendency or pattern that such a
methodology could be fruitfully used in a large-scale survey to determine
more about how people respond to warnings. Thus, warning 5 (POISON
[drawing of a skull and crossbones]) is rated strongest by all measures; it has a
mean rank of 1.95 and a mode of 1. Warning 9 (the only disease-specific
warning in the set) is rated second strongest with a mean rank of 3.79 and a
mode of 2. Close behind it is warning 4 (a clear hypothetical type), rated third
strongest with a mean rank of 4.37 and modes of 2 and 3. Warning 3 (*Miranda*)
is rated fourth strongest with a mean rank of 5.2 and a mode of 3. Competing
for fifth and sixth places are warnings 7 (the 1970 Surgeon General's Warning)
and 6 ("This is the final warning"). Warning 7 has a mean rank of 5.33 and
modes of 5 and 6, whereas warning 6 has a mean rank of 5.37 and a mode of 5.
Warning 1 is rated eighth in strength with a mean rank of 6.08 and a mode of
6. Warnings 8 and 10 have mean ranks of 5.70 and 7.87, and modes of 6 and 7,
respectively. Predictably, warning 2 ("Take heed, sweet soul") was rated
weakest with a mean rank of 9.6 and a mode of 10.

2.3. Task IV: Translation of a Warning

2.3.1. Methods

Task IV was administered to respondents as a way to obtain some information about how they understood cigarette warnings. I thought it would be

---

[11] The *mean rank* or *average* is a measure of the frequency of distribution of responses; it is
calculated by summing (adding) the individual rankings and then dividing by the total number
of responses. The *mode* is the most frequently obtained score in the data.

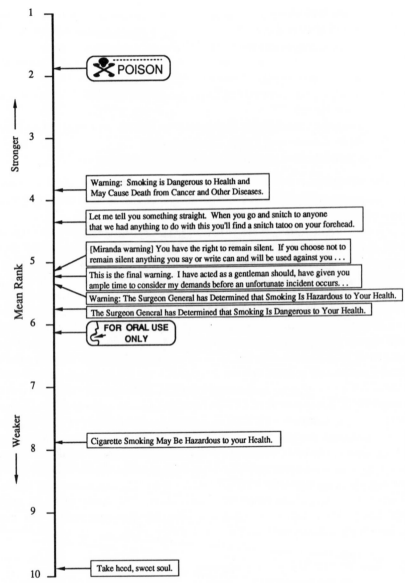

FIGURE 3. Rank-ordering of warnings in Task III of Experiment 1.

helpful to know what additions, deletions, and substitutions would be made, as well as what rearrangements of parts might occur as respondents paraphrased the words of the 1970 warning. In this task, respondents were given these instructions: "Translate the following warning into less formal language. Use your own words but try to reflect the exact meaning of the original warning." They were then given the text of the 1970 warning: "Warning: The Surgeon General Has Determined That Cigarette Smoking Is Dangerous to Your Health."

2.3.2. Data Analysis

The respondents' paraphrases of the crucial embedded clause, "Cigarette Smoking Is Dangerous to Your Health," are displayed in Table 1. The complete text of the warning consists of three parts: (1) an initial signal, *Warning:*; (2) identification of the authority whose decision is being announced, *The Surgeon General Has Determined (that)*; and (3) the crucial finding itself, *Cigarette Smoking Is Dangerous to Your Health.* In analyzing the paraphrases provided by respondents, I was most interested in the third part, which constitutes the actual warning. Table 1 shows the range of paraphrases supplied by subjects for this crucial section (followed by rewordings of the first two parts as well).

Note that although the main verb of the original warning clause is "is"— an unqualified, affirmative, present-tense form of the verb "be," 14 out of 27 respondents altered that verb in such a way as to significantly change its meaning. Many did this by adding a modal auxiliary such as "may" or "can." Some modals, of course, like "shall" and "will," serve merely to indicate simple futurity. Others, however, particularly "may," "might," "can," and "could," add notions of doubt to the predictive function of the verb *be.* Thus paraphrasing the words *is dangerous* as *may be dangerous* represents a significant semantic change in the verb phrase.

Other paraphrases added a "do" or "have" form. Also 13 changed the verb from an inflected form to the uninflected *be* or to one of the following lexical verbs: "make," "harm," "cause," "happen" (to your health), "die," "damage," "prove," "kill," or "attribute" (for "contribute?").

2.3.3. Discussion

What are the possible explanations for these changes, particularly the addition of those modal auxiliaries that inject doubt into the verb phrase? One explanation is that all cigarette package warnings are weakened by the fact that some of them contain qualifying language, sometimes in the form of the modal auxiliaries "may/might" and "can/could" (according to general hypothesis 4). The new disease-specific rotating warning, for instance, concludes with the clause "And May Complicate Pregnancy." The modal auxiliary "may"

TABLE 1. Written Paraphrases of 1970 Warning in Task IV of Experiment 1[a]

Subject	Auxiliaries (modals in caps)	Verb	Object or complement
cigarette smoking	MAY	make	you sick
smoking	WILL	be	harmful
smoking cigarettes	WILL	harm	the smoker
smoking		is	dangerous to your health
people who smoke		are	likely to get very sick
they [cigarettes]		cause	you to become sick or to get a disease
smoking cigarettes		is	dangerous
smoking		is	dangerous
something	COULD		happen to your health to seriously damage it
smoking		to be	bad for you
you	CAN	die	
smoking cigarettes	CAN and WILL	damage	your health
cigarette smoking		is	dangerous to your health
you	MAY	harm	your health
smoking		to cause	lung cancer
[you]	do not	smoke	
cigarette smoking	has been	found	to be dangerous to your health
cigarette smoking	MAY	be	very unhealthy
cigarette smoking	CAN	kill	
cigarette smoking	CAN	kill	you
the ill effects of cigarette smoking	have	prove	to be not only unhealthy, but fatal
smoking		is	unhealthy
smoking	MAY		attribute [sic] to poor health, sickness or disease

[a]Markers, qualifiers, authorities, and main clause verbs included by respondents but omitted in the display are summarized here:

  Markers: warning:, watch out, attention!, but be forewarned, please
  Qualifiers: according to, this is, studies by
  Authorities: surgeon general, the medical research, the surgeon general, surgeon general's, an authority, research, based on extensive studies
  Verbs: believes, advise, has determined, has found out, declared, prove, shows, has proved, has been proven, warn

also appears in another new rotating warning: "Smoking by Pregnant Women May Result in Fetal Injury, Premature Birth, and Low Birth Rate." These rotating warnings had been on packages in the market for several months at the time this task was administered, but packages displaying the old 1970 warning were also still available in the market. It is possible that respondents were reading into all warnings they were familiar with the qualifying language found on other warnings in current use.

It is also possible, of course, that the test instrument, the written questionnaire, was the source of contamination because it contained various examples of warnings containing qualifiers, including modal auxiliaries.

However, because the warnings on the written questionnaire mirror the fact that the new rotating warnings contain such qualifiers, it does not seem likely that the written questionnaire is the sole source of contamination. It is also quite possible that the specific circumstances of the administration of the questionnaire (its being administered in a classroom situation) presented difficulties. Though I know of no literature on the subject, it is, for instance, possible that university students use modal auxiliaries in classroom paraphrase tasks as politeness markers.

2.4. General Discussion of Experiment 1

In general, narrow hypotheses H1, H2, and H3 were supported by the data. The evidence was that the distinction between categorical and hypothetical warnings is or can be made psychologically real, that respondents were consistent in selecting one of a pair of warnings as being stronger, and that they rank-ordered warnings consistently as to strength. The specific generalizations that emerge from close examination of the pilot data are these:

1. With the exception of conventional warning labels such as the word *POISON*, respondents identified hypothetical warnings as hypothetical more often than they recognized categorical warnings as categorical.
2. Respondents perceived hypothetical warnings as stronger than categorical warnings.
3. Extralinguistic factors, such as larger type size, use of drawings, and capital letters, appeared to strengthen warnings.
4. Finally, the presence of a qualified warning in a series of rotational warnings (i.e., the series that appeared on cigarette packages at the time this research was conducted) appeared to have a contagious weakening effect in that a warning that did not contain a qualifying modal auxiliary was paraphrased by close to a third of the respondents as containing such a modal auxiliary.

3. EXPERIMENT 2: IN-DEPTH INTERVIEWS

3.1. Methods

My next step began with a heuristic phase during which I developed additional research strategies. During that phase, in order to decide what strategies to use for testing further, I purchased cigarettes, conversed with cigarette vendors in a variety of marketplaces, and observed cigarette smokers in those marketplaces opening just-purchased packages of cigarettes.

I also decided to test fabricated warnings. That decision and my need to include in my testing materials a cigarette package labeled with the original (1965) *Caution* label led me to a decision to use in my next experiments only cigarette packages that were red and white in color. I reached that decision after noting that many packages, including those of generic brands, are red and white in color. I used a red typewriter ribbon to type all the warning labels I fabricated except for those involving the word *poison* and a drawing of a skull and crossbones. For those, I obtained printed labels from the pharmacist mentioned earlier. Those printed labels were also all red and white.

The tentative conclusions reached in Experiment 1, as well as the need to test additional hypotheses, formed the basis for a second research strategy, that of conducting increasingly complex interviews in which I asked interviewees to give me their reactions to different warnings. I began by using cigarette packages labeled with five different warnings, the 1970 *Warning* and the four current rotational warnings. At a midstage, I used cigarette packages containing seven different warnings, the five described before and also the original *Caution* and a fabricated disease-specific "Surgeon General's Warning" whose final part read: "Smoking Is Addictive and Causes Lung Cancer, Heart Disease, Emphysema, and May Complicate Pregnancy." In the final interviews, I used a total of nine warnings, all those described before plus two additional ones bearing the word *POISON* between two drawings of a skull and crossbones. In warning 8, the POISON warning was on the side of the cigarette package, as is mandated by Congress. In warning 9, the POISON warning was again on the side of the package; but in addition, a smaller POISON label appeared on top of the package, where it would normally be opened. The full set of warnings explored in these interviews is shown below:

1. Caution: Cigarette Smoking May Be Hazardous to Your Health
2. Warning: The Surgeon General Has Determined That Cigarette Smoking Is Dangerous to Your Health.
3. SURGEON GENERAL'S WARNING: Cigarette Smoke Contains Carbon Monoxide.
4. SURGEON GENERAL'S WARNING: Smoking by Pregnant Women May Result in Fetal Injury, Premature Birth, and Low Birth Weight.
5. SURGEON GENERAL'S WARNING: Quitting Smoking Now Greatly Reduces Serious Risk to Your Health.
6. SURGEON GENERAL'S WARNING: Smoking Causes Lung Cancer, Heart Disease, Emphysema, and May Complicate Pregnancy.
7. SURGEON GENERAL'S WARNING: Smoking is Addictive and Causes Lung Cancer, Heart Disease, Emphysema and May Complicate Pregnancy.
8. [SKULL AND CROSSBONES] POISON [SKULL AND CROSSBONES]

9. [SKULL AND CROSSBONES] POISON [SKULL AND CROSS-BONES] [The package on which this warning was displayed also displayed a smaller, but otherwise identical warning on top, where it would normally be opened.]

My hypothesis was that warnings 2, 6, 7, 8, and 9 would be perceived as serious warnings, with 8 and 9 being the strongest and 7 the next strongest. I also hypothesized that the next strongest one would be 6. Behind it would be 2. I felt the others (1, 3, 4, 5) would be perceived as weak or ineffective, and perhaps even meaningless.

At this stage I was more interested in collecting open-ended information than I was in attempting to collect either the kind or amount of information that would be amenable to statistical analysis. I therefore conducted these interviews conversationally, jotting down comments of interviewees and noting the ordering they produced as they examined and physically rearranged the cigarette packages I showed them.

I conducted 24 of these comparative interviews, 6 at each stage. In these interviews, I showed the interviewees the cigarette packages one at a time and asked them to tell me what they noticed about the warnings. The precise questions I used are given below, in order of presentation:

1. [Show pack 2] What exactly does this warning mean to you?
2. [Show pack 1] Does this mean the same thing? The last pack said *Caution* and this one says *Warning*. Are those the same things? If not, how are they different?
3. [Show pack 3] Does this mean the same thing?
4. [Show pack 4] How about this one?
5. [Show pack 5] What does this one mean?
6. [Show pack 6] How about this one?
7. [Show pack 7] If you saw this warning on a pack of cigarettes, would it mean more or less to you—or something different—than the last one? How is it different?
8. [Show pack 8] What would you think this meant?
9. [Show pack 9] Please notice that this pack is exactly like the last one except that it has a small warning on the top also. Is the meaning of the warning the same if it's up there?

3.2. Data Analysis

The interviewees made responses to the individual questions, then often, as noted, also physically arranged the packages into various groupings, often describing to me the basis for the categorization. The categories were typically these: Very Specific, Very General, Very Exclusive (i.e., applies to only some smokers), and Meaningless (sometimes Silly). Overall, the warnings were classified as shown next:

Effective, alarming	Any variant of a warning containing the word *POISON*
Very specific	SURGEON GENERAL'S WARNING: Smoking Causes Lung Cancer, Heart Disease, Emphysema, and May Complicate Pregnancy
	SURGEON GENERAL'S WARNING: Smoking Is Addictive and Causes Lung Cancer, Heart Disease, Emphysema, and May Complicate Pregnancy
Very general	Warning: The Surgeon General Has Determined That Cigarette Smoking Is Dangerous to Your Health
	SURGEON GENERAL'S WARNING: Quitting Smoking Now Greatly Reduces Serious Risks to Your Health
Applies to few	SURGEON GENERAL'S WARNING: Smoking by Pregnant Women May Result in Fetal Injury, Premature Birth, and Low Birth Weight
Silly, meaningless	Caution: Cigarette Smoking May Be Hazardous to Your Health
	SURGEON GENERAL'S WARNING: Cigarette Smoking May Be Hazardous to Your Health
	SURGEON GENERAL'S WARNING: Cigarette Smoke Contains Carbon Monoxide

3.3. Discussion

The comments by interviewees strongly supported the thrust of both my general and task-specific hypotheses:

1. Comments by respondents suggested that the modal auxiliary "may" tends to weaken warnings.
2. Disease-specific warnings are perceived as stronger than non-disease-specific warnings.
3. Unusual syntax, as in the *double -ing* construction (e.g., *Quitting Smoking Now*), renders warnings less effective. (Alternatively, the lack of specification of positive health effects may weaken this particular warning. However, respondents' remarks about this warning label—typically something like "it sounds funny"—suggest to me that the syntax plays a role.)
4. Incomplete warnings (e.g., "Cigarette Smoke Contains Carbon Monoxide") are sometimes perceived as silly.
5. Some respondents (who were not pregnant females) commented that they did not feel addressed by the warning addressed to pregnant

women and, further, that reading that warning caused them to take other warnings less seriously. This suggests that the inclusion of limited-target warnings in a rotational series may have the effect of weakening the overall effect of the series.

6. The conventional warning label *POISON* has great power. (For example, one young male smoker, when shown the package with *POISON* on the top said, "That scares the hell out of me!") It is unclear whether the power derives from familiarity or from some inherent force of the word *POISON* in combination with the drawing of a skull and crossbones.

7. Consumers expect printed warnings on consumer products to be conspicuous with respect to such factors as type size, color contrast, and position, i.e., consumers expect that statements that otherwise constitute warnings will not be nullified or rendered ineffective by factors rendering them difficult to read.[12]

As noted, I did not ask interviewees to rank-order the warnings in this experiment. I cannot, therefore, report a strict rank ordering here.

4. EXPERIMENT 3: RAPID, ANONYMOUS INTERVIEWS

4.1. Methods

Experiment 3, like Task IV of Experiment 1, addressed the issue of how respondents understand particular warnings. Unlike Task IV of Experiment 1, it sought spoken commentary rather than written paraphrase. In it, I obtained additional information by conducting rapid anonymous interviews. Such interviews are conducted by eliciting brief responses from unidentified strangers in a public setting (Labov, 1966, 1972). In the interviews, I asked interviewees to read one of three warnings on a cigarette package (the 1965 *Caution*, the 1970 Surgeon General's Warning, or the new disease-specific

---

[12] Factors such as type size, length of warnings, distance between viewers and ads, and movement between viewers and ads are reported to play a role in the readability of the Surgeon General's warning in billboards and taxicab ads. Davis and Kendrick (1989) concluded that the Surgeon General's warning is unreadable by consumers in its current form in most billboard and taxicab ads. A similar study conducted in Australia (Cullingford, Da Cruz, Webb, Shean, & Jamrozik, 1988) analyzed the apparent size of letters, color contrast between letters and their background, and the obliqueness of angle between the warning and the horizontal message and concluded that cigarette warnings on billboards are "a minor and, in many cases, illegible component of billboard advertisements for cigarettes in both comparative and absolute terms" (p. 338). See also Fischer, Richards, Berman, and Krugman (1989) for evidence, based on the market research methods of eye tracking, aided recall, and masked recognition, that the Congressionally mandated warnings are ineffective health messages insofar as adolescents are concerned.

warning) and then tell me in their own words exactly what it meant. I interviewed 47 persons (24 females, 23 males; 18 smokers, 26 nonsmokers) on a Sunday afternoon in West Town Mall, a large shopping center in Knoxville, Tennessee, using a clearly visible tape recorder to record their responses.

4.2. Data Analysis and Discussion

Few respondents limited themselves to translation of the warning they were shown. Many respondents commented on adequacy. However, the only question put to the respondents was a request that they translate the warning into their own words and tell me exactly what it meant. Respondents' translations and comments varied widely. Although most respondents repeated words in the warnings or paraphrased them in virtually identical language, a few just said that the warning meant "exactly what it says." Others claimed not to read the warnings. One respondent offered the opinion that the new warning addressed to pregnant women is severely limited in its effect and that a label with the word *POISON* on it might deter. Another offered the opinion that the word "may" means that smoking has not been proven to be hazardous to health.

There were no strong differences between smokers and nonsmokers or between those who were shown the 1965 *Caution* and those who were shown the 1970 *Warning*. Intuitively, I think that these data present some evidence that people process general (particularly non-consequence-specific) warnings very individually, in terms of such factors as their own values and risk-taking behavior. I intend to address these issues in a later stage of research (see "Directions for Future Research"). Both the cigarette smoking and the cigarette package warning issues are highly charged emotionally. Many of the persons I interviewed wanted to know which side I was on. One particularly rabid individual, a female smoker, used the occasion of our interview to tell me how much she hated television public announcements about the dangers of smoking. She said she leaves the room when one comes on. It is difficult to think of a warning label that she would regard as usefully informative.

5. SUMMARY AND CONCLUSIONS

5.1. Legal Issues

This chapter has been concerned with the linguistic and extralinguistic adequacy of written warnings on cigarette packages. I used a variety of strategies to address the questions introduced at the outset of my discussion, the answers to which are given later. I then developed a set of general hypotheses to guide me in my research. Each of those hypotheses is also discussed briefly. First, however, I would like to review briefly some legal senses of *adequacy* and to summarize the evidence I gathered about the nature, function, and structure of warnings.

For purposes of this discussion, I will use the word "adequate" in its legal sense, insofar as its legal sense differs from its everyday sense. In law, it means "[s]ufficient; commensurate; equally efficient; equal to what is required; suitable to the case or occasion; satisfactory" or "[e]qual to some given occasion of work" (*Black's Law Dictionary* 36 (5th ed. 1979), citing *Nissen v. Miller* (1940)).

According to dicta (that is, statements that do not actually decide the case and hence have no precedential value) of the Supreme Court of the United States, "adequate" is a relative term; that is, adequacy must be assessed in the light of the facts and circumstances. In *Mullane v. Central Hanover Bank & Trust Co.* (1950), the Supreme Court decided that trying to give notice to interested parties of a pending disposition of a court case by publishing a notice in a newspaper was inadequate when there was available a way of contacting the parties directly, as from a mailing list. The Supreme Court then recognized the relative nature of adequacy when it said that notice by publication in a newspaper might be approved "as a customary substitute in another class of cases where it [was] not reasonably possible or practicable to give *more adequate warning* [emphasis added]" (p. 317).

Earlier I noted that where warning language is prescribed by Congress, it is possible that the courts may go in two directions on the issue of adequacy. In one legal interpretation of the required warnings, literal compliance with statutory law constitutes adequacy as a matter of law; cases have been and may well continue to be considered on that basis. It is also possible that a cigarette manufacturer's responsibility may be held to go beyond mere literal compliance with the statutory law and meet more stringent requirements.

I also pointed out that courts have found manufacturers in violation of the requirement of adequacy for such reasons as failure to communicate the level of the danger, failure to display the warning in a reasonable location, failure to give sufficient information about how to avoid the danger, and failure to preserve the integrity of the warning by including statements that nullify its impact. The findings from the research reported here suggest that if cigarette manufacturers were held to more rigid requirements with regard to adequacy and warning, there would be reason to hold them liable for such failure.

However the law develops with respect to this issue, there seem to be compelling reasons to understand better how warnings are perceived and processed by individuals. If it develops that cigarette manufacturers are liable for adequacy of warning, then the tobacco industry will want to protect its interests by developing warning labels that are at least legally adequate. If, on the other hand, Congress continues to mandate the wording and design of cigarette package warnings, information about how to design and word warning labels should be available to it. And as noted earlier, the whole field of product liability maintains a strong interest in the general warning issue (see also Johnson, Chapter 10 this volume).

5.2. Classification of Warnings

Although it seems true, as I noted earlier, that the formalization of semantic and syntactic rules for warnings is difficult, it now seems possible that linguistic and human factors research will eventually permit us to discover some generalizations about the nature, structure, and function of warnings.

With respect to the possible distinction between Searle's categorical (or informational) warnings and hypothetical (or predictive) warnings, the evidence from these experiments is inconclusive. Although it may be true that the distinction is in some way psychologically real, further research is needed to establish that. All I have established is that my respondents seemed to recognize hypothetical warnings with great consistency.

In particular, it is unclear whether respondents' consistency of response implicates any syntactic factors or whether it is purely a matter of logical structure. Let us consider the four hypothetical warnings once again.

1. Give me your money, or I'll shoot!
2. If you choose not to remain silent, anything you say or write can and will be used against you in a court of law.
3. When you go and snitch to anyone that we had anything to do with this, you'll find a snitch tattoo on your forehead.
4. Take heed, sweet soul.

First of all, it is clear that hypothetical warnings need not lexically express both logical operators IF and THEN, or even one of them. In 2 and 3, which have the most canonical form for hypothetical warnings of the four, the "then" is not expressed overtly, whereas "when" substitutes for "if" in 3. In 4, still more is unexpressed—the entire second (consequent) clause—which the addressee/hearer must then infer from the context. And in 2, the typical "If X, then Y" structure is replaced by a functionally equivalent structure, consisting of an imperative conjoined to a declarative—without any overt markings of the "if/then" interpretation that the structure nevertheless evokes.

Although 1 is interpretable as a warning, it is important to note that in this case, at least, it is not simply the syntactic structure that signals its illocutionary force, because this structure may be used for other kinds of speech acts that, like warnings, make a statement about the future intent of the speaker (e.g., threats—"Halt or I'll shoot," or promises—"Get an A in the course, and I'll give you a hundred dollars"). On the other hand, even an explicit "if/then" structure is not sufficient to trigger a warning interpretation, because that structure may be used in speech acts quite different from warnings (e.g., statements of natural laws—"If you heat water to 212 degrees, then it will boil").

Because the data suggest that there is no specific syntactic structure that is either necessary or sufficient to signal a hypothetical warning in these experiments, further research is necessary to decide on what basis subjects have categorized these warnings as hypothetical. Such research must then be used in further explorations of the validity of Searle's distinction between categorical and hypothetical warnings.

5.3. Summary of Findings; Conclusions

With respect to my general hypotheses, the first four were supported by the findings in Experiments 2 and 3. Responses and comments suggest that the modal auxiliaries "may" and "can" tend to weaken warnings; that disease-specific warnings are perceived as stronger than non-disease-specific warnings; that unusual syntax, as in the *double -ing* construction, may render warnings ineffective; and that incomplete warnings (*Cigarette Smoke Contains Carbon Monoxide*) are perceived as silly. There is some evidence that the inclusion of limited-target warnings in a rotational series may have the effect of weakening the overall effect of the series. There is also some evidence to suggest that people process general warnings very individually, in terms of such factors as their own values and risk-taking behavior. Much additional research is needed, however.

As stated at the outset of this chapter, my specific goal in the original trial context was to offer some linguistic and human factors evidence about the adequacy of the 1970 cigarette package warning with respect to ill-health consequences, specifically the probably negative cardiovascular effects of cigarette smoking. In order to be able to do that, I addressed eight specific questions that I had formulated on the basis of my preliminary research. The answers to those questions follow.

Q1. Can warnings be identified by the presence of specific semantic, lexical, syntactic, or other characteristics? If so, what are they?

A1. Though I did not conduct research into how individuals define the category of warnings or how they recognize that statements constitute warnings, my respondents did seem to accept as warnings statements that make reference to a future event or state that is, at least in the opinion of the speaker or writer, not in the best interests of the addressee. And they occasionally objected to labeling as *warnings* statements that clearly lack those characteristics. Although some warnings can be identified by the presence of some specific logical and lexical characteristics, many others cannot. Conventional labels (e.g., *Warning*) and words like *POISON* are among the lexical items that sometimes characterize warnings. Further, respondents' comments suggested that they expect printed warnings on consumer products to be conspicuous with respect to such factors as type size, color contrast, and position. In other words, respondents believe that statements that otherwise constitute warnings should not be nullified or rendered ineffective by factors rendering them difficult to read.

Q2. Can warnings be meaningfully classified? If so, on what bases? Do consumers respond to or evaluate warnings on such bases?

A2. Warnings can be classified in at least one meaningful way. As noted, the evidence was that the distinction between categorical and informational warnings and hypothetical or predictive warnings appears to be in some way empirically discoverable. Respondents seemed to recognize hypothetical warnings with great consistency, apparently responding to explicit or implicit IF–THEN logical structure very consistently.

Q3. Do warnings differ by degree? Do consumers classify warnings as strong versus weak?

A3. There is some evidence that, with the exception of conventional categorical words like *POISON*, English-speaking adults rank hypothetical warnings as stronger than categorical warnings. Further, external factors (type size, type color, position, etc.) play a role in the way respondents rank warnings. Warning labels that contain qualifiers (especially the modal auxiliaries "may" and "can") are ranked as weaker than other warnings.

Q4. Do the statements at issue here constitute warnings? If so, precisely what do the statements appear to warn against?

A4. The labeled warnings on cigarette packages manufactured in the United States are accepted as warnings by most respondents, though, upon being questioned, some respondents pointed out that the two new rotating warnings mentioning carbon monoxide and the advantage to *quitting smoking now* do not really warn. The different warnings are seen as warning different addressees against different dangers.

Q5. Do warnings differ by degree, that is, do consumers classify warnings as strong versus weak?

A5. Warnings differ by degree, that is, consumers classify warnings as strong or weak, effective or ineffective, inclusive or exclusive. Strong warnings are characterized by the following features, no one of which must be present, but all of which are frequently present in strong warnings:

1. They are often formulated either as hypothetical warnings or as powerful fear provokers, like *POISON*.

2. They are also frequently marked by an absence of qualifiers (e.g., *may*, *could*) and by the fact that they mention specific possible negative consequences of behavior.

3. They are generally conspicuous, for example, they are not nullified by being rendered practically invisible or easy to ignore because of type size, type color, or type position.

4. They are written in simple syntax and in ordinary, everyday language.

5. They often contain specific information about precise consequences.

Weak warnings lack one or more of these characteristics.

Q6. Are the federally mandated cigarette package warnings strong or weak? If they are weak, how could they be made strong?

A6. The federally mandated cigarette package warnings vary considerably in strength, ranging from fairly strong to silly. They could have been made stronger by following suggestions made by the FTC or by following suggestions made in market research surveys and known to the Tobacco Institute in the 1970s (Myers, Iscoe, Jenning *et al.*, 1980).

Q7. Are the warnings at issue adequate to warn consumers of possible negative effects of cigarette smoking, particularly with regard to the potentially negative cardiovascular effects of cigarette smoking? If they are not, could they have been?

A7. Some of the warnings at issue appear adequate to warn consumers of the general possible ill effects of cigarette smoking, with the exception that none of them warns of possible addiction. My research revealed no likelihood that the warning labels serve to warn against the possibly negative cardiovascular effects of cigarette smoking. Looking for such a connection was an original goal of the research.

These findings thus constitute evidence for the existence of a variety of objective criteria by means of which the relative adequacy of warnings on cigarette packages can be assessed. However, my research also shows that these objective criteria are for the most part not characteristic of present or past warnings on cigarette packages. The warnings I tested demonstrate clear inadequacies with respect to both linguistic and extralinguistic factors characteristic of strong warnings.

In particular, federally mandated cigarette package warnings display characteristics of weak warnings: (1) qualifying language (e.g., the modal auxiliaries *may* and *can*), (2) unusual syntax (e.g., the *double -ing* construction as in *Quitting smoking now*), and (3) technical and semitechnical vocabulary (e.g., *fetal injury, carbon monoxide*). The warnings lack significant information

(What are the precise dangers? Who will be affected? To what extent?) The warning labels are hard to read because of their position on the side of the package, their small type size, and the fact that they often appear in hard-to-read color combinations (e.g., gold on red).

Also, space limitations constitute a very serious problem in choosing informative wording. As mentioned, one of my graduate students reported that some pregnant women thought that *Low Birth Weight* was a desirable result of smoking and that it was unclear whether that was because they interpreted the statement to mean that *their* weight would be lower at birth or that having a baby weighing less would be desirable. Attempting to propose alternative wordings makes it clear that some problems inherent in the warning would take more words to clear up than there is room for on the package. An informationally adequate warning might read thus: "Smoking by pregnant women may cause injury to the baby before birth, as well as dangerous health problems resulting from the baby's being born prematurely." Here and elsewhere in the rotational system, brevity is accomplished by the use of typically opaque nominalizations (e.g., *fetal injury, birth weight*) made even more opaque by the omission of crucial information for which there is simply no room. This situation-required brevity is a serious obstacle to the adequacy of these warnings.

The rotating warnings present the additional problem that differences in the strength of individual warnings and in the breadth of target populations appear to have the effect of weakening stronger or more inclusive warnings. There is some evidence that two of the present rotating warnings have the effect of weakening the effectiveness of the one disease-specific warning in current use.

6. RECOMMENDATIONS

On the basis of the research reported here, I recommend that the following steps be taken in designing warning labels for consumer products, particularly where health hazards are to be warned against and where consumers will be expected to process the information given them in different ways given differing values and risk-taking stances:

1. Either formulate the warnings as hypothetical warnings or use strong conventional warning labels like *POISON*.
2. Avoid unnecessary qualifying language, for example, the modal auxiliaries *may* and *can*.
3. List specific undesirable consequences of unsafe behavior.
4. Make the warnings conspicuous in all ways, for example, color contrast, type size, and position on product.

5. Write the warnings in simple syntax and in ordinary vocabulary.
6. Include specific information about negative consequences on each label in a rotational series.
7. Do not narrow the target population by addressing specific labels to different portions of that population (e.g., pregnant women).
8. When considering the use of rotating warnings, consider that differences in the strength of individual warnings may have the effect of weakening stronger warnings.
9. Field-test all proposed warnings. (This step would appear to go without saying, but, given the history of proposed federally mandated warnings, it is clear that it does not.)

7. DIRECTIONS FOR FUTURE RESEARCH

The questions addressed here, all revolving around notions of adequacy of warning, exist in a political/economic arena in which it is often tempting to dismiss the need for and advantages of research in favor of simple or simplistic answers to the questions. During the 3 years that I have been engaged in the research described here, I have participated in many discussions, some heated, with individuals who dismiss the need for the research described here on the basis that individuals are responsible for their own fate and that any discussion of adequacy of warning is beside the real point, which is that manufacturers should not bear the financial burden for individuals who choose to engage in risky behavior.

Others have taken the almost diametrically opposed point of view and have argued that the courts must do what Congress is too cowardly to do, that is, assess the monetary damages to society of cigarette smoking to tobacco product manufacturers in the form of large awards to plaintiffs and their families.

Both these arguments have important implications for the legal questions dealt with in this chapter, particularly the very important one of whether Congressional promulgation of cigarette package warnings has preempted common-law requirements of adequacy of warning. Neither argument, however, addresses at all the indisputable facts that (1) warnings, like other speech acts, vary in communicative effectiveness and (2) it is possible to learn a great deal about the nature of the factors that promote communicative effectiveness. Although it may be questionable whether printed warnings labels are the most effective way of conveying certain kinds of health information to consumers, it seems to be true that some warning labels are superior to others. So long as we are going to require cigarette manufacturers to print warning labels on cigarette packages for the purpose of informing consumers of the probable negative consequences of smoking cigarettes, then we should also require that those warnings communicate as effectively as possible.

In the interest of continuing to advance our state of knowledge with respect to warning effectiveness, I plan to complete at least three additional research phases. In the first, I plan to explore the line of research of Kreckel's 1981 study suggesting that "[t]here is no 'natural' common core for 'warning' " (p. 87) and that ' "warnings in general' do not exist" (p. 87) (see footnote 3). I will do so by asking respondents to identify speech acts in tape-recorded conversations (using the same kind of brief instruction I described in connection with the written questionnaire). This research will have the primary goal of discovering to what extent subjects can identify warnings consistently.

In the second proposed research plan, I shall collect much larger samples of paired comparisons using many more warnings than were used in the research described here, so that my findings will be amenable to scaling analysis.[13] This research will have the primary goal of discovering the extent to which respondents display consistency in selecting the stronger of pairs of warnings. It will also shed light on the extent to which certain factors are characteristic of warnings rated as strong.

Finally, in a third phase, I plan to collect information about how respondents process cigarette warnings in the light of their own individual risk assessment techniques by making use of a computerized system, ARK, for studying the ways in which people assess risk. ARK was designed by researchers at the Oak Ridge National Laboratory for the purpose of collecting detailed information about how users assess risk in many specific domains, including cigarette smoking. Its use requires considerable computational and statistical sophistication because of the nature of the questions asked by the system. However, it is the most comprehensive system I am familiar with for gathering the kind of information it gathers. My plan is to instruct colleagues and students in its use and collect information over several years. This research will have the primary goal of discovering something about the relationship between the risk-assessing techniques of individuals and the ways in which they process tobacco product warnings.

---

[13] Among those I will add are two required on cigarette packages by the governments of Canada and the United Kingdom. Both countries mandate the use of cigarette package warnings that would, on the basis of my research findings, be rated as stronger than some of those in use in this country. The Canadian warning reads, "WARNING: Health and Welfare Canada advises that danger to health increases with amount smoked—avoid inhaling." Arguably, that gives permission to smoke; however, it also identifies the precise source of greatest health danger. The one mandated in the United Kingdom reads "DANGER: Government Health WARNING: Cigarettes Can Seriously Damage Your Health." In spite of the presence in the warning of the modal auxiliary "can," I think the warning would, on the basis of its simplicity and label, test strongly. We still have much to learn about various combinations of factors, syntactic and otherwise.

The sequence of research steps outlined should expand our knowledge of three questions, the first two of which were already discussed: (1) What does it mean to be warned? (2) What factors enhance the effectiveness of a warning? (3) How do individuals' own risk assessment techniques interact with warnings to promote or constrain behavioral response to warnings? Such knowledge may have the effect of enhancing our ability to adequately inform consumers of health risks and thus better enable all of us to make informed choices about risky behavior.[14]

8. REFERENCES

A glossary of tobacco terms. (1985). *New York State Journal of Medicine, 85,* 297–298.

Abramson, J. (1986, November 10). "Battle lines drawn in cigarette ad fight." *Legal Times 9,* p. 1.

Black's Law Dictionary (5th ed. 1979).

Breznitz, S. (1984). *Cry Wolf: The psychology of false alarms.* Hillsdale, NJ: Lawrence Erlbaum Associates.

Blasi, V., & Monaghan, H. P. (1986). The first amendment and cigarette advertising. *Journal of the American Medical Association, 256,* 502–509.

Cullingford, R., Da Cruz, L., Webb, S., Shean, & Jamrozik, K. (1988). Legibility of health warnings on billboards that advertise cigarettes. *The Medical Journal of Australia, 148,* 336–338.

Davis, R. M., & Kendrick, J. S. (1989). The Surgeon General's warnings in outdoor cigarette advertising: Are they readable? *Journal of the American Medical Association, 261,* 90–94.

De Greene, K. B. (1970). *Systems psychology.* New York: McGraw-Hill.

Deposition of Dr. Roger L. McCarthy. (1987, July 2). Frank Cusimano, Jr., Plaintiffs, vs. American Honda Motor Company, *et al.,* Defendants, in the Superior Court of the State of California in and for the County of San Diego, Docket No. 499782, Vol II.

Fischer, P. M., Richards, J. W., Berman, E. J., & Krugman, D. M. (1989). Recall and eye tracking study of adolescents viewing tobacco advertisements. *Journal of the American Medical Association, 261,* 84–89.

Fraser, B. (1975). Warning and threatening. *Centrum, 3,* 169–180.

Gidmark, D. (1986, December 1). A tobacco case activist predicts success by end of '87. *The National Law Journal, 1,* 8–9.

Kreckel, M. (1981a). Where do constitutive rules for speech acts come from? *Language and Communication, 1,* 73–88.

Kreckel, M. (1981b). *Communicative acts and shared knowledge in natural discourse.* London: Academic Press.

Labov, W. (1966). *The social stratification of English in New York City.* Washington, DC: Center for Applied Linguistics.

Labov, W. (1972). The social stratification of (r) in New York City department stores. In W. Labov, *Sociolinguistic patterns* (pp. 43–69). Philadelphia: University of Pennsylvania Press.

Lee, J. D. (1986, Winter). Three stages of tobacco litigation. *Trial Diplomacy Journal, 8,* 18–23.

---

[14]Earlier and shorter versions of this paper were delivered at The University of Tennessee (February 20, 1986), Duke University (March 25, 1986), and at the 36th meeting of the Southeastern Conference on Linguistics at Georgetown University (March 27, 1987). Requests for reprints should be directed to the author at the English Department, The University of Tennessee, Knoxville, Tennessee 37996-0430 (BITNET%"DUMASB@UTKVX").

Lehto, M. R., & Miller, J. M. (1986). *Warnings, Volume I: Fundamentals, design, and evaluation methodologies.* Ann Arbor: Fuller Technical Publications.

McCormick, E. J. (1970). *Human factors in engineering and design* (3rd ed.). New York: McGraw-Hill.

Miller, J. M., & Lehto, M. R. (1987). *Warnings: Volume II: Annotated bibliography with topical index.* Ann Arbor: Fuller Technical Publications.

Murrell, K. F. H. (1969). *Man in his working environment.* London: Chapman and Hall.

Myers, M. L., Iscoe, C., Jennings, C., et al. (1981). *Federal Trade Commission staff report on the cigarette advertising investigation.* Washington, DC: Federal Trade Commission.

Office of Smoking and Health, U.S. Department of Health, Education and Welfare (1964). *Smoking and health: A report of the Surgeon General.* Washington, DC: Author.

Restatement (Second) of Torts §§ 338, 402a (1965).

Robinson, G. H. (1977). Human performance in accident causation: Toward theories on warning systems and hazard appreciation. Washington, DC, *Third International System Safety Conference*, Oct. 17–21, pp. 55–69.

Samfield, M. (1980). *Research and manufacturing in the U.S. cigarette industry.* New York: Lockwood.

Schwartz, V. E., & Driver, R. W. (1983). Warnings in the workplace: The need for a synthesis of law and communication theory. *Cincinnati Law Review, 52,* 38–83.

Searle, J. (1969). *Speech Acts: An essay in the philosophy of language.* London: Cambridge University Press.

Weinstein, A. S., Twerski, A. D., Piehler, H. R., & Donaher, W. A. (1978). Chapter 5: Warnings and disclaimers. *Products liability and the reasonably safe product* (pp. 60–74). New York: John Wiley.

9. CASES CITED

American Optical v. Weiderhamer, 404 N.E.2d 606 (Ind.App 4 Dist. 1980).

Bituminous Casualty Corp. v. Black and Decker Corp. 518 S.W.2d 868 (Tex.Civ.App. 5 Dist., 1974).

Ford Motor Co. v. Nowak, 638 S.W.2d 582 (Tex.App. 13 Dist., 1982).

Griggs v. Firestone Tire and Rubber Co., 513 F.2d 851 (8th Cir. 1975).

Mullane v. Central Hanover Bank & Trust Co., 339 U.S. 306 (1950).

Nissen v. Miller, 44 N.M. 487, 490, 105 P.2d 324, 326 (1940).

Roysdon v. R. J. Reynolds Tobacco Co., 623 F. Supp. 1189 (E. D. Tn. 1986).

Roysdon v. R. J. Reynolds Tobacco Co., 849 F.2d 230 (6th Cir. 1988), *rehearing denied* 1988.

Wallinger v. Martin Stamping and Stove Co., 93 Ill.App.2d 437, 236 N.E.2d 755 (Ill.App. 1968).

10. STATUTES AND REGULATIONS CITED

Comprehensive Smokeless Tobacco Health Education Act of 1986, 15 U.S.C. (Supp. 1988).

Comprehensive Smoking Education Act of 1984, 15 U.S.C. (1984).

Federal Cigarette Labeling and Advertising Act of 1965, 15 U.S.C. (1965).

Public Health Cigarette Smoking Act of 1969, 15 U.S.C. (1970).

The Trade Regulation Rule for the Prevention of Unfair or Deceptive Advertising and Labeling of Cigarettes in Relation to the Health Hazards of Smoking, 29 Fed. Reg. §§ 8324, 8325, 8326 (July 2, 1964).

EPILOGUE
Where Do We Go from Here?

ANNE GRAFFAM WALKER

One of the most rewarding aspects of a developing field is the opportunity it presents for new avenues of research. As the chapters in this volume illustrate, the field of language and law is especially rich in this respect, the richness coming both from the extraordinary breadth of disciplines involved and from the wealth of challenge that lies ahead. Although the studies here deal primarily with litigation, no aspects of American law are free from the influence of language: The challenge is to identify those aspects which are appropriate for study, and once the relevant linguistic variables are isolated, to investigate their actual influence on the legal process.

To do that, however, to make those identifications and carry out those investigations, requires both that academicians be enculturated into the legal profession—knowing what is appropriate for study requires knowing how the culture works—and that legal professionals be willing to invite academicians in. For although the written law and the more sensational aspects of litigation are public, or can be made public, far more of the ways of the law are accomplished by a closed society behind closed doors. Opening those doors to empirical investigation requires that the legal community be persuaded of the value of the scholar's work, particularly when the investigation of sensitive areas necessitates the use of tools other than memory—tape recording, for

---

ANNE GRAFFAM WALKER • Forensic Linguistics Associates, 6404 Cavalier Corridor, Falls Church, Virginia 22044.

instance—for preserving the phenomenon to be studied. Fortunately, some of us *are* being invited in, and a foundation is being laid for future research.

The directions in which that research can go are varied, ranging from replication and expansion of the empirical investigations done by the authors here (and elsewhere) to wholly original studies that break new ground. Replication is probably the least enticing path for a scholar to follow, but particularly in the context of litigation, and in view of the historical resistance of the courts to "invading the province of the jury" by telling jurors something they already know (and everyone already "knows" language), it would be an intelligent course to take. Even outside the domain of litigation, a single study, no matter how impeccably done and how scientifically sound, carries less weight than several studies; it is far more credible to be able to point to replications. Each of the studies in this volume lends itself to that kind of research effort.

Each also can serve as a springboard for expansion. Interestingly enough, one direction in which expanded research might be carried out is implicit in them all: the connection articulated in the chapter by O'Barr and Conley (although not in these terms) between linguistic parity (equal access to and competence in speaking opportunities) and legal equity (equal access to legal remedies). Control of language turns out to be a significant issue, and in all of the studies in this volume it is plain that whoever controls the language has the upper hand in the legal process. Control of the linguistic code itself belongs to the foreign language interpreter (Berk-Seligson), control of speech representation in the transcript belongs to the court reporter (Walker), control of the storytelling process—before and during trial—belongs to the legal professional (Maynard, Drew, O'Barr and Conley). Law enforcement agencies control the original interpretation of surreptitiously recorded conversations (Green, Prince); control over how the law is orally interpreted to a client is in the hands of the lawyer (Sarat and Felstiner). And although their lives may be affected by their understanding of legally mandated warnings (Dumas, Johnson), the public has no control over their wording.

Beginning with the central issue of linguistic control as reflected here, research opportunities for expansion of the questions raised by these studies include at a minimum:

1. *Identification of those rules of "communicative competence" in various testimonial events (e.g., depositions, trials, administrative hearings, small claims courts) which give witnesses the greatest degree of control over the presentation of their own stories.* One specific question to ask might be what linguistic techniques (independent of intervention by the witness' own counsel, if any) are most effective for countering an opposing attorney's version of "the truth."

2. *Investigation of the interplay among the three variables of ways of speaking, impression formation, and outcome of real-life trials.* A start in this direction has been made by the Duke University project (e.g., Erickson, Lind, Johnson, &

O'Barr, 1978), but the research relied on simulated jurors as fact finders in simulated trials. A corollary line of research could focus on written speech, studying the relationship among the ways speech is represented in transcripts, impression formation, and the *actual decisions* made by appellate and other influential readers of those transcripts.

3. *Application of speech act theory to legal issues.* Early work in this area was carried out by Hancher (1976), and more recently by Kurzon (1986) and linguist-turned-lawyer Tiersma (1986, 1987). One specific research focus might be on what the mythical but legally relevant "ordinary prudent person" (or "reasonable man") understands a warning, a threat, a promise, an offer to be.

4. *Investigation of the linguistic aspects of the hazards to due process in our adversarial system for the "language and culture different," including very young children, the deaf, the developmentally impaired, nonnative, and non-English-speakers.* Published studies on some of these groups have appeared—for example, Vernon and Coley (1978) on the deaf, Gumperz (1982) on fluent but nonnative English speakers, Berk-Seligson (1990) on non-English-speakers, and Saywitz (1989) and Warren-Leubecker, Tate, Hinton, and Ozbek (1989) on young children's linguistic knowledge of the legal system—but the research is still in its infancy.

The lines of research suggested barely scratch the surface of the available opportunities for study in the field of language and law. Like many of the chapters in this volume, they focus narrowly on litigation issues and ignore broader applications of linguistics, as in, for instance, the area of evaluating the comprehensibility of legally mandated notices sent to the public by government agencies or other institutions. More seriously perhaps, they also overlook the opportunity for pure linguistic research which, by continuing the investigation of discourse in legal settings, could seek out underlying structure and regularities that might tell us more about how language itself functions.

Nevertheless, as sketchy as these suggestions are, they serve to illustrate the need for serious study of this new discipline in which linguistic theory and legal issues intersect. The judicial system in literate cultures is explicated entirely through language: It is stored in written form and is exercised in both writing and speech. Yet particularly when it comes to the *oral* and advocacy aspects of the law (e.g., questioning and preparing witnesses, conducting a *voir dire* of the jury, predicting the effects on verdicts of an attorney's speech style), such information as exists in the legal profession has until very recently been anecdotal and has thus lacked the replicability, reliability, and rigor that come with systematic study which is undergirded by theory.

Moreover, and much more dangerously, both trial and appellate courts (e.g., *California v. Brown*, 107 S.Ct. 837, 1987) are making and/or justifying their decisions by reference to "linguistic principles" which stem more from native intuition than from informed linguistic knowledge (Solan, 1990). As

Levi has so well documented in this volume and elsewhere (e.g., 1982, 1986, 1989), there is a growing body of *scientific* linguistic studies which can replace anecdotes and native intuition; it is up to the academic community to bring them to the wider attention of their juridical colleagues.

There is also a need, however, for academicians to educate themselves as to this new line of scholarly inquiry by crossing the barriers of their own domains and participating in an interdisciplinary sharing of their research goals, theories, methodologies, and results. Not only does this kind of sharing obviate the need for isolated scholars to reinvent the wheel, but it insures the availability of a wide, knowledgeable peer review in which social scientists and lawyers alike can judge the work of those who write and speak about language as it applies to the law. Further, although those who practice law could benefit from education on linguistic principles and applications, those who study language *in* the law could also profit from learning the language *of* the law: Achieving credibility in any culture or cross-discipline presupposes the ability to utilize its terms appropriately.

In the 1985 Conference on Language in the Judicial Process at Georgetown University, the groundwork was laid for the kind of sharing of research among informed and competent scholars that this volume and its authors represent. The work goes on, of course, but to date it remains primarily in the hands of academicians. What is needed now is not just increased access to, but more active participation by, legal scholars and practitioners in the design and completion of appropriate studies. With cooperation from representatives of both language and law, the ultimate benefit will be where it belongs: with all of us whom the judicial process serves.

1. REFERENCES

Berk-Seligson, S. (1990). *The bilingual courtroom*. Chicago: University of Chicago Press.
Erickson, B., Lind, E. A., Johnson, B. C., & O'Barr, W. M. (1978). Speech style and impression formation in a court setting: The effects of "powerful" and "powerless" speech. *Journal of Experimental Social Psychology, 14,* 266–279.
Gumperz, J. J. (1982). Fact and inference in courtroom testimony. In J. J. Gumperz (Ed.), *Language and social identity* (pp. 163–195). Cambridge, England: Cambridge University Press.
Hancher, M. (1976). Speech acts and the law. In R. W. Shuy & A. Shnukal (Eds.), *Language use and the uses of language* (pp. 245–256). Washington, DC: Georgetown University Press.
Kurzon, D. (1986). *It is hereby performed. . .: Exploration in legal speech acts.* Amsterdam/Philadelphia: John Benjamins.
Labov, W. (1972). *Sociolinguistic patterns.* Philadelphia: University of Pennsylvania Press.
Levi, J. N. (1982). *Linguistics, language and the law: A topical bibliography.* Bloomington, IN: Indiana University Linguistics Club.
Levi, J. N. (1986). Applications of linguistics to the language of legal interactions. In P. C. Bjarkman & V. Raskin (Eds.), *The real-world linguist: Linguistic applications in the 1980s* (pp. 230–265). Norwood, NJ: Ablex.

Levi, J. N. (1989). The invisible network: Contemporary research in the U.S.A. on language and the legal process. In P. Pupier & J. Woehrling (Eds.), *Language and law [Langue et droit]: Proceedings of the first conference of the International Institute of Comparative Linguistic Law* (pp. 519–550). Montreal: Wilson & Lafleur.

Saywitz, K. J. (1989). "Court is a place to play basketball": Children's conceptions of the legal system. In S. J. Ceci, D. F. Ross, & M. P. Toglia (Eds.), *Perspectives on Children's Testimony*. New York: Springer-Verlag.

Solan, L. M. (1990). Linguistic principles as the rule of law. In P. Pupier & J. Woehrling (Eds.), *Language and law [Langue et droit]: Proceedings of the first conference of the International Institute of Comparative Linguistic Law* (pp. 569–579). Montreal: Wilson & Lafleur.

Tiersma, P. M. (1986). The language of offer and acceptance: Speech acts and the question of intent. *California Law Review, 74*(1), 189–232.

Tiersma, P. M. (1987). The language of defamation. *Texas Law Review, 66*(2), 303–350.

Vernon, McC., & Coley, J. (1978). Violation of constitutional rights: The language impaired person and the Miranda warnings. *Journal of Rehabilitation of the Deaf, 11*(4), 1–8.

Warren-Leubecker, A., Tate, C. S., Hinton, I. D., & Ozbek, I. N. (1989). What do children know about the legal system and when do they know it? First steps down a less traveled path in child witness research. In S. J. Ceci, D. F. Ross & M. P. Toglia (Eds.), *Perspectives on children's testimony*. New York: Springer-Verlag.

2. CASES CITED

California v. Brown, 107 S.Ct. 837 (1987).

AUTHOR INDEX

SUBJECT INDEX